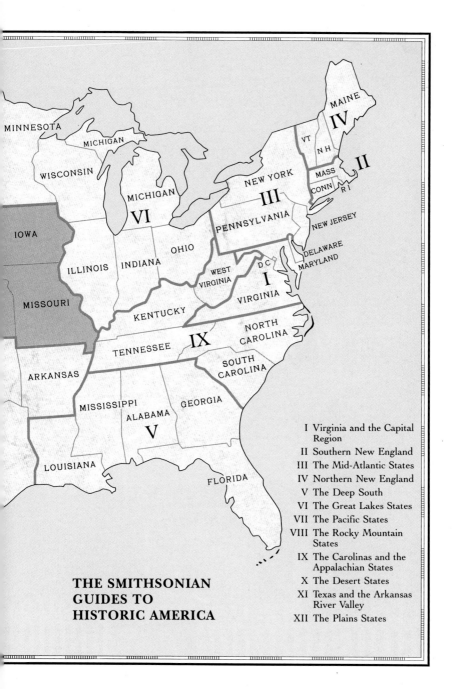

MINNESOTA
MICHIGAN
WISCONSIN
MICHIGAN
VI
IOWA
ILLINOIS INDIANA OHIO
MISSOURI
KENTUCKY
ARKANSAS
TENNESSEE **IX**
MISSISSIPPI
ALABAMA GEORGIA
V
LOUISIANA

MAINE
IV
VT
N H
NEW YORK MASS **II**
III CONN R I
PENNSYLVANIA
NEW JERSEY
DELAWARE
D C MARYLAND
WEST **I**
VIRGINIA
VIRGINIA
NORTH
CAROLINA
SOUTH
CAROLINA

FLORIDA

I Virginia and the Capital
    Region
II Southern New England
III The Mid-Atlantic States
IV Northern New England
V The Deep South
VI The Great Lakes States
VII The Pacific States
VIII The Rocky Mountain
    States
IX The Carolinas and the
    Appalachian States
X The Desert States
XI Texas and the Arkansas
    River Valley
XII The Plains States

THE SMITHSONIAN
GUIDES TO
HISTORIC AMERICA

THE
SMITHSONIAN
GUIDES TO
HISTORIC AMERICA
THE PLAINS STATES

TEXT BY
SUZANNE WINCKLER

SPECIAL PHOTOGRAPHY BY
JONATHAN WALLEN
TIM THOMPSON

EDITORIAL DIRECTOR
ROGER G. KENNEDY
Director Emeritus, the National Museum of
American History of the Smithsonian Institution,
former Director of the National Park Service

Stewart, Tabori & Chang
NEW YORK

Published in 1998 by Stewart, Tabori & Chang, a division of U.S. Media Holdings, Inc., 115 West 18th Street, New York, NY 10011.

Due to limitations of space, additional photo credits appear on page 460 and constitute an extension of this page.

Front cover: main photo—Blockhouse on hill at Fort Lincoln, Mandan, ND.
inset 1—Bolduc House, Sainte Genevieve, MO.
inset 2—Julia Lee singing with the George E. Lee band in a St. Louis, MO, club.
inset 3—St.Louis barge traffic, MO.
Half-title page: *Cradling Wheat,* by Thomas Hart Benton (detail), St. Louis, Art Museum, MO.
Frontispiece: Willa Cather House, Red Cloud, NE.
Back cover: Nebraska State Capitol, Lincoln, NE.

Series Editors: Henry Wiencek (first edition), Donald Young (revised edition)
Editor: Mary Luders

Photo Editor: Mary Z. Jenkins	**Assistant Photo Editors:** Barbara J. Seyda, Rebecca Williams
Art Director: Diana M. Jones	**Cover Design** (revised edition): Nai Chang
Designer: Lisa Vaughn (revised edition)	**Design Assistant:** Kathi R. Porter
Editorial Assistant: Monina Medy	**Cartographic Design & Production:** Guenter Vollath

Cartographic Compilation: George Colbert
Data Entry: Susan Kirby
Text revisions throughout this edition by the series editor.

Library of Congress Cataloging-in-Publication Data

Winckler, Suzanne, 1946–
    The Plains States / text by Suzanne Winckler ; special photography by Jonathan Wallen, Tim Thompson. — Rev. ed.
        p. cm. — (The Smithsonian guides to historic America ; 12)
        "Text revisions throughout this edition by Donald Young"—T.p. verso
        Includes index.
        ISBN 1-55670-643-X
        1. Great Plains—Guidebooks. 2. West (U.S.)—Guidebooks. 3. Historic sites—Great Plains—Guidebooks. 4. Historic sites—West (U.S.)—Guidebooks. I. Wallen, Jonathan. II. Tim Thompson. III. Young, Donald. IV. Title. V. Series.
        F590.3.W56   1998
        917.804'33—dc21   96-40549

Distributed in the U.S. by Stewart, Tabori & Chang, 115 West 18th Street, New York, NY 10011. Distributed in Canada by General Publishing Co. Ltd., 30 Lesmill Road, Don Mills, Ontario, Canada, M3B 2T6. Distributed in all other territories by Grantham Book Services Ltd., Isaac Newton Way, Alma Park Industrial Estate, Grantham, Lincolnshire NG31 9SD, England. Sold in Australia by Peribo Pty Ltd., 58 Beaumont Road, Mount Kuring-gai, NSW 2080, Australia.

Printed in Japan

10 9 8 7 6 5 4 3 2 1

Revised edition

C O N T E N T S

THE
PLAINS STATES

═══ HIGHWAY

○ HISTORIC SITE

NORTH

Minot

DAKOTA

BISMARCK

Little
Missouri
R.

MONTANA

Missouri R.

SOUTH

Belle Fourche R.

BLACK
HILLS Rapid
City

PIERRE

Cheyenne R.

DAKOTA

Niobrara R.

WYOMING

Scottsbluff

NEBR

North Platte R.

CHEYENNE

North
Platte

South Platte R.

DENVER

COLORADO

Arkansas R.

Dodge City

0   200 Mi.

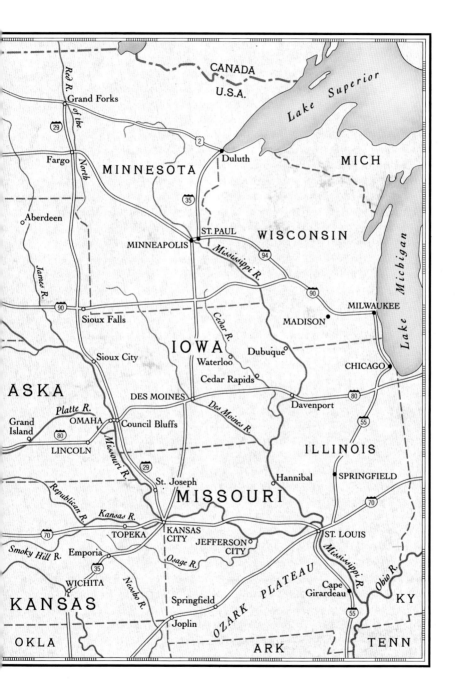

INTRODUCTION

ROGER G. KENNEDY

On July 19, 1881, Sitting Bull rode into Fort Buford, Dakota Territory. He did not surrender his .44-caliber, model 1866 Winchester to the post commander directly. Instead, he handed it to his eight-year-old son, Crowfoot, saying: "I wish it to be remembered that I was the last man of my people to surrender my rifle." He did not say: "I wish it to be remembered that I was the last man of my people to surrender my bow and arrows."

Twenty years earlier, another Sioux army, under Little Crow, had attacked Fort Ridgeley, in Minnesota. The Sioux were defeated largely because the defenders had a 24-pound howitzer, and Little Crow did not. One of Little Crow's officers watched Fort Ridgeley's 24-pounder scattering canister amid his troops, and observed: "With a few guns like that, the [Sioux] could rule the earth."

It is doubtful that he was wistful; more likely, he was making plans. They were very adaptable, these warriors of the plains. Douglas Scott has demonstrated from field cartridge cases found at the Little Bighorn that the Sioux made good tactical use of their repeating rifles against Custer. It is foolish to describe as "primitive" cavalrymen who use Winchesters and know the capability of howitzers. It is time we rid ourselves of this and other misconceptions about these shrewd and adaptable resisters to agriculturization. Sitting Bull, with his horse, his stirrups, and his Winchester, demonstrated that the Native American resistance was not technologically "primitive." With his weapons, he could have disposed of Julius Caesar or Charlemagne, with theirs.

By the time the blue-coats of the Seventh Cavalry—lithographed into our memories—arrived upon the scene, the Sioux were already making full use of the rifle and the horse; the Stone Age was long gone. The Spaniards, the first users of gunpowder upon the plains, had provided the Indians with their first horses. In the 1540s the Native Americans, pedestrian peoples of the region, witnessed the absurdity of Europeans riding encased in armor through Kansas in summer; but the Indians were not so amused as to fail to observe that the strangers were, in fact, *riding*. In the ensuing three centuries, the Cheyenne, Kiowa, Comanche, and the loosely related

OPPOSITE: *A strip farm in Iowa. In the eastern reaches of the prairie, before the deep sod was broken by the plow, natural grasses grew as high as a horseman's stirrups.*

nations of the northern plains we call the "Sioux" made themselves masters of cavalry tactics. They had learned to use muskets very soon after they first observed Europeans killing each other with them. After muskets came rifles. Artillery might have come next, but the plans conceived by Little Crow's captains never quite matured. None of the detachments of militia or of the U.S. Army that were wiped out in the succeeding years were towing howitzers or even Hotchkiss guns. The Indians were able only to add to their arsenal of rifles and carbines. They never gained cannon.

The Native Americans held off the immense numbers of their opponents for a whole generation, until nature itself, the nature of their own region, defeated them. It is suggestive of the real character of this struggle that historians cannot identify a "decisive battle" that marks the final victory of any one of the succession of generals sent against the Indians—Sherman, Sheridan, Miles, Crook, and Custer. The European tradition has a fondness for "decisive battles"—Agincourt, Waterloo, Yorktown, Vicksburg, Gettysburg. But we cannot even name a "decisive battle" in which Little Crow or Red Cloud or Sitting Bull was defeated. Most of us can name one or two, such as the Little Bighorn, that they won. Why can this be? Why, instead of scenes like that at Yorktown—stacked arms and exchanges of swords, with military bands playing in the background—do we recall a few hundred starving women and children following their warriors into acquiescence?

The bloody history of the plains records no large military encounters that settled very much. Armies decided nothing. Microbes and malnutrition settled something. Demographics, driving agriculture westward, decided more. Finally, the climate and the soil decided the rest. Red Cloud and Sitting Bull mastered the political skills necessary to build coalitions of tribal groups and were able to put several thousand men on a battlefield under coordinated leadership, just a little too late. The dry, thin soil of the western prairie could not sustain forage, game, water, and fuel sufficient to keep an army together. Such armies had to be supplied by steam-powered boats and trains.

What if the Sioux had captured some artillery? What if Native American coalition building had occurred on a large scale a little earlier? The Indians put up an extraordinary fight, using all the latest weapons they could capture, but they were starved into submission. Another way of putting the matter is to remove the military from the scene, and to visualize the Native Americans as being forced, ultimately, to give way to an ecological transformation brought about by farmers. Seen this way, the European-Americans who won the Indian wars of the plains never wore a uniform.

An ecological revolution among the humans in North America had cataclysmic consequences to the central valley. The total population of what is now the continental United States, including the invading European-Americans and the Native Americans, was about a million in 1700, as it had been in 1500. By 1750 it doubled. By 1800 it was 6 million; by the Civil War it stood at around 30 million; and it would double again by 1900. During this entire period, the number of Native Americans was declining. Furthermore, the invaders were moving into the plains in enormous numbers, shifting their nationhood west of the mountains. In 1790, 97 percent of the European-Americans lived east of the Appalachians; by 1907 about 60 percent of the people in the United States lived west of those mountains. In that same year, more immigrants appeared on these shores from Europe than the entire population in George Washington's youth. Ireland alone had provided in each of the last five years of the 1850s enough new arrivals to replace all the European settlers living in 1700. The western third of Kansas held only 38,000 people in 1885; two years later nearly 140,000 farmers were there, increasing crop acreage by 265 percent. Such transitions are seldom peaceful. It had not been an easy thing to place 2 million people in Iowa in fifty years, where a hundred thousand had been before. Nor could 1.5 million quietly crowd into Kansas around the 50,000 whose hunting required plenteous space.

As the newcomers filled the plains they radically altered its ecology, killing its animals, burning its timber, overgrazing its grass or replacing it with cultivated annuals such as wheat and corn. These farmers did what the ragtag army of the United States was never able to do in pitched battle—the Plains Indians were reduced to starvation by growers of food. In only two or three decades, agriculture replaced hunting as the chief occupation of the human race upon the plains. In 1879, three years after the Little Bighorn, 16,000 homesteads were entered in Kansas and Nebraska, covering 2,300,000 acres. It is, perhaps, symbolic that an Indian agent named Nathan Meeker precipitated a battle at Milk Creek that year by telling the Ute to plow up the land where their hunting ponies grazed, and shoot the ponies.

Neither the details nor the pacing of the Native American defeat was inevitable. Other outcomes were possible all along. If there is inevitability in the story, it arises from the massing of individual lives into population trends so great, in the aggregate, that they could not be resisted forever. Yet, even though the general direction of things was established by the different birthrates and deathrates of the Europeans and the Native Americans, by the diseases survived by some and not by others, there has always been, in the history of the Missouri Valley peoples, room for adjustment in outcomes as the result of resistance. The Missouri Valley has been the scene of intense struggles, of bloodshed and vehement politics, of a violent clash of cultures, most dramatically shown in the wars between the Native Americans and the European invaders, but just as dramatically in the political struggle of the proprietors of individual family farms against trusts and conglomerated corporations.

Even before Sitting Bull relinquished his Winchester, another rearguard action commenced. This time it was the farmers who found themselves facing antagonists coming over the horizon from the East—railroads and corporations. The railroads, engrossing millions of acres of farmland, engrossed, as well, state legislatures and worked their will in the Congress of the United States. Government was turned loose upon the farmers (and upon borrowers, in general) in the interest of corporations (and of lenders). The public's chief asset, the land in the "public domain," went to corporations in enormous grants. The public taxing power was dedicated to transferring wealth to bankers, by levying taxes to "redeem" Civil War paper money, much of it purchased in 60- or 70-cent dollars, in 100-cent dollars. The government sought to bring about a deflation of the currency that would benefit banks and other lenders and penalize farmers and other borrowers—debts would have to be repaid in dollars that were more valuable than the ones that had been borrowed. In addition, the Supreme Court of the United States began to interpret the Interstate Commerce and Contract clauses of the U.S. Constitution in entirely new ways, all resulting in the transfer of economic power to corporations. In the spring of 1880 Supreme Court Justice David Davis, a Lincoln appointee and no Populist, wrote that "The rapid growth of corporate power . . . and their corrupting influence at the Seat of Government . . . filled me with apprehension." He believed that "the corporations were maturing their plans to gain complete control of the Supreme Court."

So the farmers counterattacked, through the political process. They organized themselves as Grangers and Greenbackers in the 1870s, in Farmers' Alliances in the 1880s and as Populists in the

1890s. They began by helping each other. They did not begin by turning to the State. The alliances formed cooperatives in an attempt to regulate prices and production. Loosely related granges and alliances were linked into the People's, or Populist, party. Populist economics are not easy to read at a glance, but after reflection it becomes obvious that it would be foolish to dismiss them as intellectually "primitive." The Populists had much to teach their countrymen, and much to teach us, as well. These much-derided people believed in the governance of economic life through plebiscite—through what one might call a democratic agriculture. They also believed in the governance of industry by choice. They organized producer and consumer cooperatives. They required uniform weighing and measuring of products—both producer and consumer protection. They turned to government to establish rules for the use of children in factories and to regulate industrial hours and working conditions. They demanded a graduated income tax; that public lands be reserved for settlers and not given to railroads; and that senators be elected directly by the people, not by state legislatures.

Contrary to all the expectations of cynics then, and discomfiting to cynics now, most of the programs espoused by the People's party became law. Although the Populists fell short of two ambitious goals, those goals reveal how far-sighted they were: They were unable to forge an alliance with the remnants of the Reconstruction-era black leadership in the South in time to stave off Jim Crow, though they tried; and they were unable to forge a proto–New Deal coalition with organized labor, though they tried.

Because the Populists' modes of discourse were not genteel, it was customary for historians as late as the 1960s to make light of the remedies that they recommended. Although academic research in more recent decades has brought renewed respect to the Populists, the old misconceptions still linger in the public memory. For too long, historians (such as Richard Hofstadter), economists (such as Daniel Bell), and even playwrights had unjustly derided the Populists' understanding of their economic context, despite the fact that they understood it quite correctly: They were fighting back against the government's policy of deflation. As borrowers, they were quite correct in doing so. They observed the deployment of the power of government in the hands of their antagonists, and they resisted that attack—with remarkable success.

It was fashionable to deny the intellectual sophistication of the Populists. Yet there was as much learning upon the platform at their

convention in 1896 as there was, at the time, in the faculty of Harvard College (Ignatius Donnelly, the vice presidential candidate, might count for a faculty himself). The difference was that this was a period in which the faculty of Harvard did not include many people devoted to changing their world. The Populist intellectuals, Henry Demarest Lloyd, Clarence Darrow, Ignatius Donnelly, John P. Altgeld and, beside them, the unclassifiable Thorstein Veblen, did.

For them to gain our respect it is not necessary to prove that Donnelly, in his library at Nininger, was a better economist than Thomas Jefferson had been in his at Monticello. Reading their works, side by side, one can only be awed by the breadth of understanding of each, as against the prevailing wisdom of their times. A novelist, economist, farmer, town planner, scholar of Elizabethan drama and Icelandic myth, and a kind of proto–anthropologist, Donnelly especially was the one who understood that the government's deliberate policy of deflation was increasing the value of the dollar at the expense of the farmer. Neither Donnelly nor Jefferson was successful in bending the outcome of economic history very much in the direction he desired. But Jefferson won great office while Donnelly did not, Donnelly is often called "the wild jackass of the prairie," while Jefferson is often called "the Sage."

Native American resistance was violent, as the forces imposing unwelcome change upon them used violence to achieve it. The Greenbacker-Alliance-Populist resistance was within the conventions of constitutional politics: Theirs was an agrarian revolt, which first coincided with and then survived the Indian wars of the West. What the two had in common was a denial of the inevitability of any economic or political change, and a willingness to pay the price for resistance. We have not sufficiently honored their accomplishments or their points of view. This is not to say that the devices of Populist politics of 1890 would be precisely applicable to the requirements of 1990. The circumstances are different. But admitting that, we may ask once more: Why are we so reluctant to take them seriously? And answer once more that we find their activism, their intense expectations of each other, imply uncomfortable expectations of us.

OPPOSITE: *A poster of the early 1870s promoting the Granger movement. The motto under the farmer, I PAY FOR ALL, sums up the Granger philosophy: The country will not prosper without a thriving class of small farmers. The nostalgic farming scenes hark back to the unmechanized 1830s—all labor is being done by hand.*

A reevaluation of the plains people of the past, including the twentieth-century past, is necessary not merely because there has been much fresh learning about them. As we look to a more recent past, when the peoples of Eastern Europe demonstrated that it was possible for large numbers of people to act together to alter their history, we may be enabled to jettison some of the prejudices by which we have justified political indolence on our own part. Most Americans are politically inert today. Half of them may vote, but only a tiny percentage exert themselves to alter their circumstances through the political process. Consonant with this passivity, there has grown up a scholarship of torpor, endorsing inaction by a sophisticated disdain for the active. The indolent have been consoled by derogating those who refused to be victims.

The American tradition of self-determination survives even in nostalgia, even in such an apparently escapist film as *Field of Dreams,* a classic motion picture fresh-fledged for us in 1989, which contains a subtext of political exhortation. Embedded in this story about the pleasures of being able to play baseball in the 1920s is a message worthy of the 1960s—that civil liberties, personal idiosyncrasy, and the freedoms to act and think require constant, vigilant defense. The Iowa setting is at the heart of the matter. The central character, an Iowa corn farmer, is twice asked the same question by two ghosts. He answers it the same way each time, in case we missed it the first time, and in case it takes two tries to reinstate a national myth: "Is this heaven?" "No . . . it's Iowa." We impute to Iowa qualities of rural tranquillity and timelessness that we find sadly lacking in, say, California, or Cambridge, Massachusetts. We long for such a corn-growing agricultural Arcadia. Corn had been the crop of the pioneers; where you found thriving cornfields, you found successful pioneering. More to the point, where corn grew happily year after year, one could believe in benign, changeless, independent "family farming." This movie is likely to become an important reliquary for American nostalgia. Its message is that the American past is to be found in a cornfield. Some part of that past *is* there, surely—the part that abruptly replaced the past of Sitting Bull and Little Crow. Quirkily, in defiance of population patterns in most of the rest of the country, that part of the past has survived into our own time. It is likely that Californians are moved to make a cinematic heaven out of Iowa or Kansas, and millions of urbanites to think of going there—"they'll come!"—because the demographic and industrial histories of Kansas and Iowa have been so unlike that of, say, California. Kansas and California had the same population in 1900. Since then, Kansans have added few to their numbers, while Californians multiplied by ten by 1950 and by twenty by 1975. Iowa—changeless, heavenly, nostalgic Iowa—had about the same number of people, mostly farmers, in 1900, in 1950, and in 1980.

This apparent changelessness is rooted, of course, in the nature of the terrain itself: The natural resources do not include either waterfalls or sufficient petroleum to provide cheap, on-site energy for industry. But there is a larger lesson here, one for which there are no ecological or economic imperatives. The people of this region have, over two centuries, refused to acquiesce to changes they did not like. The most important constant quality in the political life of the Missouri Valley, a quality shared by the Native Americans, the Grangers, Greenbackers, Populists, Alliancemen, and the Cooperative Movement, is that these people do not take well to being imposed upon. This quality is discomfiting. It is abrasive to those who encounter it while enforcing the imposition; it is even less endearing to the later beneficiaries of the imposition; and it is least comforting to people who could well summon the energy to improve their circumstances, but who prefer to console themselves with a passive version of the doctrine of "progress."

"Progress" is self-justifying change, the inevitable replacement of something worse by something new. It has become as deeply ingrained in the American myth structure as the notion of Indians as "primitive" and cornfields as durable as heaven. Believers in progress derogate the past, and thus sometimes fail to resist the imposition of the worse upon the better. Indeed, they tend to be passive in the face of changes they do not entirely understand and assume to be inevitable. Sitting Bull, Red Cloud, and Little Crow did not make this mistake. Neither did the Populists; nor do the small farmers who are fighting to save their farms today; nor does the heroic, unintimidated corn farmer of *Field of Dreams,* who stands in the tradition of Sitting Bull and Ignatius Donnelly. At the end of the movie thousands of automobiles bring tourists to visit the arcadian past—what they think was and is a world apart. But this heaven has a hole in it. The corn growers of Iowa and the wheat farmers of Kansas and Nebraska were not, nor had they ever

Farmland near Rossville, Iowa, under the harvest moon. During this time of year the full moon illuminates the night from dusk to dawn for several nights in a row.

been, making lives apart from the rest of the world. Their populism arose from a determination to have something to say about how that connection operated.

The world was always ready to intrude. As early as 1790, Thomas Jefferson himself recognized that the Mississippi Valley was not intended by nature for small subsistence farms or any other self-contained agriculture. The free and independent yeoman did not farm for himself or even for his neighbors. He farmed for the urban populations of the world. Jefferson wrote George Washington that the Mississippi must be kept open for trade in order to convey the "surplus" of the valley to the rising population of Europe and the West Indies. Some six decades later Anthony Trollope strayed far enough from the Pallisers and the characters of his other novels to fulfill "the ambition of my literary life to write a book about the United States." In 1862 he observed what Americans did with their enormous surplus abundance: "I went down to the granaries, and climbed up onto the elevators. I saw the wheat running in rivers from one vessel into another, and from the railroad vans up into the huge bins on the top stories of the warehouses—for these rivers of food run uphill as easily as they do down. I saw the corn measured by the forty bushel measure with as much ease as we measure an ounce of cheese, and with greater rapidity . . . . I breathed the flour, and drank the flour, and felt myself enveloped in a world of breadstuff . . . . God [had] prepared the food for the increasing millions of the Eastern world, as also for the coming millions of the Western."

Despite the presence of those "coming millions" in cities, despite office parks and manufactories of computer chips, despite vineyards and orchards, the dominant elements of the Missouri Valley remain water and grass. There are remnants of the three general categories of natural prairie grasses to be seen even today, along with ample evidence of the hardiness of the cultivated grasses that replaced them. Near Manhattan, Kansas, lie 8,600 acres of tall-grass prairie (the Konza Preserve) and there are even 240 tall-grass acres near Lincoln, Nebraska (Nine-Mile Prairie). Not too far away, in the Willa Cather Prairie near Red Cloud, there are 600 acres of mid grass, but the glory of natural Nebraska is the Sand Hills Region, mostly mid grass and nearly 10,000 square miles in extent. Here are lakes and grassy plains as they were when the first humans came upon the scene, when horses first cropped that small portion of the vegetable systems appearing on the surface. Here the High Plains can be seen as they were when the Oregon Trail was crawling with westering Americans. Travelers today, who come in search of peace, can cross these vestiges of primitive America, as grand in their understated way as the Wind River Range or the Tetons.

The scale is very large. It was so in the 1860s when the bison herds devoured the grass of entire valleys and drank whole rivers dry. It is so today. The Missouri Valley is an ample place—it sometimes swallows us up in that amplitude, envelops us in space suspended between limitless land and infinite sky. But it never diminishes us. Because this land is so big, it comprehends without strain enormous numbers, and thereby states a rule of participation—each of us is part of the many. In the myriad, we become Franciscans—Hail, Brother Sun! Hail, innumerable cousins! A hundred million bees attend the pollination of springtime, buzzing through billions of grass-stems across a plain so straightforward that we feel—if we only climbed a stepladder—we could see a hundred miles.

MISSOURI

OPPOSITE: *The Old Courthouse in Saint Louis, framed by the Gateway Arch. Completed in 1862, the courthouse is now part of the Jefferson National Expansion Memorial and contains historical exhibits.*

On December 11, 1811, the most powerful earthquake in the nation's recorded history began to cleave the Mississippi Valley. Over the next three months, two other severe shocks and thousands of tremors rumbled through the valley, some of which were felt as far as Washington, DC, and Quebec City, Canada. The heart of the earthquakes lay in the southeastern corner of present-day Missouri, a region known as the Bootheel. "All nature seemed running into chaos," wrote John Bradbury, a Scottish naturalist camping along the river when the first quake struck. The hollow growl of the earthquake itself was accompanied by other eerie sounds—the screaming of birds, the snapping of tree limbs, the roar of earthen banks crashing into the river.

The New Madrid earthquakes—named for the thriving river town near the epicenter—devastated that city, destroying its economic vitality; reshaped the river and the nearby terrain, wreaking havoc on one of the nation's major avenues of commerce; and terrified countless people. One diarist in New Madrid wrote, "I never before thought the passion of fear so strong as I find it here among the people." The geology of the area is such that an earthquake of great magnitude is destined to strike again.

Several distinctive kinds of topography converge in Missouri. North of the Missouri River, which bisects the state, is a glaciated plain ideal for grain and livestock production; the northwest corner is especially fertile. South of the river lie the Ozark highlands, a rugged, beautiful area of mountaintop panoramas and hidden valleys poorly suited for large-scale farming but veined with lead and iron ore. The extreme southeast niche—the so-called Bootheel—was once a forest swamp but when cleared provided rich alluvial farmland. In the west and southwest is the Osage plain, a region of rolling hills and grasslands that proved appropriate for dairying and livestock grazing; the area is also underlain with deposits of zinc. The Mississippi River, which forms the eastern boundary of the state, gave rise to commercial centers, of which Sainte Genevieve was the first and Saint Louis the most enduring. Where the Missouri River forms a portion of the state's western boundary, a cluster of cities—Saint Joseph, Independence, and Kansas City—grew up as the embarkation point for famous overland trails.

OPPOSITE: *A woodcut depicting one of the New Madrid earthquakes of 1811-1812. These tremendous quakes changed the course of the Mississippi River and caused some 30,000 square miles of land to sink five to fifteen feet. Loss of life was small because the region was still sparsely inhabited.*

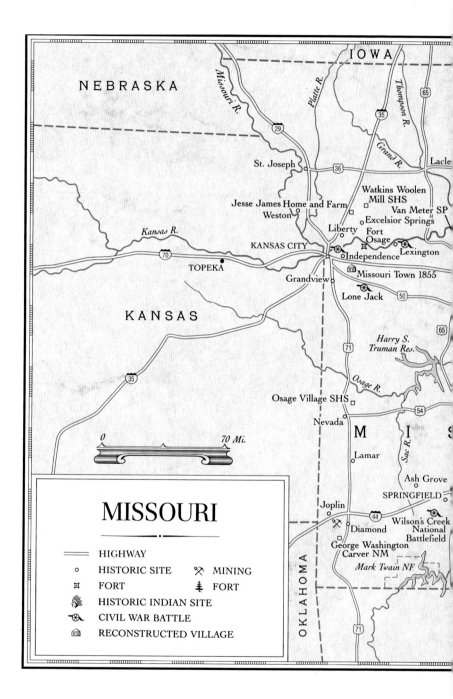

NEBRASKA

IOWA

65

Missouri R.

Platte R.

Thompson R.

29

35

St. Joseph

36

Grand R.

Lacle

Watkins Woolen
Mill SHS

Jesse James Home and Farm
Weston

Van Meter SP

Excelsior Springs

Liberty

Fort
Osage

Kansas R.

KANSAS CITY

Independence

Lexington

70

TOPEKA

Grandview

Missouri Town 1855

KANSAS

Lone Jack

50

Harry S.
Truman Res.

65

71

35

Osage R.

Osage Village SHS

54

Nevada

M   I

Sac R.

70 Mi.

Lamar

0

Ash Grove

SPRINGFIELD

MISSOURI

Joplin

44

Wilson's Creek
National
Battlefield

Diamond

George Washington
Carver NM

Mark Twain NF

——— HIGHWAY

◦   HISTORIC SITE   ⚒ MINING

⊟   FORT   ♣ FORT

HISTORIC INDIAN SITE

CIVIL WAR BATTLE

RECONSTRUCTED VILLAGE

OKLAHOMA

71

Charlton R.

Salt R.

Keokuk

61

Bethel

36

Hannibal

ILLINOIS

55

Stoutsville
Paris

Mark Twain
Birthplace SHS

Mississippi R.

Boone's Lick SHS
Arrow Rock

Graham Cave
SP
Montgomery City

61

70

Columbia

Fulton

St. Charles

70

Hermann

Defiance

ST. LOUIS

JEFFERSON
CITY

Westphalia

50

Missouri R.

Mastodon SP
Sandy Creek Covered Bridge

57

Meramec
Iron
Works

44

Meramec R.

DeSoto

Ste. Genevieve

Lake of
the Ozarks

St. James

Washington
SP

67

Gasconade R.

Missouri
Mines SHS

Bonne Terre

Mark   Twain   NF

Pilot
Knob

S
O
U
R
K
A
U
R

Dillard
Mill
SHS

Ironton

Burfordville

Trail of Tears SP

Lebanon

O
Z
A
R
K
L
A
T
E
A
U

Current R.

Cape Girardeau

Ohio R.

60

Mansfield

KY

Mark Twain NF

Iowosahgy State
Archaeological
Site

School of the Ozarks

Poplar Bluff

East Prairie

New Madrid

Big Oak Tree SP

ARKANSAS

67

Black R.

St. Francis R.

55

Mississippi R.

TENN

White R.

Little is known about Missouri's first inhabitants. A weapon found among the bone beds at Mastodon State Park, near Saint Louis, confirms the presence of nomadic hunters in the region 10,000 years ago. In more recent times—that is, about a thousand years ago—more sedentary peoples inhabited Missouri, prehistoric tribes that hunted, gathered, farmed, and were actively engaged in trade and commerce. They have been categorized broadly as the Woodland and Mississippian cultures, the latter apparently evolving from the former. They lived along major waterways that provided protein-rich fish, productive soils for farming, and a means of travel. On the fertile floodplains formed by the confluence of the Illinois, Missouri, and Mississippi rivers, many village centers flourished around A.D. 900. Cahokia, just east of Saint Louis in Illinois, was the urban core of this megalopolis. Towosahgy State Historic Site in Missouri's Bootheel region preserves several earthen mounds of a fortified village that was a satellite community of Cahokia. Around A.D. 1400 the Mississippian culture slipped into a mysterious decline.

In the late seventeenth century, when the first French explorers began to probe the area that is now Missouri, they encountered seminomadic tribes that were fairly recent migrants to the area themselves. The Sauk, Mesquakie (Fox), and Illinois, all of Algonquian linguistic stock, occupied the northeastern portion of the state. They did not get along with the various Siouan tribes—including the Oto, Ioway, Missouri, and Osage—who inhabited the rest of Missouri. By the 1730s the Osage dominated all other tribes in the Missouri area. Observers noted their vigor and imposing presence. Osage men, for example, were often six feet or taller. After migrating from the Ohio Valley onto the plains, the Osage separated into two major bands—the Great Osage, who frequented the territory around the Osage River, and the Little Osage, who tended toward the Missouri River. They became avid traders with the French, calling the hirsute newcomers *I'n-Shta-Heh,* which meant "heavy eyebrows," but their influence waned rapidly with white expansion engendered by the Louisiana Purchase. In 1808 and 1825, the Osage signed treaties relinquishing their lands in present-day Missouri and parts of Arkansas.

In the late eighteenth century, allied tribes of the Shawnee and Delaware, pushed westward by American settlement, began to regroup in the southeastern corner of the state in the vicinity of present-day Cape Girardeau. The Spanish government, happy to have the newcomers as a buffer against American advancement and the Osage, provided land grants to these Indians. But by 1825 American expansion had begun to force the two tribes to sell their Spanish land grants. The next brief stop for many Shawnee and Delaware was the eastern portion of present-day Kansas; their final destination was Oklahoma and, for some, Canada. The last Indian claims in Missouri were terminated in 1836 with the Platte Purchase, whereby the Sauk, Mesquakie, and other tribes ceded their lands in northwestern Missouri.

After Loùis Jolliet and Father Jacques Marquette's explorations of the Mississippi River in 1673, other French adventurers began to probe the eastern portions of Missouri. They were attracted by rumors of minerals, especially silver. In 1700 Pierre Charles Le Sueur led a mineralogical expedition into the Mississippi Valley. In 1715 Antoine Laumet de La Mothe, sieur de Cadillac, founder of Detroit and governor of Louisiana, explored for silver in the rugged country around present-day Bonne Terre on behalf of the French banker Antoine Crozat. He found only lead. In 1719 Mine La Motte was opened and named for Cadillac; it later became one of the richest lead-ore mines in Missouri. Other representatives of Crozat failed to find the precious metals they craved and in the process incurred heavy debts. Their dealings with the Indians, however, paved the way for the fur traders in the next wave of French entrepreneurship, who enjoyed considerably better fortune. Their first base of trade in this part of the continent was Sainte Genevieve. The village was founded in the 1740s on the west bank of the Mississippi by Creoles, primarily farmers, who had crossed the river from the east-bank town of Kaskaskia. In a few years, Sainte Genevieve was doing a brisk trade with Canada and New Orleans. Although eventually eclipsed by its upstream neighbor Saint Louis, Sainte Genevieve remains the oldest permanently occupied town in Missouri and a rare repository of French Creole culture.

In 1763 the New Orleans traders Gilbert Antoine Maxent and Pierre Laclède were granted a trade monopoly on the upper Mississippi River, and before the year's end, Laclède had ventured up the river to select the future site of Saint Louis. Laclède's child-agent,

OVERLEAF: *George Caleb Bingham's* Raftmen Playing Cards—*in the collection of the Saint Louis Art Museum—is one of a series Bingham painted in the 1840s and 1850s chronicling the boatmen of the Missouri. A self-taught artist, Bingham grew up in the river town of Franklin, Missouri (detail).*

14-year-old Auguste Chouteau, laid out the village in February 1764. Chouteau was the son of Marie Thérèse Bourgeois Chouteau. Madame Chouteau, estranged from her husband, a New Orleans innkeeper, formed a long-standing liaison with Pierre Laclède and joined him in Saint Louis, bringing along with her the son and three daughters he had fathered in New Orleans. Auguste Chouteau and his half siblings, who all maintained the Chouteau name, were Saint Louis's arbiters in both business and society, a position they strengthened by marrying into other prominent families, including the Labbadies, Gratiots, and Papins.

When Laclède and Chouteau founded Saint Louis they did not know that Louis XV had secretly ceded France's holdings west of the Mississippi to Spain in 1762. This transaction proved of little consequence to daily life in the village. French culture and language prevailed, and Spain appointed many Frenchmen to governmental offices. The events of the American Revolution proved far more disruptive. Saint Louisans sided with the Americans, aiding George Rogers Clark in his exploits in the Old Northwest and fending off an attack on the city by British and Indian forces in 1780.

With American victory and peace in 1783 came administrative and mercantile chaos in the Mississippi Valley. The victors were slow to impose order in their newly acquired possession east of the river, and for a decade British fur traders continued to intrude on American and Spanish soil, to the consternation of Saint Louis traders. At the same time, Spain, which still exercised control of the Mississippi, arbitrarily opened and closed the river to American commerce as a way of demonstrating to its new upstart neighbor who was in control of the midcontinent. Creoles and Americans alike fled the east bank of the Mississippi and in so doing kindled growth in Saint Louis and on the western—that is, future Missouri—side of the river. This realm was also attractive because of Spain's liberal land-grant policy and because slavery was not prohibited as it was after 1787 in the Northwest Territory. Daniel Boone was among the many Americans who chose to move across the Mississippi into Spanish territory.

In 1800 Spain returned the vast expanse of Louisiana to France in the Treaty of San Ildefonso. Napoleon's dreams of reestablishing a grip on the New World were dashed by the defeat of his forces

OPPOSITE: *The massive Classic Revival dome of the state capitol in Jefferson City, completed in 1917, looms over Jefferson Landing State Historic Site.*

invading Saint Domingue (Haiti), so, when American envoys went to France to negotiate the purchase of New Orleans, Napoleon offered them all of Louisiana Territory. In 1803 the United States gained the area of the present state of Louisiana plus an ill-defined tract of land lying between the Mississippi River and the Rocky Mountains for $15 million. When the American commissioners asked for a clarification of the boundaries of the purchase, Napoleon is said to have remarked: "If an obscurity did not already exist, it would perhaps be good policy to put one there."

When Meriwether Lewis began seeking out maps, charts, and advice about the territory that President Thomas Jefferson had employed him to explore, he turned to Saint Louis's leaders, Auguste Chouteau and his half brother Jean Pierre, for advice. Eager to maintain their prestige and their monopolies on Indian trade under the incoming regime, the Chouteaus actively wooed Lewis and his co-captain William Clark—for instance providing most

Henry Lewis's View of Saint Louis *(detail), painted in 1846, shows a bustling metropolis on one side of the Mississippi, the edge of the wilderness on the other. In*

of the $3,879.72 worth of Indian gifts that Lewis and Clark carried west on their expedition. The American explorers responded to courtship, to the dismay of Manuel Lisa and other competing traders in Saint Louis, and Saint Louis was set on the course of becoming the midcontinental hub of American expansion.

The War of 1812, which brought with it a flurry of Indian skirmishes in Missouri, discouraged white settlement west of the Mississippi. But after the Americans won that war and extracted promises of peace from the Indians in treaties signed in 1815 and 1816, no obstacle, excepting the thick tangle of wilderness, stood in the way of expansion. These were heady times in Missouri country. The first steamboat, the *Zebulon Pike,* arrived at the landing in Saint Louis in 1817. In that same city, the young Tennessean lawyer and editor Thomas Hart Benton was emerging as a spokesman for his adopted homeland and for the westward migration of the yeoman farmer. (Benton went on to serve as Missouri's Democratic senator

the foreground a group of pioneers, bound for Oregon as one of their wagons proclaims, makes final preparations for the trek.

for thirty years, until the fight over slavery sundered his party and ended his career.) Moses Austin, Missouri's first industrialist, who became a founder of Texas, was perfecting smelting methods in the lead-belt region just south of Sainte Genevieve. In the heart of the country, near present-day Boonville, Nathan and Daniel M. Boone, sons of Daniel Boone, were distilling and selling salt at Boone's Lick, a natural saline spring. In the early 1820s the only road in the territory was the Boone's Lick Road, which ran from the town of Franklin, near the salt spring, east to Saint Charles and the mining town of Potosi.

Having achieved territorial status in 1816, Missouri applied for statehood in 1818. Because Missouri's entry into the Union could upset the balance of power between slave states and free states, the smoldering debate over slavery came to a political climax in both Congress and the nation at large. In 1819 the northern-dominated House voted for gradual elimination of slavery in Missouri; the Senate refused to accept the proposal. In 1820 Congress struck a bargain. The so-called Missouri Compromise granted Missouri's entry into the Union as a slave state but admitted Maine, formerly a part of Massachusetts, as a free state. Slavery was banned from the remainder of the Louisiana Territory north of 36° 30' North latitude, which was the westward extension of Missouri's southern boundary. John Quincy Adams called the fight over slavery in Missouri the "title page to a great tragic volume"; the 1820 compromise soothed the troubled waters only in the short term.

Missouri entered the Union under a cloud and in a time of financial panic. In 1821 the Bank of Saint Louis and the Bank of Missouri failed. But soon Missourians were able to prime their economy with hard currency: In 1821 the trader and explorer William Becknell and a party of men left Franklin on a trading mission with Indians. They went all the way to Santa Fe, selling their wares to Mexicans eager for trade goods and with ample silver to make purchases. In 1822 Becknell put together a more organized trading party and returned to Santa Fe. The 900-mile journey to the village was not easy—in the Cimarron Desert the thirsty party was forced to drink water from a buffalo's stomach—but it was successful.

OPPOSITE: *Steamboats take on and discharge cargoes on the Saint Louis levee in 1853. Until the railroads began to replace river transport, Saint Louis was the major supply point for emigrants heading west and the major marketplace for the products of the West.*

Becknell's party turned a reported 2,000 percent profit on $3,000 worth of trade goods, and the Santa Fe Trail was officially born.

Buyers in Santa Fe purchased American goods with mules as well as hard currency. Both were useful commodities in the frontier state. By the 1830s many Missouri traders, outfitters, and merchants were benefiting from commerce on the Santa Fe Trail. Entrepreneurs found better jumping-off places on the Missouri River in the northwestern edge of the state and founded the towns of Westport—which became Kansas City—and Independence. The opening of the Oregon Trail in 1843 and the subsequent discovery of gold in California and the Rockies guaranteed the futures of these outposts. The soils and climate in northwestern Missouri proved conducive to large-scale farming. The Platte Country, as it was known, was acquired from the Indians in 1836 and annexed to Missouri the following year. Southern planters moved into the area, bringing with them their slaves. A thriving hemp and tobacco culture took hold in this corner of the state.

This mural by N.C. Wyeth, in the Missouri State Capitol, depicts cavalry units from Arkansas and Kansas charging into each other during the Battle of Westport, fought on October 23, 1864. The opposing commanders fired at one another; the Confederate was killed, the Federal commander was wounded in the arm.

In 1831 the Mormon leader Joseph Smith, Jr., selected Independence as the Mormon promised land and began leading his followers into the area. Their clannishness and opposition to slavery became sore points for many area farmers, who banded together to drive out the Mormons. The planters were abetted by the governor, who ordered the militia to exterminate the Mormons if they refused to leave the state—they were gone by 1839. Many years later the Reorganized Church of Jesus Christ of Latter Day Saints returned its headquarters to Independence.

The brief expansionist Mexican War, from 1846 to 1848, netted the United States more territory and reopened the issue of the expansion of slavery. Once again, fierce arguments raged between antislavery and proslavery factions on the matter of how to partition the new territory. The Kansas-Nebraska Act of 1854, which organized those two territories, also repealed the Missouri Compromise and put the issue of slavery into the hands of the territorial voters. A tug-of-war began immediately over Kansas. Proslavery Missourians, concentrated along the western edge of the state, jumped their state line to vote in bogus elections in Kansas Territory. Then vigilante-style warfare broke out. These Border Wars pitted extremists from both camps—Missouri's proslavery Border Ruffians (a name bestowed by Horace Greeley) against the so-called Kansas Jayhawkers. Ruthless Missouri guerrillas were led by proslavery men such as William Clarke Quantrill and William "Bloody Bill" Anderson. The abolitionists followed John Brown. Bloody deeds bespoke a predilection for violence for violence's sake. The Civil War provided the border guerrillas with a cloak of respectability. Missouri's Confederate general Sterling Price had nothing but praise for Quantrill's "gallant struggle" against Kansas despotism. Hindsight proved that the guerrilla assaults provided little more than a testing ground for outlaws who continued to run rampant after the war. Quantrill and Anderson's most proficient students were Frank and Jesse James and Cole Younger and his brothers.

Missouri was the scene of legal as well as lawless struggles over slavery. Dred Scott and his family were slaves who had resided for several years in Illinois, a free state, and a free territory before they returned with their owners to Missouri, a slave state. Scott sued for his freedom in state court, citing his prolonged residency in places where slavery was illegal—an argument that had been previously accepted by the Missouri courts. Scott lost in a first trial, won a second decision, then lost on appeals in 1852 and 1854. In 1857 the U.S. Supreme Court decided, with two dissenting votes, that Scott was subject to Missouri law and therefore remained a slave. Five of the nine justices were southern. The chief justice, Roger B. Taney, used the case as an opportunity to write an opinion declaring that blacks were not "persons" under the Constitution, were not citizens, and could not sue in Federal court. He further stated that Congress had no power to prohibit slavery from territories, and that citizens of slave states could bring their slaves into free states for an indefinite time—an opinion which many took to be a de facto legalization of slavery throughout the country. Thus an obscure Missouri lawsuit brought the national debate over slavery to a boil, and contributed to the tensions that brought on the Civil War.

On the eve of the war, Missourians elected a proslavery governor, Claiborne Fox Jackson. However, a state convention voted to stay with the Union, despite Jackson's efforts to the contrary. A strong factor in the Union's favor were the votes of Missouri's large population of German immigrants, who opposed slavery and secession. The winning of Missouri was an early strategic victory for the Union. Had the state sided with the South, Saint Louis would have been the largest city in the Confederate states. Shortly after the outbreak of the war, Jackson's government went into exile and a provisional pro-Union government was installed in Jefferson City. Missouri furnished 40,000 troops to the Confederacy and 110,000 to the Union, and a home-front militia of 50,000 was raised to help crush the guerrilla warfare within the state. Throughout the Civil War, Missouri's kin—fathers, sons, brothers, nephews, and cousins—fought against one another, a splitting of clans that made the conflict even more bitter in the minds of Missourians.

The ruthless tactics of the Confederate guerrillas provoked stern measures by the Federal commander on the Missouri border. The guerrillas were, naturally enough, provided with food, supplies, and hiding places by their families. To deny the guerrillas this support, General Thomas Ewing arrested many women in the summer of 1863 and incarcerated some of them in Kansas City. One of the buildings where the women were being held collapsed on August 14, 1863, killing five of them. Undeterred, Ewing announced plans for more arrests. Thoroughly enraged, Quantrill's men launched a bloody raid of reprisal against Lawrence, Kansas, a Union stronghold. The raid prompted a further escalation—Ewing issued his General Order No. 11, commanding the immediate forced evacuation of all civilians from three western Missouri counties. Cavalry units from Kansas drove off tens of thousands of Missourians and burned their homes.

Between 1864 and 1870 the Radical Unionists—the extremist end of the Republican party—dominated affairs in Missouri. Their ranks included a peculiar mixture of German immigrants, white subsistence farmers from the Ozarks, Saint Louis merchants, and a few abolitionists. The Radical Unionists supported rights for blacks, development of public education, promotion of business and the railroads, and punishment of their political enemies. In the early 1870s the party became stuck in the debate over its "Test Oath," which the U.S. Supreme Court had ruled was unconstitutional in 1866. The oath was intended to restrict the activities of former Confederate sympathizers. Admission of such sympathies or failure to sign the oath meant a person could not vote, hold office, teach, preach, or practice various other professions. The Democratic party filled the vacuum created by this dispute and was in power in Missouri from 1873 until 1904, when Theodore Roosevelt maneuvered the state back into the Republican fold. The post-Civil War era witnessed the decline in river and overland trail traffic and the rise of the railroads; expansion of lead and iron mines; increased industrialization; and the ascension of Saint Louis and Kansas City as trade and manufacturing centers. Growth brought prosperity and problems to both cities, and both suffered for a time under the thumb of machine politics.

The chapter begins in Saint Louis and Saint Charles. It then moves north to Hannibal, the boyhood home of Samuel Clemens, and moves through the northeast quadrant of the state to Jefferson City, the beautiful capital perched on the banks of the Missouri River. The route then leads south into the Osage Valley, introduction to Missouri's splendid Ozark hills. Next comes the Bootheel region, the squiggle of Missouri that extends into Arkansas and is part of the broad, denuded floodplain expanse of the Mississippi delta. In Big Oak Tree State Park, visitors will find remnants of ancient swamp forest that once covered these bottomlands. The route then moves through western Missouri, from Springfield on the northwestern rim of the Ozarks, to Independence and Kansas City. It proceeds north, concluding in the vicinity of Laclède.

S A I N T   L O U I S

In the summer of 1763, Jean Jacques Blaise d'Abbadie, commander of the province of Louisiana, arrived in New Orleans and proceeded to grant a number of commercial monopolies in the hopes of shoring up the economy of Louisiana, which had been severely damaged during the struggle of France and Spain against England in the Seven Years' War. To Gilbert Antoine Maxent and his partner, Pierre Laclède, he granted exclusive trading privileges with the tribes along the Missouri River and west of the Mississippi. It was this trade arrangement that stimulated the growth of Saint Louis. Two months later Pierre Laclède left New Orleans to reconnoiter this newly acquired trading domain and to select a site for a future outpost. Traveling with the group was Laclède's young lieutenant, 13-year-old Auguste Chouteau, eldest son of Madame Marie Thérèse Bourgeois Chouteau, who was estranged from her husband and had taken up with Laclède. Marie Thérèse later became the matriarch of the French village, and her offspring would reign as Saint Louis's first dynasty.

In December, while on this reconnaissance, Laclède selected a spot for his trading post on the side of a high hill on the west bank of the Mississippi, about twenty miles below the river's confluence with the Missouri. The crest of the hill above the site offered commanding views of the Mississippi Valley, but more important, it was relatively safe from flooding. In February 1764 Auguste Chouteau returned with thirty woodsmen, who began clearing the bluff for the outpost. The village was laid out in a linear grid along the river, and resembled the plan of New Orleans and other French colonial garrison-towns. In the spring Laclède named the site Saint Louis after Louis IX, thirteenth-century Crusader king of France and patron saint of Louis XV, reigning monarch in 1764. A large commons was established to provide grazing land and timber for building and fuel; it extended seven miles southward to the River des Pères. Within a few years, five common fields had been set aside for cultivation of food.

Many of Saint Louis's earliest settlers were French families living on the east bank of the Mississippi who simply ferried across the

OPPOSITE: *An allegorical representation of Saint Louis as a lovely young woman—one of the stained-glass windows created by Conrad Schmidt for Union Station.*

river in 1764 when news arrived that France had ceded to England its lands east of the Mississippi in the treaty at the end of the Seven Years' War. Unbeknownst to them, Louis XV had already given France's vast Louisiana holdings to Spain. But Spanish administrators did not take charge in Saint Louis until 1770, and even after they did, Saint Louis remained a French colonial village in culture and spirit until the Louisiana Purchase by the United States. Thereafter it was engulfed by an invasion of westward-bound American pioneers and entrepreneurs. Only pen-and-ink drawings by Clarence Hoblitzelle, commissioned in the late nineteenth century by Pierre Chouteau, Jr., give clues to the original French architecture of the city. A prominent feature of the village was a mill pond, owned by Auguste Chouteau, which stretched two miles west of present-day 9th and Poplar streets.

During the colonial period, Saint Louis grew from a population of forty in 1764 to about a thousand. It became the center of a west-

Barge traffic on the Mississippi River, passing the Gateway Arch.

ern fur-trade network controlled by a few men, among them Laclède (until his death in 1778), Auguste Chouteau, his half-brother Pierre Chouteau, and their rival, the trader Manuel Lisa. These wealthy merchants brought refined taste to the wilderness village, and they and their wives established a reputation for charm and style. Visiting Saint Louis in 1804, William Henry Harrison compared it favorably to Philadelphia and New York. Harrison was not an acute observer, but the circle about the Chouteaus was cosmopolitan and hospitable. With the Louisiana Purchase in 1803, Saint Louis was well positioned to become a hub of exploration, commerce, and military operations. In the following year, Meriwether Lewis and William Clark embarked on their expedition from nearby Saint Charles. In 1805 and 1806, Zebulon Pike departed Saint Louis on two important exploratory missions, one to find the source of the Mississippi, the other to penetrate the Rocky Mountains.

Thomas Jefferson named Lewis governor of the Louisiana Territory in 1807. During his short-lived tenure, Lewis demonstrated scant ability as an administrator; he died, apparently at his own hand, in 1809. Lewis's co-captain and friend, William Clark, was named territorial governor of Missouri in 1813, a position he held until statehood in 1821. He and his wife, Julia, were major figures in Saint Louis's social, business, and political realms. Clark was one of the investors, along with the Chouteaus, Manuel Lisa, and Sylvestre Labadie, in the Missouri Fur Company, which was organized in 1809. In 1817 the steamboat *Zebulon Pike* docked at Saint Louis, bringing a new era in commerce to the town. When Henry Shaw, founder of the Missouri Botanical Garden, arrived via steamboat in 1819, Saint Louis's riverfront was still a parklike expanse, but the levee eventually became crowded with the commercial buildings, warehouses, and foundries that characterized the area until the 1930s and 1940s. Then much of the riverfront was returned to greensward, and it was used as a parking lot until the Jefferson National Expansion Memorial was constructed.

Saint Louis took its place as the gateway to the West after the War of 1812, when the mass westward emigration began. Its location on the Mississippi (on a high bluff untouched by the river's periodic floods) just twenty miles from the mouth of the Missouri made it the ideal site for a center of trade, transportation, manufacturing, and finance. Shops and factories in Saint Louis provided fur

Firmly in the control of Federal forces, Saint Louis passed through the Civil War unscathed, as evidenced by this view of the city from Lucas Place made in 1865. The artist who made the lithograph took some liberties with the facts—the large convent in the foreground was not on Lucas Place.

traders, explorers, and emigrants with virtually everything they needed, from wagons to cooking stoves. In return, the goods of the West, such as furs, hides, lumber, meat, and grain, were sold in Saint Louis or at least shipped through it. From the 1820s through the 1860s, Saint Louis entrepreneurs virtually controlled the economy of the West from the Mississippi to the Rockies.

Until 1830 French was still the prevailing language in Saint Louis, but in the ensuing decades English speakers flooded in—the population of the city mushroomed from about 5,900 in 1830 to 16,700 in 1840, and then to 78,000 in 1850. English became the common language, while the old French colonial architectural style, with high-pitched roofs and galleries, was abandoned in favor of London- and Philadelphia-derived rowhouses and Greek Revival mansions, even by the old French-American families. The building that best embodies the confidence of the era—and the expense to which boosters would go to express that optimism—is the Old

Courthouse, a serenely poised Greek Revival edifice in the heart of downtown. Across the street once stood the equally venerable Planters Hotel, which rivaled the Saint Charles in New Orleans and Astor House in New York. In the 1830s, 5,000 Germans immigrated to Saint Louis; by the 1840s, 6,000 on average were arriving each year. To these immigrant ranks were added large numbers of Irish. By 1850 Saint Louis's foreign-born settlers, edging out American-born residents, constituted 52 percent of the population. Until Prohibition, the city's breweries were the most visible commercial indication of its strong Germanic traditions.

Saint Louis suffered during the national economic downturns in 1819, 1837, 1857, and 1873, but its blackest year was 1849, when a cholera epidemic spread through the city, killing 8,000 people. Then, on May 17, a fire spread from the docked steamboat *White Cloud* and destroyed much of the commercial center of the city. After the fire, many new buildings in Saint Louis were faced with cast-iron fronts, and the city's foundries became major suppliers of architectural ironwork. Having surpassed Cincinnati in steamboat tonnage by 1850, Saint Louis emerged as the leading city along the Ohio-Mississippi axis.

Saint Louis's large German-American population played an important role early in the Civil War. Staunch Unionists, the Germans formed military units named the Home Guard, which were called into Federal service by the local commander, Captain Nathaniel Lyon, when the secessionist state militia threatened to seize the U.S. arsenal in Saint Louis. The militia had been called out by Governor Claiborne Fox Jackson, who had been frustrated in his effort to bring Missouri into the Confederacy (although the legislature was pro-South, delegates to a special state convention voted to remain in the Union). Disguised as a woman, Captain Lyon entered the camp of the militia and found the men drilling with weapons and artillery smuggled into the city from Baton Rouge. On May 10, 1861, Lyon deployed six regiments of the Home Guard and regular soldiers—as many as 7,000 men—around the camp and forced the militia (about 700 men) to surrender peacefully. As they marched their prisoners through Saint Louis, the victors were jeered and stoned by a mob whose sentiments were not only pro-South but anti-German. A shot fired from the crowd

OVERLEAF: *A portion of the 1904 Saint Louis Exposition, held on the centennial of the Louisiana Purchase. At left is the Palace of Liberal Arts.*

provoked a fusillade from the soldiers. Some twenty-eight civilians and two soldiers died in the melee, followed by a night of rioting in which several German-Americans were murdered. On the day after the "Saint Louis Massacre," the Home Guard and soldiers firmly restored order (with another six deaths). Many secessionists fled the city. In 1862 and 1864, Confederate campaigns made Saint Louis an objective, but neither got close to the city.

Although it did not physically damage Saint Louis appreciably, the Civil War cut the city off from its traditional southern markets. The development of Chicago as a railroad center drew trade from Saint Louis. Yet by the late nineteenth century, Saint Louis was the nation's second-largest grain market, the largest inland cotton market, a major meat-packing center, and a leading manufacturer of shoes and beer. The city's chemical industry developed, especially after 1899, when John Queeny opened Monsanto and began manufacturing saccharin, formerly a German monopoly. In 1899, when Saint Louis was chosen as the site for the Louisiana Purchase Exposition, the city was given an opportunity for a civic rejoinder to its rival, Chicago (Chicago had been selected to host the World's Columbian Exposition in 1893). The exposition's planners spared no effort. When the World's Fair opened in 1904 in Forest Park, it surpassed in size not only the Chicago exposition but also those that had been held in the intervening years in Atlanta, Nashville, Omaha, Buffalo, and Charleston. Participating states and countries erected almost 1,600 buildings, and 19 million people visited the fair. "Meet me in Saint Louie, Louie" became a national refrain. (Some historians credit a food vendor at the Saint Louis World's Fair with the invention of the ice-cream cone, but ices in edible containers date back to the 1790s.)

Saint Louis claims a diverse roster of literary and musical personalities. In 1859 Samuel Clemens received his river pilot's certificate from the Saint Louis inspectors and embarked on the career on the Mississippi that later inspired his writings under the pen name Mark Twain. In 1865 the Hungarian immigrant Joseph Pulitzer arrived in Saint Louis, where he embarked on his journalism career and business enterprises. He purchased and eventually consolidated the *Saint Louis Dispatch* and the German-language *Westliche Post* newspapers in 1878, forming the *Saint Louis Post-Dispatch,* the first of the properties in the Pulitzer publishing empire. In 1903 Pulitzer announced that he would bequeath an endowment to award prizes for journalism and other publishing endeavors. The Pulitzer Prizes commenced in 1917. Although he later became a naturalized citizen of England, the eminent poet T. S. Eliot was born in Saint Louis in 1888. The poet Eugene Field was also born in Saint Louis in 1850 and spent much of his writing career here. Scott Joplin, the king of ragtime, made his home in Saint Louis in the early 1900s.

JEFFERSON NATIONAL EXPANSION MEMORIAL

This gracious green esplanade overlooking the Mississippi River commemorates the key role played by Saint Louis in the nation's westward expansion. The riverfront vista is dominated by the **Gateway Arch,** one of America's most familiar landmarks. In 1948 the Finnish-born architect Eero Saarinen won the memorial competition with his design for a stainless-steel arch. The 630-foot-high structure was completed in 1965. Space-capsule-sized elevators rise to porthole windows at the peak of the arch, providing splendid views of Saint Louis and the Mississippi River. Beneath the arch is the **Museum of Westward Expansion.** Through the use of maps, paintings, documentary photographs, and Indian and pioneer artifacts, the museum broadly surveys a hundred years of American history: the western exploration of Lewis and Clark in 1804, the Civil War, the spread of the railroads, the conquest of the Indians, and Wilbur and Orville Wright's first airplane flight in 1903. An adjacent auditorium offers a documentary film on the construction of the Gateway Arch.

On a knoll, facing east toward the river and the Gateway Arch, is the **Old Courthouse** (1839–1862). With its cruciform floor plan, columned porticos, and massive dome, the stately Greek Revival building is a typical nineteenth-century temple of justice. The initial design was by Henry Singleton, but progress was excruciatingly slow, and several architects had a hand in the project. It was not completed until 1862, when William Rumbold's Renaissance dome was erected atop the building, despite a prolonged controversy in which some engineers offered the opinion that the cast-iron dome would collapse the structure. The Old Courthouse was the scene of the first Dred Scott trials in 1847 and 1850, which led to the Supreme Court decision in 1857 that blacks were not "persons" or citizens and therefore had no right to sue in federal court. The rul-

ing helped precipitate the Civil War. Exhibits in the Old Courthouse
explain the early history of Saint Louis and of western expansion.

> LOCATION: 11 North 4th Street. HOURS: *Gateway Arch and Museum of
> Westward Expansion:* June through August: 8–10 Daily; September
> through May: 9–6 Daily. *Old Courthouse:* 8–4:30 Daily. FEE: Yes. TELE-
> PHONE: 314–425–4465.

Basilica of Saint Louis, the King (The Old Cathedral)

The Basilica of Saint Louis is the oldest cathedral west of the
Mississippi and the only structure in the area that was not razed to
make way for the Jefferson Memorial. On this site the first mass in
Saint Louis was said in 1764. A series of churches have stood here,
beginning with a log chapel constructed in 1770. The present cathedral, a handsome Greek Revival structure, was begun in 1831, at the
urging of Bishop Joseph Rosati, who noted that the previous unfin-
ished church was a "hay barn." The church was designed by the
Saint Louis architects George Morton and Joseph Laveille. When
completed in 1834, it was the most expensive structure in the city. Its
rubble limestone walls are faced with cut sandstone. Especially
impressive are the large arched and Venetian windows paned with
clear glass, which pass beautiful light into the sanctuary. A museum
on the east side of the cathedral contains the original church bell
(1772), eighteenth- and nineteenth-century religious art, and memorabilia associated with the history of the church.

> LOCATION: Jefferson Expansion Memorial, 209 Walnut. HOURS:
> *Museum:* 9:30–4 Daily (Saturday to 6:45). FEE: For museum. TELE-
> PHONE: 314–231–3250.

On a bluff behind a floodwall, the city was an eyewitness to, not a
victim of, the immense 1993 flood. One casualty, however, was the
USS *Inaugural*, a World War II minesweeper that had seen action
at Okinawa. Docked near the Memorial, it was open to the public. The flood swept it downriver and dumped it against the bank
south of the Poplar Street bridge, where it remained in the late
1990s.

EADS BRIDGE

Just north of the Jefferson National Expansion Memorial, the Eads
Bridge was the first bridge to cross the Mississippi at Saint Louis—

50,000 people came out for its dedication in 1874—and it ranks with
the Brooklyn Bridge as one of America's most celebrated achievements in engineering. Building the span required a feat of persua-
sion as well. The bridge's designer and promoter was Captain James
B. Eads, who first convinced Saint Louis of the need for a railroad
bridge and then met the criticisms of colleagues who felt his design
for the massive three-span steel and wrought-iron cantilever bridge
was preposterous. Eads orchestrated the construction of the structure between 1868 and 1874. When completed, it was unequaled in
span in America. Eads made early use of steel in the design and
employed pneumatic caissons in the construction of the masonry
abutments and piers. Eads was particularly well equipped to determine the proper placement and depth of the piers, the deepest of
which is 123 feet below water level, for his former career was as a sal-
vager, retrieving cargo from sunken ships in the Mississippi. He
understood the hazards of the river's silty, shifting floor. Though the
bridge has withstood the test of time as a marvel of engineering, it
was an immediate economic failure. Rail traffic deteriorated, and
without tolls, the Illinois and Saint Louis Bridge Company went
bankrupt. Today the bridge carries only vehicular traffic.

LACLEDE'S LANDING

North of Eads Bridge, Laclède's Landing is a precinct of renovated
nineteenth-century warehouses that line the only surviving grid
from Auguste Chouteau's original 1760s survey for the French village he helped to found. American-style buildings began to replace
the French colonial structures along the riverfront by the 1820s.
After the Civil War, as Saint Louis became a major trade center,
more and more warehouses, factories, foundries, and businesses
elbowed their way onto the waterfront, which by 1880 extended
from Biddle Street on the north to Chouteau Avenue on the south.
Laclède's Landing preserves the last stand of these nineteenth-century wharves, warehouses, and commercial buildings.

   A few remaining commercial signs, such as those for Bronson
Hide Company, Christian Peper Tobacco, and Switzer Licorice
Company, hint at the diversity of commerce in this district. The
structures themselves range from the simple brick antebellum buildings at **801–805 North 2d Street** to the richly ornamented edifices of
the **Bronson Hide Company Warehouse** (806–808 North 1st Street).

Laclède's Landing is noted for the number of its buildings with cast-iron ornamentation. Close to the iron mines of southeastern Missouri, Saint Louis emerged as a major center for the production of architectural ironwork in the nineteenth century. The facade of the **Raeder Building** (721–727 North 1st Street) is the finest cast-iron facade in Saint Louis.

DOWNTOWN

With its wide boulevards and well-placed pocket parks, downtown Saint Louis invites pedestrians. The central business district stretches west from the Mississippi River to Jefferson Avenue and is bounded on the south by Interstate 40/64 and on the north by O'Fallon Street. As with every large American city, Saint Louis has lost its share of architectural landmarks, as its downtown has seen economic decline, and money for restoration has become elusive. One mourned building was the opulent Ambassador Theater, built in 1926. The future of other buildings is in doubt, but many fine structures remain. One of the most important buildings in American architecture is the **Wainwright Building** (101 North 7th Street), a steel-frame proto-skyscraper designed in 1890–1891 by the eminent Chicago team of Dankmar Adler and Louis Sullivan. The cinnabar-red sandstone facade, embellished with brick and terra-cotta botanical and abstract motifs, is notable as an early example of Sullivan's classical discipline and poetic ornament. His architectural ideals were set forth in such writings as the *Tall Office Building Artistically Considered*. Two blocks to the north, Adler and Sullivan's **Union Trust Building** (705 Olive Street) was the tallest building in Saint Louis when it was completed in 1892. It too was adorned with Sullivan's terra-cotta designs. Sadly, much of the ornamentation on the lower levels has been removed.

Union Station

Saint Louis's magnificent Union Station is a memorial to the heyday of the railroad and a tribute to late-twentieth-century preservationist zeal. After two decades of arbitration, the terminal and twelve-acre train shed have been converted into a commercial complex. The many-turreted castle, built in the Richardsonian Romanesque style,

OPPOSITE: *Turreted, arched, and capped with pyramids, Saint Louis's Union Station is a bold statement of the power and prosperity of the railroads in the 1890s.*

was the largest railroad terminal in the world when it opened in 1894. Theodore C. Link is the architect of record, but the design was probably largely the work of Harvey Ellis, an itinerant draftsman who was also responsible for the magnificent entryway to Washington Place, which anticipated the ornament of Louis Sullivan's Wainwright Building. The waiting room, or Grand Hall, is a barrel-vaulted lobby profusely decorated with mosaics, marble, stenciling, gold leaf, and stained-glass windows by Conrad Schmidt. The train shed, engineered by George Pegram, sheltered thirty-one tracks and the loading platforms, an area that handled 300 trains and 100,000 people a day in the 1940s.

LOCATION: Market Street between 18th and 20th streets. HOURS: 10–9 Monday–Thursday, 10–10 Friday–Saturday, 11–7 Sunday. FEE: For some tours. TELEPHONE: 314–421–6655

On Market Street across from Union Station in **Aloe Plaza** is **Meeting of the Waters,** a fountain of mythical figures and aquatic creatures, all spouting water. Designed by the Swedish-born sculptor Carl Milles, the ensemble represents allegorically the marriage of the Mississippi and Missouri rivers, which meet twenty miles north of Saint Louis. The unclad bronze figures caused a sensation when the fountain was installed in 1940, but it has since become a cherished city landmark. The **Soldiers' Memorial Military Museum** (1315 Chestnut Street, 314–622–4550) has two floors of exhibits of uniforms, weaponry, photographs, and military memorabilia. The collection ranges from the Spanish-American War to the Vietnam War.

Campbell House

The Campbell House is the lone survivor of Lucas Place, where Saint Louis's affluent merchants and professionals lived from 1850 to 1880. The Irish-born Robert Campbell came to Saint Louis in 1824 and embarked on a lucrative career as a fur trader. His firm, the Rocky Mountain Fur Company, became a rival of the Chouteau-Astor interests, and Campbell established the trading post that became Fort Laramie in present-day Wyoming. He returned to settle in Saint Louis in 1836. In 1854 he purchased this handsome three-

OPPOSITE: *A parlor in the Campbell House reflects the Victorian taste for strong colors and for filling a room with a variety of decorative objects.*

story Greek Revival townhouse, which had been built in 1851. He lived here with his wife, Virginia Jane Kyle, and their three sons until his death in 1879. The Campbells' reclusive bachelor sons, two of whom lived in the house until the 1930s, preserved a virtual museum of nineteenth-century upper-class domestic life. The house contains its original Victorian furnishings, much of them bearing hand-carved Rococo Revival motifs.

LOCATION: 1508 Locust Street. HOURS: March through December: 10–4 Tuesday–Saturday, 12–5 Sunday. FEE: Yes. TELEPHONE: 314–421–0325.

Within a few blocks of the Campbell house are three churches whose congregations figured prominently in the religious fabric of nineteenth-century Saint Louis. **Centenary United Methodist** (16th and Pine streets) is a limestone Gothic Revival structure of 1869. It was built to serve the oldest (1839) Methodist congregation in the city. **Saint John the Apostle and Evangelist Catholic Church** (16th and Chestnut streets) is a twin-towered Romanesque Revival sanctuary built from 1859 to 1860 to serve a parish founded in 1848. **Christ Church Episcopal Cathedral** (1210 Locust Street) is a handsome Gothic Revival structure dedicated in 1867, noted for its carved stone altar and reredos. Established in 1819, it is the oldest Episcopal congregation west of the Mississippi.

The **Central Public Library** (1301 Olive Street) is an imposing Renaissance Revival granite structure (1912) designed by Cass Gilbert of Saint Paul and New York, who a few years previously had been a principal designer at the Saint Louis World's Fair; the very ornate interior is splendid. **City Hall** (Market Street at Tucker Boulevard) is a gargantuan Renaissance Revival civic castle modeled after Paris's city hall and constructed between 1891 and 1904.

Crouching on an entire city block, the **Old Post Office and Customs House** (815 Olive Streets) is a fortress of granite designed in 1872 by Alfred B. Mullett, supervising architect for the U.S. Treasury Department. The building, though long in coming (it was finally completed in 1884, after much legal wrangling and the expenditure of $6 million), is one of the best interpretations of the Second Empire style in the country.

During the late nineteenth and early twentieth centuries, the heart of Saint Louis's wholesale, light manufacturing, and garment districts lay along Washington Avenue and the parallel Lucas Avenue, Saint Charles Street, and Locust Street. These thoroughfares, between 9th and 18th streets, remain a virtual museum of the turn-of-the-century mercantile designs of Saint Louis's leading architects. One of the most prominent firms, that of William S. Eames and Thomas Young, designed the **Lammert Building** (911 Washington Avenue) in 1898 for the oldest dry-goods company in Saint Louis. The venerable Renaissance Revival structure is named for the furniture company that occupied the building from 1924 to 1981; one of the current occupants is the Saint Louis chapter of the American Institute of Architects (314–621–3484). The building was remodeled in 1985.

The **Scott Joplin House State Historic Site** (2658 Delmar Boulevard, 314–533–1003), which was opened in 1990, celebrates the king of ragtime, who lived in Saint Louis in the early 1900s, during which time he wrote some of his best-known works, including "The Entertainer." The child of a former slave and a free black woman, Scott Joplin was born in 1868 in Texarkana, on the Texas-Arkansas border. As a teenager, he joined with other itinerant ragtime musicians, performing in New Orleans, Nashville, Louisville, Saint Louis, and Chicago. In 1902 he lived in this modest Victorian flat with his wife, Belle Hayden, whom he had married in Sedalia, Missouri, after the success of his composition "Maple Leaf Rag."

NORTH SAINT LOUIS

The area stretching north along the Mississippi began to be settled in the 1840s. The first wave of newcomers were Germans, then Irish and Poles. In the 1910s and 1920s, the prospect of finding work brought an influx of rural people, black and white, mainly from the South and generally poor, to both North and South Saint Louis. With World War II, which created even more employment, the rural-to-urban inrush became greater.

The town of **North Saint Louis** (vicinity of North Florissant Avenue and Palm Street) was founded by Kentuckians in 1816, but by the 1850s it had become overwhelmingly German. In 1844 a group of Germans founded Bremen, which grew rapidly into a bustling manufacturing town; it was incorporated into Saint Louis in 1855. **Hyde Park** (Salisbury and North 20th streets) stands in the heart of old Bremen, and many of the handsome middle-class townhouses surrounding the park were built between 1850 and 1900. The rich ethnic complexion of North Saint Louis is borne out by the wealth of its ecclesiastical architecture. The red-brick Gothic Revival **Bethlehem Lutheran Church** (2153 Salisbury Street) was dedicated in 1893 (and rebuilt in 1894 after a fire) to serve Bremen's German-speaking congregation. Now the **Historical Christ Baptist Church** (3114 Lismore Street), the former Saint Augustine's Roman Catholic Church is a Gothic Revival structure built in 1896 by its German immigrant congregation. The **Saints Cyril and Methodius Polish National Catholic Church** (2005 North 11th Street) was built in 1857 for a Presbyterian congregation—it is one of the oldest surviving churches in Saint Louis—but in 1908 it became home to one of the Polish congregations that had split from the Roman Catholic church. **Saint Liborius Catholic Church** (1835 North 18th Street) is a red-brick Gothic Revival sanctuary and rectory built from 1888 to 1889 for its German parishioners,

The Busch mausoleum, in the Gothic Revival style, in Bellefontaine Cemetery.

who founded this parish in 1855. **Saint Stanislaus Kostka Church** (1413 North 20th Street) is a Romanesque Revival church (1891) that served the first Polish parish in Saint Louis, founded in 1880. The **Holy Cross Catholic Church** (8121–8129 Church Road) is a red-brick Gothic Revival church (1909) serving a parish founded in the 1860s by German and Irish immigrants.

The largely Protestant **Bellefontaine Cemetery** (4947 West Florissant Avenue) and its adjacent Catholic counterpart, **Calvary Cemetery** (5239 West Florissant Avenue), have commodious, park-like aspects. Many famous Saint Louisans are buried here, including Auguste Chouteau, Manuel Lisa, William Clark, the Confederate general Sterling Price, the Union general William Tecumseh Sherman, Senator Thomas Hart Benton, and the bridge engineer James B. Eads. The **Wainwright Tomb** (Prospect Avenue, in the southeast corner of Bellefontaine Cemetery) was designed in 1891 by Louis Sullivan and is one of his finest works. The Saint

Louis Sullivan designed this mausoleum for Charlotte Dickson Wainwright in 1891.

Louis promoter Ellis Wainwright commissioned the tomb for his young wife, Charlotte Dickson Wainwright. He was interred here thirty-three years later.

The **Bissell Mansion,** now a restaurant (4426 Randall Place, 314–533–9830), is a red-brick Greek Revival home built in 1830 on the 1,500-acre plantation of Captain Lewis Bissell; it may be the oldest extant brick house in Saint Louis. Much of the interior woodwork is intact. Captain Bissell, born in Connecticut, served in the War of 1812, commanded Fort Clark in Illinois, and explored the Missouri River with the Yellowstone Expedition of 1818–1819. Shortly thereafter he began acquiring 1,500 acres of land for real estate development in Saint Louis. He died in this house in 1868.

As early as 1911, a number of white Saint Louisans began drawing up covenants to restrict the sale of domestic property to blacks, who were moving into the city in increasing numbers. A house on Labadie Street became the center of controversy in 1945 when a black man, J. D. Shelley, was refused the title to it because the former owners had signed a covenant with a race clause in 1911. In 1948 these covenants were declared unenforcable by the U.S. Supreme Court in the case of *Shelley v. Kraemer.* One of the black enclaves to spring up as a result of this de facto policy of segregation was the middle-class neighborhood known as the Ville (roughly bounded by Martin Luther King Boulevard, Sarah Street, Saint Louis Avenue, and Newstead Avenue). Parents in the Ville lobbied for the relocation of **Sumner High School** (4248 West Cottage Avenue) to their neighborhood. The red-brick Georgian Revival structure was completed in 1908; it was designed by a Saint Louis School Board architect, William B. Ittner. The original Sumner High School, which dates from 1875, was the first black high school west of the Mississippi, the result of long battles to obtain public education for Saint Louis blacks.

MIDTOWN

In the 1880s a mixed-use area of businesses and residences began to spring up along Lindell Boulevard about three miles west of the river. By the 1920s the neighborhood comprised affluent homes, sophisticated residential hotels, fashionable shops, and glittering theaters and entertainment houses. One playhouse billed a precision chorus line called the Rockets, which later evolved into the Rockettes of New York's Radio City Music Hall. The building that best captures the spirit of this era is the **Fox Theatre** (527 North Grand Avenue, 314–534–1678), a 4,500-seat hall promoted by William Fox, founder of 20th Century-Fox. C. Howard Crane of Detroit designed the exotic structure, which is encrusted with Moorish and Indian motifs; Fox's wife, Eve Leo Fox, created the interior. The theater has been lavishly restored. The **Vaughn Cultural Center** (3701 Grandel Square, 314–371–0040), in the Urban League headquarters, has regular exhibits focusing on black history and culture.

A prominent businessman and philanthropist, Samuel Cupples made a fortune selling broom and ax handles and other woodware. His firm was the largest such company in the world. Now owned by Saint Louis University, the **Samuel Cupples House** (3673 West Pine Boulevard, 314–658–3025) is a Richardsonian Romanesque structure (1890) noted for its sandstone carvings. The interior is appointed with twenty fireplaces, extensive carved woodwork, stained glass, Saint Louis–manufactured ironwork, and period furnishings. It also houses an art gallery in the former bowling alley.

Cupples Station (South 10th and Spruce streets) comprises ten warehouses, built between 1894 and 1917, that were linked to the nearby railroads by an underground system of spur lines. The structures were designed by Eames & Young and represent an important grouping of turn-of-the-century commercial building.

With its huge, glittering green-tile dome, the **Cathedral of Saint Louis** (Lindell Boulevard and Newstead Avenue) is one of Saint Louis's landmarks. The immense Byzantine Revival structure takes its inspiration from the Church of Hagia Sophia in Istanbul. Designed by the Saint Louis firm of Barnett, Haynes & Barnett, it was built between 1907 and 1914, although installation of its many mosaics, which cover domes, arches, ceilings, and walls, continued until 1989.

FOREST PARK AND THE 1904 LOUISIANA PURCHASE EXPOSITION

The biggest park in Saint Louis and one of the largest urban preserve-parks in the nation, 1,300-acre Forest Park opened in 1876. It was designed by the German-trained landscape architect Maximilian Kern. The only extant nineteenth-century building in the park is the **Cabanne House** (115 Union Avenue), a Second Empire struc-

ture built in 1875 as the park headquarters. By the 1890s large numbers of Saint Louisans were taking advantage of this pleasant expanse, while many of the city's wealthier citizens were settling into quiet, deed-restricted neighborhoods on the northeastern edges of the park. **Portland** and **Westmoreland places,** where development began in 1888, are lined with well-shaded mansions, a trove of late-nineteenth-century opulence along private streets with guarded entrances. In **Fullerton's Westminster Place** (4300 and 4400 blocks of Westminster), another handsome residential area, houses date from 1892 to 1909 and were designed by Barnett, Haynes & Barnett and the other leading Saint Louis architectural firms of the period. At **4446 Westminster Place** was the residence of Henry Ware and Charlotte Stearns Eliot, whose son, the poet T. S. Eliot, intermittently resided here. Henry Ware Eliot, president of Hydraulic Press Brick Company, was the son of the Reverend William Greenleaf Eliot, founder of Washington University. The **Second Presbyterian**

The Romanesque exterior of the Cupples House (above) features a profusion of carved faces, animals, flowers, and geometric designs. The main entrance (opposite) is not at the center of a wall but on a corner, reflecting the assymetrical character of Romanesque architecture.

Church (4501 Westminster Place), with a congregation that dates from 1838, is an impressive compound of Romanesque Revival architecture; the chapel (1896) was designed by the Boston firm of Shepley, Rutan & Coolidge, while the sanctuary (1900) was conceived by the Saint Louis architect Theodore C. Link. At the confluence of North Kingshighway, McPherson, and Washington Boulevard is the **Holy Corners District,** an imposing area of turn-of-the-century religious and institutional structures in an array of noble styles.

In 1899, when Saint Louis was chosen as the site for the Louisiana Purchase Exposition, exposition planners selected Forest Park, then on the western edge of Saint Louis and well removed from the conspicuous industrial squalor of the central city, as the fair site. Development of the 1,200-acre grounds necessitated clearing a section of the park called the Wilderness, which at that time still encompassed a stand of virgin woodland. A French-born,

The Saint Louis Art Museum, designed by Cass Gilbert as part of the 1904 world's fair, is noted for its collections of pre-Columbian and German Expressionist art.

American-naturalized architect, Emmanuel Masqueray, was the exposition's chief designer; a Kansas City parks planner, George E. Kessler, was chief landscape architect. Cass Gilbert, of Saint Paul and New York, imposed his grand Beaux-Arts scheme on the fair and emerged as the most dominant of the exposition's several architects. Gilbert's fantastic French Baroque Festival Hall was dismantled after the fair, as were all exposition buildings with the exception of his Palace of Arts, which was planned from the first as a permanent facility for the **Saint Louis Art Museum** (314–721–0072). Gilbert's serene and stately Classic Revival structure commands a knoll with a sweeping view of Forest Park. The museum's American holdings range from colonial times to the present, with paintings by John Singleton Copley, Winslow Homer, Georgia O'Keefe, and Thomas Hart Benton, and sculptures by Augustus Saint-Gaudens. The museum has the nation's largest collection of paintings by George Caleb Bingham, who chronicled antebellum life along the Missouri River. There are also works by modern American artists such as Mark Rothko and Frank Stella. In front of the museum is the *Apotheosis of Saint Louis,* a bronze equestrian statue of Louis IX by Charles Niehaus, which was presented to the city in 1906 as part of the post-exposition restoration of Forest Park.

History Museum

The Missouri Historical Society's History Museum is housed in the Jefferson Memorial Building, built in 1911 on the site of the main entrance to the Louisiana Purchase Exposition. The granite-and-limestone Beaux-Arts structure was designed by the firm of Isaac Taylor, a Saint Louis architect who served as director of works for the 1904 fair. The museum's exhibits focus on the history and development of Saint Louis. The society's collection includes many documents and personal effects associated with Pierre Laclède, the Chouteau family, William and Julia Clark, and other men and women involved in the early growth of Saint Louis. There is also a photographic exhibit of the Louisiana Purchase Exposition and a display of memorabilia from Charles Lindbergh's pioneering transatlantic flight in the *Spirit of Saint Louis* in 1927.

LOCATION: Lindell Boulevard and De Baliviere. HOURS: 9:30–4:45 Tuesday–Sunday. FEE: None. TELEPHONE: 314–746–4599.

MISSOURI BOTANICAL GARDEN

Under the indefatigable Henry Shaw, a wealthy merchant turned passionate horticulturist, the Missouri Botanical Garden began to sprout from a treeless expanse of prairie in the mid-1850s. Opened to the public in 1859, it not only has beautiful public gardens but also serves as one of the world's leading botanical research institutions, particularly in the study of endangered tropical flora. Shaw drew his inspiration from gardens in England and Europe, which he intended to emulate on the edge of the American wilderness. The result has become ever more Edenic as modern Saint Louis has enveloped this serene pocket of towering trees and gardens. Shaw sought advice from the world's eminent horticulturists, including Asa Gray of Harvard, the most respected American botanist of the period, and Sir William Jackson Hooker, director of Kew Garden in England. In 1866 he hired James Gurney from London's Royal Botanical Garden at Kew to become chief gardener at both the Missouri Botanical Garden and Tower Grove Park.

Shaw commissioned the architect George I. Barnett to design two dwellings and several garden buildings. **Tower Grove,** Shaw's country home, is a gracious Italianate structure now surrounded by luxuriant gardens and old trees. His palazzo-style **townhouse,** which originally stood in downtown Saint Louis at 7th and Locust streets, was dismantled and reconstructed on the garden grounds at Shaw's behest. Both houses were completed in 1851. Tower Grove contains Victorian furnishings, some of which belonged to Shaw. The **Linnean House** (1882) is the only extant greenhouse dating to the Shaw era. The building was originally used for winter storage of Shaw's potted palms. Barnett's classically inspired red-brick building is a counterpoint to the botanical garden's most famous twentieth-century structure, the geodesic-domed **Climatron,** a greenhouse for tropical plantings completed in 1960 and rebuilt in 1988–1989.

LOCATION: 4344 Shaw Boulevard. HOURS: Memorial Day through Labor Day: 9–8 Daily; Labor Day through Memorial Day: 9–5 Daily. FEE: Yes. TELEPHONE: 314-577-5100.

Henry Shaw's other gift to Saint Louis was **Tower Grove Park,** a public preserve adjoining the Missouri Botanical Garden. Shaw donated the land to the city in 1868. In the following years, he oversaw the planting of 20,000 trees and shrubs and the construction of gazebos,

The Linnean House at the Missouri Botanical Garden. Built by Henry Shaw and dedicated to the botanist Carl Linnaeus, the Linnean is the country's oldest public greenhouse in continuous operation.

carriage entrances, and the sham ruins that were typical of eighteenth- and nineteenth-century landscape design. One of these charming fixtures, the **Arsenal Street Gatehouse** (4255 Arsenal Street, 314–771–2679), designed by George I. Barnett in 1888, now serves as the park headquarters and visitor center.

SOUTHEAST SAINT LOUIS

The wedge of Saint Louis along the Mississippi River south of downtown and Interstate 64 has served as home for wave after wave of immigrants who found work in neighborhood factories or in the nearby riverfront district. While the patterns of succession are complex and discrete for each area, it is generally correct to say that early French settlers and free blacks were followed by Germans and Central and Eastern Europeans, who in turn were replaced by rural white migrants. This part of Saint Louis is characterized by brick rowhouses arranged in compact neighborhoods that often center around a park. These residential pockets are interspersed with modest storefront businesses and the churches erected in the nineteenth and early twentieth centuries by devout ethnic congregations.

Founded in 1836, **Lafayette Square** (Park Avenue between Mississippi and Missouri avenues) was the city's first public park. It was developed from the common fields where the early French settlers from Laclède's village farmed. After the Civil War, the park was landscaped by Maximilian Kern (designer of Forest Park), and the surrounding area became a fashionable residential neighborhood of handsome stone townhouses in Second Empire, Queen Anne, Romanesque Revival, and other nineteenth-century styles.

Anheuser-Busch Brewery

The Anheuser-Busch Company is the largest beer maker in the world. Its headquarters compound contains many nineteenth-century brick structures, including the administration building (1868), an octagonal stable (1885), and the six-story brew house built in 1892. These structures are elaborately ornamented inside and out. In 1861 Eberhard Anheuser, principal creditor of Schneider Brewery, took over the small, faltering brewery on this site, which his son-in-law, Adolphus Busch, parlayed into an industrial giant. Busch married into the family in 1861 and joined the firm as a salesman. He had a knack for promotion and pioneered the refrigeration and pasteurization of beer. Anheuser-Busch weathered Prohibition by manufacturing baker's yeast and a nonalcoholic malt drink called Bevo. The Budweiser Clydesdale stable is part of the tour.

LOCATION: 12th and Lynch streets. HOURS: Tours 9–4 Monday–Saturday. FEE: None. TELEPHONE: 314–577–2626.

Chatillon–DeMenil Mansion

This farmhouse (ca. 1849) was expanded into a stately Greek Revival structure in 1863. The first owners were Henri and Odile DeLor Chatillon. She was the granddaughter of Clement DeLor Treget, the Frenchman who founded Carondelet in 1767; Henri was a guide on Francis Parkman's Oregon Trail expedition. Dr. Nicholas DeMenil

OPPOSITE: *Copper kettles, each having a capacity of more than 20,000 gallons, in the 1892 Anheuser-Busch brew house. The brewing process used today is largely the same as it was in the nineteenth century.*

purchased the house in 1856 with a partner, whom he bought out in 1861, after which he arranged for altering and enlarging the structure for his family. A Frenchman, DeMenil was married to Emilie Sophie Chouteau, great-granddaughter of Marie Thérèse Bourgeois Chouteau. Three generations of DeMenils lived in the house, until 1928, when industrial pollution from nearby factories prompted George and Ida DeMenil to leave the neighborhood. The house contains lavish period furnishings and decorative art, including two 1837 portraits by George Caleb Bingham. The crystal and china and a few items of furniture are original DeMenil pieces. Gardens and a restaurant are at the site.

> LOCATION: 3352 Demenil Place. HOURS: 10–4 Tuesday–Saturday. FEE: Yes. TELEPHONE: 314–771–5828.

The historic **Saint Louis Arsenal** (2d and Arsenal streets), which now lies within the U.S. Aerospace Center, was established in 1830. It supplied ordnance for the Black Hawk and Mexican wars but was especially important during the Civil War as a major supplier to Union troops in the Mississippi Valley. The old armory comprises an array of handsome limestone buildings and warehouses, which date to the 1830s. The Saint Louis architects George Morton and Joseph Laveille had a hand in the early planning of the arsenal.

Eugene Field House and Toy Museum

"Wynken, Blynken, and Nod" and "Little Boy Blue" are perhaps the most famous of Eugene Field's verses for children. He was also a prolific newspaper columnist in the 1880s. Field was born in this brick house in 1850 and lived here until 1864; he died in Chicago in 1895. Built as part of a row in 1845, the house contains period furnishings, a large collection of antique toys and dolls, and memorabilia of Eugene Field. Field was the son of Roswell Martin Field, a lawyer for Dred Scott.

> LOCATION: 634 South Broadway. HOURS: 10–4 Wednesday–Saturday, 12–4 Sunday. FEE: Yes. TELEPHONE: 314–421–4689.

CARONDELET

Carondelet was founded in 1767 by the Frenchman Clement DeLor Treget, who came here from nearby Sainte Genevieve. He was soon joined by other French settlers from nearby Cahokia and Kaskaskia on the east bank of the Mississippi, as well as Creole, French, and Canadian farmers and mountain men. Carondelet lay along the Mississippi south of Saint Louis, an area that is now roughly bounded by Delor Street on the north, the River des Pères Drainage Channel on the south, and Route I-55 on the west. All vestiges of the early French colonial village are gone, but there are several handsome limestone structures built by the German immigrants who made Carondelet their home in the 1840s, including the **Jacob Steins House** (Steins and Reilly streets, private), the **Charles Schlichtig House** (300 Marceau Street, private), and the **Henry Zeiss House** (7707–7713 Vulcan Street, private).

Jefferson Barracks Historical Park

Overlooking the Mississippi River, this bluff-top military post was carved out of the common fields of Carondelet in 1826, the year that its namesake, Thomas Jefferson, died. Jefferson Barracks served as a crucial military outfitting and training center during the era of westward expansion. In 1832 the Sauk leader Black Hawk was brought to Jefferson Barracks after the Black Hawk War, and during his incarceration George Catlin painted his portrait. Many men who served here became prominent figures in the Civil War, including Jefferson Davis, Robert E. Lee, Braxton Bragg, Ulysses S. Grant, William Tecumseh Sherman, and Philip Sheridan. Four of the stone-and-brick buildings dating from the 1850s have been restored, and a museum in the old powder magazine contains pertinent maps, photographs, weapons, uniforms, and flags.

LOCATION: 533 Grant Road, at the end of south Broadway. HOURS: 10–5 Tuesday–Saturday, 12–5 Sunday. FEE: None. TELEPHONE: 314-544-5714.

The **Provincial House of the Sisters of Saint Joseph of Carondelet Convent** (6400 Minnesota Avenue) is the oldest foundation of the Sisters of Saint Joseph in America. The order of nuns came from Lyons, France, to Saint Louis in 1836, to teach the deaf. In 1845 they started a school for the daughters of free blacks. The construction of the convent's compound began in 1841. The **Quinn Chapel A.M.E. Church** (227 Bowen Street) is a Greek Revival brick structure of the 1860s that originally served as a market for blacks, some of whom purchased the building from the city in the 1880s and converted it to a church. It is named for William Paul Quinn, first black bishop of the African Methodist Episcopal church.

The **Carondelet Historic Center** (6303 Michigan Avenue, 314–481–6303) is housed in the **Des Pères School,** where in 1873 Susan Blow initiated an experimental kindergarten based on her observations of Friedrich Froebel's early-childhood teaching methods in Germany. Blow's pilot program became a nationwide institution. By 1880 more than 8,000 children in Saint Louis were enrolled in kindergarten classes, and her educational model had been duplicated throughout the country. The handsome red-brick Italianate building was designed by Frederick Raeder. The kindergarten room at the Des Pères School has been restored to its appearance in the nineteenth century, and there are exhibits of early textbooks and teaching aids.

SAINT LOUIS ENVIRONS

ULYSSES S. GRANT'S FARM

After his resignation from the army in 1854 Grant and his wife, Julia, lived on a tract of land near Saint Louis given to them as a wedding present by Julia's father. Grant farmed and sold cordwood and worked for awhile in Saint Louis selling real estate. He was not successful at any of these endeavors, and in 1860 the family moved to Galena, Illinois, where Grant's father owned a tannery. During their time in Missouri, Grant built this large Southern-style log home. It was commodious but ugly. As Julia wrote, "The little house looked so unattractive that we facetiously decided to call it Hardscrabble." Hardscrabble is now part of the August A. Busch, Jr., estate, on which Anheuser-Busch operates a game preserve and facilities for the brewery's Clydesdale horses. Tours of the grounds include a stop at Grant's Farm.

> LOCATION: 10501 Gravois (Route 30), in southern Saint Louis County. HOURS: June through August: 9–3 Tuesday–Sunday; mid-April through May, September through mid-October: 9–3 Thursday–Sunday. FEE: None. TELEPHONE: 314–843–1700.

In **Crestwood**, the **Thomas Sappington House** (1015 South Sappington Road, 314–957–4785) is a fine example of the persistence of Renaissance architecture into the nineteenth century and one of the oldest extant structures in the state. It was the home of Thomas and Mary Ann Sappington, who came to Missouri from Kentucky. The brick structure was built by slaves in 1808. The furnishings in the house are early American antiques from Missouri, Pennsylvania, and the South.

The suburb of **University City** was promoted in the early twentieth century by the visionary Edward Gardner Lewis, who wanted to make this planned community a center for the arts, a dream that evaporated with the financial collapse of his publishing business. A champion of women's rights, Lewis published the popular *Woman's Magazine* and organized the American Women's League and the American Women's Republic. A reminder of Lewis's aspirations is the **Magazine Building** (6801 Delmar Boulevard), a splendid domed octagonal structure in the French Renaissance style, which has housed the municipal offices of University City since 1930.

FAUST COUNTY PARK/THORNHILL AND THE SAINT LOUIS CAROUSEL

About thirty miles west of downtown Saint Louis, Faust County Park is situated on a ninety-eight-acre remnant of the nineteenth-century plantation Thornhill, which was owned by Frederick Bates. The native Virginian arrived in Missouri in 1807 to serve as secretary and land commissioner of the Louisiana Territory. In 1824 he was elected the second governor of the state but died several months after taking office. During his years in Missouri, Bates acquired about a thousand acres of land, on which he built a home in the style of a southern plantation. The structure (ca. 1819), constructed of hewn and sawn oak timbers, has a handsome two-story central portico. It has been restored and contains period furnishings on the first floor. Several outbuildings, including a barn and granary, have also been restored or rebuilt. Also in Faust Park is the Saint Louis Carousel, which was made by the Dentzel Company of Philadelphia in about 1920. The hand-carved carousel has been restored and put back into operation.

LOCATION: 15185 Olive Boulevard, Chesterfield. HOURS: 12–5 Wednesday–Sunday. FEE: Yes. TELEPHONE: 314–532–1030.

The **Museum of Transportation** (3015 Barrett Station Road, Kirkwood, 314–965–7998) is a fifty-acre compound that contains a large assortment of locomotives and railroad rolling stock dating from the pre-Civil War era to the 1950s. There are also exhibits of automobiles, streetcars, buses, tractors, horse-drawn vehicles, airplanes, a Mississippi River towboat, and other conveyances. The grounds encompass the **Barretts tunnels,** the first two railroad tunnels bored west of the Mississippi River.

SAINT CHARLES

This picturesque river town was founded in 1769 as *Les Petites Côtes*—the Little Hills—by French-Canadian fur trader Louis Blanchette. A succession of now-famous people and events are associated with Saint Charles and the area. In 1798 Daniel Boone was attracted to the region by the offer of a Spanish land grant. Jean Baptist Point du Sable, the trader of African and French descent who helped found Chicago, spent the last years of his life in Saint Charles, dying here in 1818. At about 4 PM on May 21, 1804, amid a blustery rain, the Lewis and Clark expedition began its official ascent up the Missouri River from the landing at Saint Charles. The Corps of Discovery battled the current for three miles before making their first camp.

Pockets of nineteenth-century Saint Charles remain well preserved, especially along South Main Street, which parallels the Missouri River. Particularly handsome is **Stone Row** (314–330 South Main Street), a group of gable-roofed stone houses that date to the early settlement of Saint Charles.

First State Capitol State Historic Site

From 1821 to 1826 Saint Charles served as the temporary seat of government for the new state of Missouri while the permanent capital, the future Jefferson City, was being carved out of the wilderness in the center of the state. The First State Capitol is a row of brick structures constructed in the early nineteenth century, with fenestration and brickwork derived from London and Philadelphia townhouses and French-inspired rear galleries. They housed the General Assembly, the governor's office, and the residence and general store of two bachelor brothers. The restored capitol complex contains

The First State Capitol in Saint Charles, where the Missouri legislature met in second-floor chambers in the early 1820s. In the 1960s the state purchased the deteriorating complex of buildings and began a restoration program.

furnishings and fixtures from the 1821–1826 period. The Peck brothers' store and dwelling have been restored to the mid-nineteenth century.

> LOCATION: 200–216 South Main Street. HOURS: Mid-April through October: 10–5 Monday–Saturday, 12–6 Sunday; Rest of year: 10–5 Monday–Saturday, 12–5 Sunday. FEE: Yes. TELEPHONE: 314-946-9282.

DANIEL BOONE HOME

The Daniel Boone Home stands on the outskirts of Defiance about eighteen miles southwest of Saint Charles. In 1797, at the age of 63, after a long and colorful career as an officer, scout, surveyor, woodsman, legislator, and magistrate, Boone moved his family from Kentucky across the Mississippi River to the beautiful valley of Femme Osage, territory that was then held by Spain. Boone and his son Nathan built this handsome stone house between 1816 and 1820. The structure is patterned after the Georgian-style house in Pennsylvania where Boone was born in 1734. The famous frontiersman continued to hunt and explore in the region and lived here until he died in 1820. The house contains Boone family heirlooms.

LOCATION: 5 miles west of Defiance on Route F. HOURS: Mid-March through November: 9–5 Daily; Rest of year: 11–4 Saturday–Sunday. FEE: Yes. TELEPHONE: 314–987–2221.

MASTODON STATE PARK

Mastodon State Park contains one of the largest Pleistocene bone beds in North America. Excavations in 1839 and the early 1900s revealed a cache of bones of mastodons and other mammals that roamed the continent at the end of the last ice age 10,000 years ago. In 1979 archaeologists discovered a stone spear point dating to the Clovis period, 10,000 to 14,000 years ago. The find provided the first conclusive evidence of the coexistence of humans and mastodons in eastern North America. The excavation site, which is called the **Kimmswick Bone Bed,** is open to the public, and interpretive signs explain the history of the archaeological work that has been done here. The visitor center has displays of bones, tusks, teeth, and human artifacts from the site, photographs of archaeological explorations, and a full-size replica of a mastodon skeleton.

LOCATION: 1551 Seckman Road, Imperial. HOURS: *Visitor Center:* 9–4:30 Monday–Saturday, 12–4:30 Sunday. *Park:* 8–Dusk Daily. FEE: Yes. TELEPHONE: 314–464–2976.

Located about twenty-five miles southeast of Saint Louis, the **Sandy Creek Covered Bridge** (Old Goldman Road, six miles north of Hillsboro off Route 21) was first built in 1872 and rebuilt in 1886.

NORTHEAST MISSOURI

BETHEL

Bethel, situated on the banks of the North River about fifty miles west of Hannibal, is one of the utopian communities that sprang up in the United States in the nineteenth century. Its founder, the charismatic Prussian-born Wilhelm Keil, came to Missouri in 1844 from Philipsburg, Pennsylvania. Some of those who followed Keil to Bethel came from the ranks of the German Methodist Church, which had evolved from George Rapp's utopian Harmony Society. Bethel had no written laws; all directives, both religious and civil, came from Keil. By 1855 the Bethel German Colony, which was non-denominational, had a population of 650 and owned almost 5,000 acres of land in the area. Farming was the primary activity; the colonists were also noted for their arts and crafts and built many fine structures of local brick and stone. The community had its own shops, canneries, mills, and stores, which were patronized by out-siders. All property was owned in common; individuals were not allowed to keep money, which went into a common treasury.

The colony weakened as it prospered; some members resisted giving up their earnings and left. In the 1850s Keil sent scouts to the

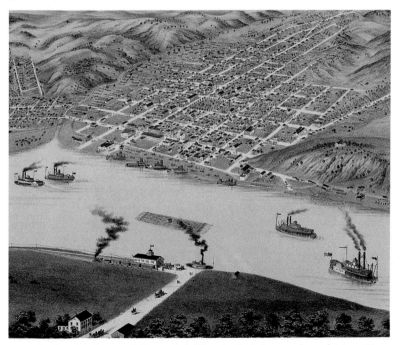

Many landmarks of Samuel Clemens' childhood, which he transformed into settings in Tom Sawyer *and* Huckleberry Finn, *are visible in this 1869 bird's eye view of Hannibal, Missouri, drawn by Albert Ruger.*

Far West to find a location for a sister colony. In 1855 about seventy-five people, including Keil, left Bethel for the Willamette Valley in Oregon, where they established Aurora. In the 1860s more Bethel colonists migrated to the new colony. The bonds of the Missouri colony were further weakened in 1877 with the death of Keil. Lacking a leader of Keil's authority, Bethel Colony was dissolved in 1879, and its common property divided among the remaining residents. In 1883 the town of Bethel was incorporated. Many handsome structures built by members of the colony can still be seen in town.

HANNIBAL

Hannibal rests on the west bank of the Mississippi River. Proximity to this omnipotent watercourse determined the town's development in the nineteenth century and made a mighty impression on Hannibal's most famous denizen, Samuel Langhorne Clemens, who lived here as a boy and later wrote under the name of Mark Twain.

The site of Hannibal was first granted to a farmer as part of a government effort to recompense those who had lost land during the 1811 New Madrid earthquake. The town was founded in 1819. Meat packing and milling of lumber and grain were important early industries. During the California gold rush, many area residents were lured west. The Hannibal & Saint Joseph Railroad, completed in 1857, was the first rail line to cross Missouri. In the 1870s and 1880s lumbermen began cutting the vast forests of Wisconsin and Minnesota and floating rafts of pine down the Mississippi, and Hannibal became a booming lumber mill town. **Rockcliffe** (1000 Bird Street, 573–221–4140) was the home of Hannibal lumber baron John Cruikshank. **Garth Woodside Mansion** (New London Road, 573–221–2789), a lavish summer home with a three-story flying staircase, now a bed-and-breakfast, contains period furnishings.

Mark Twain Boyhood Home and Museum

On cobblestoned Hill Street, one block from the Mississippi River, stands the simple white clapboard house where Samuel Clemens grew up. This neighborhood was the source of many of the experiences and characters described in Mark Twain's writings, especially *The Adventures of Tom Sawyer* (published in 1876) and *The Adventures of Huckleberry Finn* (1884).

In 1839 John Clemens, chronically beset with financial worries, moved his family from nearby Florida, Missouri, to Hannibal, where he enjoyed some measure of success as a justice of the peace. He died in 1847, when Samuel was about 12 years old. Shortly thereafter Samuel was apprenticed to the publisher of the *Missouri Courier,* and in 1853, at the age of 17, he left Hannibal and embarked on his adventures as journeyman printer, reporter, and apprentice to a riverboat pilot. John Clemens built the house at 208 Hill Street in about 1843. The family occupied it until 1853, except for a period in 1846–1847, when they lived across the street. The small frame house contains pioneer furnishings and explanatory notes indicating the items of literary significance, including the whitewashed fence that figures prominently in the early pages of *Tom Sawyer.* A museum contains editions of Samuel Clemens's writings, family furniture, and memorabilia, and the visitor center offers

The 1898 Rockcliffe Mansion in Hannibal was designed by Barnett, Haynes, and Barnett, an architectural firm from Saint Louis.

documentary photographs and additional items associated with his life and career. Across the street stands **John Clemens's law office;** the **Pilaster House and Grant's Drug Store,** where the family lived from 1846 to 1847 and where John Clemens died; and the **Becky Thatcher Bookshop,** which occupies the house where Laura Hawkins, model for *Tom Sawyer*'s Becky Thatcher, lived as a child. Portions of these structures contain period furnishings.

LOCATION: 208 Hill Street. HOURS: Open Daily, hours vary by season. FEE: Yes. TELEPHONE: 573–221–9010

One mile south of Hannibal is the **Mark Twain Cave** (Route 79, 573–221–1656). This large limestone cave was a popular destination for Hannibal's nineteenth-century residents, including the young Samuel Clemens. Mention of the cave occurs in *Innocents Abroad, Tom Sawyer, Huckleberry Finn,* and other writings by Twain.

The birthplace of Mark Twain, a small house in Florida, Missouri, is now preserved in its entirety inside the Mark Twain Birthplace State Historic Site. Of the town, Twain later commented "I was born in the almost invisible village of Florida. . . . The village contained a hundred people and I increased the population by one percent." OPPOSITE: *A portrait of Twain. After his humble upbringing and years in gold-rush towns, Twain built his family a magnificent home in West Hartford, Connecticut, the heart of Yankeedom.*

MARK TWAIN BIRTHPLACE
STATE HISTORIC SITE

The Mark Twain Birthplace State Historic Site stands on the shores of Mark Twain Lake, about thirty miles southwest of Hannibal, between the towns of Stoutsville and Paris. The damming of the Salt River in the twentieth century has obscured the presettlement terrain, but when John and Jane Clemens came here in 1835 they found a landscape of rolling hills and rugged limestone bluffs. Known as the Salt River Hills, the area resembles the Ozarks of southern Missouri. Samuel Clemens was born on November 30, 1835, on the Salt River in the village of Florida. His parents had arrived just six months earlier from Tennessee. The birthplace—a small two-room cabin—is now housed within the museum at the historic site. Despite its modest proportions, the house sheltered John and Jane Clemens, five children, and a slave. Finding it difficult to earn a living in the area, John Clemens moved the family to Hannibal in 1839. For over a decade, however, Samuel continued to visit an uncle in Florida during the summers, and his boyhood experiences amid the Salt River Hills provided sources and background for his later writings. The museum contains first editions of Clemens's works, a handwritten manuscript of *The Adventures of Tom Sawyer*, memorabilia, furnishings from Clemens's Connecticut home, and a full-size replica of a steamboat pilothouse.

> LOCATION: Mark Twain State Park, off Route 107. HOURS: April through October: 10–4 Monday–Saturday, 12–6 Sunday; November through March: 10–4 Monday–Saturday, 12–5 Sunday. FEE: Yes. TELEPHONE: 573–565–3449.

The **Union Covered Bridge,** eight miles southwest of Paris on County Route C, is one of four extant covered bridges in Missouri. The first patent for a covered bridge was issued in 1797, and construction of the bridges became commonplace during the nineteenth century. Engineers believed that covering a bridge increased its longevity by protecting its framework from the elements. The Union Covered Bridge, built in 1871 to span the Elk Fork of the Salt River, is an oak timber structure and is the only surviving example in Missouri of the Burr-arch truss system, a bridge type designed by engineer Theodore Burr. Burr employed large wooden arches to reinforce the triangular trusses.

CENTRAL MISSOURI

COLUMBIA

Columbia is situated in the heart of Missouri, midway between Saint Louis and Kansas City. The town was founded in 1821, and its largest institution, the **University of Missouri,** was established in 1839. The **Francis Quadrangle Historic District** (Conley Avenue and Elm, 6th, and 9th streets) encompasses the nineteenth-century core of the university. The focal point of the quadrangle is an ensemble of six Ionic columns, the remains of the original Academic Hall, which was destroyed by fire in 1892. The historic district contains an assortment of academic buildings that reflect nineteenth-century architectural styles. The **Chancellor's Residence,** a brick Italianate structure built in 1867 on the east side of the quadrangle, is the oldest extant building on campus. The university's **Museum of Anthropology** (104 Swallow Hall, 573–882–3764) has exhibits focusing on Missouri cultures from the prehistorical inhabitants through historical Indians; pioneer life in the 1800s; and Native American cultures such as Eskimo, Plains Indian, and Southwest Indians, including the Pueblo and Navajo.

ARROW ROCK

In 1808 William Clark noted in the journal of his trip to build Fort Osage that the bluffs on the west bank of the Missouri River where the village of Arrow Rock now stands would make "a handsome spot for a town." After the first settlers arrived in 1815, there followed a steady influx of Kentuckians, Virginians, and Tennesseans who were likewise impressed with the setting. Many of these newcomers were slaveholders who transplanted their southern culture along the Missouri River. Arrow Rock grew into a thriving trade center for local farmers and a supply stop for expeditions heading west on the Santa Fe Trail, booming in the mid-1800s. As railroads, and later, highway bridges across the Missouri, bypassed Arrow Rock, it became a sleepy backwater village.

Arrow Rock State Historic Site

Six structures that date to the town's heyday have been preserved within this district. These include the **George Caleb Bingham Home**

(1st and High streets), a simple brick structure that served as the periodic residence of the famous portrait and landscape artist from 1837 to 1845, and **Arrow Rock Tavern** (Main Street), a massive brick Federal-style building constructed in 1834 to serve travelers on the Santa Fe Trail. The tavern is still in business. The other four restored structures—two houses, a jail, and a store—also contain period furnishings. Throughout the summer, artists demonstrate a variety of nineteenth-century crafts at Arrow Rock.

> LOCATION: Route 41, 13 miles north of Route I-70. HOURS: 10–5 Monday–Saturday, 12–5 Sunday. FEE: Yes. TELEPHONE: 816–837–3231.

Several other restored sites in the town may be visited by arrangement with the Friends of Arrow Rock (816–837–3231), including the **John P. Sites Gun Shop** of 1844, the white frame **Christian Church** (1872), the **Odd Fellows Lodge Hall** built in 1868, and a one-room **log house,** built in the 1830s, containing a pioneer doctors' museum.

Located amid a cedar grove five miles west of Arrow Rock, the **Sappington Cemetery State Historic Site** (816–837–3330) contains the graves of three prominent Missourians. Dr. John Sappington (1776–1856) practiced medicine in the Arrow Rock area and is remembered for his early use of quinine to treat malaria. One of his daughters married Meredith Miles Marmaduke (1791–1864), a Unionist who had served as eighth governor of the state. Sappington's three other daughters were the successive wives of Claiborne Fox Jackson (1806–1862). As the pro-Confederate fifteenth governor, he served only six months of his term before Union forces seized Jefferson City. Along with other Confederate-leaning politicians, Jackson fled the capital. He died shortly thereafter in Arkansas.

A few miles northeast of Arrow Rock, **Boone's Lick State Historic Site** (Route 87, 816–837–3330) preserves the natural saline spring, or salt lick, that provided early settlers with a source of the important mineral and preservative. Nathan and Daniel M. Boone, sons of Daniel Boone, manufactured salt here from 1806

OPPOSITE: *Six Ionic columns from the University of Missouri's first Academic Hall, built in 1841, remained standing after the building was consumed by fire in 1892. Jesse Hall, constructed in 1895, replaced the earlier building.*

President Harry S Truman, Winston Churchill, and Westminster College president Dr. Franc L. McCluer walking from the chapel to the gymnasium on the occasion of Churchill's "Iron Curtain" speech on March 5, 1946.

until 1811, when they sold their interests in the business to their partners, James and Jesse Morrison, who continued the business until 1833. Approximately sixty pounds of salt could be obtained by boiling 300 gallons of brine. At peak operation the outfit employed twenty men and produced 100 bushels of salt a day, which sold in the nearby river towns for $2 to $2.50 per bushel.

WINSTON CHURCHILL
MEMORIAL AND LIBRARY

In 1946 Winston Churchill, at a lecture at Westminster College in Fulton, warned of Soviet expansion in Eastern Europe. His oration, which he delivered in the college gymnasium, came to be known as the "Iron Curtain Speech," for it included these words: "From Stettin in the Baltic to Trieste in the Adriatic, an iron curtain has descended across the continent." As a memorial to Churchill, Westminster College resurrected the **Church of Saint Mary the Virgin, Aldermanbury,** on its campus, where it serves as the college chapel. Dating to the twelfth century, the church stood at the corner of Love Lane and Aldermanbury Road in London. After the Great Fire of 1666, the eminent English architect Christopher Wren rebuilt Saint Mary Aldermanbury along with some fifty other fire-ravaged churches in London. The sanctuary remained in service for almost 300 years, until World War II, when it was gutted by a German incendiary bomb. In 1965 the remains of the English Baroque church were dismantled and reassembled at Westminster College. Used as a nondenominational place of worship, the church houses an undercroft museum that exhibits Churchill memorabilia; artifacts, photographs, and microfilm relating to World War II; and material pertaining to the work of Christopher Wren. The museum is the only center devoted to Churchill studies and the only building in the United States that was unquestionably designed by Wren. A part of the Berlin Wall has been relocated at the memorial.

LOCATION: 7th Street and Westminister Avenue. HOURS: 10–4:30 Daily. FEE: Yes. TELEPHONE: 573–592–1369.

The twelfth-century church of Saint Mary the Virgin, Aldermanbury, was rebuilt by Christopher Wren after London's Great Fire of 1666, gutted by a German bomb in 1940, and moved stone by stone and rebuilt in Fulton, Missouri, as a memorial to Winston Churchill.

Archaeologists have found evidence of human habitation dating back at least 10,000 years in **Graham Cave,** a sheltered bluff in **Graham Cave State Park** (north of Route I-70, 2 miles west of Danville, 573–564–3476). Although the cave itself is not open to the public, interpretive signs at the mouth of the shelter explain archaeological discoveries that have been made there.

HERMANN

Hermann sits in a beautiful valley on the south bank of the Missouri River. It was laid out in 1838 by members of the German Settlement Society of Philadelphia who hoped that in the isolation of the frontier they could preserve the language and customs of their homeland. During the nineteenth century a swath of the Missouri River valley from Boonville to Saint Louis became a stronghold of German settlement, and Hermann became a center of the immigrants' culture, music, and wine making. Many handsome brick structures from that period remain, built in German Neoclassical and vernacular styles. Set on a hilltop on the western edge of town, the **Old Stone Hill Historic District** includes several nineteenth-century brick buildings, a Greek Revival residence, warehouses, and stone-lined cellars. From 1847 until Prohibition, the second largest winery in the country was in Hermann. For many years after Prohibition, mushrooms were cultivated in the underground labyrinth, but the **Stone Hill Winery** (Stonehill Highway, 800–909–9463) is again vinting wine and is open for tours.

Deutschheim State Historic Site

Deutschheim State Historic Site is a German cultural history museum that preserves two nineteenth-century structures that figured prominently in the founding and growth of Hermann. The **Pommer-Gentner House** (108 Market Street) was built and occupied by the Pommers and later purchased by the Gentners, two of the town's founding families. Constructed in 1840, the house is an exceptional example of German Neoclassicism (*Klassisismus*). The **Strehly House and Winery** (109 West 2d Street), a fine example of German vernacular, was constructed in stages from 1842 to 1869. A prominent German Freethinker operated a press here, publishing books and the first German-language newspapers west of Saint Louis. In 1857 his brother-in-law added a winery and tavern to the complex. Both offer exhibits on German immigrant life and culture in Missouri.

LOCATION: 109 West 2d Street. HOURS: 10–4 Daily. FEE: Yes. TELE-PHONE: 573–486–2200.

JEFFERSON CITY

Missouri's capital was founded in the heady years following the Louisiana Purchase and was named for Thomas Jefferson. The city was established by legislative act on December 31, 1821, and town planners soon set to work laying out the capital atop the bluffs along the south bank of the Missouri River. Events in Jefferson City in the 1860s reflected the turmoil in Missouri during the Civil War era. Elected governor in 1860, Claiborne Fox Jackson called for secession, but Missourians demonstrated their pro-Union sentiments in a special 1861 convention held in Saint Louis. Governor Jackson abandoned the capital, and on his heels General Nathaniel Lyon and a troop of Unionist volunteers claimed Jefferson City. Hamilton Gamble, named provisional governor, kept the state within the Union camp until his death in 1864, although he was never able to stop the bloody guerrilla warfare that wracked Missouri. Jackson established rump governments in Arkansas and Texas but never seriously threatened the authority in Jefferson City; he died in 1862. A more potent menace was Jackson's ally, the former governor and Mexican War hero, General Sterling "Pap" Price, who repeatedly tried to seize Missouri for the Confederacy.

Jefferson Landing State Historic Site

Jefferson Landing, on the banks of the Missouri, comprises three structures built when the capital city was a bustling river port. The **Lohman Building** (ca. 1839) is a rare early example of Missouri River commercial architecture. The three-story limestone structure was Jefferson City's trading center for almost fifty years. German-born Charles Lohman, a Jefferson City merchant, owned the building from 1852 until the mid-1870s. A visitor center in the Lohman Building has exhibits dealing with the settlement of Jefferson City.

With increased rail and river traffic in the 1850s, another Jefferson City entrepreneur, Charles Maus, built a hotel across the

street from the Lohman Building in about 1855. First called the
Missouri Hotel, it was renamed the **Union Hotel** in 1865, after Maus
returned from the Civil War. Now undergoing restoration, the red-
brick **Christopher Maus House,** directly behind the Union Hotel,
was built about 1854 by Charles Maus's brother. In the rear a grace-
fully sloping roof covers a large gallery.

> LOCATION: 101–102 Jefferson Street. HOURS: *Lohman Building:*
> 8:30–4:30 Daily. *Union Hotel:* 8:30–4:30 Daily. FEE: None. TELE-
> PHONE: 573–751–3475.

Overlooking Jefferson Landing, the **Missouri Governor's Mansion**
(100 Madison Street, 573–751–4141) sits atop the bluffs of the
Missouri River amid beautifully landscaped grounds. The Second
Empire brick residence, built in 1871, has striking stone quoins and
iron grillwork cresting the mansard roof. Across the street is the **Cole**

*The Second Empire Missouri Governor's Mansion was designed by George Ingham
Barnett, an architect from Saint Louis. The columns for the portico, which were
quarried in Ironton, Missouri, arrived several inches too short, and had to be set on
bases to reach the necessary height.*

County Historical Museum (109 Madison Street, 573–635–1850), housed in a rowhouse erected in 1871 by then-governor B. Gratz Brown. The museum exhibits inaugural gowns of the governors' wives, nineteenth-century furnishings, glassware, and Civil War relics. To the rear of the museum is the **Upschulte House,** a brick residence built about 1840, which is used as the office for the historical society. Built in 1896, the **Cole County Courthouse and Jail–Sheriff's House** (Monroe and High streets) are stone structures in the Richardsonian Romanesque vein. The complex, along with the first bridge across the Missouri River, was part of a city improvements package initiated to keep legislators from moving the capital elsewhere.

Missouri State Capitol

Jefferson City's first two capitols were destroyed by fires in 1837 and 1911. The third and current capitol, built between 1915 and 1917, is a colossal edifice in the Classic Revival style. Its most prominent external features are the towering dome and a central portico supported by Corinthian columns. Commanding this entryway is a statue of Thomas Jefferson. The capitol's best-known, and at one time quite controversial, interior fixture is the Thomas Hart Benton mural entitled *A Social History of the State of Missouri,* a bold portrayal of Missouri's small towns and industries that shocked many when it was painted in 1935. Prior to this, the historical art in the capitol had been allegorical in nature and conservative in approach. Benton's mural depicts dance hall girls, strippers, a mother diapering a bare-bottomed child, and such typical but cheerless daily scenes as poor blacks picking through coal piles. Benton's brand of realism angered many lawmakers; there was even talk of whitewashing some of the offending parts of the mural, such as the bare-bottomed infant. The mural is on the third floor in the building's west wing. The **Missouri State Museum** on the first floor has exhibits explaining the natural history of the state and its cultural evolution from the period of the Indians to the present day. Dioramas, artifacts, and other displays examine the customs, traditions, and experiences of four cultural groups of Missourians—the French, blacks, Anglo-Southerners, and Germans.

LOCATION: High Street between Broadway and Jefferson streets. HOURS: 8–5 Daily. FEE: None. TELEPHONE: 573–751–4127.

Another handsome Jefferson City landmark is the 1883 Gothic **Saint Peter's Roman Catholic Church** (216 Broadway), which stands just to the west of the capitol.

Route 63, south of Jefferson City, leads across the Osage River, a major tributary of the Missouri River, and into the beautiful hill country of southern Missouri. In the mid-nineteenth century many German immigrants settled in the Osage Valley. One of their villages is **Westphalia,** a charming hilltop town about fifteen miles south of Jefferson City. Its dominant edifice is the stone **Saint Joseph Catholic Church** (1848), with its commanding bell tower and steeple.

The **Meramec Iron Works,** active from 1829 into the 1870s, is located six miles southeast of Saint James in **Meramec Spring Park** (Route 8, 573–265–7124). Remnants of the cold-blast furnace and five refinery forges are preserved in the park. Also on the site are the **Ozark Agriculture Museum,** which houses an array of turn-of-the-century farm machinery and implements, and the **Meramec Museum,** which traces the history of the mine, the iron-manufacturing process, the daily life of the miners and their families, and the culture of the Shawnee Indians, who first pointed out the iron-ore deposits to white entrepreneurs. The ore bank, where miners extracted iron ore to feed the blast furnace, is located on the park's west end. Nearby is the site of **Stringtown,** where the miners lived. There are no remaining dwellings, but interpretive signs depict the types of housing that the miners built.

The **Dillard Mill State Historic Site** (one mile south of Route 49, 573–244–3120) is hidden in the forest-clad Ozark hills between the towns of Dillard and Viburnum. Standing at the confluence of Indian and Huzzah creeks, the structure is a beautifully preserved example of a nineteenth-century water-powered gristmill. The first mill on the site was built in the 1850s and operated by a succession of owners, including James and Joseph Dillard Cottrell. Between 1900 and 1908, Emil and Mary Mischke, brother and sister immigrants from Poland, rebuilt and modernized the mill, which was in operation until 1956. The steel roller mills and other original machinery remain intact.

OPPOSITE: *The rotunda of the Missouri State Capitol is decorated with murals by Thomas Hart Benton, which, when painted in 1935, were criticized for the "lack of refinement" in their depiction of Missouri history.* OVERLEAF: *This panel on the East Wall of the Capitol depicts scenes of farm life, industry, and law in Missouri.*

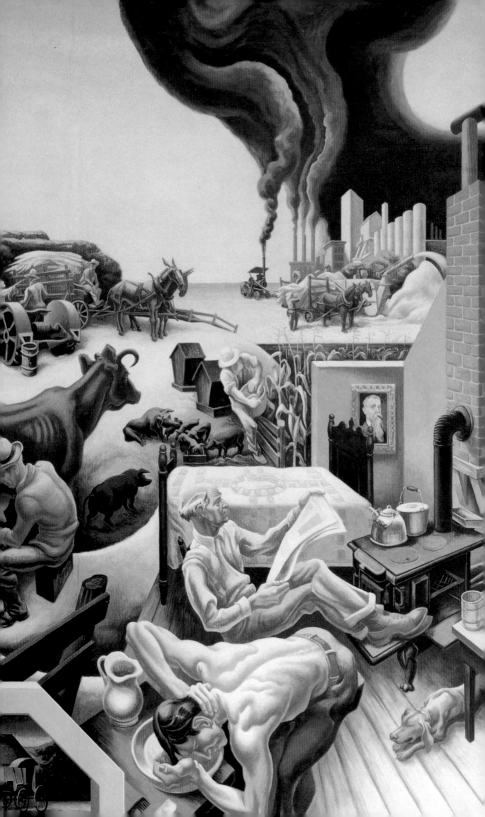

SOUTHEAST MISSOURI

Washington State Park (314–586–2995), six miles southwest of De Soto, preserves hundreds of prehistoric petroglyphs amid the beautiful forests of the Ozark hills. The rock carvings, which depict human figures, footprints, claws, birds, arrows, and various geometric designs, date from between A.D. 1000 and 1600.

BONNE TERRE

The Saint Joseph Lead Company was a powerful economic force in the Old Lead Belt, particularly in the town of Bonne Terre, where the firm began mining on a 950-acre tract in 1865. Work went slowly at first, but with innovations in ore smelting and deep-rock drilling technology, business began to flourish. The Saint Joseph Lead Company dug its first shaft in 1870 at the **Bonne Terre Mine** (Route 47, 573–358–2148), which was in operation until 1962. Today it features exhibits of minerals and mining equipment and memorabilia. The first two levels of the mine are open for walking tours; the lower three levels comprise a huge underground lake, which can be viewed by boat or by scuba diving. In 1909 carpenters employed by the lead company built the **Bonne Terre Depot** (Oak Street, 314–731–5003), a beautiful wooden structure of the Queen Anne and Stick styles. It is now a bed-and-breakfast inn.

MISSOURI MINES STATE HISTORIC SITE

The Missouri Mines State Historic Site in Flat River is situated at the former **Federal Mill Number 3** in the heart of Missouri's Old Lead Belt. The rugged hill country west of the Mississippi River and south of Saint Louis is honeycombed with almost a thousand miles of underground mining tunnels. A French explorer, Pierre Charles Le Sueur, led a mineralogical expedition into the area in the early 1700s and uncovered rich lodes of lead ore. Full-scale mining began in 1869 with the introduction of the diamond drill, and for a hundred years the area supplied much of the nation's lead ore. After World War II, as lead deposits were being depleted around Flat River, Bonne Terre, and Mine La Motte, mining operations began to move to the Viburnum or New Lead Belt, which lies just to the west in the Mark Twain National Forest.

Federal Mill Number 3 is an impressive example of early-twentieth-century industrial architecture. The compound of twenty-five buildings was built from 1906 to 1907 and taken over in 1923 by the Saint Joseph Lead Company, the major mining corporation in the area. Lead ore was processed here until 1972. The powerhouse contains a museum that explains the history and technology of lead mining in Missouri through exhibits of pneumatic tools, a Saint Joe shovel, diamond drills, and other examples of mining equipment along with displays of minerals, gems, and fossils.

LOCATION: Route 32, Park Hills. HOURS: May through September: 10–4 Monday–Saturday, 12–6 Sunday; October through April: 10–4 Monday–Saturday, 12–5 Sunday. FEE: Yes. TELEPHONE: 573–431–6226.

FORT DAVIDSON STATE HISTORIC SITE

Fort Davidson State Historic Site is located in Pilot Knob, a small town situated in the well-named Arcadia Valley, an area of lovely forested hills and spring-fed streams about ninety miles south of Saint Louis. In 1861 federal troops established a small garrison here to protect the area's iron mines and smelters. In 1863 Union soldiers constructed a hexagonal earthen fortress in the cleft of the valley, a site that was secure against infantry assault but vulnerable to artillery.

In 1864 President Jefferson Davis of the Confederacy decided to mount an operation to recapture Missouri while Union troops were preoccupied east of the Mississippi River. The leader of this campaign was Major General Sterling Price, a colorful Missourian who had joined the Confederacy at the outbreak of the war. Under Price's command were 12,000 cavalry, one of the largest mounted forces ever assembled by the Confederacy. The troops entered southeastern Missouri in September 1864 and during the ensuing weeks moved west along the Missouri River to Kansas City. Despite the size of the force, the men were ill equipped and ill trained, their morale was low, and there were many desertions. Price was defeated in Missouri, and in early November his troops retreated south along the Kansas-Missouri border, concluding the Confederacy's attempts to seize Missouri.

The Battle of Pilot Knob, the first major confrontation of the campaign, occurred on September 27 at Fort Davidson when some 7,000 Confederates advanced on the Union earthworks, which were manned by only about 1,000 soldiers. While trying to storm the fort, about 500 Confederate infantry were killed, and Union fire knocked out Confederate artillery positions established on promontories overlooking the fort. During the night, the Union troops, under Brigadier General Thomas Ewing, Jr., staged a daring and successful evacuation of Fort Davidson. Faced with an elusive enemy and shaken by losses, Price gave up on taking Saint Louis and marched west. The campaign ended in defeats at Westport (in present-day Kansas City), and in Kansas. In its sheltering valley, Fort Davidson, like many battlefields, is a paradoxically beautiful site; it is hard to conjure up scenes of bloody combat. The fort's earthworks are intact.

LOCATION: Route 21, Pilot Knob. HOURS: *Visitor Center:* April through October: 10–4 Monday–Saturday, 12–6 Sunday; Rest of year: 10–4 Monday–Saturday, 12–5 Sunday. FEE: None. TELEPHONE: 573–546–3454.

In nearby **Ironton** is a beautifully preserved example of Gothic Revival architecture, **Saint Paul's Episcopal Church** (East Reynolds and North Knob streets). Completed in 1871, the white frame structure has a steeply pitched roof with a painted plaid pattern, vertical batten siding, a bell tower, lancet windows, and other classic Gothic Revival elements.

SAINTE GENEVIEVE

Looking for fresh lands to cultivate, French farmers from nearby Kaskaskia, on the east bank of the Mississippi in present-day Illinois, crossed the river and founded Sainte Genevieve, Missouri's oldest permanent settlement, in the late 1730s. The new site also provided settlers with better access to the west-bank Saline Spring, where they could process that precious frontier commodity—salt. The village developed strong trade ties with New Orleans. Sainte Genevieve prospered and—despite its remoteness—took on an air of gentility. After the Louisiana Purchase, the town became Americanized. A remarkable number of structures from this transitional period are preserved in a charming blend of French and American architectural styles. The original Sainte Genevieve was on *le grand champ*—the fertile bottomlands along the Mississippi—but after a disastrous flood in 1785 virtually destroyed the village, the French inhabitants moved to higher ground about two miles to the north and continued to farm. *Le grand champ,* which is still being farmed, and a few of the pecan trees that the French planted to demark the boundaries of the common field can still be seen along Saint Marys Road on the southern edge of Sainte Genevieve.

By 1804 there were ten working lead mines in the region, and Sainte Genevieve became a warehouse and shipping point for the valuable mineral. Connecticut-born Moses Austin came to Sainte Genevieve in 1796, where he became a leader in the lead-mining business. In 1798 he took over operations of Mine à Breton near Potosi; he sank the first deep shaft in the area and introduced a furnace that improved the smelting process of lead ore. After the depression of 1818, Austin began to consider the notion of establishing an Anglo-American colony in the Spanish-held province of Texas. Although he died in 1821—he is buried in Potosi—and the province passed from Spanish into Mexican hands, his son, Stephen F. Austin, secured a land grant from Mexico and carried out his father's plan to colonize Texas. Transporting the lead from the mining district to the landing at Sainte Genevieve was a difficult and tedious activity before the advent of the railroad. From 1835 until the arrival of the Iron Mountain Railroad in 1857, lead was hauled on a forty-two-mile-long plank road (present-day Market Street) built between Sainte Genevieve, Iron Mountain, and Pilot Knob.

Some homes in town were underwater during the Great Flood of 1993, and historic houses barely escaped damage. Responding to media reports of the town's plight, volunteers from Memphis and other distant points helped fill 750,000 sandbags and pile up 100,000 tons of rock. Water reached the base of the 1790 **Green Tree Inn,** a structure built almost entirely of walnut.

Many structures are fine examples of eighteenth-century French Creole styles. These residences have vertical log construction that is either *poteaux en terre* (posts in ground) or *poteaux sur sole* (posts on stone foundation); massive trusses typical of fifteenth-century Normandy, which originally supported thatched roofs; and wraparound galleries, where colonists found relief from sultry summers. Examples of this type include the **Bequette–Ribault House** (private) and the **Saint Gemme–Amoureux House** (573–883–7102), both on Saint Mary's Road; the **Bolduc House** (125 South Main Street, 573–883–3105); and the **Guibourd–Valle House** (4th and Merchant streets, 573–883–7544). The Bolduc

ABOVE *and* OPPOSITE: *The Bolduc House in Sainte Genevieve is constructed with vertical log walls and a large overhanging hipped roof which shades the encircling gallery, both distinctive features of French Colonial architecture in the Mississippi Valley.*

House has handsome frontier furnishings, many of which belonged to Louis Bolduc (1734–1815), a French–Canadian lead miner, merchant, and planter. The small chairs are a reminder of the small stature of many people in the eighteenth century.

Felix Valle State Historic Site

This classic residence demonstrates the growing American influence in Sainte Genevieve in the early nineteenth century. The native stone structure combines a private house and commercial space and was built in 1818 by a Philadelphia merchant, Jacob Philipson. He sold it in 1824 to a prominent Sainte Genevievean of French-Canadian lineage, Jean Baptiste Valle, who used the mercantile side of the house for his various business interests, which included mining and trade with Indians in Missouri and Arkansas. In the 1830s Jean Baptiste passed the house on to his fourth son, Felix, and his

wife, Odile. They lived in the residential part, while Felix used the commercial portion to conduct business, and for many years the house was a social and mercantile center of Sainte Genevieve. It contains furnishings, some of which are original Valle family pieces.

> LOCATION: 198 Merchant Street. HOURS: 10–4 Monday–Saturday, 12–5 Sunday. FEE: Yes. TELEPHONE: 573–883–7102.

Sainte Genevieve's devout French Catholics established their first church on *le grand champ* in 1759. After the 1785 flood, parishioners moved to the new town, where they erected bigger and more lavish churches as their congregation grew. They built the current large brick **Church of Sainte Genevieve** (49 Dubourg Place) in 1876, appointing it with stained-glass windows and French paintings. It contains relics, art, and furnishings from the original log church. The **Sainte Genevieve Museum** (Merchant Street and Dubourg Place, 573–883–3461) displays prehistoric and historic Indian artifacts, implements from the Saline Spring, Catholic documents and ecclesiastic objects, items associated with the plank road, and riverboat memorabilia. The **Great River Road Interpretive Center** (66 South Main Street, 573–883–7097) offers exhibits relating to Sainte Genevieve history and provides maps for self-guided walking tours.

TRAIL OF TEARS STATE PARK

This state park comprises an area of majestic hardwood forests on the bluffs of the Mississippi River. In 1838 General Winfield Scott, at the behest of President Andrew Jackson, began the forced removal of some 13,000 Cherokee from their homelands in North Carolina, Georgia, and Tennessee. During the winter of 1838–1839, they were herded 1,200 miles west to Indian Territory—present-day Oklahoma. As a result of the hardship of this exodus, which became known as the Trail of Tears, more than 4,000 people died. The winter ice in the Mississippi made crossing the river very treacherous, and many Cherokee, despite the bitter cold, were forced to camp on the east bank of the Mississippi. When they began to cross in January, a number of them landed at Moccasin Springs, a site that

OPPOSITE: *The Bolduc House, one of the largest and most comfortable houses in eighteenth-century Sainte Genevieve, contains many original family furnishings.*

lies within the state park. The visitor center has exhibits recounting the history of the Trail of Tears.

LOCATION: Route 177, 12 miles north of Cape Girardeau. HOURS: April through October: 9–5 Daily; November through March: 9–5 Wednesday–Sunday. FEE: None. TELEPHONE: 573–334–1711.

BOLLINGER MILL STATE HISTORIC SITE

Bollinger Mill stands on the Whitewater River in the small town of Burfordville. The first mill was built of wood in about 1800 by George Frederick Bollinger, a settler from North Carolina who received a Spanish land grant in the area in 1797. Besides running his mill, Bollinger became active in Missouri politics, serving as a member of the first territorial assembly as well as a state senator. After Bollinger's death in 1842, the mill was extensively expanded and operated by his daughter, Sarah Daugherty, and her sons. During the Civil War, Union troops burned the frame upper structure because the Daugherty family was suspected of supplying Confederates. In 1866 Solomon Burford, for whom Burfordville is named, bought the mill site and rebuilt it, using local brick. From the late nineteenth century until the 1940s, the mill was a focal point of the local economy. The massive structure, which closed in 1953, has been restored and the water-powered machinery put back into working order.

Spanning the Whitewater River adjacent to the mill is the **Burfordville Covered Bridge.** The 140-foot bridge is built of local yellow poplar. The Civil War interrupted construction of the structure, which was begun in 1858 but not finished until a decade later.

LOCATION: Route 34, Burfordville. HOURS: 10–4 Monday–Saturday, 12–4 Sunday. FEE: Yes. TELEPHONE: 573–243–4591.

NEW MADRID

The extreme southeast corner of Missouri is shaped like the heel of a boot. Here the Ozark hills drop off into the flat floodplains of the Mississippi River. This expanse was once covered with wet prairies and swamp forests where giant oaks and bald cypresses grew. Lumbermen were attracted to the area by the rich stands of timber.

Settlement began in the late eighteenth century—the town of New Madrid was laid out on the Mississippi where the river takes a large horseshoe bend—but was temporarily halted because of the New Madrid earthquake of 1811–1812. Over the course of several months, land from Cape Girardeau south into Arkansas sank ten to fifty feet and there was extensive flooding in the Bootheel region. Much of the area has since been drained and put into cultivation.

Hunter-Dawson Home State Historic Site

The Hunter-Dawson Home is an antebellum mansion set amid giant oaks and gum trees on the north edge of New Madrid. One of the town's most successful entrepreneurs was William Washington Hunter, a Virginian who came to the area in 1830. Hunter devised the idea for the house but died in early 1859 before construction. It was built by the family, using slaves and craftspeople from the area, for his widow, Amanda, and their seven children between 1859 and 1860. The home is a two-story, fifteen-room frame structure with Greek Revival and Italianate elements. It contains many of its original Rococo Revival and Eastlake furnishings, including a large collection of furniture from the late 1850s by Mitchell and Rammelsberg, a Cincinnati, Ohio, maker of inexpensive, machine-made furniture in the Rococo Revival style. Many middle-class households in the Midwest ordered furnishings from this company.

LOCATION: Dawson Road. HOURS: 10–4 Monday–Saturday, 12–4 Sunday. FEE: Yes. TELEPHONE: 573–748–5340.

The **New Madrid Historical Museum** (1 Main Street, 314–748–5944) has exhibits on the New Madrid earthquake, the Civil War, and prehistoric Indian Mound Builder cultures of the area. Also displayed are turn-of-the-century household articles and items relating to the Civil War Battle of Island No. 10. Adjacent to the museum, an observation deck overlooks the twenty-mile-long oxbow of the Mississippi River called New Madrid Bend.

Fourteen miles south of East Prairie on Route 102, **Big Oak Tree State Park** (314–649–3149) preserves a remnant of the magnificent bottomland forests that flourished along the Mississippi prior to white settlement. The forest canopy averages 120 feet in height, with some individual trees reaching 130 feet. Eighty acres of the park contain virgin hardwood, and a boardwalk traverses a swamp forest. Thirteen miles east of East Prairie, **Towosahgy State Historic Site** (573–649–3149) contains the remains of a fortified village and ceremonial center occupied between A.D. 1000 and 1400. The Osage Indians, who lived in this area in later times and were familiar with the ancient village, called it *Towosahgy,* meaning "old town." Using the nearby Mississippi as a thoroughfare, it is thought the inhabitants of the village traded with Indians living upriver at Cahokia (present-day East Saint Louis, Illinois), which was the largest prehistoric metropolitan center in North America. Today there are remnants of seven mounds at Towosahgy; the largest is 250 feet long, 180 feet wide, and 16 feet high. It probably served as a platform mound for another structure. Also visible are several pits, from which workers removed earth to build the mounds, and numerous depressions that indicate house sites.

WESTERN MISSOURI

Children's author Laura Ingalls Wilder lived most of her adult life on a farm near **Mansfield,** forty miles east of Springfield. In 1894, at the age of 27, she moved from De Smet, South Dakota, to the Missouri Ozarks with her husband, Almanzo Wilder, and their daughter, Rose. Here the family farmed and raised livestock, and Wilder began to write her series of books on pioneer life on the Great Plains. The **Laura Ingalls Wilder–Rose Wilder Lane Museum and Home** (Route A, 417–924–3626) preserves the Wilder family farmhouse. An adjacent museum contains memorabilia pertaining to the life and writing careers of Wilder and her daughter.

SPRINGFIELD

Springfield lies on a plateau surrounded by the Ozark Mountains in the southwestern corner of Missouri, a zone that the government had reserved for the Delaware and Kickapoo Indians. However, their removal west, beginning in 1830, cleared the way for white settlers, who began trickling into these remote hills. The establishment of a land office in 1835, and the Butterfield Overland Stage route, which began in 1858, helped transform Springfield into a bustling trade and transportation center, a surge that made the town of some strategic importance at the outbreak of the Civil War.

Missouri remained in the Union, but Springfield contained many southerners with Confederate sympathies. The town was on the brink of the first major conflict west of the Mississippi, the 1861 Battle of Wilson's Creek, which gave the Confederates a tenuous hold on Springfield. A few months later, Union forces regained control of the city and held it until the end of the war. In 1867 the **Springfield Confederate Cemetery** was established alongside the **National Cemetery,** separated by a high stone wall. After the turn of the century the wall was removed, and today the cemetery is one of only a handful that contain the remains of both Union and Confederate soldiers. The railroad industry figured prominently in the economy and politics of nineteenth- and early-twentieth-century Springfield. Despite much protest, the town of North Springfield sprang up in the 1870s, when the Atlantic & Pacific Railroad was routed a mile north of the original settlement, but the two towns were consolidated in 1887. The **History Museum for Springfield–Greene County** (830 Boonville Street, 417–864–1976), in the 1894 City Hall, has collections on Springfield and Ozark history, including 20,000 photographs. The **Air and Military Museum of the Ozarks** (AMMO, 2305 East Kearney, 417–864–7997) features memorabilia from of the U.S. armed forces. The museum building is also home to the Ozark Mountain Squadron of the **Confederate Air Force,** which preserves historical aircraft.

WILSON'S CREEK NATIONAL BATTLEFIELD

The Battle of Wilson's Creek occurred on August 10, 1861, at a time when the state was precariously under Union control. The Confederacy coveted the state for its strategic position between two great rivers, its rich lead and iron mines, and other natural resources such as cattle, hemp, corn—and manpower.

Pro-Confederate governor Claiborne Jackson called out the state troops but failed in his attempt in May 1861 to seize the U.S. arsenal in Saint Louis. With the failure of this and other plans, Governor Jackson, Major General Sterling Price, and elements of the new Missouri State Guard retreated to southwestern Missouri. They were joined by regular Confederate troops under General Ben McCulloch and N. Bart Pearce, commanding the Arkansas State Guard, yielding a combined force of over 12,000 men. In vigorous pursuit of the Confederates was the commander of the U.S. arsenal, Brigadier General Nathaniel Lyon, and about 5,000 Union soldiers.

General Nathaniel Lyon is shot through the chest leading a charge at the Battle of Wilson's Creek. He was the first Union general to be killed in action in the Civil War. Although the battle was a victory for the Confederates, they were unable to take control of Missouri.

On August 2, 1861, Union troops, now grown to some 5,865 men, overwhelmed a vanguard of Confederate soldiers near Springfield, but during the encounter Lyon learned he was severely outnumbered. Nevertheless, at dawn on August 10, he launched a surprise two-pronged attack on the Confederates, who were encamped near Wilson's Creek. In the Ray cornfield, Union forces supporting Lyon's column were defeated and driven back to Lyon's main force, securing the east side of Wilson Creek for the Confederates. Colonel Franz Sigel led his German-American U.S. Volunteers in a flanking attack on the Confederate camp and caught the Rebels by surprise; but his attack faltered when he mistook some gray-clad Confederate units for Iowans (who also wore gray uniforms) and allowed them to approach his position. The Confederates tore into Sigel's command, throwing them into a panicky retreat. The Confederates were then able to shift the full weight of their numbers against Lyon's men on the crest of a ridge that came to be called Bloody Hill.

By 9:30 AM Nathaniel Lyon had been killed, and by 11 AM the Union troops were in an orderly withdrawal to Springfield. The Federals lost 1,317 men and the Confederates 1,222 in the heavy fighting. General Price followed this victory with another at Lexington, but the Confederates were never able to turn their raids into occupation of the territory. Missouri had two state governments during the war, one Union, one Confederate. The Unionists, in control of the capital, put Jackson out of office and took charge of the government. Jackson, however, continued to be recognized as the state's governor by the Confederacy.

Major points on the battlefield are accessible by car, and each stop has exhibits, maps, and historical information on the battle. There are also trails to Bloody Hill and the sites of other important confrontations, to various military encampments, and to both the **Ray House** and **Springhouse,** the only extant structures associated with the battle. A farmhouse and post office (ca. 1852) served as a Confederate field hospital during and after the battle. The visitor center features an orientation film, maps, and interpretive displays.

> LOCATION: Routes ZZ and 182, 10 miles southwest of Springfield. HOURS: Memorial Day through Labor Day: 8–9 Daily; Labor Day through Memorial Day: 8–5 Daily. FEE: Yes. TELEPHONE: 417–732–2662.

The **Ralph Foster Museum** and **Edwards Mill** (417–334–6411), part of the **College of the Ozarks,** are at **Point Lookout,** about fifty miles south of Springfield. The liberal-arts college teaches Ozark crafts such as weaving and basket making. The museum contains exhibits of Indian crafts and artifacts, firearms, Civil War items, Ozark music, and natural history of the area. The Edwards Mill is a working replica of a late-nineteenth-century water-powered gristmill.

GEORGE WASHINGTON CARVER NATIONAL MONUMENT

The eminent botanist and agronomist George Washington Carver was born into slavery on the Moses Carver farm near the village of Diamond in the early 1860s. One evening during the Civil War, he and his mother were kidnapped by Confederate bushwhackers. She was never found, but the infant George was returned to Moses and Susan Carver, who raised him and his brother Jim.

George developed an early interest in gardening and native plants. At about the age of 12, he went to nearby Neosho to attend a school for black children. In Kansas and Iowa, Carver continued his education, pursuing his own self-guided plant experiments and attending the few institutions that accepted blacks. In 1894 he received a degree in agriculture from Iowa State and joined the faculty of the college. Two years later, Booker T. Washington invited Carver to become director of agriculture at Tuskegee Institute in Alabama. One of Carver's goals at Tuskegee was to help fellow blacks face the new economic conditions in the South, and it was here that the charismatic teacher and agronomist made his important contributions regarding the cultivation and uses of the peanut and sweet potato. Carver died in Tuskegee in 1943, where he is buried next to Booker T. Washington.

The George Washington Carver National Monument comprises Carver's birthplace site, the Moses Carver House (1881), the ceme-

The modest 1881 house of Moses and Susan Carver, who raised George Washington Carver after his mother was kidnapped and disappeared during the Civil War. The house is preserved at the George Washington Carver National Monument near Diamond.

tery where Moses and Susan Carver are buried, and the woodlands where George roamed as a child. The visitor center contains exhibits pertaining to Carver's life and career, during which he developed 400 byproducts from the peanut and potato.

LOCATION: County Route V off Route 71A, 2.5 miles southwest of Diamond. HOURS: 9–5 Daily. FEE: None. TELEPHONE: 417-325-4151.

JOPLIN

Joplin sits upon a high, undulating prairie, which halts abruptly on the southern edge of town at Shoal Creek, where the rugged terrain of the Ozarks commences. The first settlers arrived in the late 1830s, and one of them, Methodist minister Harris Joplin, is remembered in the town's name. Rich deposits of lead were discovered in the vicinity around 1850, and after the Civil War the mining of galena went into full swing in the southwestern corner of Missouri and adjacent parts of Oklahoma and Kansas, an area that came to be called the Tri-State District. Unlike the development of the lead belt in southeastern Missouri, which was an orderly, rather sober event, here towns sprang up overnight, prospectors could make a fortune in a matter of days and lose it just as quickly, and law and order were practically nonexistent. Zinc ore, also known as jack, occurs in the Tri-State District six to ten times more abundantly than lead ore. After the railroads reached the district, the zinc ore could be marketed profitably, and the zinc industry expanded rapidly. In the boom years of the 1870s, Joplin was known as "the town that jack built." These free-wheeling days are depicted in the Thomas Hart Benton mural in Joplin's **Municipal Building** (303 East 3d Street). In **Schifferdecker Park,** on Joplin's western edge, the **Tri-State Mineral Museum** (417–623–2341) displays rocks and minerals from the region as well as mining machinery and tools. Also in the park is the **Dorothea B. Hoover Historical Museum** (417–623–1180), which contains period rooms appointed with Victorian furnishings, Indian artifacts, and a collection of dolls.

HARRY S TRUMAN
BIRTHPLACE STATE HISTORIC SITE

Located in the small southern Missouri town of Lamar, the Harry S Truman Birthplace preserves the modest house where the nation's thirty-third president was born on May 8, 1884. His parents, both reared in the vicinity of Kansas City, moved here in 1881, where John Anderson Truman farmed and dealt in livestock. Harry's tenure in his birthplace was brief; when he was eleven months old, his family returned to the Kansas City area, and by 1890 they had settled in nearby Independence, where Truman grew up. The one-and-a-half-story frame house was built about 1881 and contains furnishings of the period.

LOCATION: 1009 Truman Avenue, Lamar. HOURS: 10–4 Monday–Saturday, 12–4 Sunday. FEE: None. TELEPHONE: 417–682–2279.

In the town of **Nevada,** the **Bushwhacker Museum** (231 North Main, 417–667–5841) is housed in the former Vernon County Jail (ca. 1860), one of the few structures left standing when the town was burned to the ground by Union soldiers. Exhibits include photographs and memorabilia on the Confederate guerrillas who roamed western Missouri during the Civil War and who came to be called bushwhackers.

OSAGE VILLAGE STATE HISTORIC SITE

In 1719 the fur trader Charles Claude du Tisne came upon a village of Osage Indians on this hill overlooking the Osage River. The archaeological remains of this village constitute the earliest known Osage settlement in western Missouri. The Osage migrated from the Ohio Valley to the eastern Great Plains in the late seventeenth century, just prior to European exploration of the area.

In 1774 the community that lies within Osage Village State Historic Site supported from 2,000 to 3,000 people, who lived in about 200 lodges. Several trading posts and one Christian mission sprang up within a five-mile radius of the Osage village, in the midst of a network of trade that developed in the region. The trading posts included **Fort Carondolet,** built on the Osage River in 1795 by the Chouteau family of Saint Louis, and another fort built at the confluence of the Little Osage and Marmaton rivers in 1802 by another prominent Saint Louis trader, Manuel Lisa. A walking tour affords vistas of these outposts.

LOCATION: Route C, 15 miles northeast of Nevada, between Walker and Fair Haven. HOURS: Always open. FEE: None. TELEPHONE: 417–682–2279.

HARRY S TRUMAN FARM HOME

Harry S Truman lived in this late-nineteenth-century frame house in what is now Grandview from 1906 to 1917, while operating the family's 600-acre farm. As a young bachelor he gained firsthand knowledge of both the pleasures and vicissitudes of agrarian life, which enabled him later to garner the votes of farmers and to shape federal farm programs. The farmstead contains original Truman family items and period furnishings. The site contains 525 acres. Tours of the farm may be taken in summer.

LOCATION: 12301 Blue Ridge Boulevard, Grandview. HOURS: 9–4 Friday–Sunday. FEE: None. TELEPHONE: 816–254–2720.

MISSOURI TOWN 1855

Missouri Town 1855, set in Fleming Park just southeast of Independence, is a group of more than thirty buildings dating from 1820 to 1860. These have been relocated from the surrounding area

Walls of a hewn-log church built in the 1850s, preserved at Missouri Town 1855.

to create a village and farmscape typical of the southern culture that predominated in this corner of frontier Missouri prior to the Civil War. The structures include Greek Revival houses of affluent southern farmers, simple slave quarters, various types of barns, and a cruciform church built in 1844 of hickory and linden logs. The buildings have been furnished with period items, and several also house special collections of such things as farm equipment and land-grant documents. Emphasis is placed on prevailing frontier building techniques, and cutaway sections reveal such procedures as post-and-beam construction and brick nogging for insulation. Throughout the town is a variety of nineteenth-century fencing, including stake-and-rider fence, Virginia snake fence, rustic palisade fence, and an Ohio post-and-rail. Staff in clothing of the 1850s demonstrate an array of nineteenth-century chores and crafts. Farm animals add a touch of reality to the scene.

LOCATION: 7 miles south of Blue Springs in Fleming Park, near Lake Jacomo. HOURS: 9–4:30 Wednesday–Sunday. FEE: Yes. TELEPHONE: 816–795–8200.

The **Civil War Museum of Jackson County** in **Lone Jack** (Routes 50 and 150, 816–566–2272) explains the events surrounding the Battle of Lone Jack, which took place here on August 16, 1862. Some 2,000 Confederates fought 800 Federals in an eight-hour battle. Neighbors and friends fought against each other, as many of the soldiers on both sides were from this area. Over one hundred Confederates and 43 Federals were killed.

KANSAS CITY AND INDEPENDENCE

Kansas City and Independence grew up in tandem at a time of growth and turmoil on the edge of the frontier. The two cities, along with Saint Joseph to the north, are fascinating cases of urban development because these cities were not sustained by water—an ocean or lake or river—in the way that the other trade centers to the east were. They were not ports but trailheads.

Kansas City and Independence stand where the Missouri River takes a big swing to the northwest. This area became the jumping-

OPPOSITE: *A schoolhouse built about 1860, a store, a worker's house from the 1830s, and a barn of the 1840s are some of the other buildings at Missouri Town 1855.*

off place for pioneers and gold seekers bound Southwest and West, as beyond this point there were no reliably navigable rivers to move goods to Santa Fe or the masses of people pressing to go to Oregon and California. While Saint Louis is known as the Gateway to the West, the term more accurately describes these outposts in western Missouri. It was here that all the rules of the game changed, where a culture accustomed to traveling on a network of rivers adapted to an ocean of prairie. It was here that people got off the steamboats that had carried them up the Missouri from Saint Louis and packed their goods into the ox- or mule-drawn covered wagons that jostled 2,000 miles across the Oregon and California trails.

Independence began to be settled in 1827, after the federal government acquired title to Indian lands in the area. It became the chief outfitting point for Santa Fe Trail traffic after Franklin—the town in central Missouri where William Becknell launched the famous trail in 1821—was swallowed up by the capricious Missouri River. In 1826 Francois Chouteau, of the influential Saint Louis Chouteaus, relocated his trading post near the Missouri and Kansas rivers in order to deal with the Kansa, Osage, and Wyandot Indians. In 1834, four miles to the south, John Calvin McCoy opened a store with the intention of snagging Santa Fe Trail business from merchants and outfitters in nearby Independence. He was successful; a town sprang up around him, which he called Westport. Westport and Independence became hives of activity in 1843 with the opening of the Oregon Trail. In the meantime Chouteau's fur post had grown into a thriving trade center in its own right, and in 1838 McCoy organized the Kansas Town Company to buy the area surrounding the depot's landing. He platted the village in 1839 and named it Kansas. McCoy's second settlement, known variously as Town of Kansas and City of Kansas, annexed Westport in 1889 and officially changed its name to Kansas City. An outbreak of cholera in 1849, followed by the Civil War, severely dampened trade and traffic in the area. Nonetheless, McCoy's City of Kansas began to eclipse Independence, the main reason being that its citizens secured the much-coveted Missouri Pacific Railroad, which arrived in 1865.

KANSAS CITY

Between 1865 and 1870 Kansas City's population grew from 6,000 to 20,000. For the most part, the city experienced unabated prosperity

until the Great Depression of the 1930s. Kansas City became a great
hub, where manufactured goods were shipped from the East in
exchange for cattle and wheat from the West. In 1869 the Hannibal
Bridge was completed across the Missouri; in 1870 the first stockyards were constructed; and in 1876 the Kansas Board of Trade
introduced the practice of futures trading in grain.

Kansas City's developers held the standard nineteenth-century
attitude that riverfront property was best reserved for commercial
use. They were prescient, however, in initiating the extensive system
of parks and boulevards that distinguishes Kansas City as one of the
country's most beautiful cities. A vocal champion in this and a
broad range of other civic issues was William Rockhill Nelson,
founder in 1880 of the *Kansas City Star*. From his arrival in Kansas
City—which he described as "incredibly commonplace and
ugly"—until he died in 1915, Nelson worked to transform the raw-
boned frontier town into a paradigm of the City Beautiful
Movement. "I decided," he said, "that if I were to live here, the
town must be made over." Kansas City's riverfront encompasses the
site of Francois Chouteau's landing—it stood at the foot of present-
day Grand Avenue—which McCoy purchased and platted in 1839.
Here is where Kansas City began. Only the street grid, oriented
toward the river, remains as evidence of the city's origins, but the
few surviving Romanesque Revival and Italianate commercial buildings, especially those along Delaware Street, suggest the area's nineteenth-century mercantile hustle.

A few blocks away, one of America's most distinctive bridges
spans the Missouri River. The **A. S. B. Bridge**—an abbreviation for
Armour, Swift, and Burlington, the packing houses and railroad that
jointly financed the project—was completed in 1911. Designed by a
Kansas City resident, J. A. L. Waddell, the double-decked bridge
(railroad below) lifts upward to accommodate the passage of barge
traffic on the river. The bridge is no longer in use.

Kansas City's historic industrial district, which remains vibrant,
sits on an isolated wedge of floodplain at the confluence of the
Missouri and Kansas rivers. Its existence here is something of a marvel because access has always been a problem: it is cut off from the
city to the east by an imposing palisade of bluffs. Cable railroad
lines, built in 1885, provided the first direct passage, but it was not
until the completion of the **12th Street Viaduct,** in 1915, that a
direct roadway linked the West Bottoms with the city proper.

Railroads, not rivers, dominate the scene, and the district's chief architectural glory is its profusion of terra-cotta-encrusted red-brick Romanesque Revival warehouses and factories. After the Hannibal Bridge was completed in 1869 and Kansas City emerged as the mid-continental trading hub, the West Bottoms became the central distribution point for livestock. The **Stockyards** (Genessee between 14th and 16th streets), with its rambling maze of pens and chutes, started going up in 1870. Other landmarks associated with the cattle industry include the **Live Stock Exchange Building** (16th and Genessee streets), built in 1910; the **West End Hotel** (1619 Genessee Street), of 1911, which once served a crowd of cattlemen and railroad workers; and the **American Royal Building** (23d and Wyoming streets), a vast livestock exposition hall constructed in 1922.

South of the riverfront, and evolving from it, the central business district, which is now hemmed in by Routes I-70, I-35, and I-29,

The maze-like Kansas City Stockyards, teeming with activity in the 1880s.

began to attract the attention of developers in the 1860s. By the 1890s it was the commercial heart of the city, which it remained until the 1950s, when the automobile and inexorable suburban growth began to shift people and money from the core to the rim of the city. The structure that best embodies Kansas City's late-nineteenth-century boom years is the **New York Life Building** (20 West 9th Street), a brownstone office designed by the New York architectural firm of McKim, Mead & White. The exterior is appointed with masonry and terra-cotta detailing and a large bronze eagle from the studio of Augustus Saint-Gaudens. At the time of construction, 1887–1890, this ten-story Renaissance Revival building was the tallest in the city. The building is interesting from an engineering standpoint because it is a late example of load-bearing wall construction. It is architecturally almost identical to the New York Life building in Omaha, built at the same time by the same firm. The insurance

The Kansas City stockyards today.

company, which was expanding its regional operations at the time, wanted to save money by using the same plans twice.

Several other structures reflect the city's irrepressible spirit of optimism at the turn of the century. The **New England Building** (112 West 9th Street) of 1888 is a Renaissance-style brownstone office with an elegant two-story oriel bay on its southwest corner. Two hotels catered to notable out-of-towners, including several presidents, and fashionable Kansas City residents. The **Savoy Hotel** (219 West 9th Street) is noted for its Savoy Grill with its Art Nouveau leaded-glass windows. It was built and expanded from 1888 to 1906. The **Coates House Hotel** (1005 Broadway) by Van Brunt & Howe is a brick structure with ornamental sheet-metal cornices. It was constructed between 1886 and 1891 and takes its name from Kersey Coates, the Philadelphia-born entrepreneur who initiated the first development in the central business district and who platted the nearby affluent residential neighborhood called **Quality Hill,** where Kansas City's wealthiest citizens lived at the turn of the century. A few remnants of their occupation remain, including the 1888 **George Blossom Mansion** (1032 Pennsylvania Avenue, private), a stately brick residence with terra-cotta trim and sandstone lintels and sills.

During the early twentieth century engineers and architects, with an eye cocked toward Chicago, began experimenting with the latest building materials and styles in the central business district. The area remains a showcase for the work of Kansas City's most accomplished architect, Louis S. Curtiss. His **Standard Theater,** now called the **Folly Theater** (300 West 12th Street, 816–842–5500), is a gem. Built in 1900, it stood at the center of Kansas City's early-twentieth-century theater district. The **Boley Clothing Company** (1124–1130 Walnut Street), completed in 1909, is a handsome blend of Commercial-style and Art Nouveau elements and is one of the country's earliest examples of metal-and-glass curtain-wall construction. Built at the same time as the Boley Building, **Louis Curtiss's Studio** (1118–1120 McGee Street) is another curtain-wall structure. The terra-cotta cornice bears a shield with the architect's initials.

The **Kansas City Power & Light Building** (northwest corner of 14th Street and Baltimore Avenue), built in 1930–1931 by Hoit,

OPPOSITE: *Kansas City's first skyscraper, the New York Life Building designed by McKim, Mead & White, is decorated with a bronze eagle cast in the studio of the sculptor Augustus Saint-Gaudens.*

Price & Barnes, and, one block east, the 1936 **Municipal Auditorium** (211 West 13th Street), by Gentry, Voscamp & Neville, with Hoit, Price & Barnes, are superior examples of Art Deco design. The thirty-four-story Kansas City Power & Light Building was the tallest structure in the state when it was completed. It is particularly impressive at night, when a system of floodlights illuminates its facade and crowning shaft. **City Hall** (414 East 12th Street), another Art Deco structure dating from 1937, offers a panorama of Kansas City and the Missouri River from its thirtieth-floor observation deck.

Two nineteenth-century churches stand as reminders of the time when the area sustained vibrant residential neighborhoods. **Saint Patrick's Catholic Church** (800 Cherry Street) was completed in 1875 to serve a predominantly Irish congregation. The exuberant Italianate structure was designed by the pioneering Kansas City architect Asa Beebe Cross. **Saint Mary's Episcopal Church** (1307 Holmes Street) is a commanding structure in the Victorian Gothic style, built in 1888. It is noted for its high altar of painted marble, which was made in Italy by a process now considered a lost art.

With Kansas City's post-Civil War prosperity, affluent families began to move eastward onto the forested bluffs overlooking the Blue and Missouri rivers. The **Gladstone Boulevard mansions** (3200–3600 blocks), many of them palaces of stone and brick, serve as bold reminders of the turn-of-the-century boom years. Skirting the bluffs, Cliff Drive affords sweeping vistas of the Missouri River from **Scarritt Point** and **Prospect Point.** The road winds through **Kessler Park,** formerly North Terrace Park, which was established in 1899. The park and Cliff Drive were both designed by George Kessler.

Kansas City Museum

This museum is housed in the **Robert A. Long Residence,** designed by Henry F. Hoit and one of the most sumptuous of the Gladstone Boulevard estates. Exhibits deal with the history of Kansas City from the time of the Osage Indians to the time of the Civil War. These include a replica of François Chouteau's trading post (1821) and a drugstore (1910) with a functioning soda fountain. The museum has an extensive collection of clothing and textiles dating from the 1700s, a large collection of American Indian artifacts, and a natural-history hall with dioramas of North American flora and fauna. In

The Kansas City Museum is housed in the former Robert A. Long Residence, designed by Henry F. Hoit and completed in 1910.

addition there is a planetarium and the Challenger Discovery Center, where visitors can take simulated space-shuttle trips.

LOCATION: 3218 Gladstone Boulevard. HOURS: 9:30–4:30 Tuesday-Saturday, 12–4:30 Sunday. FEE: Yes. TELEPHONE: 816–483–8300.

The City Beautiful Movement finds its best expression in midtown Kansas City, where handsome public and commercial buildings are interspersed with engaging residential neighborhoods, and the whole is served by a large urban park, Penn Valley. Here also is where William Rockhill Nelson held sway, and the efforts of his civic sermonizing can be seen everywhere. One of his legacies is the *Kansas City Star* **Building** (18th Street and Grand Avenue). Nelson commissioned the Chicago architect Jarvis Hunt to design a facility for his newspaper. The result, completed in 1911, is a palatial Renaissance Revival structure faced with tapestry brick and topped with a red-tile roof. Jarvis Hunt also designed **Union Station** (Pershing Road and Main Street), the premiere structure in midtown. Completed in 1914, the immense Beaux-Arts building is a classic example of the City Beautiful Movement and one of the largest train depots in the United States. On a stifling day in June 1933, the terminal was the backdrop for a bloody shootout that came to be called the Union Station Massacre. In the melee three machine-gun-toting gangsters, including Charles Arthur "Pretty Boy" Floyd, were attempting to rescue a friend, a convicted felon who was in the custody of three lawmen and two unarmed FBI agents. Before fleeing, the hoodlums gunned down four of the officers and accidentally killed their friend as well.

To the south of Union Station lies the 176-acre **Penn Valley Park,** one of the first in the parks-and-boulevards plan adopted by Kansas Citians in the 1890s. The landscape architect George E. Kessler, an adherent of the concepts of Frederick Law Olmsted, drafted the comprehensive urban plan and designed this park, which is situated amid rugged hills and ravines.

Liberty Memorial

The Liberty Memorial, located in Penn Valley Park across from Union Station, has the only museum and archives in the United States to specialize in the World War I period. Dedicated as a monument to peace, the memorial commemorates the service of those who served during the Great War. Memory Hall, the east building, houses several murals including the *Pantheon de la Guerre,* which was completed by more than forty French artists during World War I and was originally over 400 feet long. This is the only remaining section of the mural on display in the world. The 217-foot "Torch of Liberty" observation tower affords a fine view of the city. The museum houses an excellent collection of military and home-front artifacts. The memorial, at 100 West 26th Street, was scheduled to reopen in 2000 after restoration. Until then, the museum exhibits were housed in two temporary locations.

LOCATION: (Museums): *Town Pavilion,* Main Street between 11th and 12th streets; *Ward Parkway Center,* 8600 Ward Parkway. HOURS: *Pavilion:* 10–6 Monday–Friday; *Parkway:* 10–6 Tuesday–Sunday. FEE: None. TELEPHONE: 816–221–1918.

OPPOSITE: *The Cathedral of the Immaculate Conception on West 11th Street in Kansas City was designed by T. R. Tinsley, a local architect. Built in 1882, it has an elaborate cupola that was covered with gold leaf during renovations in the 1960s.*

Julia Lee, one of Kansas City's notable jazz musicians, singing in a local club with her brother's band in 1924. She performed at the White House during Truman's presidency.

During the free-wheeling Pendergast era, which fell roughly between the two world wars, money was loose and people stayed up late spending it. Nightlife flourished in Kansas City, and the night music of the time was jazz. This hothouse environment nurtured musical talents including Charlie Parker and Count Basie. Kansas City came to be known for its own hard-driving brand of jazz. The area around 18th and Vine streets is considered the cradle of Kansas City jazz, and one of the landmarks of this historic period is the modest building at 1823 Highland Avenue that housed the **Musicians Union Local 627.** During this same time, the six-block area surrounding 18th and Vine was the commercial and social heart of Kansas City's black community, a crowded neighborhood of churches, hotels, nightclubs, lawyers' and doctors' offices, and the local headquarters for the NAACP and Urban League. The **Black Archives of Mid-America** (2033 Vine Street, 816–483–1300), begun in 1974, traces black history and culture from slavery to the Kansas City jazz era by way of an extensive collection of photographs and documents from the Missouri–Iowa–Oklahoma–Kansas areas.

Included are the papers of Scott Joplin, Langston Hughes, Don Brown, Count Basie, Charlie Parker, and others.

Westport

Visitors to this area, which lies to the south of midtown, will note that some of the streets run diagonally to the standard north–south grid, a vestige of John McCoy's original plat of this pioneer town. Westport Road is a relic of the Santa Fe Trail. Architecturally, Westport encompasses a range from charming **rowhouses** (1–7 East 34th Street) to Frank Lloyd Wright's **Clarence W. Sondern Residence** (3600 Belleview Avenue, private) and the lavish estates of wealthy Kansas Citians. At this end of the spectrum is the **August R. Meyer Residence** (4415 Warwick Boulevard), a Flemish-gabled mansion of 1897 that now serves as administrative offices for the Kansas City Art Institute. Meyer made his fortune in mining and smelting and was an early promoter of Kansas City's parks system. He also kindled interest in the development of the Paseo, the major north–south boulevard in Kansas City that was inspired by the Paseo de la Reforma in Mexico City. A high concentration of mansions can be found in **Janssen Place** (East 36th Street and Janssen Place), a planned community developed by a local railroad magnate in the late 1890s. The Italianate, Shingle, Queen Anne, Arts and Crafts, and Georgian Revival styles can be seen in beautifully landscaped lots facing a private boulevard. Many lumber industry moguls lived in Janssen Place, hence its alternate appellation, Lumberman's Row. On a more modest scale, the **Rockhill Neighborhood** (46th Street to Pierce Street, Locust Street to Troost Avenue) is William Rockhill Nelson's vision of a City Beautiful community. The thoughtfully planned neighborhood is characterized by simple clapboard and limestone houses built between 1901 and 1910. Two antebellum structures associated with influential denizens of early Westport include the **Reverend Nathan Scarritt Residence** (4038 Central Street, private), built about 1897, and the **John Harris Residence** (4000 Baltimore Avenue, private), a fine Greek Revival home that dates from about 1855.

Thomas Hart Benton Home and Studio State Historic Site

For thirty-five years the artist Thomas Hart Benton lived in this cloistered stone house with his wife, Rita Piacenza Benton, and used the carriage house in the rear as his studio. Born in Neosho, Missouri, in 1889, he spent some time in New York before returning to Missouri, where he spent the rest of his life painting realistic works dealing with regional history, rural life, and folk themes. He is noted for his large murals in public buildings, some of which sparked controversy for Benton's bold and unsentimental treatment of his subject matter. Benton, who took a lively interest in politics, was the son of a Missouri congressman and the grandnephew and namesake of Missouri's first senator, Thomas Hart "Old Bullion" Benton (1782–1858). The residence was built in 1903 for an executive of the Kansas City Electric Light Company. It contains furnishings and personal effects of the Bentons, while the studio holds many of the artist's tools and equipment. Benton died in his studio while painting on a winter day in 1975.

LOCATION: 3616 Belleview: HOURS: Mid-April through October: 10–4 Monday–Saturday, 12–5 Sunday; November through mid-April: 10–4 Monday–Saturday, 11–4 Sunday. FEE: Yes. TELEPHONE: 816–931–5722.

The studio of the noted Missouri artist, Thomas Hart Benton, in Kansas City.

Nelson–Atkins Museum of Art

William Rockhill Nelson, who had no personal art collection, provided the money and the idea for this one. It was further endowed by his wife, daughter, and son-in-law, a close family friend, and Mary Atkins, a reclusive former schoolteacher who developed a love of fine art late in life. When ground was broken for the museum in 1930 there was nothing to put in it. Those acquiring a collection were fortunate, however, to be making their initial purchases during the depth of the Depression. Laurence Sickman, one of the buyers, was studying in China at the time, and his early purchases form the nucleus of the Oriental collection, which is one of the finest in the country. The Classic Revival building, which opened late in 1933, was designed by the Kansas City firm of Wight and Wight. It stands on the former estate of the Nelsons, whose residence was razed to make way for the museum. The exterior has sculptured panels by Charles Keck depicting Midwestern exploration and settlement.

> LOCATION: 4525 Oak Street. HOURS: 10–4 Tuesday–Thursday, 10-9 Friday, 10–5 Saturday, 1–5 Sunday. FEE: Yes. TELEPHONE: 816–751–1278.

Three days of skirmishes and engagements, known as the **Battle of Westport,** culminated on October 23, 1864, in fighting across hills and dales now occupied by quiet neighborhoods. The last important Civil War clash in Missouri, it marked the end of Major General Sterling Price's attempt to seize the state from Union control, a campaign that had begun a month earlier in southeastern Missouri at the Battle of Pilot Knob. To stop Price's drive, Major General Samuel R. Curtis led a large force of regular soldiers and Kansas militia to the Kansas-Missouri border. In addition, about 20,000 Union soldiers under General Alfred S. Pleasanton were pursuing Price's column. Some 8,000 of Curtis's men crossed the border and dug entrenchments along the Big Blue River several miles east of Westport.

The Federal plan to trap Price between two armies seemed to go awry when the Confederate cavalry leader Jo Shelby outflanked Curtis's entrenchments and drove off the Federals. Price thereupon occupied the abandoned defenses and confidently awaited the arrival of his pursuer, Pleasanton. On the morning of October 23, Price attacked Curtis's men once again and threw them back; but the Federals counterattacked. Then Pleasanton's men crossed the

Big Blue and punched through a strong point in Price's line, putting the Confederates to rout. Now truly caught between two onrushing Federal attacks, Price began a long retreat to the south, his campaign a failure. A series of markers note important points of the battle. Some of the fiercest fighting occurred in the vicinity of Ward Parkway and 55th Street, on the estate of William W. Bent, the founder of Bent's Fort in Colorado and a principal Westport trader and wagon-train impresario. In 1870 the trader and trapper Seth E. Ward bought the house and a portion of Bent's Westport property on which to retire. The expanded and remodeled **Seth E. Ward Residence** (1032 West 55th Street, private) was designed by Asa Beebe Cross in 1871. During the Battle of Westport, the Wornall House was used as a hospital by Union and Confederate troops successively. The home (1858) is the finest Greek Revival structure in Kansas City. Now maintained by the Jackson County Historical Society as the **John Wornall House Museum** (146 West 61st Terrace, 816–444–1858), it contains period furniture and examples of nineteenth-century textiles, glass, silver, and ironware.

Swope Park (63d Street and Gregory Boulevard), a 1,770-acre park situated along the Blue River, was donated to the city in 1896 by real estate mogul Thomas H. Swope when the surrounding terrain was still the province of bucolic farms and orchards. The park's benefactor is buried here in the **Swope Memorial and Mausoleum,** a Classic Revival portico flanked by lions designed by Wight and Wight and constructed in 1916–1917. One of the most charming sites in the park is the **Swope Park Shelter,** a Spanish Mission–style structure built in 1904–1905.

Alexander Majors House

Alexander Majors began hauling freight from Independence to Santa Fe in 1848. Seven years later he joined ranks with William H. Russell and William B. Waddell to form a business that became the premiere freighting firm on the frontier. Securing contracts to haul government as well as private goods, Russell, Majors & Waddell lured business to Kansas City and helped to develop and settle far-flung portions of the western United States. At the height of its operation, the company owned 3,400 wagons and 40,000 oxen and employed 4,000 men. In addition, Russell, Majors & Waddell founded the Pony Express, the overland mail service that was headquartered in Saint Joseph during its brief but celebrated existence. One of the company's riders was William F. "Buffalo Bill" Cody. In the 1890s Buffalo Bill, by then a wealthy and renowned entertainer, found his former boss living alone in a shack in Denver, where he was writing an account of his life. Cody financed the publication of these memoirs, which provided Majors with royalties toward the end of his life. He died in 1900 at the age of 86.

Alexander Majors conducted business from this handsome Greek Revival home, which was built in 1856. It has been restored and furnished with period items. Replicas of the barn and smokehouse stand on their original sites. A wagon room and a blacksmith shop contain a variety of nineteenth-century vehicles, including a Conestoga wagon.

LOCATION: 8201 State Line Road. HOURS: April through December: 1–4 Thursday–Sunday. FEE: Yes. TELEPHONE: 816–333–5556.

INDEPENDENCE

The sobriquet Queen City of the Trails was not a reference to an excess of civility in Independence but rather an indication of its early dominance as a trailhead. Much of the action in this rough-and-tumble town centered on **Independence Square** (Liberty, Maple, Main, and Lexington streets). It was here that wagon trains lined up for their westward departure, an event that often required a full day of assembly. In the antebellum days, some of the area's largest slave auctions took place on the square. Dominating Independence Square is the **Jackson County Courthouse,** a building first erected in 1836 on an older foundation and expanded five times in the nineteenth century. The 1859 **Marshal's Home, Jail, and Museum** (217 North Main Street, 816–252–1892) is a brick compound that has been restored to its condition in the Civil War era; it contains period furnishing and exhibits of local history. On August 11, 1862, during the Battle of Independence, the guerrilla raider William Quantrill and his followers stormed the jail and released its Confederate prisoners. Frank James was incarcerated here during the winter of 1882–1883. The **1827 Log Courthouse** (107 West Kansas Street, private) functioned as temporary government quarters for Jackson County and subsequently served a variety of mercantile, religious, and philanthropic uses.

Independence Square, the location of the Jackson County Courthouse, in 1857.
Wagon trains heading west on the Santa Fe Trail, the California Trail, and the
Oregon Trail lined up here to start their journeys.

   The **Bingham-Waggoner Estate** (313 West Pacific Avenue,
816–461–3491) takes its name from its better known occupants.
Portions of the house were built about 1855 by an Independence
saddle maker. In 1864 the artist George Caleb Bingham purchased
the estate, and it was here in his log cabin studio that he painted
one of his most famous paintings, *Order No. 11,* which depicts the
forced evacuation of civilians from sections of northwestern
Missouri ordered by Federal authorities following Quantrill's raid
on Lawrence, Kansas. Bingham and his wife, Eliza, lived in the
house until 1870. In 1879 it was purchased by Peter and William
Waggoner, Pennsylvania millers who had also bought the long-established mill complex just north of the estate. In 1883 they joined with
George Porterfield Gates (maternal grandfather of Bess Wallace
Truman) to form the Waggoner-Gates Milling Company, which
became known for its Queen of the Pantry flour. With their growing
prosperity, the Waggoners transformed the original Italianate villa
into a mansion with Queen Anne elements. The period furnishings
now on display in the home are from the Waggoner estate.

In 1831 the Mormon prophet Joseph Smith, coming from church headquarters in Kirtland, Ohio, selected Independence as the new promised land. Many of his followers migrated to the town, and by 1833 the Mormons constituted about a third of the population in the area. Local resentment increased with the brisk increase in their numbers. Mob violence erupted, forcing the Mormons to relocate north of Independence, first to adjacent Clay County (ca. 1833–1836) and next to Caldwell and Davies counties (1836–1839). Their ranks in northwestern Missouri continued to swell, as did local rancor. In 1838 Governor Lilburn Boggs issued the Extermination Order, pronouncing that Mormons must be killed or driven from the state. Many Mormons fled to Illinois, where in 1839 they established the city of Nauvoo, on the banks of the Mississippi. Again they encountered local prejudice, which culminated with the murder of Smith near Nauvoo in 1844. The prophet's death precipitated yet another exodus as well as a major doctrinal split within the church. Brigham Young led one group to Salt Lake City, Utah, where they retained the formal name The Church of Jesus Christ of Latter-day Saints. Among many splinter groups, a small group started a church in the 1850s that it named New Organization of the Church of Jesus Christ of Latter Day Saints. In 1860 the group asked Joseph Smith III to head up the church under a new name—The Reorganized Church of Jesus Christ of Latter Day Saints. The reorganized church eventually returned its headquarters to Independence, where it remains today.

Two museums in Independence deal with the history of Mormonism in Missouri: the **Independence Visitors Center** (937 West Walnut Street, 816–836–3466), which is affiliated with The Church of Jesus Christ of Latter-day Saints, and the **Temple** (West Walnut Street, 816–833–1000) of the Reorganized Church of Jesus Christ of Latter Day Saints, which is across the street from the RLDS world headquarters. The **Vaile Mansion** (1500 North Liberty Street, 816–325–7111) is a towering Second Empire structure liberally encrusted inside and out with decorative details and appointed with period furnishings. This thirty-one-room mansion was built in 1881 for Harvey M. Vaile, who made his fortune in the construction of the Erie Canal and in U.S. mail route contracts.

The **National Frontier Trails Center** (318 West Pacific Avenue, 816–325–7575) stands on the site of the spring where wagon trains topped off their water kegs, an important finale before departing

The Vaile Mansion in Independence was designed in the Second Empire style by Asa Beebe Cross, a noted architect from Kansas City, and built in 1881.

Independence on one of the west-bound trails. The center is housed in two warehouses of the Waggoner-Gates Milling Company and contains exhibits and archives dealing with the history of the Santa Fe, Oregon, and California trails.

Independence is closely associated with the childhood and early political career of Harry S Truman, the thirty-third president of the United States. Truman, the epitome of the plain-spoken midwesterner, was described by Winston Churchill as "a man of immense determination. He takes no notice of delicate ground, he just plants his foot down firmly on it." His command of the rural vernacular and his lack of a formal college education endeared him to the electorate. John Anderson and Martha Ellen Truman moved from their farm near Grandview to Independence when their eldest child, Harry, was 6 years old. As a young adult he worked for the Santa Fe Railroad, in the mail room of the *Kansas City Star,* and as a bookkeeper in two banks. At the age of 35, after living as a bachelor farmer and serving in World War I, he married Bess Virginia Wallace, whom he had known since she was 5 years old.

Following a brief venture in the men's retail clothing business, Truman entered local Democratic politics at the encouragement of Mike and Jim Pendergast, a brother and nephew of Kansas City's infamous Tom Pendergast. Elected county judge, Truman championed honest government and also saw to such practical things as the building of much-needed roads. Tom Pendergast tapped Truman for the U.S. Senate race in 1934, which he won. Truman's candor and no-nonsense approach to government saved him from being tarred by his association with the Pendergast machine. In 1944, while serving in the U.S. Senate, he was drafted as Franklin Delano Roosevelt's vice-presidential running mate. They won the election handily. Upon Roosevelt's death in April 1945, Truman assumed the presidency along with the responsibility for bringing World War II to its conclusion and for determining the U.S. role in the postwar era. In July and August, Truman met with British prime minister Winston Churchill and Soviet marshal Joseph Stalin at

The Independence house in which Harry and Bess Truman lived from their marriage in 1919 until their deaths was built by Mrs. Truman's grandfather in 1867 and extensively remodeled in 1885.

Potsdam to discuss Germany's future. In those months Truman also made the decision to use the atomic bomb against Japan. In 1947 he declared the so-called Truman Doctrine, making it American policy "to help free peoples to maintain . . . their national integrity against aggressive movements that seek to impose upon them totalitarian regimes." This doctrine overturned the traditional U.S. policy of avoiding foreign entanglements, a policy that had been formulated by George Washington. Truman was elected president in 1948. In 1950 he ordered U.S. occupation troops in Japan, under General Douglas MacArthur, into Korea to repulse a North Korean invasion of South Korea. After MacArthur publicly criticized the president's decision not to allow attacks against bases within China, Truman (with the support of top military officers) relieved the general of his command. Truman chose not to seek re-election in 1952 and retired to Independence, where he died in 1972.

The **Harry S Truman Library and Museum** (Route 24 and Delaware Street, 816–833–1400) contains personal papers and historic documents pertaining to the presidency as well as personal and family memorabilia. Harry and Bess Truman are buried in the courtyard of the museum. A Thomas Hart Benton mural entitled *Independence and the Opening of the West* is located in the foyer of the library. The **Harry S Truman National Historic Site** (219 North Delaware Street, 816–254–9929) preserves the house where Harry and Bess Truman lived after they were married in 1919. They shared the home with Bess's mother and maternal grandmother, and their only child, Mary Margaret, was born here in 1924. Originally a small farmhouse, it was expanded over time into a quite large and comfortable home—progress that paralleled the growth of the Waggoner-Gates Milling Company, in which Bess's grandfather was a partner. The house contains many furnishings and personal possessions of the Trumans.

The **Harry S Truman Office and Courtroom** (Main and Lexington streets, 816–795–8200) are located in the **Jackson County Courthouse,** where Truman served as county judge from 1922 to 1924 and from 1926 to 1934. The **Harry S Truman Railroad Station** (Grand and Pacific streets, renovated) recalls the excitement of Truman's 1948 "Whistle Stop" campaign. It was widely predicted that Truman would lose the 1948 election to Thomas E. Dewey, but Truman took his campaign directly to the voters in a tour by train, speaking to large crowds at each stop, criticizing a "do-nothing" Congress to cheers of "Give 'em hell, Harry!" He won the election by a narrow margin.

FORT OSAGE

A reconstruction of Fort Osage stands on the south bank of the Missouri River fourteen miles northeast of Independence. It was one of the first frontier outposts built after the Louisiana Purchase. William Clark, whom Thomas Jefferson had appointed overseer of Indian affairs in the Louisiana Territory, ordered construction of the fort in 1808 as part of a treaty with the Osage. The agreement offered these Indians federal protection from their enemies, the Sauk and Mesquakie (Fox), if the Osage would in turn relinquish part of their Missouri lands for white settlement. Under the management of George C. Sibley, the fort grew into a thriving outpost, and its inhabitants developed strong and friendly ties with the Osage, a number of whom built their lodges around the fort. As the frontier was pushed farther west and the fur trade was divided among private traders, Fort Osage ceased to have a mission and was abandoned in 1827. The fort has been reconstructed using War Department records and information from archaeological digs. It includes five blockhouses, officers' quarters, enlisted men's barracks, and the factory where fur trade business was conducted. All are furnished with items from the early nineteenth century; costumed staff members serve as guides. Inside the visitor center are artifacts found during excavations of the site.

LOCATION: Route 24 east to Buckner, then north on Sibley Street (Route BB) about 2.5 miles to Sibley, then follow signs. HOURS: Mid-April through mid-November: 9–4:30 Daily; mid-November through mid-April: 9–5 Saturday–Sunday. FEE: Yes. TELEPHONE: 816–795–8200.

BATTLE OF LEXINGTON
STATE HISTORIC SITE

After the Confederates' success at the Battle of Wilson's Creek, General Sterling Price's troops marched north toward the Missouri River town of Lexington, where they found Colonel James A.

Mulligan's Union troops hastily constructing an earthen fortress. On the morning of September 18, 1861, fighting began. The Confederates advanced behind a portable breastwork of water-soaked hemp bales, and the clash is sometimes referred to as the Battle of the Hemp Bales. At nightfall on September 20, the overwhelmed Union troops raised a white flag. The **Oliver Anderson House** was used as a field hospital by the Union, but during the battle the house alternated between Union and Confederate control. The brick Greek Revival structure (1853) is peppered with battle damage and contains original furnishings and Civil War artifacts.

LOCATION: 4 miles off Route 24. HOURS: Mid-April through October. 9–4:30 Monday–Saturday, 12–5:30 Sunday. FEE: None. TELEPHONE: 816–259–4654.

Built in 1847, the **Lafayette County Courthouse** on the public square in **Lexington** is a brick Greek Revival building, a handsome remnant of antebellum Missouri.

The Watkins Woolen Mill, which began operations in 1861, produced blankets and cloth from some forty to sixty thousand pounds of woolen fleece annually during the 1860s. The goods it produced were sold in a small general store on the ground floor.

Fourteen miles northwest of Marshal, **Van Meter State Park** (Route 122, 816–886–7537) preserves important archaeological areas associated with prehistoric and historic Indian cultures of Missouri. The most significant of these areas, the **Utz Site,** is not open to the public, but visitors can see the so-called **Old Fort,** an earthwork on a hill in the northern half of the park that is thought to have been built by the Missouri Indians. The visitor center has exhibits explaining the natural and cultural history of the area and displays of artifacts from the Utz Site.

In **Excelsior Springs** the **Hall of Waters** (201 East Broadway, 816–630–0750) is a splendid Art Deco building constructed in 1937. It houses mineral baths, a water-bottling facility, and an indoor swimming pool, as well as offices for the municipal government.

WATKINS WOOLEN MILL STATE HISTORIC SITE

The Watkins Woolen Mill, which contains all its original machinery, is a wonderful relic of nineteenth-century frontier industrial ingenu-

The Watkins Mill, the only nineteenth-century textile factory in the United States with its original machinery intact, is equipped with a ring-frame ply-twister and other machinery that is still in operating condition.

ity. The textile mill was in operation from 1861—it did a brisk business in blankets and cloth during the Civil War—until the late 1880s, when the advent of ready-made clothing forced the mill out of business. Plantation owner Waltus Watkins conceived of the mill when he was 55 years old. He constructed the three-and-a-half-story structure of bricks made on his farm and equipped it with looms, carding and spinning machines, a huge boiler, and a steam engine. These pieces of machinery, ordered from Philadelphia and Saint Louis, were shipped via railroad and steamboat, then hauled twenty miles from the river landing to the mill by teams of oxen.

Watkins had come to western Missouri from Kentucky in 1830. He expanded his initial eighty-acre landholding in Clay County to a 3,660-acre livestock farm. In its heyday, Bethany Plantation, as it was called, was virtually a self-contained community. It consisted of Watkins's handsome brick Greek Revival home, the mill, a general store where the woolen goods were sold, farm buildings, a blacksmith shop, school, church, sawmill, brick kiln, and cabins for the families of the some forty mill workers. Several of these structures have been restored and are open to the public, including the fully equipped mill; portions of the 1850 Watkins home and outbuildings containing original furnishings; the 1871 Mount Vernon Church; and the Franklin School, built in 1856 and noted for its unusual octagonal design.

LOCATION: Route 69, 6 miles north of Excelsior Springs. HOURS: April through October: 10–4 Monday–Saturday, 12–6 Sunday; November through March: 10–4 Monday–Saturday, 11–4 Sunday. FEE: Yes. TELEPHONE: 816–296–3357.

LIBERTY

The **Jesse James Bank Museum** (103 North Water Street, 816–781–4458) was the scene of a robbery on Valentine's Day 1866 that is thought to have been the work of the James gang. The perpetrators got away with over $60,000 and shot and killed a young bystander. If the James boys were in fact the culprits, this was their first robbery. It was also the first daylight robbery of a U.S. bank in peacetime. The **Clay County Historical Museum** (14 North Main Street on Courthouse Square, 816–781–8062) is housed in a drugstore dating to 1865. It has exhibits of patent medicines, medical equipment, pioneer farm tools, nineteenth-century furnishings,

Civil War memorabilia, and Indian artifacts. **Lightburne Hall** (301 North Water Street), the largest standing antebellum mansion in Missouri, was built around 1850. The Greek Revival plantation was home to one of the region's prosperous hemp growers. The **William Jewell College Library** (Jewell Street, 816–781–7700) has collections relating to Missouri history.

In the winter of 1838–1839, Joseph Smith and five other members of the Mormon church were incarcerated in the Liberty Jail. The old stone jail has been reconstructed within the **Liberty Jail Visitors Center** (Mississippi and Main streets, 816–781–3188), which contains other artifacts associated with Mormon history.

In 1836, during their settlement of Caldwell County, the Mormons founded the town of **Far West**. During the nineteenth century, the Mormons demonstrated a talent for designing and building beautiful temples, but the one proposed for Far West was never constructed. All that remains of the long-abandoned town are the cornerstones of the temple. A monument and markers explain the significance of the site. Far West is about five miles west of Kingston on Route D.

JESSE JAMES HOME AND FARM

Jesse James and his older brother Frank are Missouri's most notorious figures. Born in 1843 and 1847 respectively, the two boys came of age in Clay County, a stronghold of southern sentiment, in a household dominated by their mother, the fiercely matriarchal and decidedly pro-South Zerelda Cole James. Their father, the Reverend Robert James, died in California in 1850. Several years later Zerelda married the mild-mannered physician Reuben Samuel.

At the beginning of the Civil War, Frank, at age 18, first joined Major General Sterling Price's Confederate forces and then William Quantrill's guerrillas. In 1864 Jesse, at age 16, joined his brother with Quantrill. Frank and Jesse also rode with William "Bloody Bill" Anderson's raiders. On September 27, 1864, they were among the 225 guerrillas who looted the town of Centralia, Missouri, stopped a train, and murdered 25 unarmed Federal soldiers who were passengers. On the same day, Anderson's men defeated a detachment of 200 cavalrymen who tried to capture them, killing almost every one of their pursuers, some after they had surrendered. Frank James was with Quantrill on his last, unsuccessful foray—an expedition to assassinate President Lincoln. Quantrill's men, disguised in blue uniforms, set out from Missouri for Washington in January 1865; their mission came to an end when Quantrill was fatally wounded in a skirmish in Kentucky.

At the end of the war, guerrillas were not included in the general amnesty extended to Confederates and were regarded as outlaws. Trying to surrender under a white flag, Jesse James was shot by soldiers. The next year he and his brother began their career as peacetime robbers. The James gang was active for about fifteen years, from 1866 to 1881, and is credited with about twenty-six raids and holdups in eleven states and territories. Frank and Jesse took up with Cole, James, and Robert Younger, also alumni of Quantrill's raiders, and committed a series of sensational robberies across the Midwest. They performed their first train robbery in Iowa on July 21, 1873. The James and Youngers staged their last joint heist at a bank in Northfield, Minnesota, in 1876. The Youngers were captured and summarily convicted and imprisoned. Frank and Jesse escaped, but by now the brothers were married with families, and life was becoming an increasingly grim affair of hide-and-seek from law officers, Pinkerton agents, and people hoping to obtain the reward on their heads.

In 1882, while living under an assumed name in Saint Joseph, Jesse was killed by Robert Ford. Fearing for his own life, Frank surrendered to Governor Thomas T. Crittenden. In 1883 he stood trial for murder and train robbery in a court in Gallatin, another predominantly southern community about forty miles north of the James farm. The trial was steeped in Confederate nostalgia and included the dramatic appearance of the Confederate general Joseph Shelby, who testified as a character witness. Asked to point out Frank James in court, Shelby exclaimed, "Where is my old friend and comrade in arms? Ah, there I see him! Allow me, I wish to shake hands with my fellow soldier who fought by my side for Southern rights!" The jury voted for acquittal. Subsequent trials were held, but charges were dropped in 1885. James retired to the family farm, where he died in 1915.

The James farmstead was often under surveillance and was the scene of two grisly incidents. In 1863, in the aftermath of Quantrill's bloody raid on Lawrence, Kansas, a group of Federal soldiers hanged Dr. Samuel, leaving him for dead, and beat Jesse James. Both survived, and after this episode Jesse joined Quantrill's band.

In 1875 Pinkerton operatives threw a bomb into the James kitchen, where the explosion severed Zerelda's right arm and killed 8-year-old Archie Samuel. Portions of the simple log-and-clapboard farmstead were built in 1822. The house has been restored and contains original furnishings. The adjacent museum contains the guns and personal effects of Jesse James, the original tombstone on his grave, the family Bible, and various historical documents, including Frank James's letter of surrender to Governor Crittenden. Across the road stands the **Claybrook House,** a handsome rural antebellum structure, where Jesse's daughter, Mary James Barr, lived, 1900–1921.

LOCATION: 3 miles northeast of Kearney. HOURS: June through September: 9–4 Daily; Rest of year: 9–4 Monday–Friday, 12–4 Saturday–Sunday. FEE: Yes. TELEPHONE: 816–628–6065.

WESTON

Weston, with its wealth of beautifully preserved homes and commercial buildings, is a classic antebellum river town. Founded in 1837 at an ideal landing on the Missouri, Weston soon grew to be the area's central shipping point for hemp and tobacco, the two economic mainstays in this corner of Missouri before the Civil War. The town's boom years were curtailed in 1881 when the fickle Missouri River took a radical change of course and left Weston a few miles inland. In the 1890s, with the comeback of tobacco production, Weston became a warehousing and bartering center for the crop and remains the only tobacco market west of the Mississippi. The **Weston Historical Museum** (601 Main Street, 816–386–2977) contains documents and artifacts pertaining to the history of the town and surrounding area.

Limestone springs near Weston proved useful for the distilling of bourbon. The **McCormick Distilling Company** (McCormick Lane, 816–640–2276) has been manufacturing whiskey for over a century excluding a pause during Prohibition. The distillery was one of many enterprises of Weston's most famous citizen, Ben Holladay, whose primary ventures were in shipping and overland freight. In 1861 Holladay gained control of Russell, Majors & Waddell, because of large loans he had advanced the floundering freight company. He in turn made a great deal of money selling portions of this business to Wells Fargo, a fortune he lost in the Panic of 1873.

Burley tobacco growing near Weston, the site of the only tobacco market west of the Mississippi.

SAINT JOSEPH

Saint Joseph spreads from bottomlands on the east bank of the Missouri River up onto the flanking bluffs in an area of northwestern Missouri known as the Blacksnake Hills. In 1826 the American Fur Company dispatched Joseph Robidoux III to the site to open a fur-trading station. In 1799, while trading with Indians at the site of present-day Kansas City, 16-year-old Robidoux had apparently made a trip farther north along the Missouri and reconnoitered the spot where he would later return.

Robidoux was born in Saint Louis in 1783. His parents were French-Canadians, and his father was a prominent Saint Louis trader. Robidoux and his brothers followed in their father's footsteps and by the 1820s had established a wide-ranging family trade network in the West. During his years on the Missouri River, Robidoux gained a reputation as a shrewd trader with a penchant for gambling and an ability to get along with local Indians. In 1830 Robidoux bought the Blacksnake Hills outpost from the American Fur Company. Six years later the Sauk, Mesquakie, and Ioway Indians in the area sold their land—a tract along the Missouri River north of Robidoux's Post—to the United States. In contradiction to the 1820 Missouri Compromise, the strip was annexed to the state of Missouri as slave territory, which prompted a land rush among slaveholders, many of whom came from Virginia, Tennessee, Indiana, and Ohio. The newcomers began raising hogs and cattle and, with their attendant slaves, established a thriving tobacco and hemp culture. Robidoux's Post became the principal trade center for this agrarian community. In an effort to secure his town as county seat, Robidoux platted his land in 1843 and renamed it after his patron saint.

After the discovery of gold in California in 1848, Saint Joseph began to rival Westport and Independence as a major supply depot and outfitter for westward-bound wagon trains. Traffic through Saint Joseph increased even more after an outbreak of cholera in 1849 ravaged the Westport-Independence area. During the gold rush, a city of tents sprang up along the bluffs, and in one month in 1849 some 1,500 prairie schooners crossed the river at Saint Joseph. The travelers' demand for meat—both processed and on the hoof—gave rise to Saint Joseph's meat-packing and livestock industries. Another surge of migration came in 1859 with discovery of gold in Colorado. That same year, Joseph Robidoux drove a final golden spike in the Hannibal & Saint Joseph Railroad, the first passenger train across Missouri, which guaranteed a steady influx of travelers into the river town. As the western terminus of the rail line, Saint Joseph was the natural departure point for the short-lived (April 1860–August 1861) but renowned Pony Express, whose riders carried mail from Saint Joseph to Sacramento, California, in ten or fewer days.

Business dwindled in Saint Joseph during the Civil War but picked up again after it. In the late 1860s, Texas cattle ranchers began herding their livestock to the railhead at Saint Joseph; in 1873 a bridge was completed across the Missouri River; in 1887 the Saint Joseph Stock Yards Company was organized; and by the 1890s the city's flour-milling and meat-packing industries and its mule and horse market were booming. Saint Joseph contains a wealth of historic structures from its boom days before and after the Civil War.

The chief glory of Saint Joseph is its collection of magnificent residences built between 1888 and 1893 in the amalgam of

Richardsonian Romanesque and Francois Premier, or Chateauesque, styles. Most of these were the products of the local firm of Eckel and Mann, but their chief designer was the vagrant genius of Midwestern design, Harvey Ellis. Ellis was born in Rochester, New York, in 1857 and died there in 1904, but his best work was done in Minneapolis, Saint Paul, and Saint Joseph. Only in Saint Joseph is much of it still preserved, with the result that this small city is a museum of his exuberant work. The chief surviving examples are two civic buildings, the **American National Bank** (1889) at 7th and Felix and the **Police Station** at 7th and Messanie; and the following private residences (some now converted to institutional use): **J. B. Moss House** (1889) at 9th and Sylvanie; **J. W. McAlister House** at 101 North 19th (1889); **J. D. McNeely House** at 701 South 11th (1889); **A. T. Smith House** at 802 Hall Street (1890); and **Nave House** (ca. 1891), at 22d and Clay.

Robidoux Row Museum

Joseph Robidoux began constructing this row of brick buildings in the 1850s as temporary housing for travelers to the west. After his wife died in 1857, he took over one of the quarters and lived here until his death in 1868. The complex is an early example of East Coast urban rowhouse styling transplanted onto the frontier. Four of the original seven units remain, restored to reflect the history of the structure. One room is furnished as Robidoux's bedroom and contains some of his personal effects. Another contains pioneer furnishings typical of transient quarters. The third is a kitchen, and the fourth, a family room, is dominated by a large, rustic fireplace.

> LOCATION: 3d and Poulin streets. HOURS: May through October: 10–4 Tuesday–Friday, 12–4 Saturday–Sunday; Rest of year: 10–4 Tuesday–Saturday. FEE: Yes. TELEPHONE: 816–232–5861.

Neighboring structures in this commercial area, which date from the 1850s to the 1860s and reflect elements of the Italianate and Renaissance Revival styles, are the **Missouri Valley Trust Company Building** (4th and Felix streets) and the **Corby Building** (5th and Felix streets). Nearby, at the foot of Francis Street, is the site of **Robidoux's Landing,** where the original town and the ferry and riverboat landings were established in the 1840s, and where thousands of immigrants departed on their westward journeys in the nineteenth century.

The **Buchanan County Courthouse and Jail** (Courthouse Square) is an interesting mix of architectural styles and one of the largest county government compounds in the state of Missouri. The brick courthouse, built in 1873, is in the High Victorian Italianate style, while the jail, which was built about 1909, reflects elements of the Prairie School style. In 1882 the Buchanan County Courthouse was the site of the trial of two men, Robert and Charles Ford, who had been planning to deliver the James gang into the hands of the law. Themselves members of the gang, the Fords plotted with a sheriff to trap the criminals in the act. Robert Ford ended up fatally shooting Jesse James instead and was hauled into court with his brother for conspiring to murder that notorious public enemy. Ford pleaded guilty and was sentenced to hang; but a few hours later a telegram arrived from Governor Thomas Crittenden declaring Ford pardoned. Ten years later Ford was gunned down by one of Jesse's men.

Patee House Museum/Jesse James House

The Patee House Hotel is a brick Italianate building that was constructed from 1856–1858 as a luxury hotel. In 1860 the building served as the headquarters for Russell, Majors & Waddell, the firm that inaugurated the Pony Express mail service from Saint Joseph to Sacramento, California. Mail that had been sorted in a special mail car on the Hannibal & Saint Joseph Railroad was then carried on horseback to Sacramento in grueling 2,000-mile trips. Russell, Majors & Waddell suggested that applicants for the job be young, skinny, not over eighteen, and preferably orphans. Before this service began, the greatest volume of mail to California went by ship via the isthmus of Panama, a trip that took twenty-two days. Other California-bound mail was sent on the Butterfield Stage, which went to San Francisco on a circuitous course through Memphis and El Paso.

The Pony Express began amid great fanfare and lived up to its claims of providing quicker service than either the Panama or Butterfield Stage routes. Nevertheless, nineteen months after the Pony Express began, it was defunct, partly because of the advent of the telegraph, but also because the government, which relied heavily on the service, was not able to come up with the funds to pay its bills, forcing Russell, Majors & Waddell into bankruptcy. The museum in the Patee House exhibits the last Hannibal & Saint Joseph

Railroad Locomotive and Railway mail car, Pony Express memorabilia, Civil War items, Victorian furnishings, and horse-drawn buggies and wagons.

The **Jesse James House,** which originally stood two blocks north of the Patee House at 1318 Lafayette Street, was the last home of the notorious guerrilla, bandit, and pathological killer, whose gang perpetrated daring bank and train robberies across the Midwest for a decade after the Civil War. Under the alias Tom Howard, James retreated to Saint Joseph as a fugitive, where he lived in this simple frame house with his family. On April 3, 1882, Robert Ford, a 21-year-old gang member who was planning to betray James to the sheriff for a $10,000 reward, instead shot him in the back of the head when James became suspicious. In Ford's own account, he shot James as he was straightening a picture on the wall: "As he stood there, unarmed, with his back to me, it came to me suddenly, 'Now or never is your chance. If you don't get him now he'll get you tonight.' Without further thought or a moment's delay I pulled my

The Pony Express Museum in Saint Joseph, which was the eastern terminus of the overland mail service to California.

revolver and levelled it as I sat. He heard the hammer click as I cocked it with my thumb and started to turn as I pulled the trigger. The ball struck him just behind the ear and he fell like a log, dead." James was 34 years old. The house contains period furnishings, many of which are original to the house, and exhibits of the era.

LOCATION: 12th And Penn streets. HOURS: *Patee House:* April through October: 10–4 Monday–Saturday, 1–5 Sunday; February through March, and November: 10–4 Saturday, 1–4 Sunday. *Jesse James Home:* June through August: 10–5 Monday–Saturday, 1–Sunday; Rest of year: 10–4 Monday–Saturday, 1–4 Sunday. FEE:: Yes. TELEPHONE: 816–232–8206.

Pony Express National Memorial

Pony Express National Memorial is in the reconstructed brick stables from where the company's first westbound rider embarked on April 3, 1860, on a bay mare named Sylph. The rider carried about a

The fully equipped blacksmith shop at the Pony Express Museum, Saint Joseph.

hundred letters, bound mostly for California, which each sender had paid $5 to post. The 1858–1861 building, formerly Pike's Peak Stables, has Italianate ornamentation. The stable has blacksmith and wheelwright shops and Pony Express memorabilia.

LOCATION: 914 Penn Street. HOURS: April through September: 9–5 Monday–Saturday, 2–5 Sunday. FEE: Yes. TELEPHONE: 816–279–5059.

The Psychiatric Museum of Saint Joseph State Hospital

The museum, opened in 1967 by the hospital museum committee, traces the history of treatment for mentally ill patients from the fifteenth century to present times. It is the only such museum in Missouri and one of about a half dozen in the nation. Exhibits include a reproduction of a "tranquilizer chair"—in which patients were kept strapped for as long as six months—developed in Philadelphia by Dr. Benjamin Rush, the noted eighteenth-century physician, and a swing in which patients were strapped and then spun in an effort to stimulate circulation in the brain. Also on display are nineteenth-century hospital furniture, and weaving, painting, and ceramic works created by patients. An intriguing exhibit displays a collection of 1,446 items such as thimbles, nails, screws, metal tops of pepper shakers, spoon handles, and other objects that a single patient swallowed over time in the 1920s.

The museum is in the 1874 hospital administration building.

LOCATION: 3400 Frederick Avenue. HOURS: 8:30–4 Monday-Friday, 1–5 Saturday–Sunday and holidays. FEE: None. TELEPHONE: 816–387–2300.

The **Saint Joseph Museum** (11th and Charles streets, 816–232–8471) is housed in a Gothic Revival sandstone mansion of 1879, overlooking the Missouri River. The interior is appointed with lavish walnut woodwork and stained glass. The museum maintains the largest collection of American Indian arts and crafts in the region, natural-history exhibits, and displays that chronicle Saint Joseph's growth as a transportation, trade, and agricultural center.

The **Albrecht–Kemper Museum of Art** (2828 Frederick Boulevard, 816–233–7003) contains eighteenth-, nineteenth-, and twentieth-century American art by such artists as Gilbert Stuart,

Albert Bierstadt, Mary Cassatt, Edward Hopper, and Thomas Hart Benton. It is housed in the Georgian Revival mansion (1935) of William Albrecht, founder of Westab, a tablet and stationery company, today known as Meade Products.

Just west of Laclede off Route 36 is the 151-foot **Locust Creek Covered Bridge,** the longest of the four extant covered bridges in Missouri. When it was built in 1868, it was part of Route 8, the main east–west thoroughfare in northern Missouri. The creek it spanned has since been diverted.

GENERAL JOHN J. PERSHING BOYHOOD HOME STATE HISTORIC SITE

John J. Pershing was born in 1860 near Laclède, the oldest of nine children. When he was 6, his family moved into town, where he lived until 1882 when he left to attend the West Point Military Academy. Pershing's long and distinguished military career began in 1886 as the army campaigns to subdue the Indians were drawing to a close. He served with the Sixth Cavalry against the Apache in New Mexico and during the last stirrings of the Sioux on the Dakota–Nebraska border. In 1898 he fought in the Spanish–American War and in 1900 he was assigned to the Philippines. He married Frances Warren in 1905, and they had three daughters and a son. In 1915, while Pershing was commanding a brigade against Pancho Villa along the Mexican border, Frances and their daughters were killed in a fire in California. With the outbreak of World War I, Pershing served as commander-in-chief of the American Expeditionary Forces, and in 1919 he was named General of the Armies. Pershing won a Pulitzer Prize for his memoir, *My Experiences in the World War* (1932). The general died in 1948 and is buried at Arlington National Cemetery.

The house (ca. 1857) where Pershing grew up is a simple structure with Gothic ornament. It contains period furnishings, exhibits of local history, and Pershing memorabilia. The **Prairie Mound School,** where Pershing taught before leaving for West Point, has been moved onto the grounds.

LOCATION: Worlow Street and Pershing Drive, Laclede. HOURS: 8–4 Monday–Saturday, 12–5 Sunday. FEE: Yes. TELEPHONE: 816–963–2525.

CHAPTER TWO

KANSAS

Carl Becker, a New England professor of history, went out to Kansas to teach at the turn of the century and became an eloquent spokesman for his adopted state. In 1910 he wrote this appraisal of Kansas's unruly story: "To the border wars succeeded hot winds, droughts, grasshoppers; and to the disasters of nature succeeded in turn the scourge of man. . . . Until 1895 the whole history of the state was a series of disasters, and always something new, extreme, bizarre, until the name Kansas became a byword, a synonym for the impossible and the ridiculous." Becker's observations are distilled in the state's motto, *Ad astra per aspera*—"To the stars via adversity." Few states possess so candid a maxim.

Kansas is a place of beautiful vistas. The eastern third is serrated with rugged, scenic stream valleys. Prior to settlement this part of the state was covered with majestic expanses of tall grass—vegetation that easily towered over the heads of humans. West of the 100th meridian is the High Plains, a vast semiarid area of treeless short-grass prairie. Kansas's straight-arrow boundaries are contrived, except for a nibble out of the northeast corner formed by the Missouri River. Competing ideologies accounted for some development. The origin of such places as Atchison (proslavery) and Lawrence (free-state) illustrates the flurry of passion-spawned town building in Kansas on the eve of the Civil War. But climate and the evolution of overland transportation better explain the long-term configuration of cities and towns on the Kansas map. The largest urban areas cluster east of the ninety-eighth meridian, where more ample rainfall made initial settlement less arduous. Even today the High Plains of western Kansas is sparsely populated. Several Kansas towns, including Leavenworth, Baldwin City, Great Bend, Larned, and Dodge City, sprang up along the southwest curvature of the Santa Fe Trail, which cut a 400-mile swath through present-day Kansas. The Atchison, Topeka & Santa Fe Railroad later followed the general course of the trail, prolonging the life of these towns and spurring the growth of others. (By comparison, the Oregon Trail, which arched through the northeastern corner of Kansas, was never shadowed by a railroad line, and the only reminders of its presence in the state are two Pony Express stations near the villages of Hanover and Marysville.) A succession of other rail lines prompted the growth of other Kansas towns.

Kansas has always been a crossroads. Seminomadic bands of Indians converged on the Great Plains long before the arrival of the

A painting by E.L. Spybuck shows the signing of the 1825 treaty between the United States government and the Osage Indians at Council Grove, which secured right-of-way for U.S. citizens traveling across Osage lands on the Santa Fe Trail.

first Europeans. In 1541, after abandoning his search for the seven cities of Cibola, Francisco Vásquez de Coronado went looking for Quivira, a region that later became Kansas. The explorer failed to find the gold and silver that an Indian slave had promised (the man was later executed for his misleading tip), but Coronado did encounter various tribes, of which he mentioned the Kaw (or Kansa), Wichita, and Pawnee.

The state and its largest river are named for the Kansa, an appellation that means People of the South Wind. Of the Siouan language group, these Indians settled along the Kansas River at an unknown time, having migrated onto the plains from the Ohio Valley. The Pawnee and Wichita, who share a Caddoan ancestry, moved onto the plains from the southwest, likewise at unknown periods. While the Wichita moved in and out of Kansas at intervals—they were present, for example, when the town that bears their name was founded—the Pawnee stayed in the area of Kansas and Nebraska. A powerful tribe, they developed strong ties first with the French and later with the Americans. They once numbered approximately 25,000.

The demographics of Kansas's Indians became increasingly complicated in the early nineteenth century. In the 1820s the Osage

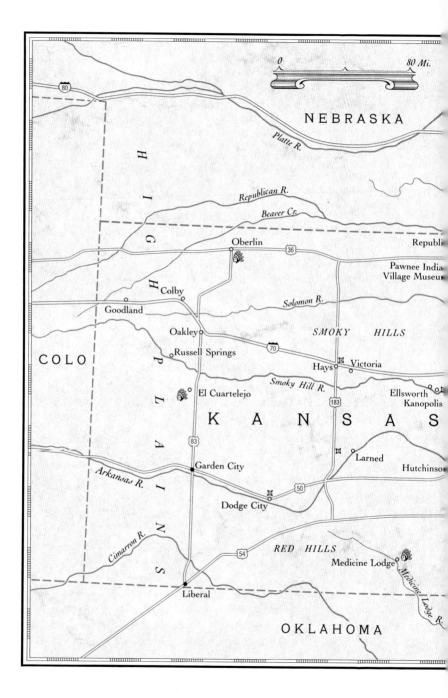

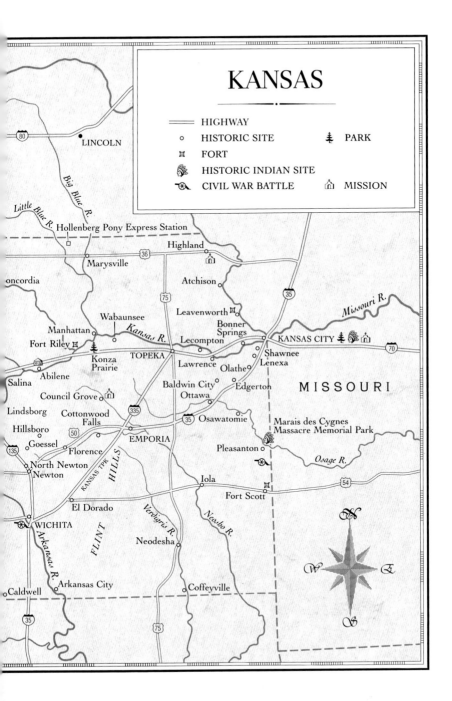

KANSAS

- ═══ HIGHWAY
- ○ HISTORIC SITE
- ⊟ FORT
- HISTORIC INDIAN SITE
- CIVIL WAR BATTLE
- ♣ PARK
- ⌂ MISSION

LINCOLN

Big Blue R.

Little Blue R.

Hollenberg Pony Express Station

Highland

Marysville

36

oncordia

Atchison

75

Leavenworth ⊟

35

Missouri R.

Wabaunsee

Kansas R.

Bonner
Springs

Manhattan

Lecompton

KANSAS CITY ♣

70

Fort Riley ⊟

TOPEKA

Konza
Prairie

Lawrence

Olathe

Shawnee
Lenexa

Salina

Abilene

Council Grove ⌂

Baldwin City

Edgerton

MISSOURI

Lindsborg

Cottonwood
Falls

335

Ottawa

Hillsboro

50

Osawatomie

Marais des Cygnes
Massacre Memorial Park

Goessel

135

EMPORIA

Florence

Pleasanton

Osage R.

North Newton

Newton

KANSAS TPK

FLINT HILLS

Iola

54

Fort Scott

El Dorado

Verdigris R.

Neosho R.

WICHITA

FLINT

Neodesha

Arkansas R.

Caldwell

Arkansas City

Coffeyville

35

75

PAWNEE FAMILY

migrated west from Missouri into the Neosho River valley in the southeastern part of what later became Kansas. The nomadic Arapaho and Cheyenne, pushed west by the Sioux, began roaming the High Plains. In the Treaty of Fort Laramie, of 1851, the federal government allowed them to retain their hunting grounds in western Kansas and eastern Colorado—then gold was discovered in the Rockies in 1858. The Kiowa of the upper Missouri country, also displaced by the Sioux, were shoved south to the Arkansas and Canadian rivers. These tribes did not all get along: The Pawnee were in constant conflict with the Kaw and Osage, while the Arapaho and Cheyenne, allies with each other, were enemies of the Pawnee.

In the 1820s settlement pressure in the Ohio Valley gave rise to the notion that eastern tribes should be relocated in perpetuity to Kansas. Two American explorers, Zebulon Pike in 1806 and Stephen H. Long in 1819, had concluded that Kansas was a desert, of little use to white agrarians. The movement of Indians commenced. The Kaw and Osage ceded lands that became home in 1825 to the Shawnee (who published the first newspaper in Kansas) and a progression of other eastern tribes, including the Sauk, Mesquakie, Potawatomi, and Kickapoo. The last of these, the Wyandot, who arrived in 1842, started the first free school in the territory and founded the town that became Kansas City.

These eastern tribes did not remain long in their new "permanent" home. The Kansas–Nebraska Act of 1854 set in motion the next phase of resettlement, resulting in the final exodus of Indians from Kansas. This law established the territories of Nebraska and Kansas and repealed the Missouri Compromise of 1820, replacing that act with popular sovereignty, whereby territorial residents would vote to determine the slavery issue in their future states. People of opposing persuasions rushed into Kansas to stake out their philosophical position as well as land, and some thirty-five tribes of Indians were caught in the middle of the controversy. During the intense moral debate over slavery, the rights of Indians were virtually ignored. By 1880 virtually all Indians in the state had ceded their lands and retreated to Oklahoma. Today small reservations are held in Kansas by the Ioway, Sauk, Mesquakie, Kickapoo, and Potawatomi.

OPPOSITE: *A family of Pawnee, a Plains tribe that lived in Kansas along the Arkansas River. The man is wearing a peace medal, which had probably been passed down in his family. These medals, given out by the U.S. government at treaty signings, were greatly prized by the Indians.*

The Kansas–Nebraska Act drove a wedge through the national Democratic party, which paved the way for the growth of the nascent Republican party and the election of Abraham Lincoln; it set the nation on the road toward the Civil War; and as a prelude to that war, it ignited the ten-year era of Bleeding Kansas. While advocates of slavery from Weston and other Missouri towns were hopping the river to establish beachheads in Kansas Territory, Eli Thayer of Massachusetts was organizing the New England Emigrant Aid Company with the plan of sending free-soil settlers into Kansas. Although the organization never mobilized the large numbers of immigrants anticipated, Thayer and his associates were articulate spokesmen for their cause and had ready access to the Eastern press. Departures of Kansas-bound parties were well-publicized events at which John Greenleaf Whittier's poem "The Kansas Emigrant's Song" often reverberated to the refrain of "Auld Lang Syne." Its first stanza ran, "We cross the prairies as of old / The pilgrims crossed the sea, / To make the West, as they the East, / The homestead of the free."

In the early months after the formation of Kansas Territory, the proslavery forces held the upper hand. They orchestrated two infamous elections, in the fall of 1854 and spring of 1855, in which armed toughs from Missouri invaded the territory, harassed free-state settlers, and stuffed the ballot boxes. The legislators brought to power in these bogus elections went on to enact the so-called Bogus Laws, which called for such extreme measures as punishment by death for any person who aided or abetted the rebellion of slaves or free blacks. The free-state faction countered by rattling pen and sword—they published four newspapers, organized militias, and imported Sharps rifles from the East. Violence was perpetrated by extremists on both sides. The antislavery town of Lawrence was sacked by a proslavery faction in 1856; in the same year the abolitionist John Brown murdered five proslavery men on Pottawatomie Creek, which in turn incited the Battle of Osawatomie, involving several hundred adversaries. At Marais des Cygnes Creek in 1858 a group of proslavers killed five men. Abolitionists made raids into Missouri against slaveholders, an activity that came to be known as jayhawking. The abolitionists garnered national publicity in excess

OPPOSITE: *The 2d Kansas State Militia marching toward Missouri on October 21, 1864, on their way to attack a Confederate army under Major General Sterling "Pap" Price. This depiction was done from memory by Samuel J. Reader (detail).*

30 1906 x

S.J.R.

2'OND K.S.M. INVADING Mo.

With grub and baggage, flag and gun —
(The State line no obstruction —)
The forward movement has begun,
To compass "Pap's" destruction.

7. 06 x

of their actual political strength within the territory. The bulk of the settlers, from Ohio, Indiana, Illinois, and eastern Missouri, opposed the introduction of slavery on pragmatic economic grounds and out of a general apprehension of blacks. Struggling farmers were attracted by the promise of land and did not want to compete with slaveholding plantation owners or, for that matter, with free blacks. By their sheer numbers these agrarians finally prevailed. Kansas became a free state, ratifying a constitution prohibiting slavery in 1859. Statehood followed, in January 1861. The first governor was Dr. Charles Robinson, a Massachusetts physician who was the principal agent for the New England Emigrant Aid Company and a founder of the anti-slavery strongholds of Lawrence, Topeka, and Manhattan.

While the state was embroiled in political intrigue, the Civil War rehearsed in Kansas was largely waged elsewhere. No significant battle occurred on Kansas soil. Nonetheless, the state was firmly in the Union camp, and of all Union states, it supplied the largest percentage of soldiers in proportion to its population of fighting-age males; its troops also had the highest battle mortality rate. As a brigadier general assigned to raise regiments of Kansas volunteers, James Lane was the first Union commander to recruit blacks for combat service. Most of these men were Missouri slaves freed by force from their owners by Lane's brigade of white volunteers, many of whom were experienced jayhawkers. In September 1861 Lane raided and burned the town of Osceola, Missouri, presaging the terrible bloodshed that would take place along the border during the war.

Kansas's post-Civil War period was marked by prosperity, optimism, and some setbacks: the Panic of 1873, a scourge of grasshoppers in 1874, and renewed attacks on homesteader incursions upon the Great Plains by the Cheyenne and Arapaho. By the 1870s the Kansas Pacific, the Missouri, Kansas & Texas, and the Atchison, Topeka & Santa Fe had laid tracks across the state, providing access to markets to farmers and livestock producers, who were until 1885 chiefly longhorn cattle drovers from Texas. In the late 1870s, Kansas received many rural blacks, driven from the South by poverty and an escalation of racially motivated violence. The wave constituted the first major migration of former slaves out of the South. They became known as Exodusters, and the largest number came to Kansas, attracted by reports of bountiful agricultural lands and by the state's symbolic role in the freeing of their race. The peak of the migration, known as the Kansas Fever Exodus, occurred in 1879 when some 6,000 blacks arrived in the state from Louisiana, Mississippi, and Texas. In 1880 approximately 15,000 Exodusters remained in Kansas, working as domestics, as laborers on farms and the railroads, and in mines and factories.

The railroads' aggressive courtship of European immigrants accounts for much of the ethnic diversity in Kansas and elsewhere on the Great Plains. The railroads obtained a great deal of land from the government as enticement to lay tracks across the West—in Kansas alone they owned more than 10 million acres, which they advertised in sales campaigns across Europe. By 1890 one Kansan in every ten was foreign-born. The small towns of Scandia, in north-central Kansas, and Lindsborg, in central Kansas, lie amid areas still farmed by descendants of Swedish immigrants. Beginning in the 1870s, after the Russian government announced a policy of universal conscription, a large number of pacific German-Russians of Lutheran, Roman Catholic, and Mennonite faiths purchased 100,000 acres from the Santa Fe Railroad and immigrated to central Kansas. These newcomers had perfected techniques of dry-land farming on the steppes of Russia that transposed well to the Great Plains climate, and the Mennonites popularized a drought-resistant strain of hard red winter wheat known as turkey red. Wheat began to replace corn as the staple crop, and today Kansas ranks first in the nation in wheat production.

In 1872 Kansas farmers organized a local group of the National Grange of the Patrons of Husbandry, or the Grange, which had been founded in 1867 in hopes of bettering the lot of farmers. The Grange provided the nucleus for the Farmers' Alliance, which in turn became the Populist party, the most effective of the agrarian movements in Kansas. The party formed in 1890 at a time when national monetary policy, drought, and a national depression were forcing many farmers into foreclosure. The Populist party secured a majority in the state legislature for a few years and elected two governors, who served in 1893–1895 and 1897–1899, as well as a U.S. senator and several congressmen. One of the most popular of the Populist orators was Mary Elizabeth Lease, wife of a druggist, mother of four, and one of Kansas's first female lawyers, whose advice was to "raise less corn and more hell!"

OVERLEAF: *A wheat field in Kansas. Much of the land on the Great Plains could not be farmed profitably until late in the nineteenth century, when dry-farming techniques and a drought-resistant strain of wheat were introduced.*

In the early twentieth century, agricultural mechanization and the food demands of World War I brought boom times to farmers in the Great Plains. After the war, however, demand slackened, grain prices fell, farmers produced more rather than less in an attempt to offset their losses, and inevitably prices fell even lower. Farmers were in their own economic slump when the stock market crash in 1929 ushered in the Great Depression. Then came a prolonged drought, producing huge dust storms. The southwestern corner of Kansas was in the heart of the Dust Bowl. The "black blizzards" that boiled up from this region between 1932 and 1939 darkened the skies for days at a time. A storm in May 1934 removed 300 million tons of soil from the Dust Bowl region, depositing the dirt not only over the eastern half of the United States but also on ships 500 miles out to sea.

While President Dwight D. Eisenhower, the state's most famous citizen, embodied the foursquare, plain-spoken Kansas ideal, a native-born journalist, William Allen White, explained the state's mores to the nation in his editorials and essays. As a boy in the small Kansas town of El Dorado, White witnessed drought, grasshoppers, and a tornado that destroyed the town. As a young man, he purchased the *Emporia Gazette* and in 1896 wrote the editorial that established his national reputation as a journalist. "What's the Matter with Kansas?" blamed much of the state's problems on the Democrats and Populists, a bout of conservatism that White later repudiated. In the early twentieth century, White became a confidant and spokesman for President Theodore Roosevelt and the Progressive movement and backed Roosevelt's Bull Moose party in 1912. In the 1920s he helped quash the Ku Klux Klan in Kansas and backed striking miners, and in the 1930s he supported much New Deal legislation while managing to remain within the ranks of the Republican party. As one biographer wrote, White was the spokesman of "rank-and-file, first-name, commonsense, God-fearing, good-neighbor, small-town, Main Street America."

This chapter begins in eastern Kansas where early missionaries worked among the Indians and the first pro- and anti-slavery towns sprang up in the aftermath of the Kansas–Nebraska Act. It then moves to the central part of the state, the heartland of Mennonite and German-Russian settlement and the location of the state's largest city, Wichita. Finally the chapter ventures onto the High Plains, the vast and sparsely populated western third of the state.

E A S T E R N   K A N S A S

Missionaries coming to work with Indians on the Western reservations formed the vanguard of white settlement in this area. Many reminders of their ardent energy remain in eastern Kansas, and some of the oldest extant structures in the state are associated with their ministry. In and near the small town of **Highland** in extreme northeastern Kansas, the Presbyterian minister Samuel Irvin evangelized among the Indians and early white settlers. In 1837 he founded the **Native American Heritage Museum** (Route 36, 913-442-3304), which was active until 1866. The brick-and-stone building, built in 1846, was originally 106 feet long and served as classroom, chapel, and dormitory. Part of the mission has been restored as a museum containing chapel furnishings, Indian artifacts, and items of local history. In 1858 Irvin went on to establish Highland University, the first institution of higher learning in Kansas, now **Highland Community College. Irvin Hall** was built of brick between 1858 and 1859 on the college campus. The **Doniphan County Courthouse** (Walnut and Liberty streets) is a brick rendition of Richardsonian Romanesque designed by the nineteenth-century Kansas architect George P. Washburn, who built a dozen other monumental courthouses in the state.

ATCHISON

Atchison, along with Leavenworth, sprang up as a proslavery enclave in the summer of 1854, a few months after the passage of the Kansas–Nebraska Act. It soon became a busy outfitting point for westward-bound wagon trains. In 1897 Amelia Earhart was born in her grandparents' house here. The simple Alexander Jackson Downing–inspired Gothic Revival **Amelia Earhart Birthplace** (223 North Terrace, 913-367-4217) was built in 1861 atop a bluff with a fine view of the river. Earhart purportedly used her inheritance from the sale of the house to buy her first airplane. The house contains period furnishings and memorabilia associated with the famous aviatrix. Atchison has two fine interpretations of Richardsonian Romanesque architecture: the **Atchison Post Office** (621 Kansas Avenue) built from 1892 to 1894, and the **Atchison County Courthouse** (5th and Parallel streets). The latter, which dates to

1896, is another product of George P. Washburn. A number of handsome Queen Anne and Second Empire private residences survive in Atchison, a reminder of the town's prosperity in the late nineteenth century.

The large monastery building of the **Saint Benedict's Abbey** overlooks the Missouri River on the northeast edge of Atchison. The architecture of the monastery—its corridors are more than 300 feet long—is modified Tudor Gothic. Constructed of Waverly Ledge limestone quarried locally, it was built from 1927 to 1929 to designs by E. Brielmaier and Sons of Milwaukee.

LEAVENWORTH

In 1827 Colonel Henry Leavenworth established a military outpost on the banks of the Missouri River to protect traffic on the Santa Fe Trail. A few farmers and missionaries lived around the fort, but real settlement began abruptly in 1854, shortly after passage of the Kansas–Nebraska Act on May 30. A group of proslavery advocates from Weston, Missouri, just across the river, decided to hop the river and squat on land that was then part of a Delaware Indian preserve. By June they had organized a town company, thereby securing for Leavenworth the title of first incorporated town in Kansas Territory. A major commercial coup occurred in 1856, when the firm of Majors, Russell, and Waddell made Leavenworth headquarters for its overland freight-hauling business. Numerous blacksmiths, wainwrights, merchants, outfitters, and traders, many lured from Missouri, settled in Leavenworth as a result. By the onset of the Civil War, Leavenworth's original constituency was outnumbered by pro-Union settlers. Leavenworth's prominence as a frontier transportation center began to wane when it lost its bid as a railhead. The **Leavenworth County Historical Museum** (1128 Fifth Avenue, 913–682–7759) is housed in a sixteen-room Victorian mansion of 1867, containing antique furnishings, toys, china, and porcelain from area homes. The **Fred Harvey House** (624 Olive Street) was home to the entrepreneur who established a chain of restaurants and hotels along the Santa Fe Railroad. The residence was constructed in 1875 of limestone ashlar and has Italianate touches; it is now used for county offices.

OPPOSITE: *The federal penitentiary at Fort Leavenworth, a Classic Revival complex known to its denizens as "The Big House."*

Fort Leavenworth and the Frontier Army Museum

Dating to 1827, Fort Leavenworth is the oldest permanent military post west of the Missouri River. In the 1830s, after the region was declared Indian Territory, the Kickapoo and Delaware migrated into the traditional homeland of the Kaw Indians. The fort protected travelers on the Santa Fe Trail and played a peace-keeping role among the Indians. During the Mexican War, it was a major supply depot and launching point for campaigns. Post commander Colonel Stephen Kearny left here in 1846 with 1,700 troops, who ultimately occupied Santa Fe and captured Los Angeles. In 1854 the fort served as temporary capital of the newly formed Kansas Territory. During the Civil War, Fort Leavenworth was an enlistment and train-ing center for Kansas volunteers. Troops at the outpost were called upon to track down William Quantrill and his Confederate raiders, but the guerrillas always eluded their pursuers. In 1867 Colonel Benjamin H. Grierson organized the famous Tenth Cavalry at Fort Leavenworth, a regiment composed of some 700 black soldiers. The men of the Tenth saw extensive duty on the frontier. In 1874 a mili-tary prison was established at Fort Leavenworth, which after 1916 was called the **U.S. Disciplinary Barracks**. A federal civilian prison was also established near the fort in 1895, the mammoth compound of **Leavenworth Penitentiary.** More than a hundred buildings at Fort Leavenworth date to the nineteenth and early twentieth centuries. The oldest of these, and one of the oldest extant structures in the state, is the **Rookery** (12–14 Sumner Place), a barracks built in 1832 and still in use. Indians camped on the **Main Parade Ground** (Kearny, McClellan Avenue, Sumner Place) during negotiations with federal authorities. The **Frontier Army Museum** (Reynolds Avenue) focuses on westward expansion and military life on the frontier. It contains military clothing and equipment of the nine-teenth century, a variety of carriages and wagons, and a stagecoach.

LOCATION: Metropolitan Avenue (Route 73) and Grant Avenue. HOURS: Fort: Open all year. *Museum:* May through August: 10:30–4:30 Monday–Saturday, 1–4:30 Sunday; Rest of year: 1–4:30 Daily. FEE: None. TELEPHONE: *Fort:* 913–684–5604; *Museum:* 913–684–3767.

National Agricultural Center and Hall of Fame

Created by an act of Congress in 1960, the site encompasses 270 acres and has three buildings of exhibits. Its comprehensive collections include a 1780s Indian plow, antique toys and dolls, a large assortment of barbed wire, a wheelwright shop, blacksmith shop, steam threshing engines, and an array of other historical farm equipment, including a plow used by Harry Truman.

LOCATION: 630 North 126th Street, Bonner Springs. HOURS: March through November: 9–5 Monday–Saturday, 1–5 Sunday. FEE: Yes. TELEPHONE: 913–721–1075.

KANSAS CITY

Kansas City, Kansas, spreads into three counties—Wyandotte, Leavenworth, and Johnson—and forms one seamless metropolitan area with its larger counterpart, Kansas City, Missouri. The city stands at the confluence of the Missouri and Kansas rivers. The latter watercourse is frequently referred to as the Kaw River. A succession of Indian nations came into this region. The Shawnee are the first from whom written records remain, followed by the Delaware, who were in turn replaced by the Wyandot. One of the most famous of the Shawnee migrants—though at the time he was shunned by many of his peers—was Tenskwatawa, the Shawnee Prophet. He is buried on private property on the south side of Kansas City at a historic watering place for Indians and early settlers called Whitefeather Springs.

The founders of Kansas City were Wyandot, who purchased this undulating parcel of bluff-top prairie from the Delaware in 1843, calling it Wyandot City. With the 1849 California gold rush, its citizenry began to anticipate the inevitable onslaught of white settlers. The Wyandot sold their Kansas property, and Wyandot City became a white settlement and the nucleus for future Kansas City. In 1867 the Indians were forced to relocate in the new Indian Territory in present-day Oklahoma, where they have long shared reservation lands with the Cherokee. Several other settlements grew up in the area. One was Quindaro, founded in 1856 by a mixed-blood Shawnee and Wyandot man, who named the town for his Wyandot wife. A free-state port that competed with the proslavery river towns of Weston and Leavenworth, Quindaro boomed for a few years until Wyandotte—as the white settlers now called their town—won the title of county seat. Other places along the river grew because of the railroads and the stockyard industry. They included Kansas City, along the Kansas River, platted in 1868; Armourdale, named for the Armour meat-packing house, founded in 1871; and Riverview, established in 1879. These converging towns were consolidated into Kansas City in 1886.

In the heart of Kansas City, the **Huron Cemetery** (Minnesota Avenue between 6th and 7th streets) contains some forty headstones and hundreds of unmarked graves of Wyandot Indians. The first to be interred died in an epidemic shortly after arriving here from Ohio. In 1906, when attempts were made to sell the cemetery, three fervent sisters, Ida, Lyda, and Helena Conley, of Wyandot and English heritage, who had family members buried in the cemetery, locked the gates and stood guard over the cemetery until they were arrested. Litigation ensued, and in 1910 the matter reached the U.S. Supreme Court. Lyda Conley, a lawyer, argued and won the case. She was the first American Indian and one of the first women to argue before the Supreme Court.

Jobs in the packing houses lured Exodusters and European immigrants to Kansas City in the late nineteenth century. One of the Slavic enclaves was **Strawberry Hill,** which was part of old Riverview. The **Strawberry Hill Museum** (720 North 4th Street, 913–371–3264) contains displays of Croatian artifacts and other exhibits explaining the neighborhood's ethnic history. It is housed in the former Saint John's Children's Home, a High Victorian structure built in 1873.

The **Westheight Manor District** (roughly between 18th and 25th streets and Wood and State avenues) was developed as a residential area in the early twentieth century, with plans prepared by Hare and Hare, well-known landscape architects from Kansas City, Missouri. The neighborhood retains many frame, cement block, and stucco houses. Several Prairie-style structures were designed by Louis Curtiss, the most distinguished architect to practice in Kansas City. One of his designs, the rough-stone **Jesse A. Hoel Residence** (2108 Washington Boulevard, private) is the finest work of domestic architecture in the city.

Grinter House

A Kentuckian, Moses Grinter, established the first ferry across the Kansas River in 1831. He arrived in the midst of the Delaware Indians' migration here (the area had been set aside as the Delaware Indian Reserve in 1829) and was probably the first permanent white settler in Wyandotte County. Grinter married Anna Marshall, who was part Delaware, in 1836; they had ten children. In 1857 he built

The Moses Grinter House, built in 1857 by the first permanent white settler in Wyandotte County.

this handsome brick house with Greek Revival elements, using local walnut for timber, walnut and white pine for woodwork, and linden wood for the floors. The house contains period furnishings.

LOCATION: 1420 South 78th Street. HOURS: 10–5 Tuesday–Saturday, 1–5 Sunday. FEE: None. TELEPHONE: 913–299–0373.

Shawnee Methodist Mission and Indian Manual Labor School

The Reverend Thomas Johnson, a young minister from Virginia, founded the Shawnee Methodist Mission in 1830. It became the most influential religious outpost in the region and its leader one of the most respected early settlers (Johnson County is named for him). In 1838 the federal government provided funds for expanding the mission into a manual labor school for Indian children. At its peak of operation, the school consisted of sixteen buildings on 2,000 acres and had an enrollment of 200 boys and girls from many different tribes. The peripatetic first territorial legislature, having

The girls' classroom at Shawnee Methodist Mission contains a teacher's desk from the mid-nineteenth century and students' desks that were reproduced as a WPA project in the 1930s. On the wall is a map of the United States in 1845.

decamped from the first capital (near present-day Fort Riley), convened at the Shawnee Mission in 1855. At this second capital they enacted the "Bogus Laws" in an attempt to keep slavery in Kansas Territory. Their next meeting place was Lecompton, near Lawrence. With increasing border strife, the mission went into decline and the school closed in 1862. In the winter of 1865, Johnson was shot and killed on his farm near Westport, Missouri, by an unknown assailant. He is buried in a family cemetery near the Shawnee Mission. Three handsome brick structures remain on the mission grounds: the **Superintendent's House** (1839), a **School and Chapel** (1839), and a **Girls' School and Dormitory** (1843–1844). Together they form one of the oldest ensembles of buildings in the state. Several rooms contain period furnishings, and there are exhibits of the instructional methods taught at the school and of items made by students.

LOCATION: 3403 West 53d Street, Fairway. HOURS: 10–5 Tuesday–Saturday, 1–5 Sunday. FEE: None. TELEPHONE: 913–262–0867.

Located in the suburb of **Bonner Springs,** the **Wyandotte County Historical Museum** (631 North 126th Street, 913–721–1078) features a collection of Plains Indian artifacts, as well as nineteenth-century clothing, furnishings, decorative arts, and vehicles. It is also the repository for many archaeological items from the **Trowbridge Site,** a village of the Hopewell period (about A.D. 200). The site, which is located in Kansas City, is not open to the public.

The **Johnson County Museum** (6305 Lackman Road, Shawnee, 913–631–6709) has an array of letters, diaries, tools, household items, weapons, toys, and clothing that illuminates the history of the area, from the time of the Kansa and Shawnee Indians to the border wars over slavery to agricultural settlements and on to contemporary times. In **Edgerton,** the museum maintains the **Lanesfield School Historic Site** (18745 South Dillie Road, 913–893–6645). It is the only remaining structure on the town site of Lanesfield, a mail stop on the Santa Fe Trail. The one-room stone building, constructed in 1869, contains period furnishings and operates as a living-history classroom. Located in **Sar-Ko-Par Park** in the city of **Lenexa,** the **Adam Legler Barn Museum** (14907 West 87th Street Parkway, 913–492–0038) is a beautiful stone structure built by a Swiss immigrant in 1864. Legler's property stood on the Santa Fe Trail; it is said that William Quantrill and his guerrillas stopped here for a meal on their way to raid Lawrence in 1863. The barn contains displays of local historical artifacts. Also on site are a restored **Lenexa Railroad Caboose** and **Depot,** containing exhibits on the late 1800s.

In **Olathe,** the **Mahaffie Farmstead** (1100 Old Kansas City Road, 913–782–6972) was the home of J. B. Mahaffie, who came to the area in 1857 and became a prosperous farmer with the biggest herd of livestock in the area. He built this handsome two-story stone house in 1865. It served as a stagecoach stop on the Santa Fe Trail for the next four years. The restored home contains period furnishings.

LAWRENCE

In the 1850s Lawrence was the chief bastion of free-soilism in Kansas, and the focus of the wrath of proslavery forces. Straddling the banks of the Kansas River, Lawrence was founded in 1854 in a hotbed of proslavery sentiment by the antislavery New England Emigrant Aid Company and named for the Boston philanthropist and abolitionist Amos A. Lawrence. One of its chief organizers was a founder of the Free State party, Dr. Charles Robinson, who went on to be elected the first governor of Kansas in 1861. Robinson was married to Sara Lawrence, whose 1856 book, *Kansas: Its Interior and Exterior Life,* offers a free-stater's firsthand account of the territory.

For eight years Lawrence was the scene of much oration and of frequently violent outbursts. In November 1855, as the Free State party and proslavery forces vied for power, a young free-stater was murdered near Lawrence by a proslavery settler. In the aftermath, some 1,500 proslavery Missourians marched on Lawrence, where 1,000 heavily-armed free-soilers stood at the ready. After last-minute negotiations, violence was avoided. In the spring of 1856, 800 Missourians, deputized as a posse by a proslavery judge, descended upon Lawrence to arrest antislavery legislators who had been indicted for treason by a grand jury. This time the citizens of Lawrence decided not to fight. They stood by as the Missourians demolished two newspaper offices, attempted to destroy the Free State Hotel, set Robinson's house afire, and plundered several others. Amazingly, only one person died—a proslavery man who was hit on the head by a falling brick. The "Sack of Lawrence" provoked outrage in the antislavery states, and prompted Massachusetts Senator Charles Sumner to make his famous two-day "Crime Against Kansas" speech, excoriating the proslavery forces in general and the "murderous robbers from Missouri" in particular. In response Congressman Preston Brooks of South Carolina severely beat Sumner with a cane on the floor of the Senate. The violence in Lawrence also inflamed John Brown, who carried out his threat to "fight fire with fire," and murdered several "slave hounds" at Pottawatomie Creek.

At the dawn of the Civil War, the free-staters prevailed, and in 1861 Kansas was admitted to the Union with a constitution declaring the equal and inalienable rights of all men. This milestone did not spell peace for Lawrence. On August 21, 1863, William Quantrill and 450 Confederate raiders stormed the town. As they rode into Lawrence, they gunned down a black minister as he sat milking a cow. In the next three hours the raiders murdered more than 180 men and boys, some of whom were pulled from their houses and shot as their families watched. Others were burned alive as the raiders torched the town. The Jayhawk leader whom Quantrill had hoped to drag off to Missouri for lynching, Senator James Lane, escaped. After the raid, the town selected for its seal a phoenix rising from the ashes and the motto "From Ashes to Immortality." They rebuilt in brick and stone; in three years some sixty buildings, many of which still stand in downtown Lawrence, were erected.

The Richardsonian Romanesque Douglas County Courthouse in Lawrence.

After the Panic of 1873, Lawrence emerged as a center for education and a busy trade hub for the surrounding grain-producing areas. Many of the commercial and public buildings on Massachusetts Street, the main thoroughfare in town, date from the optimistic turn of the century, including the **Douglas County Courthouse** (Massachusetts and 11th streets), constructed in 1903–1904. The Richardsonian Romanesque limestone building was a collaborative design by John G. Haskell and Frederick C. Gunn, two well-known turn-of-the-century Kansas architects.

Watkins Community Museum of History

Another fine building on Massachusetts Street, the Richardsonian Romanesque Watkins Land Mortgage and National Bank of 1888, houses the Elizabeth M. Watkins Community Museum. It is named for the wife of Jabez B. Watkins, the prosperous owner of a land and

mortgage company and subsequently this bank. Watkins's office on the third floor is intact, as are the beautiful burley pine wood, brass, marble, and stained-glass embellishments in the bank's interior. The museum's collections include agricultural tools and equipment, textiles, antique toys and dolls, a cannon from the Mexican War used during the Bleeding Kansas period, and many nineteenth-century illustrations, photographs, maps, and pamphlets.

LOCATION: 1047 Massachusetts Street. HOURS: 10–4 Tuesday–Saturday, 1:30–4 Sunday. FEE: None. TELEPHONE: 913–841–4109.

The **Old West Lawrence Historic District** (bounded by Tennessee, 8th, Indiana, and 6th streets) is an affluent residential neighborhood that sprang up after Quantrill's raid. Early stone structures and later Queen Anne and Italianate houses date from the midnineteenth to the early twentieth centuries. One of its most impressive residences is the **George Innes House** (701 Louisiana Street, private), a three-story Queen Anne-style structure built in 1889. Innes was a leading dry-goods merchant of the city. His home features a mahogany entryway, seven fireplaces, and a third-floor ballroom.

Haskell Institute, or **Haskell Indian Junior College** (23d and Barker streets), built in 1884, is one of the few surviving nonreservation schools for Indians in the country and draws Native Americans from more than 120 tribes. The campus contains late-nineteenth- and early-twentieth-century buildings constructed of stone or brick.

Museum of Natural History

This museum on the campus of the **University of Kansas** is housed in the splendid Romanesque Revival **Dyche Hall**, a huge castlelike limestone structure designed in 1901 by Walter Root and George Siemens of Kansas City, Missouri. The ornate exterior is decorated with large stone gargoyles, and the arched main entrance is modeled after the portal of Saint Trophime in Arles, France. The building is named for Lewis Lindsay Dyche, a colorful outdoorsman, avid naturalist, and gifted taxidermist. He mounted 112 large mammals for the Kansas Exhibit of the 1893 Chicago World's Columbian Exposition, which attracted wide attention and are now showcased

OPPOSITE: *The tellers' side of the bank counter at the Watkins National Bank, now the Elizabeth M. Watkins Community Museum, holds a collection of early business machines. The building was designed by the Chicago firm of Cobb and Frost.*

in Dyche Hall as the Panorama of North American Plants and Animals. Dyche was one of a group of brilliant and indefatigable nineteenth-century characters who established the University of Kansas's fine reputation in field biology and the natural sciences.

The museum has four floors of exhibits emphasizing vertebrate animals from Kansas and the Great Plains. Its most celebrated exhibit, mounted by Dyche, is Comanche, the horse ridden by Captain Myles Keogh in the Battle of the Little Bighorn. Comanche was the only Seventh Cavalry survivor of that rout left on the battlefield.

LOCATION: 14th Street and Jayhawk Boulevard, University of Kansas Campus. HOURS: 10–5 Monday–Saturday, 12–5 Sunday. FEE: None. TELEPHONE: 913–864–4540.

Jayhawk Boulevard, which crests the top of a hill known as **Mount Oread,** is lined with an impressive array of campus buildings in the Romanesque, Gothic, and Classic Revival styles, constructed from the 1890s to the 1930s.

The University of Kansas's Dyche Hall, which houses the fourth largest natural history museum in the United States, is constructed of locally quarried Oread limestone.

LECOMPTON

The picturesque village of Lecompton sits amid corn and wheat fields on the south bank of the Kansas River just northwest of Lawrence. It was established in 1854 and named for Samuel Lecompte, first chief justice of Kansas Territory. It was Lecompte who deputized the posse of 800 proslavery Missourians that sacked the town of Lawrence in 1856. From 1855 until 1861, when Kansas gained statehood, Lecompton was the seat of the territorial government. The historic clapboard **Constitution Hall** (North Elmore Street) was the meeting place of the second territorial legislature. In 1857 a separate convention was called here to draw up a state constitution permitting slavery in Kansas Territory. The document was the subject of national controversy and served to sunder the Democratic party along Northern and Southern lines. Although the proslavery constitution was endorsed by President Buchanan, it was ultimately rejected by the territorial electorate and the U.S. Congress. The building (785–887–6520) has been restored.

Lane University was established by the United Brethren Church in 1865. Its founders named the institution after the largest donor, James Lane, who pledged $3,000. The **Territorial Capitol–Lane Museum** (Lane University, 785–587–6148 or 785–887–6285) stands on the foundation of the proposed Kansas state capitol building. President Dwight Eisenhower's parents were married here. The three floors feature territorial, Victorian, and Eisenhower memorabilia. Nearby, the pre-Civil War headquarters of the Democratic Party, a small rock structure, is being restored.

TOPEKA

Topeka, capital of Kansas, was founded by Colonel Cyrus K. Holliday of Pennsylvania, who came to Kansas Territory as a young man with the intention of building a railroad. One of the people whom he interested in his scheme was the New England Emigrant Aid agent Charles Robinson, who funneled immigrants from that region into Topeka, giving it a free-state bias. After statehood and some jostling between Topeka and Lawrence, Topeka was selected state capital. Meanwhile, Holliday was developing the Santa Fe Railroad, and in 1869 construction began on the Atchison, Topeka & Santa Fe west of the city. Offices and machine shops were established in Topeka in 1878. Railroad jobs attracted Exodusters as well as Russo-Germans,

Swedes, and Mexicans. At the same time, the town was becoming a terminal for the fertile grain-growing regions of Kansas. Testimony to the town's railroad-agriculture linkage can be seen in the looming grain elevators lining the north bank of the Kansas River along West Gordon Street. Le Corbusier described such elevators as "the magnificent first fruits of a new age."

Kansas State Capitol

The Kansas State Capitol was built in stages between 1866 and 1903. The finished product is a classic American statehouse—that is, an immense stone building with a floor plan in the form of a Greek cross, each wing featuring columned porticos and the whole topped with a massive dome. The architect of record was E. Townsend Mix, although many hold that a Kansas architect, John G. Haskell, contributed to the plans. It is known that Haskell, along with L. M.

Inside the Kansas State Capitol, John Steuart Curry's famous mural "The Settlement of Kansas" depicts the confrontation of free-soil and proslavery forces, with the apocalyptic figure of John Brown brandishing a rifle and a Bible (detail). OPPOSITE: *The Classic Revival capitol is the work of many architects.*

Wood, designed the capitol's most stunning precinct—the Senate Chamber on the third floor in the East Wing. The room is richly adorned with marble, wood, hand-hammered copper, cast-iron grillwork, and elaborate plasterwork. Throughout the building beautiful murals depict historical themes, including those by John Steuart Curry, whose painting of a maniacal, goggle-eyed John Brown is a well-known Kansas icon.

LOCATION: 8th, 10th, Jackson, and Harrison streets. HOURS: 8–5 Daily. FEE: None. TELEPHONE: 785–785–3966.

The **Charles Curtis House** (1101 Topeka Avenue) was home to the influential Kansas politician who served as vice president under Herbert Hoover. Curtis was also an important figure in formulating federal Indian policy (he was part Kaw) in the early twentieth century while serving in the U.S. Congress. The 1880s brick house, now used for offices, is noted for its elaborate and eclectic fenestration and exterior ornamentation.

Historic Ward–Meade Park

This bluff-top park overlooking the Kansas River was part of the 240-acre farmstead of early Topeka settlers Anthony and Mary Jane Ward. The Wards moved here in 1854, a few months after the city was laid out. In 1870 they started building a bona fide mansion—a large brick-and-limestone Victorian residence, which eventually became the home of a daughter, Jennie, and her husband, John Mackey Meade, a civil engineer for the Atchison, Topeka & Santa Fe Railroad. Added to over the years, the house is an amalgam of Greek Revival, Italianate, and Prairie styles. The mansion has been restored and a grouping of log cabins assembled to suggest the Wards' original log house. Both contain period furnishings. A turn-of-the-century Kansas town is being re-created in the park to the west of the Ward–Meade House, including a Santa Fe depot and one-room schoolhouse. The complex includes botanical gardens.

LOCATION: 124 Northwest Fillmore Street. HOURS: 10–4 Tuesday–Saturday; Tours: Tuesday–Sunday. FEE: Yes. TELEPHONE: 785–295–3888

Standing on a river bluff on the western edge of Topeka is the **Kansas Governors' Mansion,** known as **Cedar Crest** (1 Cedar Crest

In Ward-Meade Park, three connected log cabins with plank siding re-create the original Topeka residence of Anthony Ward, an early settler.

Road, 785–296–3636). The large Norman-style estate was built in 1928 and has been the home of Kansas's governors since 1962. In 1919 Dr. Charles Frederick Menninger and his doctor sons, Karl Augustus and William Claire, founded the Menninger Clinic, which gained an international reputation for its work in psychiatry. The **Menninger Museum** (5800 West 6th Street, 785–350–5915) has displays on the history of psychiatry; it also houses a large collection of Sigmund Freud's papers.

Kansas Museum of History

Housed in a Postmodern facility built in 1983, the museum is the state's central repository for artifacts; its galleries chronicle the history of the state, beginning with its prehistoric dwellers. A log house of 1866 has been reconstructed within the museum and furnished with period items. One section is devoted to the Bleeding Kansas period and the Civil War. There are many Indian artifacts and several domestic structures, including a Southern Cheyenne buffalo-hide tepee and a replica of a Wichita grass lodge. The centerpiece of the collection is the restored 1880 Baldwin locomotive number 132. The museum is located on the grounds of the old Pottawatomie Indian Baptist Mission and Manual Labor Training School (1849), the exterior of which has been restored. A one-room schoolhouse dating to the 1870s is also on the grounds and contains period fixtures.

> LOCATION: 6425 Southwest 6th Street. HOURS: 9–4:30 Monday–Saturday, 12:30–4:30 Sunday. FEE: None. TELEPHONE: 785–272–8681.

In the history of American civil rights and constitutional law, **Sumner Elementary School** (330 Western Avenue) is one of the most important landmarks. The Sumner school refused to enroll 10-year-old Linda Brown because she was black. Topeka attorneys Charles and John Scott filed suit in federal district court on behalf of Linda's father, an assistant pastor at Saint Mark's AME Church, and twelve other black parents. The case, *Brown v. Board of Education of Topeka,* worked its way up to the U.S. Supreme Court, which ruled in 1954 that separate educational facilities were inherently unequal. The unanimous decision, written by Chief Justice Earl Warren, redefined the meaning of citizenship. It energized the civil rights movement and put into motion the task of integrating public schools. **Brown v. Board of Education National Historic Site** was established in 1992 at Monroe School, 1515 Monroe Street, the segregated school Linda Brown attended.

The **Combat Air Museum** (Forbes Field off Route 75, 785–862–3303) houses a wide variety of aircraft, from biplanes to a pair of C-47s and an F-11F Tiger jet flown by the Blue Angels. There are also exhibits of military and aviation memorabilia.

BALDWIN CITY

From 1821 to 1860, the site of Baldwin City was the second stop on the Santa Fe Trail. One of the best places to see vestiges of the deep wagon ruts on the historic trail is in the **Dr. Ivan Boyd Prairie Preserve,** three miles east of town. The small settlement was first called Palmyra but was later named for John Baldwin, who arrived in

1857 to build a sawmill and gristmill. The **Old Castle Museum** (515 5th Street, 785–594–6809) is housed in a three-story stone structure constructed in 1858 as the first building of the Methodist Episcopal Church's Baker University, one of the oldest colleges in the state. The soaring building was a landmark for travelers on the Santa Fe Trail. The museum contains Indian artifacts, a doctor-dentist exhibit, china, quilts, pottery, pewter, a replica of an old grocery story, and a working nineteenth-century print shop. Composed of early-twentieth-century coaches, the **Midland Railway** (High Street, 785–594–6982) travels six-and-a-half miles through rolling eastern Kansas farmland and woods. The railroad was originally built in 1867 by Chinese laborers and Civil War veterans. The train departs from the former **Santa Fe Depot** (1906) in Baldwin. The handsome Prairie-style terminal contains displays pertaining to the history of the railroad, the town, and the Santa Fe Trail.

OTTAWA

Baptists founded the city of Ottawa in 1864 and Ottawa University in 1865, a direct result of the Baptist mission established nearby among the Ottawa Indians by the Reverend and Mrs. Jotham Meeker in 1837. Meeker brought the first printing press to Kansas in 1833. Ottawa's Forest Park was the home of the famous Ottawa Chautauqua from 1883 to 1914, the second-oldest and second-largest Chautauqua in America, after the original one at Chautauqua, New York. Ottawa was also where the Underwood and Underwood photography studios began in 1883. The Underwood brothers established one of the world's major stereopticon companies and later were pioneers in photojournalism and aviation photography. The **Old Depot Museum** (Tecumseh and Main streets), a stone Santa Fe depot of 1888, houses displays of these and other subjects of local historical interest, including a French silk-producing utopian community and John Brown. In City Park is the **Dietrich Cabin,** built in 1859 by a German immigrant, one of the few remaining early log structures in the state.

OSAWATOMIE

Osawatomie is closely associated with the Kansas activities of the abolitionist John Brown. Five of Brown's sons, who lived near pre-

The John Brown Museum, housed in a mid-nineteenth-century log cabin that belonged to Brown's brother-in-law, the Reverend Samuel Adair. By the wall is a melodeon, a small keyboard organ, which was played at Brown's funeral.

sent-day Rantoul, summoned their father to Kansas Territory in 1855. Shortly after the sack of Lawrence in 1856, partly in retaliation, John Brown made his famous strike against several of the more threatening proslavery men of the area. On the night of May 24, 1856, Brown and his men murdered five proslavery men near Dutch Henry's crossing on Pottawatomie Creek, where Lane is today. This led to the Battle of Osawatomie, in August 1856, in which several hundred proslavery men attacked Brown and his followers in the village, burning the settlement and killing one of Brown's sons. Brown left Kansas shortly thereafter and did not return for any length of time until the summer of 1858, when he again participated in border wars and liberated several slaves, who escaped to freedom in Canada. From Canada he began to plan the raid on the federal arsenal at Harpers Ferry, Virginia, the exploit for which he was tried, convicted, and hanged in 1859. The **John Brown Museum** (10th and Main streets, 913–755–4384) is housed in the **Adair Cabin,** a log structure built in 1854 that originally stood northwest of Osawatomie but was moved and reassembled at this site in 1912. Reverend Samuel Adair's wife, Florella, was John Brown's stepsister. John Brown was a frequent visitor at their cabin during several journeys to the area between 1855 and 1858. The cabin contains many original furnishings, including a melodeon that was played at Brown's funeral, firearms, and other John Brown memorabilia. The nearby **Old Stone Church** (6th and Parker streets) was built in 1861 to serve the Reverend Adair's small congregation.

MARAIS DES CYGNES MASSACRE MEMORIAL PARK

John Greenleaf Whittier's poem lamenting the Marais des Cygnes massacre—one of the incidents of the Bleeding Kansas era—captures the nation's shock over the episode: "The foul human vultures / have feasted and fed; / The wolves of the Border / have crept from the dead." On May 19, 1858, near present-day Pleasanton, Charles Hamelton, a native of Georgia and proponent of slavery, entered Kansas with some thirty followers. They rounded up eleven free-staters whom they happened to encounter on the roads, herded them into a ravine, and shot them, firing-squad style. Five men died. In 1863 one raider was apprehended and hanged for the murders. Hamelton returned to Georgia, where he died in 1880. A museum in a stone house built after the incident contains Civil War documents, Indian artifacts, and pioneer tools.

> LOCATION: 5 miles north of Pleasanton on Route 69, then 3 miles east on Route 52. HOURS: 10–5 Wednesday–Saturday, 1–5 Sunday. FEE: None. TELEPHONE: 913–352–6174.

Historical **markers** on Route 69 trace the action of the **Battle of Mine Creek,** the only Civil War military engagement between regular Union and Confederate forces in Kansas. It came near the end of Confederate Major General Sterling Price's failed campaign to recapture Missouri for the South (a final defeat took place a few days later in Missouri). The battle occurred on October 25, 1864, two days after Price's defeat at nearby Westport in Missouri. About 300 Confederates were killed or wounded, and 900 were taken prisoner. Price retreated to Arkansas.

FORT SCOTT NATIONAL HISTORIC SITE

Located in the small town of Fort Scott on the Kansas–Missouri border, this frontier outpost was established in 1842 at a time when eastern Indian tribes were relocated here, supposedly to land that was to be theirs in perpetuity. The fort, which was named for General Winfield Scott, stood on a high bluff overlooking rolling prairie that was the traditional homeland of the Osage Indians. The outpost was intended to keep peace among these intermingling tribes and white squatters, but the Indians never posed any serious threat. The fort was a unit of the permanent Indian Frontier, which marked the boundary of Euro-American settlement and stretched from Fort Leavenworth to Fort Towson on the Red River in Texas. A military road connecting these forts was built between 1839 and 1844.

Fort Scott's role evolved with westward expansion. During the 1840s the U.S. Dragoons guarded caravans on the Santa Fe Trail and patrolled far into Indian country. The dragoons, organized in 1833, were an elite mounted regiment trained to fight on foot or horseback. Their companies were designated by the color of their horses, black, gray, chestnut, or bay, preferably with no nose or hoof markings. Dragoons from Fort Scott fought in the 1846 Mexican War campaigns under Stephen Kearny and Zachary Taylor. Although the fort closed in 1853 and its buildings were auctioned off in 1855, federal troops returned to the town of Fort Scott in 1857 and 1858 to quell the unrest among settlers fighting over the slavery issue. The fort was reactivated during the Civil War, when it served as an important supply depot for Union armies in the West, a refugee center for Indians, and a base for one of the first black regiments raised during the war. In the 1870s its soldiers helped to protect railroad workers laying tracks through southeast Kansas to the Gulf of Mexico. The fort closed in 1873.

Several of the original frame-and-brick structures at Fort Scott have been restored, and others have been reconstructed. One of the original buildings is the **hospital** (1843), which now contains the visitor center and a refurnished wardroom. The reconstructed **infantry barracks** contains a museum that details the primary periods of the fort's history, the Indians of the area, Bleeding Kansas and Civil War history, and archaeological investigations at the fort. In the reconstructed **dragoon barracks** are exhibits of uniforms and other items

OPPOSITE: *The hospital (with double porch) and barracks at Fort Scott.*

associated with the infantry and dragoons who manned the fort in the 1840s. Thirty-three rooms in various fort buildings are furnished with period pieces that reflect military life at this frontier fort.

LOCATION: Old Fort Boulevard, in Fort Scott. HOURS: 8–5 Daily; June through August: Interpretive and living-history programs and events. FEE: Yes. TELEPHONE: 316–223–0310.

Four miles north of **Iola** on Route 169 is the **Edward H. Funston House,** a frame farmstead (ca. 1860) that was home to two prominent Kansas figures. Edward Funston was a state legislator, and U.S. representative, and his son, Frederick Funston, was a journalist and a field botanist for federal expeditions in Death Valley and Alaska. He had a career in the military, fighting in the Philippines, serving as military governor of Veracruz, Mexico, and rising to the rank of major general. The Kansas State Historical Society is restoring the property. In **Neodesha** the **Norman Number 1 Oil Well and Museum** (109 South 1st Street, 316–325–5316) commemorates the vast Mid-Continent Oil Field, which became a major producing field by 1900 and yielded more than half the U.S. petroleum supply into the 1930s.

COFFEYVILLE

On October 5, 1892, the Dalton Gang—three Dalton brothers and two of their sidekicks—attempted to rob two Coffeyville banks at the same time. Townspeople jumped them as they tried to escape, and a gunfight ensued in which four citizens and all the robbers but Emmett Dalton were killed. He served fourteen years of a life sentence in a Kansas penitentiary and died in California in 1937. Robert and Gratton Dalton are buried in **Elmwood Cemetery,** two blocks west of Route 169. The **Condon National Bank** (811 Walnut Street), site of one of the robberies, is still standing—a brick building with a stamped metal facade built in 1890. The **Dalton Museum** (113 East 8th Street) displays items associated with the Daltons and the robbery, as well as memorabilia of baseball great Walter Johnson, pitcher for the Washington Senators for twenty-one years and a native of the Coffeyville area. The **W. P. Brown Mansion** (South Walnut and Eldridge streets, 316–251–0431) was built in 1904 for a wealthy lum-

OPPOSITE: *The adjutant's office at Fort Scott has been restored to its appearance in the 1840s. Above the ledger table is an 1847 map of the United States, showing the area that is now Kansas as part of Indian Territory.*

The Dalton Gang came to a violent end in a gunfight after the gang attempted to rob two banks in Coffeyville, Kansas. The bodies of the robbers were lined up on the street and photographed as a graphic illustration that crime does not pay.

berman and investor in Kansas's oil and natural gas fields. The Georgian Revival mansion contains original family furnishings.

SOUTH–CENTRAL KANSAS

Some fifty miles south of Wichita, **Arkansas City** was incorporated in 1872. It was one of the five staging points in Kansas for the Cherokee Outlet Land Rush, which took place on September 16, 1893. The Cherokee Outlet, also called the Cherokee Strip, was a swath of land in Oklahoma 200 miles long and 57 miles wide, an area larger than the state of Vermont. The federal government purchased it from the Indians for about $1.38 an acre, divided it into 40,000 homesteads, and then opened up the lands to white settlement at high noon on that day. At the sound of pistols and bugles, some 100,000 people made a mad dash southward; a lucky few crammed onto trains. By the following dawn every square foot of the Cherokee Outlet had been claimed. The **Cherokee Strip Land Rush**

Bullet holes made in the doors of the Condon Bank in Coffeyville during the fierce gun battle between townspeople and members of the Dalton Gang. The unarmed residents quickly commandeered guns from local stores when they learned of the gang's presence.

Museum (South Summit Street Road, 316–442–6750) in Arkansas City features memorabilia associated with the land rush, Indian artifacts, and exhibits of area history.

El Dorado, twenty miles northeast of Wichita, was the site of an oil discovery in 1915 that led to the largest oil boom in Kansas's history. The **Kansas Oil Museum** (383 East Central, 316–321–9333), which is part of the **Butler County Historical Society Museum,** has a re-created oil field with a 100-foot derrick, pumping units, and a railroad tank car.

WICHITA

The peaceable Wichita were living in the Arkansas River country of present-day central Kansas when Coronado made his foray into the territory in 1541. Over the next 300 years, sundry hostilities and treaties pushed the Wichita southward to the Red River region in present-day Oklahoma and Texas. Then, in 1864, the refugee

Wichita, stirred by tribes that had joined the Confederacy, were moved by the federal government to their old home on the banks of the Arkansas River, this time near its confluence with the Little Arkansas. They were guided here by Jesse Chisholm, a trader of Scottish and Cherokee descent who established the trade route through Indian Territory. This later became part of the famous cattle trail, which bears his name, from the Wichita village to the Red River in Texas. Chisholm died in 1868.

By the late 1860s the Wichita were once again forced to decamp to Indian Territory. The site they vacated in 1867 became the town of Wichita. The federal government still had to bargain with the Osage, who had a treaty claim to the territory; negotiations lasted until 1870. People came to the nascent village, anticipating that it would become the next cattle boomtown. The one missing ingredient, a railroad, arrived in May 1872. Wichita promoters had chartered the Wichita & South Western Railroad as a subsidiary of the Santa Fe in time to replace Abilene as the premier Kansas cattle-shipping point. In that inaugural season, Wichita shipped some 80,000 head of cattle to Eastern markets—a number far greater than that sent from its main competitor, Ellsworth. Just as in Abilene, however, Wichita's cattle town days were brief. Changes in the state quarantine line regulating cattle drives ensured that in 1875 Texas longhorns were much reduced in numbers at the Wichita railhead. In 1877 the Kansas legislature moved the quarantine line farther west of Wichita, and Dodge City was well on its way to becoming the next bustling Kansas cow town. Wichita fairly smoothly turned into a prosperous trade and milling center for the fertile outlying wheat farms. During and immediately after World War I, the discovery of oil in the vicinity and the launching of the commercial and military airplane-manufacturing industries set Wichita on a course to becoming the state's largest city, which it remains today.

The **Wichita-Sedgwick County Historical Museum** (204 South Main Street, 316–265–9314) is housed in the former **Wichita City Hall,** a massive multiturreted Richardsonian Romanesque structure completed in 1892. On exhibit are items of local history, Indian artifacts, costumes, and toys. In addition, the museum's extensive furniture collections are displayed in period settings. The **Mid-America**

OPPOSITE: *The Arkansas Valley Elevator, the only fully restored wooden grain elevator in the United States, is preserved in Wichita's Old Cowtown Museum. In the late 1870s, there were eight grain elevators in Wichita.*

All Indian Center and Museum (650 North Seneca, 316–262–5221) features permanent exhibits of Plains, Southwest, Northwest Coast, and Inuit Indian art and artifacts.

Old Cowtown Museum

This seventeen-acre site re-creates the old cattle town of Wichita. Some forty structures contain period furnishings, tools, decorative arts, and textiles. Numerous buildings are original to the cattle era, including the 1869 **Munger House,** which was a hostelry of log construction, and the elegant **Murdock House** (1874). There are a variety of living-history programs, including blacksmith demonstrations and reenactments of nineteenth-century county fairs and Fourth of July celebrations.

> LOCATION 1871 Sim Park Drive. HOURS: March through October: 10–5 Monday–Saturday, 12–5 Sunday; Rest of year: 10–5 Saturday, 12–5 Sunday. FEE: Yes. TELEPHONE: 316–264–0671.

THE MENNONITE REGION

The Mennonites, a wing of the Dutch Anabaptists, were named for their sixteenth-century leader Menno Simons. In the late eighteenth century, Catherine the Great of Russia invited the Mennonites then living in Prussia to settle in the Ukraine. In the 1870s, however, after compulsory military training was introduced, thousands left the steppes of Russia for the Great Plains of America. The immigrants brought with them distinctive notions of community life, pacifism, and religious worship. Mennonites have a long tradition of performing mission and relief work, and today almost as many of them live in Asia and Africa as in the United States.

Mennonite religious beliefs have roots in the Anabaptist movement in Western Europe during the sixteenth century. While the movement had different factions and permutations, all Anabaptists eschewed infant baptism in favor of adult baptism. Many also supported the idea of separation of church and state. In Catholic countries many Anabaptists were imprisoned, banished, tortured, and killed for their beliefs. To escape persecution, the first Dutch Mennonites migrated to America in 1683 from the Krefeld, Germany, area. In 1874 a group of Mennonite farmers from Russia bought land from the Santa Fe Railroad and settled in the central plains of Kansas just north of Wichita. The Dutch Mennonites from the Netherlands who had previously migrated to Polish Prussia and in 1820 to Russia left Russia in 1874. They built an array of handsome structures including the "longhouse," in which the house and barn were joined. And they planted turkey red, a resilient strain of hard winter wheat brought from Russia, which became a mainstay in the Kansas agricultural economy. Numerous museums and examples of nineteenth-century Mennonite architecture can be seen in the towns of Newton, North Newton, Goessel, and Hillsboro.

In **Hutchinson,** the **Reno County Museum** (100 South Walnut, 316–662–1184) has a permanent exhibit on settlement in the area from 1871 to the early 1920s. It includes pioneer artifacts, domestic items, farm implements, frontier educational materials, musical instruments, toys, and a history of each community in Reno County.

NEWTON

This town is the location of the commodious **Warkentin House** (211 East 1st Street, 316–283–3113), the home of Bernard Warkentin, a Russian immigrant who aided in the resettlement of fellow Mennonites in Kansas. He also helped introduce turkey red wheat to this country. Warkentin built this house for his family in 1887. In 1886 he had bought the **Warkentin Mill** (3d and Main streets), a massive brick-and-stone structure built in 1879.

In 1871, when Newton was the westernmost terminus of the Santa Fe Railroad, it ballooned into the largest cattle-shipping center on the Chisholm Trail. It developed a reputation as a rowdy cow town, but the cattle and the notoriety fled as soon as the Santa Fe tracks pressed west to Dodge City. The **Harvey County Historical Society Museum** (203 North Main, 316–283–2221) has exhibits of local history, including a collection of railroad memorabilia. Five miles north of Newton on Route 15 is a **Chisholm Trail Marker.** From 1867 to 1871, more than half a million Texas longhorns were driven over the trail to the railhead in Abilene.

KAUFFMAN MUSEUM

This museum is affiliated with **Bethel College,** the oldest of ten Mennonite colleges in North America. The museum contains

This barn, built by the Ratzlaff family in the Mennonite community of Buhler, Kansas, in 1886, was moved to the Kauffman Museum at Bethel College a century later.

exhibits on the natural history of North American prairies; the history of food production, from hunting and gathering and peasant agriculture to farming in the industrial age; and the cultures of Plains and Southwestern American Indians. The focus is on the Mennonite immigrant societies of central Kansas. Numerous exhibits display Mennonite textiles, clothing, household furnishings, kitchen utensils, and religious effects. The museum complex, situated on five acres, includes a grouping of historic buildings that form a nineteenth-century farmstead. This ensemble includes a homesteader's log cabin from South Dakota, a frame farmhouse (1875) furnished with period pioneer items, a barn (1886), and a windmill (ca. 1900).

LOCATION: Bethel College campus, off Route 135, North Newton. HOURS: 9:30–4:30 Tuesday–Friday, 1:30–4:30 Saturday–Sunday. FEE: Yes. TELEPHONE: 316–283–1612.

MENNONITE HERITAGE MUSEUM

Located in Goessel, this museum is composed of two exhibit halls: The **Mennonite Immigrant House** is a facsimile of the long barracks erected by the Santa Fe Railroad to house the immigrants until they built their own homes, and the **Turkey Red Wheat Palace** commemorates the famous strain of Russian wheat. Both halls display clothing, household goods, family memorabilia, and nineteenth-century vehicles and farm machinery, especially equipment related to the wheat industry. Several historic Mennonite structures have also been moved to the site from the surrounding area. These include a one-room schoolhouse of 1875, the Goessel Preparatory School (1906), a barn (1902), and a residence (1911), all of which have been restored and furnished with period items.

LOCATION: 202 Poplar, Goessel. HOURS: May through September: 10–5 Tuesday–Friday, 1–5 Saturday–Sunday; March through April and October through December: 12-4 Tuesday–Friday, 1–4 Saturday–Sunday. FEE: Yes. TELEPHONE: 316–367–8200.

One mile north of **Goessel** on Route 15 lies the beautiful white frame **Alexanderwohl Church.** It is named for the Mennonite village in the Ukraine whose citizens migrated to Kansas in 1874. The current structure was built in 1928.

HILLSBORO

In Hillsboro, **Pioneer Adobe House Museum** (501 South Ash Street, 316–947–3775) is an example of European housing adapted to the American Great Plains. It is a longhouse—the barn is attached to the living quarters—built of adobe bricks. Peter Loewen, a Mennonite immigrant, built the home in 1876. The original thatch roof has been replaced with shingles, and the house contains pioneer furnishings and a grass-burning oven, a distinctive heating device designed to utilize the most abundant fuel on the prairie. The shed contains horse-drawn farm equipment. Also in Hillsboro, the **William Schaeffler House** (312 East Grant Street, 316–947–3775) is a handsome residence built in 1909 by a prosperous businessman of German Lutheran background. The period furnishings include the original family china and a few pieces of Schaeffler furniture.

In **Florence,** the **Harvey House Museum** (3d and Marion streets, 316–878–4296) preserves a portion of the old Clifton House, an early acquisition in Fred Harvey's expanding chain of restaurant-hotels along the Santa Fe Railroad. He purchased it in 1878 with profits from his first restaurant in Topeka. The first Harvey House to offer sleeping accommodations, it was in operation until 1900. The museum contains Santa Fe and Harvey House memorabilia.

THE   FLINT   HILLS

In **Cottonwood Falls**, the **Chase County Courthouse**, designed by John Haskell, an architect who worked on the Topeka capitol, is notable for its black walnut staircase and balustrade. Just to the north, near **Strong City**, is the 10,894-acre Z Bar/Spring Hill Ranch, now converted by Congress, in 1996, to the **Tallgrass Prairie National Preserve**, operated jointly by the National Park Service and the National Park Trust. The house and prairie, never touched by the plow, are open for tours.

EMPORIA

Emporia is situated between the Neosho and Cottonwood rivers at the edge of the tall-grass prairie and the Flint Hills. The town was established in 1857 by free-state advocates from Ohio who were opposed to the activities of the border ruffians and other proslavery forces. They named the village after the ancient Mediterranean marketplace on the coast of North Africa. The citizens of Emporia helped attain stability for their town by securing the construction of railroads in 1869 and 1870. The first train arrived in 1870, and the line later became a branch of the Missouri–Kansas–Texas Railroad. Shortly afterward the Atchison, Topeka & Santa Fe Railroad arrived.

The eminent journalist and essayist William Allen White was born in Emporia in 1868 and spent most of his adult life there. He was owner and editor of the *Emporia Gazette* from 1895 until his death in 1944, when his son, author and World War II correspondent William Lindsay White, became editor. From his small town on the prairie, William Allen White wrote on many topics, from American mores, racism, and social change to the death of his only daughter in a riding accident at age 17. He won the ear of presidents and congressmen and captured the imagination of the reading public. The **William Allen White House** (927 Exchange Street, private), or **Red Rocks**, was built in 1885 and purchased by William and Sallie White in 1899. After a fire in 1920, the Whites had the house remodeled; they chose a design by the Kansas City firm of Wight and Wight, but the plan incorporates two distinctive elements from an initial design submitted by Frank Lloyd Wright—the handsome sandstone verandah and the staircase in the foyer. The red sandstone and brick

OPPOSITE: *The Second Empire Chase County Courthouse, completed in 1873, replaced a small log cabin that had served as the county's first courthouse and school. It is the oldest courthouse still in use in Kansas.*

structure is a blend of Queen Anne and Tudor elements. It remains in the White family. The **Lyon County Historical Museum** (118 East Sixth Avenue, 316–342–0933), housed in the Carnegie Library (1904), contains costumes, photographs, and an extensive scrapbook collection of local memorabilia.

COUNCIL GROVE

Council Grove figures prominently in the history of the Santa Fe Trail. In 1825, while conferring under a canopy of trees, agents of the federal government secured from the Osage the all-important right-of-way across their lands for the Santa Fe Trail. Situated on the banks of the Neosho River, near abundant water, grass, and timber, Council Grove became the final jumping-off place for southward-bound travelers on the trail. Caravans stocked up at the **Last Chance Store** (West Main and Chautauqua), which was also an Indian trading post. Built in 1857, the simple limestone building is one of the oldest extant structures in town.

The first permanent white settler in Council Grove was Seth Hays, who built a home and trading post in 1847 just north of the Santa Fe Trail. Soon followed by other traders, he came to the area not just because of trail traffic but to do business with the Kaw Indians, who had acquired reservation lands here as part of an 1846 treaty. The **Seth Hays House** (203 Wood Street, private), a brick residence, was built in 1867; Hays lived here until his death in 1873.

Kaw Mission Museum

In 1850 the Methodist Episcopal Church, whose ministers had been working among the Kaw for two decades, established a mission and school at Council Grove for the tribe. Construction of the facility was completed early in 1851, and in the spring of that year Thomas Sears Huffaker opened the school. It never flourished as its missionaries had hoped, in part because the Kaw, who were skeptical of white pedagogy, sent only orphaned boys to the school. Instruction ceased in 1854, and by the 1870s the Kaw had been removed to reservation lands in Oklahoma. The handsome limestone building contains period fixtures.

LOCATION: 500 North Mission Street. HOURS: 10–5 Tuesday–Saturday, 1–5 Sunday. FEE: None. TELEPHONE: 316–767–5410.

ABILENE

Abilene sits on the banks of Mud Creek near its confluence with the Smoky Hill River. Its two most famous citizens were the frontier lawman Wild Bill Hickok and Dwight David Eisenhower, Allied supreme commander in World War II and thirty-fourth president of the United States. Abilene was platted by a town speculator in 1861, but after several years the site had just a handful of log huts. The fortunes of the sleepy frontier village took an abrupt change in the summer of 1867 with the beginning of the great overland cattle drives in Kansas. During the first half of that decade, Texas cattle had been forbidden entry into Kansas and southwestern Missouri during the summer because the animals carried a fever that was lethal to northern livestock. In 1867 Kansas legislators—watching the Kansas Pacific Railroad move westward across their state—amended the statute to allow the longhorns into the sparsely populated western half of Kansas. The politicians established a quarantine line—or "deadline," as it came to be called—that cut north–south through Ellsworth County, just west of Salina.

Plans were afoot to establish the town of Ellsworth as the main terminus for cattle from Texas. Then Joseph McCoy, a livestock dealer from Springfield, Illinois, noted for his wealth, energy, and ego, became involved. Through shrewd political maneuvering, he got Abilene in Dickinson County—east of the quarantine line—approved as a livestock shipping point. Over the next five years nearly 3 million head of cattle tramped over the Chisholm Trail from Texas to Abilene. But the first major Kansas cow town was also the first to expire. By 1872 the anti-cattle fence-the-range movement, orchestrated by real estate dealers, had forced cattle drovers out of Abilene to Ellsworth and Wichita, and farmers were settling on open grazing land. The transition had not been tranquil. Life in Abilene was subsequently embellished in pulp fiction and Hollywood movies, and although greatly exaggerated, this romantic notion of the cattle town has taken on a life of its own. The now immortalized Abilene lawmen were Thomas J. Smith, a former New York policeman who was murdered by two outlaws, and James Butler "Wild Bill" Hickok, who was later killed during a card game in Deadwood, South Dakota.

The **Old Abilene Town and Western Museum** (6th Street and Buckeye, 785–263–4194) is a reconstruction of legendary Texas

Street, the main thoroughfare in Abilene, complete with cancan dancers in the saloon and gunfights in the street. There are replicas of various businesses from the cattle drive era, including the Merchant's Hotel and Alamo Saloon, a favorite haunt of Wild Bill Hickok. Several log structures and the schoolhouse are original buildings, which have been moved onto the site. Housed in the 1887 **Rock Island Depot** (1887), the Western Museum exhibits an array of Western memorabilia. The **Dickinson County Heritage Center** (412 South Campbell Street, 785–263–2681) has a museum with exhibits on the Plains Indians, railroads, Abilene's cattle-drive period, and westward expansion. Also on site is the **Museum of Independent Telephony,** which displays antique telephones, insulators, switchboards, and other artifacts of the telephone industry. One of the center's most prized possessions is the C. W. Parker Carousel, one of only three surviving hand-carved carousels built at the turn of the century by the Abilene-based Parker Amusement Company.

Dwight D. Eisenhower Center

Early in his military career, the future president Dwight David Eisenhower became known for two enduring attributes: he was a workaholic with a disarming smile. Eisenhower was born in Denison, Texas, in 1890, but he grew up in Abilene. He was the third of seven sons of David Jacob and Ida Elizabeth Stover Eisenhower, who had come to Abilene in the late 1870s with a colony of River Brethren, a Mennonite sect from Pennsylvania. Dwight Eisenhower was graduated from West Point in 1915 and was sent to Fort Sam Houston in San Antonio, Texas. Here he met the Iowa-born and Colorado-reared Mamie Doud, whom he married several months later. The Eisenhowers had two sons, Doud Dwight, who died of scarlet fever at the age of 3, and John Shelton Doud. In 1933 Eisenhower became an aide to General Douglas MacArthur, who was then chief of staff of the army. He was an executive officer at Fort Ord in California when Pearl Harbor was bombed. In the summer of 1942, then a major general, Eisenhower was given command of the newly established European theater of operations for U.S. forces. He oversaw the invasions of North Africa, Sicily, and Italy. In 1944, as a full general, he was named Supreme Commander of the Allied Expeditionary Force, with responsibility for Operation Overlord—the invasion of Normandy. After the war he served as

The back parlor of the Eisenhower family home in Abilene contains a patchwork pillow made by Ida Eisenhower, stitched with the names of her seven sons. Visible in the front parlor is a secretary brought from Pennsylvania to Abilene by Frederick Jacob Eisenhower, General Eisenhower's grandfather.

president of Columbia University and in 1952 was nominated and elected thirty-fourth president of the United States. He served two terms. Eisenhower died in 1969.

The **Eisenhower Home,** a white frame structure, was occupied by family members from 1898 until the death of Ida Eisenhower in 1946. It contains original furnishings. The visitor center has a film and exhibits recounting the life and career of President Eisenhower. The museum, decorated with murals depicting Eisenhower's life, contains an array of memorabilia, including gifts given to the Eisenhowers from heads of state. Dwight D. Eisenhower, Mamie, and Doud Dwight are interred in the adjacent chapel.

LOCATION: South Buckeye and 4th Street. HOURS: 9–4:45 Daily. FEE: Yes. TELEPHONE: 785–263–4751

The residential areas along North Buckeye, 3d, and North Vine streets retain numerous turn-of-the-century homes, including the Georgian Revival **Seelye Mansion** (1105 North Buckeye,

Abilene's Second Empire Kirby House, built in 1885 by a prosperous local banker.
OPPOSITE: *The staircase of the A.B. Seelye Mansion, built by the owner of the largest patent medicine company in the midwest.*

785–263–1084) of 1905 and the **Lebold-Vahsholtz Mansion** (106 North Vine Street, 785–263–4356), a beautiful stone Italianate structure built in 1880. The **Kirby House** (205 Northeast 3d Street, 785–263–7336) is a restored mansion, built in 1885, that now serves as a restaurant.

FORT RILEY

Fort Riley, located where the Smoky Hill and Republican rivers converge to form the Kansas River, was established in 1852 to provide protection to caravans on the Santa Fe and Oregon trails. In 1855 it was expanded to a cavalry post, and in 1866 the famous Seventh Cavalry was organized here. Second in command of the newly created unit was General George A. Custer. The first assignment of the Seventh Cavalry was to protect Union Pacific Railroad laborers from Indians. After the Plains Indians were subdued, Fort Riley became the headquarters for the U.S. cavalry.

The Kansas First Territorial Capitol, where legislators elected in the so-called bogus election met on July 2, 1855. The building served as the capitol for five days.

The **U.S. Cavalry Museum** (Building 205, Sheridan Avenue, 785–239–2737), housed in an 1855 building that served as the post hospital and headquarters, contains murals depicting the cavalry in action on the Western frontier, as well as exhibits of cavalry uniforms from 1833 to 1950, cavalry headgear, and military saddles and horse equipment. In addition there is a gallery of Western art and sculpture; an exhibit on the black soldiers who helped tame the West; a weapons gallery; and a gallery on the twentieth-century cavalry.

Quarters 24, also called the **Custer House** (24 Sheridan Avenue, 785–239–2737), is a large and handsome native limestone structure that dates to the 1855 building phase at Fort Riley. The house actually occupied by George and Elizabeth Custer stood nearby but was destroyed by fire. Quarters 24 has been furnished to reflect an officers' quarters during the 1880s, the decade Fort Riley was selected as the site for a cavalry school. The quarters reflect the relative gentility of life at a frontier army post in transition.

The Territorial Capitol at Fort Riley has been restored to its appearance in 1855, with a thirty-one star American flag.

First Territorial Capitol

The First Territorial Capitol was the site of the notorious July 1855 conclave of territorial legislators, most of whom had been selected in a bogus election the previous spring. In that election, held on March 30, 1855, hordes of Missourians, many bearing arms, had crossed the border into Kansas to stuff the ballot boxes. Investigation later disclosed that there were 4,968 fraudulent votes cast and only 1,210 legal ones. Governor Andrew Reeder, the appointee of President Franklin Pierce, convened the meeting in the town of Pawnee, which sat amid a hotbed of free-state activity. The main item on the agenda was to move the capital to the eastern border of the territory, where sentiments were more strongly proslavery. Reeder's veto of this plan was overturned by the legislators, and a few weeks later the politicians convened at the Shawnee Mission in present-day Kansas City, where they drew up the "Bogus Laws," which were intended to make

Kansas a slave state. The stone warehouse where the Pawnee legislators met was barely completed in time for the convention, and its role as a statehouse was short-lived. It later served as a carpenter shop, hostelry, bachelors' club, occasional church, and army warehouse. Everything in Pawnee—except the capitol—was absorbed by Fort Riley as it began to grow in 1855. The old stone building has been restored and contains territorial-period furnishings.

LOCATION: Huebner Road. HOURS: 10–5 Thursday–Saturday, 1–5 Sunday. FEE: None. TELEPHONE: 785–784–5535.

MANHATTAN

Manhattan stands near the confluence of the Big Blue and Kansas rivers amid the beautiful Flint Hills and bountiful farm and grazing lands. It is home to the state's land-grant college, Kansas State Agricultural College (now **Kansas State University**), which opened in 1863. The site of Manhattan previously supported a large Kaw Indian village. The city sprang from three settlements that took root here in the mid-1850s. The earliest of these, Polistra and Canton, were founded in late 1854. In the spring of 1855, representatives of the New England Emigrant Aid Company consolidated the two villages, calling it New Boston. That same spring, a group of settlers from Cincinnati, called the Cincinnati and Kansas Land Company, was working its way to Kansas via steamboat on the Ohio, Mississippi, Missouri, and Kansas rivers. They were detained in Saint Louis on the grounds that the party was an abolitionist mission. The Cincinnati group bought into New Boston and persuaded their new associates to rename the settlement Manhattan. One of the town's early settlers was David Butterfield, founder of the Butterfield Overland Despatch Route, which went from Atchison to Denver. From its earliest days, Manhattan had a free-state bent. It became an agricultural trading center with development of the outlying farm lands, and its prosperity was assured with the arrival in the 1860s and 1880s of the Union Pacific and Rock Island railroads.

Goodnow House

One of Manhattan's first settlers, Isaac Tichenor Goodnow was a devout Methodist and an opponent of slavery who left a professor-

OPPOSITE: *The Isaac T. Goodnow House in Manhattan, home to an important early Kansas educator.*

ship in Rhode Island to come to Kansas Territory. He became active in promoting free-state issues and organizing the state's common school educational system. He helped found Bluemont Central College, the institution that later became Kansas State University, and he established the Kansas State Teachers Association. In 1861 Goodnow purchased six acres of land and built this stone house adjacent to the college. Many original furnishings are on display.

LOCATION: 2301 Claflin Road, Pioneer Park. HOURS: 10–5 Wednesday–Saturday, 1–5 Sunday. FEE: None. TELEPHONE: 785–539–3731.

Also in Pioneer Park, the **Riley County Historical Museum** (2309 Claflin Road, 785–565–6490) contains Indian artifacts and extensive displays of pioneer furnishings, musical instruments, glass, china, and school and church memorabilia. The historical society also maintains the nearby **Hartford House,** one of the prefabricated houses that members of the Cincinnati and Kansas Land Company brought on the steamboat *Hartford* when they came to Kansas in 1855. The restored house contains pioneer furniture. The **Wolf-Butterfield House Museum** (630 Fremont, 785–565–6490), another property of the historical society, served as a stage stop on the Butterfield Overland Despatch Stage route. Built about 1865, it contains nineteenth-century furniture, glass, and china.

The western edge of east Kansas is a picturesque area of rolling uplands notched with limestone bluffs, of which the most prominent are the Flint Hills. Rain is plentiful enough here to encourage the growth of timber, especially in the valleys, while the uplands support stands of tall grass. One of the largest extant tallgrass prairies in the United States is the 8,616-acre **Konza Prairie Research Natural Area** (785–532–6659), which is owned by The Nature Conservancy and is operated by Kansas State University. It is located ten miles south of Manhattan, west of Route 177 and north of Route I-70. Much of the prairie is reserved for research, but there is a self-guided nature trail on the northern edge.

The abolitionist minister of the Plymouth Church in Brooklyn, New York, Henry Ward Beecher, preached that the Sharps rifle was a greater instrument of moral teaching than the Bible, which is how this firearm came to be called Beecher's Bible. Ten miles east of

The Konza Prairie Research Natural Area preserves one of the largest remaining tallgrass prairies in the United States.

Manhattan in **Wabaunsee** is the **Beecher Bible and Rifle Church** (Chapel and Elm streets, off Route 18). Built in 1862, the limestone building served a group of antislavery Congregationalists from Connecticut. One of the original Bibles and rifles are on display.

The original Home Station of the Pony Express, just before Hollenberg Station, was in **Marysville,** fifteen miles east of Hanover. The **Marysville Pony Express Barn** (106 South 8th Street, 785–562–3825) was built in 1859 and used as a livery stable until 1914. Now a museum, it houses a few Pony Express artifacts and antiques gathered from the area. The **Charles Koester House** (919 Broadway, 785–562–2417) is an Eastlake residence containing the original furnishings of the locally prominent banker who built the house in 1873. The **Marshall County Courthouse** (1207 Broadway), of 1891, is another of the impressive Richardsonian Romanesque buildings that distinguish many of Kansas's rural county seats.

The weathered board walls of Hollenberg Pony Express Station near the Nebraska–Kansas border in Hanover, built around 1858.

HOLLENBERG PONY EXPRESS STATION

Gerat Hollenberg, a German immigrant and far-ranging prospector who had looked for gold in California, Australia, and Peru before coming to Kansas in 1857, built this long frame structure about 1858. It stood on the Oregon–California Trail, which skirted the northern tier of Kansas, and like many nineteenth-century frontier ventures, it served multiple purposes. In the downstairs rooms, Hollenberg ran a dry-goods and grocery store, kept a tavern, and quartered his family; the loft was a sleeping area for stagecoach drivers and for Pony Express riders during the eighteen months that this overland mail service was in business. The Hollenberg Station, 123 miles from Saint Joseph, was the westernmost relay stop in Kansas, after which the route swung north into Nebraska. The different rooms in the restored station are furnished to reflect their use in 1860.

LOCATION: 2889 23rd Road, northeast of Hanover. HOURS: 10–5 Wednesday–Saturday, 1–5 Sunday. FEE: None. TELEPHONE: 785-337-2635.

CENTRAL KANSAS

PAWNEE INDIAN VILLAGE MUSEUM

Migrating northward from what is now Texas, the Pawnee Indians were early inhabitants of the Great Plains. Spanish explorers, such as Coronado, encountered them in the sixteenth century. Though they roamed over the plains to hunt bison, they lived on terraces overlooking rivers, where they farmed and built large sod and timber lodges. Four distinct bands of Pawnee had formed by the early 1700s, and these were associated with specific river drainages, from the Platte and Loup rivers in Nebraska to the Arkansas River in Kansas. From the opening of the American frontier, the Pawnee remained peaceful with white traders and settlers, in part because they sought an ally against their traditional foes, the Sioux, Cheyenne, Arapaho, Kiowa, and Comanche. The Pawnee became the most famous of the Indian scouts for the U.S. Army. By the mid-1800s they had signed over most of their traditional homelands to the United States, except for a reservation along the Loup River, which they gave up in 1876. They were subsequently relocated to Indian Territory in Oklahoma. This Pawnee Indian village was probably inhabited in the 1820s and 1830s. The population is estimated to have been about 1,000. Today twenty-six lodge sites can be seen on the grounds of the museum. The museum building encloses one of the larger lodge sites. The floor, almost 2,000 square feet in size, has a ceramiclike finish formed by puddling wet clay and then building fires on it to create a hardened surface. In situ are the remains of stone, bone, and metal trade goods, such as an ax and hoe blade, and pieces of mussel shell and corn.

LOCATION: 8 miles north of Route 36 on Route 266. HOURS: 10–5 Wednesday–Saturday, 1–5 Sunday. FEE: None. TELEPHONE: 785–361–2255.

MCPHERSON COUNTY OLD MILL MUSEUM AND PARK

This complex of historic buildings is located in the village of Lindsborg in the valley of the Smoky Hill River. The town was settled by the Chicago Swedish Company in 1868, and many descendants of the original immigrants still live in this rich wheat-growing area. The twelve structures on the site contain an array of furnishings, Indian artifacts, pioneer tools, and items associated with the region's Swedish heritage. The **Smoky Valley Roller Mill** is a three-story brick structure built in 1898 for a German immigrant miller; all of its original machinery is intact and operable. The **Swedish Pavilion** was prefabricated in Sweden and assembled at the Saint Louis World's Fair in 1904. The three-building U-shaped compound resembles a Swedish manor house.

LOCATION: 120 Mill Street, Lindsborg. HOURS: June through August: 9–5 Monday–Saturday, 1–5 Sunday; Rest of year: 9-5 Tuesday–Saturday, 1-5 Sunday. FEE: Yes. TELEPHONE: 785–227–3595.

Five miles east of Ellsworth in the village of **Kanopolis** is the site of Fort Harker, one of three forts established in the Smoky Hill River valley to protect the stagecoach route to Denver. It was active from 1866 until 1873. One of several extant buildings, the **Fort Harker Guardhouse** (Wyoming and Ohio streets, 785–472–5733), built in 1867, houses a military museum, which exhibits Indian artifacts, firearms, and uniforms.

ELLSWORTH

Beginning as a fort on the Smoky Hill River, Ellsworth tried mightily in the late 1860s to lure Texas cattle to its Kansas Pacific railhead, but floods, cholera, and marauding Indians, among other things, conspired against the town's promoters. Not until 1871, when Abilene could no longer fend off the advance of fence-building farmers, did the cattle business come to Ellsworth, and then only briefly. By 1875 settlement was encroaching upon the town, laws were passed in favor of local farmers and stock raisers, and the railroads were advancing toward Texas, thereby eliminating the need for the long cattle drives to Kansas. That same year much of Ellsworth burned down. The **Hodgden House Museum** (104 West Main Street, 785–472–3059) occupies a stone structure, one of the first residences built after the fire. Inside are exhibits of Indian artifacts, pioneer tools and clothing, a 1909 caboose, and local memorabilia. Several nineteenth-century buildings have been moved onto the grounds, including a church, log cabin, and rural school.

MEDICINE LODGE PEACE TREATY SITE

Located on the southeastern edge of Medicine Lodge, this natural amphitheater near the banks of the Medicine River was the scene in October 1867 of a great peace council between some 600 federal officials (mostly military escorts) and the chiefs and 15,000 members of five Plains tribes—the southern Cheyenne, Kiowa, Comanche, Arapaho, and Apache. It was the largest gathering of Indians and whites in American history. The main Indian spokesmen included the Arapaho Little Raven; Satanta, chief of the Kiowa; the Comanche leaders Young Bear, Iron Mountain, and Painted Lips; and Black Kettle, Bull Bear, and Slim Face of the southern Cheyenne. The federal commissioners were led by N. G. Taylor, with a cast of advisers and onlookers that included Colonel James Leavenworth, Kansas governor Samuel Crawford, Kit Carson, and Jesse Chisholm. Henry M. Stanley covered the event for the national press. Negotiations went on for two weeks for a treaty calling for peace between all parties. The Indians agreed to relinquish claims to ancestral lands in Kansas, Colorado, and Texas in return for federal economic and edu-

At a council at Medicine Lodge in 1867, five Plains tribes agreed to move to reservations in western Oklahoma Territory. This view was painted by Private Hermann Stieffel, who witnessed the signing of the treaty (detail).

cational assistance on reservation lands. The Medicine Lodge Treaty marked a departure from the previous federal Indian policy of expelling and isolating the Indians in that it attempted to assimilate them into a sedentary agrarian culture. Since 1927 a reenactment of the council has been held on the treaty site every three years.

In **Medicine Lodge** the **Carry Nation Home** (211 West Fowler Avenue, 316–886–3553) has furnishings and memorabilia of the temperence leader, who staged her first public protest here in 1899.

T H E   H I G H   P L A I N S

In the nineteenth century, the western third of Kansas evoked rapture in those who beheld it. "The whole surroundings," remarked one observer, "make the traveler feel that the country had been abandoned a thousand years ago, and that all traces of an inhabitation had faded away." Said another witness, "The landscape of those pristine plains was a power so tremendous that no wholly well man could escape its enchantment." Westering settlers, land speculators, and railroad tycoons assumed they could transform the western half of the state into a replica of the eastern half. This proved impossible, the limiting factor being rain. There is too little precipitation west of Route I-135—old U.S. Highway 81—and this north–south thoroughfare is the state's cultural dividing line. To the east are the undulating tall-grass prairies, rain, trees, cities, and people. West of Salina, Concordia, and Wichita, the land is higher and drier, the grass gets short, the horizon is jagged with buttes, cliffs, and mesas. There are no major north–south thoroughfares and, even more obvious, no cities. The largest towns are along the two historic railroad routes, the Kansas Pacific and the Santa Fe. The smaller towns line up along easterly flowing rivers—the Solomon and Republican rivers in the north; the Smoky Hill and Pawnee rivers and Walnut Creek in the middle; and the Arkansas and Cimarron rivers in the south.

DODGE CITY

Dodge City stands on a magnificent bluff of the Arkansas River. It was near here that the Santa Fe Trail swung south across the river. In 1865 the army established Fort Dodge to protect commerce on the trail, and a small settlement of traders and teamsters took root just upstream from the outpost. In 1872, a few months before the Santa

Fe Railroad was scheduled to arrive, the post commander and some local merchants and army contractors formed a corporation and founded the town of Dodge City. The frontier town lay in the heart of buffalo country, and in 1870, after a tanning process was developed for bison hide, hunters descended on the High Plains. Dodge City became the capital of the massacre of the buffalo; the arrival of the Santa Fe Railroad increased the slaughter. One merchant shipped out 200,000 hides the first winter after the railroad opened.

The bison, which were exterminated by 1876, were replaced by Texas longhorns. In that year, the quarantine line was pushed west of Wichita, and Dodge City became the next wild and woolly cow town. It held this distinction for almost a decade, longer than any of its predecessors. One pundit termed Dodge City the "Beautiful Bibulous Babylon of the Frontier." Famous lawmen associated with the town include Wyatt Earp, the Masterson brothers (Bat, Ed, and Jim), and Doc Holliday. At the same time, farmers were pouring into the area—except during the drought years of 1878 to 1881—and they were lobbying vociferously for protection from the livestock disease and general havoc that came with the cattle drives. The vast plain around Dodge City proved ideal for ranching, and as locals began developing their own herds, they cast a jaundiced eye on the invading longhorns from Texas. In the summer of 1884, cattle prices slumped, and splenic fever—the disease carried by longhorns—infected northern cattle in the stockyards at Kansas City, Saint Louis, and Chicago. Economics and an array of state laws turned against the Texas cattle drovers. The last cattle drive into Dodge City was in 1885.

Boot Hill Museum and Front Street

Front Street is a reconstruction of the main street in Dodge City during the cattle-drive era. It includes replicas of original structures as well as nineteenth-century buildings moved onto the site. The visitor center is in a reconstruction of the **Great Western Hotel.** Other buildings include the original **Fort Dodge Jail,** which formerly stood at the military outpost five miles east of Dodge City; a replica of the **Long Branch Saloon,** one of sixteen such establishments in Dodge City in 1877 and the one made famous in the television series "Gunsmoke"; and the **Hardesty House,** a residence (1878) typical of a prosperous cattle rancher's home of the period. The **Boot Hill Building** contains exhibits on the presettlement history of the area,

Dodge City's Front Street, re-created from photographs taken between 1876 and 1878, is part of the Boot Hill Museum. The original buildings burned in 1885.

Indians of southwestern Kansas, buffalo hunting, and early settlers. The **Boot Hill Cemetery** lies behind the museum. A number of living-history events take place on Front Street, including medicine shows and gunfights.

> LOCATION: Front Street. HOURS: Memorial Day through August: 8–8 Daily; September through Memorial Day: 9–5 Monday–Saturday, 1–5 Sunday. FEE: Yes. TELEPHONE: 316–227–8188.

The **Mueller–Schmidt House,** or the **Home of Stone,** (112 East Vine Street, 316–227–6791) is built of native stone. Its first owner was John Mueller, a prominent Dodge City bootmaker who went to cattle ranching. Its next occupant, Adam Schmidt, was a blacksmith. The house contains original furnishings and pioneer items.

Fort Dodge was active from 1865 until 1882. Several native stone structures from the old fort still stand on the grounds of the **Kansas Soldiers' Home** (five miles east of Dodge City on Route 154). Vestiges of the Santa Fe Trail can be seen nine miles west of Dodge City on Route 50.

George Masterson, the brother of Bat Masterson, tends bar at the Varieties Dance Hall in the "Beautiful Bibulous Babylon of the Frontier," Dodge City, about 1878.

FORT LARNED NATIONAL HISTORIC SITE

This site preserves numerous stone structures from the military outpost that was a principal guardian of Santa Fe Trail commerce. The fort was established in 1859, and in 1860 it was named for Colonel Benjamin F. Larned, U.S. Army paymaster general. Throughout the 1860s Fort Larned also served as an agency of the Indian Bureau Under the Treaty of Fort Wise (1861) and the Treaty of Medicine Lodge (1867), the federal government agreed to pay annuities to the Cheyenne, Arapaho, Kiowa, and Comanche Indians if they in turn promised to remain on their reservations and keep the peace. Fort Larned was a distribution point for these payments. Settlers proceeded to squat on Indian lands, bands of Cheyenne continued depredations on the Santa Fe Trail, and, in 1868, Major General Philip Sheridan launched a winter offensive against the Indians on the southern Plains. In November 1868 General George A. Custer, in a battle at the Washita River in Oklahoma, defeated Cheyenne chief Black Kettle. The Battle of Washita ended the organized Indian threat in the vicinity. In the 1870s soldiers from Fort Larned provided protection for workers on the Santa Fe Railroad as it pushed west

An army escort wagon, used to transport soldiers on the Kansas frontier, in front of the stone quartermaster storehouse at Fort Larned, built in 1868.

from Topeka. With the Indians removed, the railroad completed, and the overland trail obsolete, the fort was abandoned in 1878.

The first structures at Fort Larned were adobe. These were replaced in the late 1860s by ten stone buildings clustered around a parade ground. The first barracks now houses the visitor center. The second barracks, post hospital, shops building, and officers' quarters contain authentic or reproduction furniture from the 1860s.

LOCATION: Route 156, 6 miles west of Larned. HOURS: June through August: 8–6 Daily; Rest of year: 8:30–5 Daily. FEE: Yes. TELEPHONE: 316–285–6911.

Five miles east of the fort is a forty-acre tract where wagon ruts of the old Santa Fe Trail are still visible. The **Santa Fe Trail Center** (Route 156, two miles west of Larned, 316–285–2054) is a regional museum with exhibits of prehistoric and historic Indian artifacts, a full-size mounted buffalo, a replica of a Wichita Indian grass lodge, a freight wagon, and pioneer furnishings, firearms, and religious items. Many nineteenth-century structures, including a sod house, dugout, and schoolhouse, are preserved or reconstructed on site.

HAYS

The town of Hays, in the valley of the Smoky Hill River, came into being in 1867 with the arrival of the Union Pacific, Eastern Division Railroad (which became the Kansas Pacific). It also served nearby Fort Hays. Like other "end-of-the-track" towns, it supported a number of saloons, gambling houses, and brothels. From 1867 to 1873, there were over thirty homicides in and around Hays, which earned a reputation as one of the most violent of the Kansas frontier towns. For several months in 1869, Wild Bill Hickok was the acting sheriff of Ellis County, apparently serving at the will of a vigilante committee. The **Ellis County Historical Society Museum** (100 West 7th Street, 785–628–2624) has extensive exhibits of pioneer artifacts. On the grounds of the museum are a Gothic Revival stone church of 1879 and a replica of the native stone housing constructed by the German-Russian immigrants who came to the area in 1875. On the campus of Fort Hays University, the **Sternberg Museum of Natural History** (relocating; call 785–628–4286) has exhibits of geology; paleontology, including a "fish within a fish"; archaeology and ethnology; natural history; and area history.

The surgeon's bedroom in the south officer's quarters at Fort Larned has been restored to its appearance in 1867-1869, when it was occupied by Captain Forwood, an Army doctor who took great interest in the local natural history.

FORT HAYS

Fort Fletcher, the precursor of Fort Hays, was established in 1865 about fifteen miles to the southeast. It was intended to protect stage and freight traffic along the Smoky Hill Trail to Denver. With the closing of the trail in the spring of 1866, Fort Fletcher was abandoned. In the fall of that year, the fort reopened to help protect workers building the Union Pacific Railway's Eastern Division from Kansas City to Denver. That winter the post was renamed Fort Hays, after General Alexander Hays, killed in the Battle of the Wilderness during the Civil War. As the railroad approached, it became clear that the fort would need to be moved closer to the intended path, and in the spring of 1867 a new spot was found. Before the post could be moved, however, it was greatly damaged by a flood. In June the fort moved to its present site along Big Creek, and in October of that year the railroad finally arrived. The town of Hays City sprang up, and the fort immediately became a supply depot serving posts farther south along the Santa Fe Trail. At its height, 565 troops were stationed here. It was host to such illustrious military leaders as George Custer, Nelson Miles, and Philip Sheridan and such well-known civilians as Buffalo Bill Cody and Wild Bill Hickok. Fort Hays was abandoned as a military post in 1889. Four of the original structures remain: The blockhouse, a hexagonal stone structure built in 1867 and used primarily as headquarters; two frame officers' quarters, also built in 1867; and the stone guardhouse built in 1872. The buildings contain furnishings, uniforms, military accoutrements, firearms, Indian artifacts, and artifacts excavated at the site.

LOCATION: Exit 157 off Route I-70, then 4 miles south to Route 183 Bypass. HOURS: 9–5 Tuesday–Saturday, 1–5 Sunday–Monday. FEE: None. TELEPHONE: 785–625–6812.

Cathedral of the Plains (1911), a beautiful Romanesqe Revival structure built of native limestone, is in **Victoria. Russell** is the birthplace and longtime home of Robert J. Dole, who was U.S. Senate majority leader and Republican nominee for president in 1996.

In **Oakley,** the **Fick Fossil and History Museum** (700 West 3d Street, 785–672–4839) has an extensive collection of fossils and fossil art, rocks, minerals, and wildflowers, a sod house, an 1886 depot, and pioneer memorabilia. **Russell Springs** was a stop on the Butterfield Overland Despatch. The **Logan County Courthouse** (1888) on the main square in Russell Springs houses the **Butterfield Trail Historical Museum** (785–751–4242), which has antique Indian artifacts, fossils, furniture, pioneer memorabilia, and agricultural implements.

Ten miles north of Scott City is **El Cuartelejo,** located in **Lake Scott State Park** (316–872–2061). This important archaeological site contains the restored ruins of a stone pueblo that was occupied between 1650 and 1720 by Taos and Picuris Indians. They migrated here from their homeland in the Southwest to take refuge with the Plains Apache. In **Colby** the **Prairie Museum of Art and History** (1905 South Franklin, 785–462–4590) contains a large collection of antique dolls, glass, china, furniture, textiles, silver, and memorabilia associated with area homesteaders. There is also a sod house, farmhouse, and other buildings dating to the pioneer period.

In the town of **Goodland,** the **High Plains Museum** (1717 Cherry, 785–899–4595) features pioneer exhibits and a life-size automated replica of America's first patented helicopter, built here in 1910. Dioramas tell the story of the region, beginning with the Kidder Massacre. In the northeast quadrant of Sherman County on the South Fork of Beaver Creek, Lieutenant Kidder and a small detail of men accompanied by an Indian scout were searching for General George Custer to deliver an urgent message. The men were ambushed by a large war party and killed when they mistakenly fled into a blind canyon on the creek. Custer and a party found the bodies and buried the remains in a common grave.

In the town of **Oberlin,** the **Last Indian Raid Museum** (258 South Penn Avenue, 785–475–2712) has items of pioneer history and memorabilia related to the last Indian raid in western Kansas. In 1878, the northern Cheyenne leader Dull Knife and 255 followers, after a miserable year in Indian Territory, came through Kansas, bound for home in Montana. Many Kansans sympathized with them. But the Indians killed forty-one settlers and generally terrorized western Kansas. Apprehended, many died in captivity or trying to escape. Seven, tried for murder, were acquitted when witnesses failed to appear on time.

Nicodemus National Historic Site, in Nicodemus (402–221–3432), preserves the only remaining Western town established by African Americans during the Reconstruction era after the Civil War. These men and women dared leave the only region (the South) that they knew to seek freedom and opportunity elsewhere.

CHAPTER THREE

NEBRASKA

In *My Antonia,* Willa Cather's novel about turn-of-the-century life on the Great Plains, young Jim Burden steps off the train from Virginia in the middle of the night and is bowled over by the vastness of his new Nebraska home: "There was nothing but land: not a country at all, but the material out of which countries are made. . . . I had the feeling that the world was left behind, that we had got over the edge of it, and were outside man's jurisdiction." The terrain still evokes similar responses. The largest cities in Nebraska, Omaha and Lincoln, cling to the eastern edge of the state, barely fifty miles apart. Most towns of any size line up along the state's main thoroughfare, Route I-80, as it slices west for 450 miles across the lower third of the state. Away from this corridor lies sparsely populated ranch and farm country.

Archaeologists speculate that nomads stalked mammoths across these plains 12,000 years ago. The hunters then adapted their methods to other prey after increasingly arid conditions pushed the mammoth to extinction. About 2,000 years ago, prehistoric hunters began to settle down to farming. Then, 500 years ago, a series of droughts and other environmental changes dramatically altered horticultural practices over much of what we now call Nebraska. For a hundred years, the region's population declined. As the climate improved, farming tribes returned to eastern Nebraska, where they were prospering when Spanish and French explorers and traders penetrated the area in the late seventeenth century. These Indians clustered along the lower reaches of the Loup River valley where it joins the Platte, living in large, round earthlodges. Their economy and culture centered on the cultivation of corn. These so-called Lower Loup people are the likely ancestors of the Pawnee, who by the 1820s were the most powerful Indian nation on the central Great Plains. The Pawnee lived along the Platte, Republican, and Loup rivers and controlled a huge territory stretching from the Niobrara River in northern Nebraska to the Arkansas River in southern Kansas.

The Pawnee lived in villages of earthlodges, where women cultivated the corn and other crops; periodically the males went out to hunt bison, raid (particularly for horses), and barter. The Pawnee participated in a large trade network included the Arikara, Mandan, and Hidatsa on the upper Missouri River; French and Americans in Saint Louis; the Caddoan-speaking Indians of Texas and Oklahoma;

OPPOSITE: *A portrait of an Arikara warrior by the Swiss artist Karl Bodmer, whose portraits and scenes of daily life, made on a 3,000-mile journey up the Missouri in the early 1830s, are an invaluable record of Plains Indian culture.*

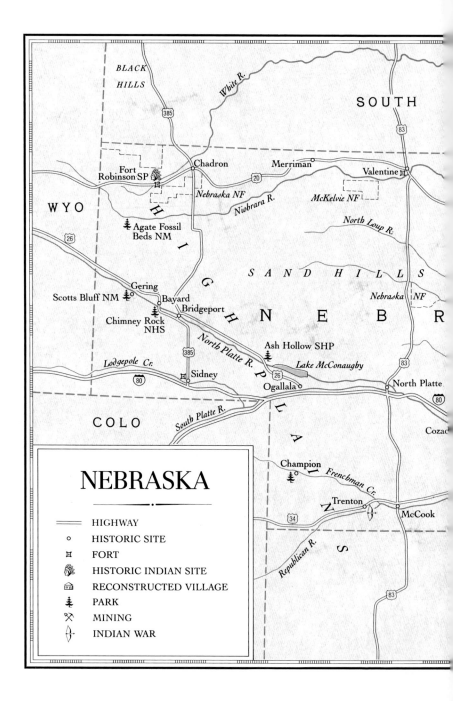

BLACK
HILLS

White R.

SOUTH

385

83

Fort
Robinson SP
Chadron

Merriman

Valentine

20

WYO

Nebraska NF

Niobrara R.

McKelvie NF

Agate Fossil
Beds NM

North Loup R.

26

S A N D   H I L L S

Nebraska   NF

Gering

Scotts Bluff NM

Bayard

N   E   B   R

Bridgeport

Chimney Rock
NHS

H

Ash Hollow SHP

North Platte R.

Lake McConaughy

83

Lodgepole Cr.

Sidney

North Platte

80

26

Ogallala

80

COLO

South Platte R.

Cozad

Champion

Frenchman Cr.

Trenton

McCook

34

N

Republican R.

83

NEBRASKA

━━━━━   HIGHWAY
   ○   HISTORIC SITE
   ⌷   FORT
        HISTORIC INDIAN SITE
        RECONSTRUCTED VILLAGE
        PARK
   ✕   MINING
        INDIAN WAR

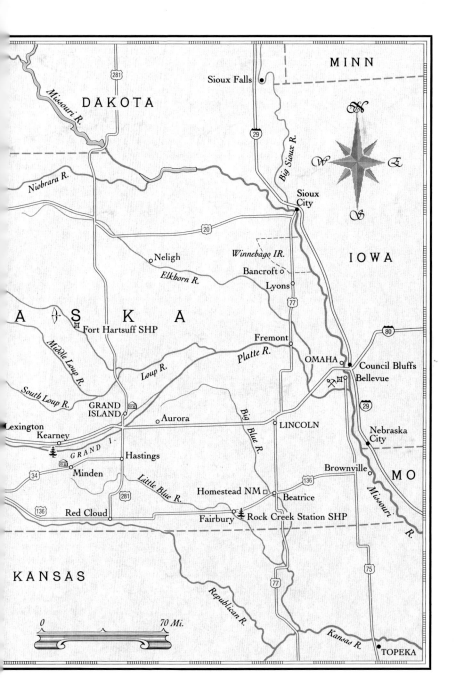

and Spaniards and Mexicans in Santa Fe. These were times of prosperity for the Pawnee, who probably numbered between 10,000 and
15,000. John Dougherty, the government agent assigned to the
tribe, observed in 1828, "The Pawnee have great confidence in their
own strength, believing themselves to be more numerous, warlike,
and brave than any other nation on earth." But in the summer of
1831, large numbers of Pawnee died of smallpox. Cholera took additional lives in 1849.

Perhaps as early as the 1500s, a succession of eastern tribes had
begun to push west to the river systems of Nebraska. Here they
embraced many Pawnee customs, most notably the construction of
earthlodges. The allied Oto and Missouri, Siouan-language speakers
from the Great Lakes region, established villages along the Platte
River near its confluence with the Missouri. The Omaha Indians and
their close relatives, the Ponca, are part of a Siouan-language group
thought to have been centered in the Ohio Valley. The Omaha

A sod house in Oglala National Grassland, a preserve in western Nebraska.

established themselves along the Missouri River and its nearby tributary, the Elkhorn, while the Ponca lived farther north, at the confluence of the Missouri and Niobrara rivers.

The acquisition of Spanish horses in about 1750 drastically changed the customs of many North American tribes, among them the Sioux, Cheyenne, and Arapaho. These semisedentary peoples became nomads on the Great Plains: As the Cheyenne legend describes it, they "lost the corn." With an improved means of hunting buffalo, the Indians' standard of living rose quickly. They became bold warriors, and the source of their new-found way of life acquired religious significance. The Sioux called their mounts *shunka wakan*—"sacred dogs."

As the Indians competed for the best hunting grounds and for favor with white traders, the Great Plains became an immense stage of shifting tribal alliances. The Cheyenne and Arapaho united against the Kiowa and Comanche, and in time the Cheyenne and Arapaho joined the Sioux against the Crow. In the 1830s the Oglala and Brule bands of the Sioux, along with the Cheyenne and Arapaho, began to move into the buffalo-rich plains surrounding the Niobrara, North Platte, and Republican rivers of western Nebraska. Here they bumped up against the Pawnee, and a fierce animosity developed between the long-established Nebraska tribe and the loosely allied Sioux, Cheyenne, and Arapaho. In 1873 a large party of Sioux slaughtered a hunting party of Pawnee, including women and children, in the valley of the Republican River in Massacre Canyon, near present-day Trenton. It was the last great intertribal confrontation in North America. In 1875 the Pawnee ceded their Nebraska lands and settled in Indian Territory in Oklahoma.

The first whites to establish themselves along the Missouri River in present-day Nebraska were fur traders, who had followed on the heels of Lewis and Clark's 1804–1806 expedition. Fur traders were also the first whites to travel along the wide, sandy river that French explorers in the 1700s had aptly named the Platte. This term, meaning "flat," was the French equivalent of *Nebraska,* the Oto word for "flat water." In 1812 Robert Stuart and six other employees of John Jacob Astor were the first whites to traverse the length of the Platte River in Nebraska. Heading east from Fort Astoria on the Columbia River, they discovered South Pass, the most important pass in the entire Rocky Mountain chain. In 1824 the Rocky Mountain fur trader William Ashley and a party of twenty-five men traveled from Fort

Atkinson on the Missouri River to the Rocky Mountains. Newspaper accounts of the trip informed a broad audience that the Platte River valley was a good route west. In 1830 the fur traders Jedediah Smith, David Jackson, and William Sublette, on their way from Saint Louis to the Wind River, led the first wagon train west along the Platte River. In 1842 a government-sponsored expedition led by John C. Frémont—with counsel from scouts Kit Carson and Lucien Maxwell —provided the first accurate map and guidebook for traveling along the Platte River. The trickle of traders, trappers, mountain men, and government explorers became a flood of settlers and gold seekers. In 1843 the first large caravan of settlers left Independence, Missouri, for Oregon. In 1847 Brigham Young and the first of his Mormon followers traced the Platte to the Great Salt Lake. Two years later the California gold rush commenced; in 1850 approximately 65,000 people headed west along the Platte bound for California. In 1858 the discovery of gold in Colorado spurred even more traffic along the trail. An estimated 500,000 people traversed Nebraska between 1841 and 1866. Between 1820 and 1880, the federal government established a number of forts in Nebraska, the most important being Forts Atkinson, Kearny, and Robinson.

The Oregon Trail followed the valley of the Platte River, one of the richest of the Indians' hunting grounds. But despite their worst fears, overland emigrants were rarely attacked by Indians during the peak migration years, in the 1850s. In the summer and fall of 1864, Cheyenne, Arapaho, and Brule Sioux launched coordinated attacks on travelers and settlers in the Platte Valley. Arapaho leaders began to withdraw their people from the conflict with whites, but many Sioux and Cheyenne made this a fight to the bitter end. Under the leadership of Crazy Horse and Sitting Bull, they campaigned so effectively that they were able to keep their freedom and their hunting grounds for several years, to the frustration of the U.S. Army. But in 1875 the Oglala and Brule Sioux, by then removed to reservations in Dakota Territory, agreed to surrender their last hunting rights in western Nebraska. In the spring of 1877, Crazy Horse at last agreed to join his brethren on their reservation lands; he marched into Fort Robinson with almost a thousand followers and surrendered. A few months later, Crazy Horse was stabbed to death in a scuffle with soldiers at the fort—probably a deliberate assassination.

Nebraska Territory, when it was organized in 1854, encompassed a huge and desolate expanse that included parts of the present states of Colorado, North and South Dakota, Idaho, Montana, and Wyoming. The 1854 census counted only 2,732 people in this region, and many of them were thought to be transient. Growth in the early years of the territory was steady but not rapid; by 1860 the population was 28,841. Always a place on the way to someplace else, Nebraska became a place to settle in the 1860s. The passage of the Homestead Act in 1862 furnished the economic incentive—free land—that attracted yeoman farmers to try their luck in Nebraska. The conclusion of the Civil War in 1865 provided a large body of young men looking for land, and the construction of the Union Pacific Railroad through the Platte Valley from 1865 to 1867 attracted workers. Most important, a railroad in Nebraska afforded a means of occupying a land with no navigable rivers, as well as a method of getting one's goods to market.

The Homestead Act was frequently amended to extend entitlements. The Timber Culture Act of 1873, introduced by a Nebraska

The Shores family at their homestead near Westerville in Custer County, photographed by Solomon Butcher in 1887. Many former slaves settled in this county after the Civil War. Some came to Nebraska from Canada, where they had earlier found refuge via the Underground Railroad.

senator, allowed homesteaders to acquire an additional section (160 acres) by planting part of that land to trees and tending it for ten years; while the Kinkaid Act of 1904, named for the Nebraska congressman who promoted it, permitted homesteaders to obtain 640 acres in the arid Sand Hills of north-central Nebraska after five years' tenancy. The Kinkaiders, as they came to be called, practiced dryland farming, lived in tar-paper shacks or soddies, and became fiercely loyal to the beautiful if marginal Sand Hill country where they settled.

The federal and state governments gave Union Pacific and Burlington, Nebraska's two major railroads more than 7 million acres as an incentive to build; ultimately one-sixth of Nebraska's acreage was given to the dozen or so railroad companies that crisscrossed the state. As in other midwestern states, the rail companies disposed of this land by means of aggressive advertising campaigns in major cities in the East and in northern and central Europe. The Union Pacific, for example, sold land in the Platte Valley west of Omaha to a group from Sweden, and German Russians acquired railroad land near Sutton.

Virtually every town west of Omaha and Lincoln owed its existence, location, and layout to a railroad. Railroad sidings, around which towns sprouted, tended to be six to ten miles apart—a distance, wrote the Nebraska historian Frederick Luebke, that was "governed by the number of miles a farmer could drive his horse-drawn wagon to town, loaded with grain or hogs, and return home on the same day." Villages did not grow up around a central business district but instead in a line along the tracks. Many railroad-spawned towns have disappeared, while others have been altered by modern suburban accretions, but some still retain their linear scheme. Their majestic grain elevators best define Nebraska's rural landscape.

The 1880s were boom years for Nebraska. The region received above-average rainfall, which encouraged an influx of settlers. The state's population surged from half a million to a million between 1880 and 1890 (the state's 1996 population was about 1.65 million. In the eastern and central portions of the state, where rainfall has always been more predictable, farming became the principal industry and corn the prevailing crop.

The western half of Nebraska became cattle domain. Texas longhorn drovers began moving their herds onto Nebraska's ranges, attracted by the Union Pacific's offer of lower hauling rates, compared to those of the Kansas Pacific. From 1873 until the mid-1880s, Ogallala was the terminus of these trail drives and a ripsnorting cowboy town, Nebraska's equivalent of Kansas's Dodge City. When settlers in northwestern Kansas and southwestern Nebraska began petitioning for herd and quarantine laws, they effectively blocked the path of these cattle drives. By the 1880s, however, ranching had taken root in western Nebraska. One of the state's early stock raisers was Edward Creighton, an Omaha millionaire and builder of the transcontinental telegraph. Among the first ranchers to graze livestock in the bleak Sand Hills were Frank North and his partner William F. "Buffalo Bill" Cody. Others soon realized that the grass-covered dunes made the best range land in the West. James S. Brisbin's *The Beef Bonanza; or, How to Get Rich on the Plains,* published in 1881, promoted the notion of quick and easy profits in the cattle business. Eastern and European investors responded to the lure, but shaky financing, overgrazing, and the blizzards of 1885–1886 and 1886–1887 ended the Great Plains cattle bonanza. The ranching business revived in western Nebraska twenty years later on a smaller but sounder scale. Fenced land supplanted the open range; pure-blooded stock, such as Hereford, Shorthorn, and Angus, were bred instead of the Texas longhorn; and hay was harvested to supplement the standard grass diet, a feeding regimen that proved particularly beneficial during harsh winters. All of these practices continue today.

This chapter begins in Omaha, on the west bank of the Missouri River, and proceeds north to historic Fort Atkinson and west to Neligh Mills, an old gristmill on the Elkhorn River in rural Nebraska. The route then moves to Lincoln, the capital, and the southeastern part of the state. From here the route swings through the Republican River valley along the southern tier of the state, an area that includes the picturesque town of Red Cloud, childhood home of Willa Cather and a fictional backdrop in much of her writing; the home of Nebraska's great twentieth-century progressive politician, Senator George Norris; and Massacre Canyon, scene of the last battle between the Pawnee and Sioux in 1873. The route then retraces the trail of the pioneers along the Platte River Road from Grand Island to Courthouse and Jail Rocks, Chimney Rock, and Scotts Bluff, the majestic landmarks on the edge of the Sand Hills that guided caravans west on the Oregon Trail. The last section of the chapter, the Sand Hills, is the location of Nebraska's ranch country.

MAGNOLIA PLANTATION AND GARDENS

Magnolia Plantation has belonged to the Drayton family for 300 years. There have been three plantation houses on the site; the first was accidentally destroyed by fire, and the second was deliberately torched by Union soldiers in 1865. The gardens and the original family tomb survived, though the cherubs adorning the monument were used for target practice.

After the war the family disassembled a pre–Revolutionary War summer cottage in Summerville, floated it down the Ashley River, and set it on the foundation of the previous structure. In the 1880s Victorian elements, including a tower, were added. The house was occupied by the family until 1976. The plantation gardens fared better than the residence. The earliest portion, known as Flowerdale, dates to the 1680s. In the years prior to the Civil War, Reverend John Drayton married and greatly expanded this original garden, hoping, he wrote, "to create an earthly paradise in which my dear Julia may forever forget Philadelphia and her desire to return there." By the 1870s tourists journeyed up the Ashley by steamboat to view the lush plantings. Today the fifty-acre gardens, planted for year-round color, are at the heart of a 500-acre-estate, which includes a waterfowl refuge and cypress swamp. canoe and foot trails.

> LOCATION: 10 miles northwest of downtown Charleston on Route 61. HOURS: 8–5 Daily. FEE: Yes. TELEPHONE: 803–571–1266.

MIDDLETON PLACE

Henry Middleton and his bride moved to Middleton Place in 1741 and immediately began the creation of a formally landscaped garden. It took 100 slaves ten years to complete Middleton's grand design, which incorporated a canal, terraces, and twin lakes. Henry Middleton served in the First Continental Congress, and his son, Arthur, was a signer of the Declaration of Independence.

Prior to the Civil War, the Middleton residence consisted of a brick main house built sometime before 1741 and two flanking buildings constructed in 1755. A detachment of Sherman's army ransacked and burned the mansion on February 22, 1865. The family salvaged what they could of the south flank, which had been

encompasses the site of the Bellevue fur-trading post established in 1822. A diorama at the interpretive center includes a scale model of the post and a reproduction of Karl Bodmer's 1833 painting of it. A **log cabin** (1805 Hancock Street), constructed of hand-hewn cottonwood logs in about 1840, was originally on the riverbank but was moved to higher ground in the 1850s. The brick **Fontenelle Bank** (2212 Main Street), built in 1856, has Greek Revival and Italianate touches. The bank failed during the Panic of 1857. The **Reverend William Hamilton House** (2003 Bluff Street), built around 1856, was the home of a leading misssionary, who started the **Presbyterian Indian Mission,** devoted much of his life to the Omaha, and oversaw construction of the stone rubble and stucco Presbyterian Church (2002 Franklin), the state's oldest (ca. 1856) extant church. The **Strategic Air Command Museum** (2510 SAC Place, 402–292–2001) displays military aircraft next to the nation's defense "nerve center." The **Sarpy County Historical Museum** (2402 SAC Place, 402–292–1880) has Indian artifacts and period rooms.

During the 1850s the new settlement at Omaha became the site of the territorial capital (1854), the Union Pacific rail route (1865), and the bridge across the Missouri (1868)—consequently Omaha grew while Bellevue shrank. The Union Pacific Railroad fueled the growth of both Omaha and Nebraska. The railroad attracted workers and had land to sell to homesteaders. Liberal land-grant legislation passed in 1864 allotted 12,800 acres of land to the railroad for every mile of track built. By 1869 the Union Pacific had earned over $2 million from the sale of 480,000 acres. In 1880 a third of Omaha's population was foreign-born. Germans predominated, followed by Irish and Swedish.

The 1880s were boom years for Omaha: The city's population grew from 30,000 to 102,000, and there were plenty of jobs to be had. The Omaha and Grant Smelting Company, founded in 1870, processed silver, lead, and copper from Western mines. By the end of the decade, it was the largest smelter in the world. Continuing the pattern begun in other midwestern cities, German settlers developed a thriving brewery industry in Omaha. Peter and Joseph Iler's Willow Springs Distillery grew to become the third-largest in the country by the 1890s. In 1883 a group of businessmen organized the Union Stockyards Company. Their facilities just south of Omaha attracted the meat-packing firms of Swift, Armour, and Cudahy, as well as a host of job-seeking immigrants.

Although the early twentieth century was a time of agricultural prosperity for Nebraska, the city of Omaha's political landscape and industrial sector were dismal. From 1900 to 1930, the city was run by a political machine headed by Tom Dennison. The mayor, "Cowboy" Jim Dahlman, was a Texas-born stockman-turned-politician who preferred demonstrating his rope tricks to curbing vice in Omaha. Labor unrest began in the 1880s at the city's smelter and spread to the stockyards and packinghouses by the turn of the century. Ethnic and racial tensions were high, especially after recent immigrants were hired as strike breakers. A riot broke out in 1909 when a Greek packinghouse worker shot a policeman; the violence was directed against not only Omaha's Greeks but its Hungarian, Italian, and Polish communities as well. In 1919, 6,000 Omahans stormed the courthouse, set it on fire, and abducted a black man who had been arrested for allegedly assaulting a white woman. They tried to hang the mayor on a traffic light (he barely survived) and hanged the black man from a telephone pole, where the mob shot him repeatedly, then burned the body. The city had to be placed under martial law to restore order.

Many of Omaha's finest residences and commercial buildings that were erected between 1890 and 1930 were designed by three local architectural firms. The most influential of the group—and Nebraska's preeminent architect—was Thomas Rogers Kimball, whose firm of Walker and Kimball served as chief designer for the Trans-Mississippi Exposition. John Latenser, Sr., was a German-educated immigrant whose two sons, John, Jr., and Frank, later joined him in his business. The Latensers designed many public buildings and schools in Omaha. John McDonald and his son Alan developed a practice with domestic commissions from wealthy Omahans, in particular from George and Sarah Joslyn.

DOWNTOWN

Downtown Omaha faces the Missouri River to the east and is bounded by Route I-480 on the north and west and Leavenworth Street on the south. Within this area are remnants of nineteenth-century mercantile and industrial Omaha as well as the city's major historical museums. The heart of the business district contains several architectural landmarks. The **Trinity Cathedral** (113 North 18th Street) is a late Gothic Revival structure (1883) with interior wood carving and bronze relief work. Its Episcopal congregation was established in 1856. Reflecting the aspirations of Omaha at the turn of the century are three commercial buildings designed by nationally prominent firms from Chicago and New York. The 1889 **New York Life Insurance Building** (17th and Farnam streets), designed by the New York firm of McKim, Mead & White, is virtually identical to the New York Life building in Kansas City, Missouri, by the same architects. The **First National Bank** (16th and Farnam streets) is a fourteen-story steel-frame building designed by Graham, Burnham & Company of Chicago and built in 1917. The **City National Bank** and the **Creighton Orpheum Theater** (16th and Harney streets) form an engaging complex. The Chicago firm of Holabird & Roche designed the sixteen-story bank, Omaha's first steel-frame skyscraper when it was completed in 1910. In 1927 the architects Rapp & Rapp rebuilt the interior of the adjacent theater, which dated to 1892. The cavernous, lavishly decorated interior remains the grandest entertainment space in the city. Typical of 1920s theatrical architecture, the **Astro Theater** (2001 Farnam Street) is a brick and terra-cotta confection with Moorish motifs, built in 1926. The **Douglas County Courthouse** (1700 Farnam Street) is a monumental Renaissance Revival structure of 1912, designed by John Latenser, Sr.

A baby named Leslie King was born at 32nd Street and Woolworth Avenue on July 14, 1913. Two years later his parents divorced, and his mother moved to Grand Rapids, Mich., where she married Gerald Ford, a businessman. The boy took his stepfather's name, went on to a career in public service, and became the 38th president. **Gerald R. Ford's Birthplace and Gardens** preserves the site—the house burned in 1971—and includes memorabilia.

Kenefick Park (6th Street and Abbott Drive) contains two Union Pacific locomotives that were the largest of their types ever built: the steam-powered *Big Boy* (1944) and the diesel-electric engine *Centennial* (1969). Both are open for inspection.

Near the south edge of the Central Park Mall, just east of the business district, are several buildings from the era when the area was a thriving commercial and warehouse district serving the railroads. The Italianate **Burlington Headquarters Building** (1004 Farnam Street) was built in 1879 and remodeled in 1899 by Thomas Rogers Kimball to resemble the Chicago, Burlington & Quincy Railroad Building in Chicago. The Italianate **Poppleton**

Block (1001 Farnam Street) was designed by the Omaha architect Henry Voss and built in 1880 by the Omaha attorney Andrew Jackson Poppleton, who won the landmark case for the Ponca chief Standing Bear in 1879. Two blocks south of the mall lies the **Old Market Historic District** (between Farnam, Jackson, 10th, and 13th streets), an assemblage of turn-of-the-century Italianate buildings along cobblestone streets. Included is the **Anheuser-Busch Beer Depot** (1207–1215 Jones Street), a charming Romanesque Revival structure (1887) that is the only remaining building from a complex designed by Henry Voss.

Western Heritage Museum

The Western Heritage Museum is housed in the beautiful **Union Station,** an Art Deco building of 1931, sheathed in cream-colored glazed terra-cotta. The waiting area is intact, and the striking details in the room include stained-glass windows, murals, and chandeliers. Gilbert Stanley Underwood, a Los Angeles architect, designed this and several other terminals for the railroad. The museum's exhibits

The Western Heritage Museum occupies the former Union Station, a building of cream-colored terra cotta erected in 1931.

recount the development of Omaha from 1880 to 1954: Highlights include a model train layout eighty-five feet in length with 40 cars, as well as an archival photography collection of 200,000 negatives and prints. The collection of coins assembled by the nineteenth-century Omaha businessman Byron Reed includes many rare early pieces from the United States and Europe. The Reed collection also includes many historic American documents.

LOCATION: 801 South 10th Street. HOURS: 10–5 Tuesday– Saturday, 1–5 Sunday. FEE: Yes. TELEPHONE: 402–444–5071.

Adjacent to the Western Heritage Museum is **Burlington Station** (925 South 10th Street), which was a terminal for both passengers and freight. The original Classic Revival structure, designed in 1898 by Thomas Rogers Kimball, was greatly admired. In 1930 the station was redesigned by the Chicago firm of Graham, Anderson, Probst, and White. The USS *Hazard,* a World War II navy minesweeper, and the USS *Marlin,* a target submarine active from 1953 to 1973, are berthed at Freedom Park (402–345–1959). Their systems are virtually intact and open to the public.

Capitol Hill (Dodge between 20th and 24th streets) affords a lovely panorama of the city and river flats below. From 1857 until 1867, when the state capital was moved to Lincoln, Nebraska's second territorial capitol stood on this hilltop. Since 1900 **Central High School** (124 North 20th Street) has commanded the bluff. The enormous Classic Revival building, designed by John Latenser, Sr., and built between 1900 and 1912, is still in use as a school.

Joslyn Art Museum

The pink-marble Joslyn Art Museum, on Capitol Hill just west of Central High School, is Nebraska's finest example of Art Deco design. Sarah Joslyn established the museum as a memorial to her husband George, a prominent Omahan who made a fortune in the patent medicine business and as president of the Western Newspaper Union, which supplied printing equipment to small newspapers. The Omaha architects John and Alan McDonald designed the building, which opened in 1931. The eight bas-relief panels on the exterior were done by Chicago sculptor John David

OPPOSITE: *The beautifully beaded clothing of an Omaha, perhaps a chief, in the collection of the Joslyn Art Museum. The clothing may have been made in the 1870s.*

Brcin. The museum's Western American collection includes works by Alfred Jacob Miller, George Catlin, and Frederic Remington. The watercolors and drawings of Swiss artist Karl Bodmer documenting his journey with Prince Maximilian of Wied through upper Missouri country in the 1830s form the focal point of the collection. The museum also has sections devoted to the Plains Indians and westward expansion, Victoriana, nineteenth-century Omaha, and European art.

LOCATION: 2200 Dodge Street, HOURS: 10–5 Tuesday–Wednesday, Friday–Saturday, 10–8 Thursday, 12–5 Sunday. FEE: Yes. TELEPHONE: 402–342–3300.

WEST-CENTRAL OMAHA

The first urban pioneer on the bluff-top prairie west of downtown was Bishop James O'Connor, who purchased twelve acres of land at Burt and 36th streets in 1880 for the Academy of the Sacred Heart (now Duchesne). The girls' school was soon surrounded by the comfortable, often palatial, homes of wealthy Omahans. The West Farnam District, as it was called, also came to be known as the Gold Coast. After World War I, many residents moved to neighborhoods farther west, but opulent structures remain in an area roughly bounded by Hawthorne Avenue on the north, Route I-480 on the east, Harney Street on the south, and 40th Street on the west. **Saint Cecilia's Cathedral** (701 North 40th Street) dominated the early-twentieth-century Omaha skyline and was Thomas Rogers Kimball's masterpiece. The Spanish Colonial Revival church, with its two domed towers, barrel-vaulted ceiling, and fine interior ornamentation, was built in 1901. It is among the ten largest cathedrals in the United States.

In 1902 John McDonald designed the **Joslyn Castle** (3902 Davenport Street, 402–595–2199) to simulate a Scottish baronial fortress, complete with battlements and turrets. The **West Central Cathedral District,** 38th Street between Cuming and Davenport streets, begins two blocks to the east of the castle. The architects John and Alan McDonald settled here amid their clients: The senior McDonald's Jacobean Revival residence of 1911 stands at 515 North 38th Street; his son's Georgian Revival home (1920) is down the street at Number 509. The McDonalds also designed the **First Unitarian Church of Omaha** (3114 Harney Street). This Georgian

Revival structure of 1918 resembles the eighteenth-century churches of New England, where Unitarianism originated. In 1907 Thomas Rogers Kimball designed the handsome Jacobean Revival **Gottlieb Storz Mansion** (3708 Farnam Street, 402–345–0620) for one of Omaha's prominent German brewers. The house contains period furnishings; the domed gazebo, or *bierstube*, in the garden was part of the 1898 Trans-Mississippi Exposition.

NORTH OMAHA

Two mid-nineteenth-century settlements, **Florence** and **Sarasota,** were early challengers to Omaha. Florence was established by the Nebraska Winter Quarters Company in 1854 on the site of the town that the Mormons built on the river bluffs in 1846. It prospered as the last outfitting spot for westward-bound Mormons, who trekked through the village until 1863. The **Bank of Florence** (8502 North 30th Street), built in 1856, played an important role in the development of the town. Sarasota was founded in 1856 by the Sulphur Spring Land Company, whose promoters hoped to capitalize on the curative powers of the mineral spring on the site. But the Panic of 1857 brought financial ruin to Sarasota and Florence.

In the 1880s the Omaha banker Herman Kountze began developing a suburb in the vicinity of old Sarasota. **Kountze Place** (Locust and Pratt between 16th and 24th streets) quickly became an enclave of Omaha's rising professional class. The 1898 Trans-Mississippi Exposition, located nearby, renewed development here and **Kountze Park** (Pratt and Pinkney between 19th and 21st streets) was laid out on the Grand Court of the 1898 exposition. During World War II, many of the large homes in this neighborhood were divided into apartments, and Omaha's growing black population began to take up residence in North Omaha. A North Omaha landmark and emblem of this transition is the **Calvin Memorial Presbyterian Church** (3105 North 24th Street), a Classic Revival structure built in 1910 that carried over the predominant architectural style of the Trans-Mississippi Exposition. Another handsome community church is **Saint John's African Methodist Episcopal Church** (2402 North 22d Street), a Prairie-style structure built in 1921. **Sacred Heart Catholic Church** (2218 Binney Street) is a late Gothic Revival structure completed in 1902. A **marker** at 3448 Pinkney Street indicates the birthplace of the black leader Malcolm X, who was born Malcolm Little on May 19, 1925.

*The commanding officer's quarters at Fort Omaha, built for General George Crook.
During the Civil War Crook led a corps under Philip Sheridan in the Shenandoah
Valley. In 1876, during the Sioux Wars, he was defeated by Crazy Horse and Sitting
Bull. In the 1880s, Crook twice captured Geronimo, who escaped both times.*

Fort Omaha and the General Crook House Museum

The Civil War officer and Indian fighter George Crook was commander of the U.S. Army's Department of the Platte from 1875 to 1882
and from 1886 to 1888. Crook's Italianate residence, built in 1878,
was designed to entertain dignitaries inspecting the Western frontier,
including Presidents Ulysses S. Grant and Rutherford B. Hayes. The
house is furnished with Victorian pieces and suggests what army life
on the edge of the frontier was like.

Fort Omaha was established in 1868 as a frontier outpost for
deploying and supplying the army troops that protected the settlers,
the railroad, and the telegraph during the Indian Wars. The post
became a permanent fort in 1878. The Ponca chief Standing Bear
was held at the fort awaiting trial in the case of *Standing Bear v.
Crook*. His lawyers, Andrew Jackson Poppleton and Webster, successfully argued Standing Bear's right to live off reservation land. The
case set important precedents in granting Indians the right of
habeas corpus and recognizing them as "persons" under the law for

the first time in the history of the United States. The fort has been used for other military purposes in the twentieth century, including a Balloon Training School during World War I. It now serves as one of the campuses for Metropolitan Community College.

LOCATION: 30th and Fort streets. HOURS: *Crook House:* 10–4 Tuesday–Friday, 1–4 Sunday. FEE: For Crook House. TELEPHONE: 402–455–9990.

The **Great Plains Black Museum** (2213 Lake Street, 402–345–2212) chronicles the black experience during the settling of the Great Plains. The exhibits document the experience of black women on the Great Plains and the service of blacks in the frontier military.

The Winter Quarters and Mormon Pioneer Cemetery

In the fall of 1846, Brigham Young and the first wave of Mormons heading west from Nauvoo, Illinois, established a base camp on the western bluffs of the Missouri River. They secured permission from the resident Omaha Indians to use the land for two years, quickly

Mormon pioneers prepare to depart from Winter Quarters, their camp on the Missouri, in the spring of 1847 (detail). The scene was painted by Carl Christensen, a Dane who had converted to Mormonism. In the 1850s he retraced the path of the Mormon migration and painted several scenes of the trek as inspirational works.

built 600 dugouts and log houses, and dubbed the village Winter Quarters. The Mormons, who numbered nearly 3,500, were exhausted by their trek across Iowa; hundreds succumbed to malaria, typhoid, diphtheria, and scurvy. The survivors remained at Winter Quarters for another winter, while Brigham Young searched for an appropriate western destination. In the spring of 1848, many of the Mormons resumed their journey west. Those who remained recrossed the river to Kanesville, which became Council Bluffs. By the end of the year, Winter Quarters was abandoned, although the site formed the base for the village of Florence in 1854. Successive waves of Mormons passed through the area on their way to Great Salt Lake for another fifteen years. Perched on a peaceful wooded hilltop, the Mormon Pioneer Cemetery is a poignant reminder of the perseverance of these pilgrims on their westward odyssey. The nearby visitor center has interpretive displays on the Mormon trek.

LOCATION: 3215 State Street. HOURS: *Visitor Center:* 9–Dusk Daily. FEE: None. TELEPHONE: 402–453–9372.

Boys Town

In December 1917, after spending several years running a residence for transient men, Father Edward J. Flanagan opened a home with five boys who had been placed in his care by the juvenile probation officer of Omaha's school system. By Christmas he was taking care of twenty-five boys; in another month he had fifty. In 1921 Father Flanagan moved his charges to a farm he purchased outside of Omaha. To raise money the boys formed a "traveling circus," which performed around the state. In 1936 Boys Town was legally incorporated as a municipality. Two years later the institution became famous when MGM released the motion picture *Boys Town.* The story of Boys Town is chronicled in the Hall of History; Father Flanagan's residence, built in 1927, displays some personal memorabilia.

LOCATION: 132d and West Dodge Road. HOURS: 9–4:30 Daily. FEE: None. TELEPHONE: 402–498–1140.

FORT ATKINSON STATE HISTORICAL PARK

With great ceremony, Lewis and Clark convened a group of Oto and Missouri on these bluffs on August 3, 1804, the first formal meeting with Indians that the explorers held on their famous expe-

In 1822 a foreign visitor described Fort Atkinson as a group of "good-looking white-washed buildings" located on "one of the most picturesque points" on the Missouri River. The fort is being reconstructed on the basis of archaeological investigations.

dition. Lewis and Clark dubbed the spot Council Bluff and recommended it as a site for a fort. The first and largest U.S. military post west of the Missouri River was established here in 1820. The commandant of Fort Atkinson had two missions: to protect American fur-trading interests in the upper Missouri country and to forge alliances with the Indians. Built on a grand scale, the fort garrisoned a thousand soldiers. Its log barracks formed the exterior walls, which measured 455 by 468 feet. The roster of fur-trade explorers and mountain men associated with Fort Atkinson includes William Ashley, Jedediah Smith, Jim Bridger, Mike Fink, William Sublette, and Hugh Glass. Several early explorations of the Mexican settlements at Taos and Santa Fe embarked from the fort. Fort Atkinson turned out to be too far north of the overland path along the Platte River used by emigrants and was abandoned in 1827. Although all physical evidence of the fort has disappeared, it is being reconstructed based on archaeological findings. Several rooms in the west barracks and council house are furnished with reproductions; there are periodic demonstrations of riflery, carpentry, and barrel making. The visitor center displays dishes and hardware excavated at the site, along with uniforms and an exhibit about the Lewis and Clark expedition.

LOCATION: 1 mile east of Route 75 in Fort Calhoun. HOURS: *Park:* 8–5 Daily. *Visitor Center:* June through Labor Day: 9–5 Daily; Labor Day through October: 10–4:30 Wednesday–Sunday. FEE: Yes. TELEPHONE: 402–468–5611.

DE SOTO NATIONAL WILDLIFE REFUGE AND BERTRAND MUSEUM

De Soto National Wildlife Refuge, located twenty-five miles north of Council Bluffs and Omaha on the Missouri River, provides important feeding and resting areas for ducks and other migratory birds on the Central and Mississippi flyways.

During the heyday of steamboating in the nineteenth century, 400 vessels were wrecked along the treacherous Missouri River. About sixty sank in the vicinity of Council Bluffs and Omaha. Efforts began in 1967 to salvage the steamboat *Bertrand,* a fully loaded shallow-water stern-wheeler that sank on April 1, 1865, en route from Saint Louis to Fort Benton in Montana Territory. The *Bertrand* was purportedly carrying a valuable cargo of mercury. Using old maps and newspaper articles and a magnetometer, treasure hunters located the steamboat buried under twenty-eight feet of sand and river silt. A two-year excavation project recovered only nine iron canisters of mercury—most of the mercury was probably retrieved in 1865 as the boat sank—but netted a cache of nineteenth-century merchandise, including clothing, shoes, canned foods, patent medicines, wine, glass, ceramics, black powder, and farming equipment. Artifacts from the *Bertrand* are now housed in the visitor center at the refuge.

LOCATION: Route 30, east of Blair. HOURS: *Visitor Center:* 9–4:30 Daily. *Excavation Site:* Sunrise–Sunset Daily. FEE: Yes. TELEPHONE: 712–642–2772.

In **Fremont,** about thirty-five miles northwest of Omaha, the **Louis E. May Historical Museum** (1643 North Nye Avenue, 402–721–4515) preserves the handsome Theron Nye House (1874). In the early twentieth century, Nye's son commissioned the

Milwaukee architectural firm of Ferry & Clas to alter the structure from Italianate to Classic Revival. The house contains lavish furnishings and items of local history.

The **Love-Larson Opera House** (545 North Broad Street) recalls the days when Fremont was a bustling railroad, grain-freighting, and farm center. Built in 1888, the brick and stone structure has Richardsonian Romanesque touches. It has been restored as a community performance hall.

NORTHEAST NEBRASKA

JOHN G. NEIHARDT CENTER

With his shock of wavy hair and piercing eyes, John G. Neihardt had the demeanor of a lyric poet. Seldom far from the Great Plains, which were his subject, Neihardt wrote poems that drew on the traditions of the Plains Indians and the legends of the mountain men. Neihardt was born in Illinois in 1881 and moved to Wayne, Nebraska, with his sisters and widowed mother when he was 10. In 1900 he moved to nearby Bancroft, a village on the edge of the Winnebago-Omaha Indian Reservation, where he worked for an Indian trader and edited the *Bancroft Blade*. In Bancroft he began his life's work, the epic poem *A Cycle of the West,* and married the sculptor Mona Martinsen. In 1920 the family moved to Missouri, where Neihardt was a literary editor for the *St. Louis Post-Dispatch* and poet in residence at the University of Missouri. Late in life he returned to Lincoln, Nebraska, where he lived until shortly before his death at the age of 92. His ashes, along with those of his wife, were scattered from an airplane over the Missouri River. The Neihardt Center has first editions of his work, original manuscripts, and memorabilia. The study where Neihardt worked is in a simple clapboard building that contains period furnishings. In 1921 Neihardt was named poet laureate of Nebraska; in 1982 the title was extended in perpetuity.

LOCATION: Elm and Washington streets, Bancroft. HOURS: 9–5 Monday–Saturday, 1:30–5 Sunday. FEE: None. TELEPHONE: 402–648–3388.

One of the finest rural churches in Nebraska stands southeast of Bancroft near the town of **Lyons.** A white frame Gothic Revival structure with German folk detailing, the **Saint John's Lutheran Church** (three miles south of Lyons on Route 77; one mile east on the gravel road), also known as the *Deutsche Evangelische Lutherische Saint Johannes Kirche,* was built in 1902 by German immigrants who settled in the area in the 1870s.

NELIGH MILLS HISTORIC SITE

The small town of Neligh stands on the banks of the Elkhorn River in rural northeastern Nebraska. Like many frontier towns, it sprang up along a watercourse that afforded power for milling. The earliest gristmill in Nebraska was built in 1821 by the soldiers at Fort Atkinson. By the 1870s flour milling was the biggest industry in the state. As the railroads penetrated the plains in the 1880s, small-town mills installed grain elevators, and many of these majestic towers still punctuate the landscape. The 1930s brought drought, the Depression, and a demand for uniform-quality flour that the small-roller mills could not provide, and so these rural mills began to close. Neligh Mills, one of two extant nineteenth-century mills in Nebraska

The Neligh Mills Historic Site preserves a complex of grain elevators and water-powered mills that produced flour for an international market.

(the other is in the far southwest at Champion), was started in 1873 by the town's founder, John D. Neligh. In 1886 the stone burrs of the grindstone were replaced with steel rollers; this improved the quality of the flour and increased capacity. The 1880s milling equipment is in place and the mill office contains the original furniture.

LOCATION: N Street and Wylie Drive, Neligh. HOURS: May through September: 8–5 Monday–Saturday, 1:30–5 Sunday; October through April: By appointment. FEE: Yes. TELEPHONE: 402-887-4303.

SOUTHEAST NEBRASKA

LINCOLN

Lincoln is the home of the state government and the University of Nebraska. Visitors to the city can hardly miss the two large symbols of these institutions—the towering capitol, which dominates the city's skyline, and the 76,000-seat Memorial Stadium, where an estimated 6 percent of the Nebraska population gathers each autumn to watch their beloved Cornhuskers play football. Lincoln lies in a basin about fifty miles south of the Platte River, where Salt Creek and other streams once converged. Indians used to gather salt deposits from the area's saline springs, and prior to settlement, some early entrepreneurs did a brisk business harvesting and selling the salt. In 1859 pioneers founded the town of Lancaster, named after Lancaster County, Pennsylvania. The town did not flourish; in fact, when Lancaster was selected as the new state capital in 1867, it had fewer than fifty inhabitants. During the search for a capital, the Omaha delegation pushed through legislation requiring that the new capital be called Lincoln. The Omahans hoped that having to bear the name of the Great Emancipator would rile Nebraska Democrats, who tended to concentrate south of the Platte. South Platters, as they were called, took the name change in stride. In 1869 the legislature established the University of Nebraska. The first railroad to Lincoln—the Burlington & Missouri from Plattsmouth—arrived in 1870.

Nebraska State Capitol

In the early 1900s, the capitol building in Lincoln began to sink and crumble. After much debate a committee headed by Thomas Rogers

Kimball selected a New York architect, Bertram Grosvenor Goodhue, to design a sturdier structure. Ground was broken in 1922. Two years later Goodhue died, but his associates executed the design that was to be his masterpiece. Known as the Tower of the Plains, the Nebraska State Capitol is a 400-foot spire topped with a bronze statue of a man sowing grain. The building marks a radical break with traditional statehouse architecture. Goodhue selected durable but costly Indiana limestone as his building material—one of the items that brought the cost of the capitol to $10 million. The artwork throughout the building stresses Nebraska's Indian heritage and the history of its agrarian pioneers. Lee Lawrie designed the bas-relief exterior sculptures as well as the sower atop the building, and Hildreth Meiere executed the spectacular mosaic murals in the interior.

LOCATION: 15th and K streets. HOURS: 9–4 Monday–Friday, 10–4 Saturday, 1–4 Sunday. FEE: None. TELEPHONE: 402–471–0448.

The Nebraska State Capitol (opposite), was designed on a heroic scale by Bertram Grosvenor Goodhue, who also designed the campus of West Point. The North Vestibule of the capitol (above) features murals done in 1965 by James Penney, The First Furrow and The First Camp Fire. On the ceiling is a series of mosaics in a style suggestive of the Bible, The Gifts of Nature, by Hildreth Meiere.

The Italianate-style Thomas P. Kennard House, built in 1869. Kennard, one of the commissioners who had selected the site of the capital, built the house as a display of faith in the new city—an Omaha newspaper had asserted that, except on business, "Nobody will ever go to Lincoln."

Thomas P. Kennard and William J. Ferguson Houses

Standing side by side on H Street southeast of the Capitol, the Kennard and Ferguson houses preserve a sense of life in early Lincoln. Secretary of State Thomas Kennard was one of three commissioners appointed in 1867 to select a site for the new capital. The Ohio-born, Indiana-reared Kennard had come to Nebraska as a young man and became involved in politics. To exhibit confidence in the fledgling capital, each of the commissioners built a commodious Victorian home designed by the Chicago architect John Winchell. Of the three, only the Kennard residence remains. Kennard lived in the yellow-painted brick house until his wife's death in 1887. The house contains 1870s American furnishings including a cylinder desk used by Nebraska's first governor, David Butler. The Ferguson House (1910), a brick Renaissance Revival mansion, has tourist information but is not open for tours.

LOCATION: 1627 H Street. HOURS: 9–12, 1–4:30, Tuesday–Friday; June through August: also 1–5 Saturday–Sunday. FEE: Yes. TELEPHONE: 402–471–4764.

O Street, the main thoroughfare in downtown Lincoln, features several interesting structures. The **U.S. Post Office and Courthouse,** at 920 O Street, was constructed between 1874 and 1879 and served for many years as the city hall. The handsome Second Empire limestone building was designed by Alfred B. Mullett and William Appleton Potter, supervising architects of the U.S. Treasury. The **Terminal Building** (947 O Street), a ten-story reinforced-concrete tower sheathed in white glazed terra-cotta, was completed in 1916. It served as the headquarters for the Lincoln Traction Company, the city's main streetcar company from 1909 to 1943. **Gold's Galleria** (1033 O Street) is a handsome six-story commercial structure with Gothic Revival motifs; the first portion, called Gold's Department Store, was built in 1924. The **Rock Island Depot** (1944 O Street) is a graceful Chateauesque red-brick building of 1893 that now houses a bank.

Museum of Nebraska History

This museum chronicles the history of plains people from prehistoric times through the 1950s. Exhibits document the immigration of Europeans to Nebraska and the 1862 Homestead Act. Period settings include a Pawnee earthlodge from about 1865, a Winnebago Indian reservation house of 1915, a Victorian parlor of the 1860s, a sod-house interior from about 1885, and a walk-through turn-of-the-century general store. Shell ornaments, bone tools, projectile points, and ceremonial objects are also on display.

LOCATION: 15th and P streets. HOURS: 9–5 Monday–Saturday, 1:30–5 Sunday. FEE: None. TELEPHONE: 402–471–4754.

On the downtown campus of the **University of Nebraska,** the **Sheldon Memorial Art Gallery** (12th and R streets, 402–472–2461) houses one of the region's most important collections of twentieth-century American art in an "impeccable box" designed in 1962 by Philip Johnson. The **Center for Great Plains Studies Art Collection** (second floor of Love Library, 13th and R streets, 402–472–6220) includes paintings, drawings, and sculptures by Albert Bierstadt, Charles M. Russell, Frederic Remington, and Solon Borglum. The oldest extant building on the campus is the lovely Richardsonian Romanesque **Architecture Hall,** which was originally built as the Old University Library in 1895.

The **Museum of American Historical Society of Germans from Russia** (631 D Street, 402–474–3363) has exhibits of artifacts and memorabilia associated with the mass migration to America of Germans from Russia in the late nineteenth century. The museum is located in the **South Bottoms Historic District** (bounded roughly by A, 9th, 2d, and M streets and Salt Creek), where the Volga Germans concentrated when they emigrated from Russia in the 1870s. Several structures typical of their culture have been gathered on the museum's grounds, including a small house, summer kitchen, chapel, and country store. All are furnished with turn-of-the-century items. One highlight in this ethnically rich neighborhood is the simple **German Evangelical Lutheran Freidens Church,** located directly behind the museum.

Fairview: The William Jennings Bryan House

William Jennings Bryan was Lincoln's most famous citizen. A rumpled, earnest man with a golden voice, Bryan had an uncommon knack for articulating the hopes and fears of the common people. He was an advocate for farmers and the working class, an avowed enemy of the rich, and a three-time Democratic candidate for president. During his lifetime, Bryan was the highest-paid lecturer in America. Born in 1860 in Salem, Illinois, he moved to Lincoln in 1887 as a young lawyer with his wife, Mary Baird Bryan. In 1890 he was elected to Congress as a Democrat in a largely Republican district and held that office until 1894, when he lost a bid for the Senate. Next he became editor-in-chief of the *Omaha World-Herald* and embarked on the Chautauqua lecture circuit. His vehement opposition to the gold standard, expressed most eloquently in his famous "Cross of Gold" speech at the Democratic national convention in 1896, catapulted him into presidential politics. Bryan was only 36 years old when he was nominated for president, and although his exhausting 18,000-mile campaign across America failed to win him the presidency, it secured his fame as an orator. He was defeated by William McKinley in the 1896 and 1900 elections and by William Howard Taft in 1908.

In January 1901 Bryan produced the first issue of the *Commoner,* a weekly newspaper wherein he railed against the influence of wealth in politics. The paper was widely subscribed and a financial success for Bryan. Having orchestrated Woodrow Wilson's nomination in 1912, Bryan was selected to be his secretary of state, a position he held from 1913 to 1915. Bryan's last crusade was against the teaching of evolution. In 1925 he served as a prosecuting attorney in the Scopes trial, during which, in an unusual move, defense attorney Clarence Darrow summoned the great orator as a witness. Scopes's conviction was overturned on a technicality, but Bryan had undergone a withering cross-examination by Darrow and died in his sleep five days after the trial.

Bryan's country estate is situated on a knoll southeast of Lincoln. The brick house, completed in 1903, combines the Queen Anne and the Classic Revival styles. The Bryans' three children grew up in this house, which contains family mementoes along with original and period furnishings.

LOCATION: 4900 Sumner Avenue on the campus of Bryan Memorial Hospital. HOURS: 1–4 Tuesday–Friday. FEE: None. TELEPHONE: 402–483–8303.

One of the largest expanses of virgin tall grass in Nebraska, **Nine-Mile Prairie** (West Fletcher Avenue, one mile west of Northwest 48th Street, 402–472–2720) is maintained by the University of Nebraska. This beautiful prairie was the site of pioneering research by the plant ecologist John E. Weaver in the 1920s.

NEBRASKA CITY

This handsome old river town began in the 1850s as a trading post on a cutoff of the Oregon Trail. A variety of nineteenth-century Greek Revival, Gothic Revival, Italianate, Georgian Revival, and Queen Anne commercial structures are preserved within the **Nebraska City Historic District** (3d and 19th streets and Fifth and Central avenues). The Greek Revival–Italianate **Otoe County Courthouse** (11th Street and Central Avenue), built in 1865, is the oldest public building in use in the state. The **U.S. Courthouse and Post Office** (202 South 8th Street) was designed by W. E. Bell, a supervising architect for the U.S. Treasury. The red-brick structure of 1889 combines Chateauesque and Richardsonian Romanesque elements. The **Wildwood Period House** (Steinhart Park Road, 402–873–6340) is a Gothic Revival country home built for Jasper Ware in 1869.

Arbor Lodge State Historical Park

Arbor Lodge encompasses the grounds, greenhouse, and home of Julius Sterling Morton, the frontier politician and newspaper editor who introduced a resolution establishing the first Arbor Day in Nebraska in 1872. Subsequently the lower forty-eight states and numerous foreign countries adopted special days for planting trees. Morton moved to Nebraska Territory from Michigan in 1854 as a young man and remained for the rest of his life. It is appropriate that an advocate of trees should hail from the treeless plains. In the nineteenth century, Nebraska pioneers planted trees to fight soil erosion, provide windbreaks, protect livestock, and perhaps to remind them of the eastern woodlands they left behind. Some agrarians even believed, erroneously, that planting trees would increase rainfall on the semiarid plains. Morton codified the passion of frontier Nebraskans for trees. He and Governor Robert Furnas helped to establish fruit orchards in the southeastern corner of Nebraska. Morton's farmstead began in 1855 as a modest four-room frame house and evolved into a fifty-two-room Georgian Revival mansion. Expansions continued after his death in 1902. The house contains original furniture, documents, and memorabilia.

> LOCATION: 2d and Centennial avenues. HOURS: Park: 8–Dusk Daily, Weather Permitting. June through August: 9–5 Daily; Spring and Fall: Shorter hours; January through February: Closed. FEE: Yes. TELEPHONE: 402–873–7222.

The quaint village of **Brownville** was once a booming steamboat landing, ferry crossing, and overland freight terminus. This river town was founded in 1854, just a few months after the Oto surrendered title to their lands in the area. Brownville failed to secure a railhead and relinquished the county seat to nearby Auburn; by the turn of the century it had slipped into quiescence. There are many charming domestic, commercial, and religious structures in the **Brownville Historic District** (1st, 7th, Nemaha, and Richard streets) dating from the town's heyday. The **Brownville Historical Society Museum** (Main Street, 402–825–6001), located in the **Captain Bailey House** (ca. 1858), displays Indian artifacts, costumes, glass, and farming implements. The *Captain Meriwether Lewis,* docked at the Brownville land-

OPPOSITE: *Arbor Lodge, the home of Julius Sterling Morton, a lover of trees who found himself on the treeless prairie and became the founder of Arbor Day.*

ing, is a 1931 U.S. Army Corps of Engineers steam-powered side-wheel dredge that was used until 1969 to maintain the Missouri River channel as part of the flood-protection program. The vessel is now the **Museum of Missouri River History** (402–825–3341), and it features exhibits on geology, Indian culture, and steamboat history.

HOMESTEAD NATIONAL MONUMENT

Tucked away on a country road in southeastern Nebraska, Homestead National Monument captures the primeval quiet that confronted pioneers on the Great Plains in the 1860s. The park is situated on the quarter-section (160-acre) claim of Daniel Freeman, thought to be one of the first applicants to file under the Homestead Act of 1862. None of the Freeman structures remains, but the 1867 **Palmer–Epard Cabin** was relocated to the site from a nearby homestead. The log structure is typical of frontier houses in the eastern portion of Nebraska, where timber was available. A trail winds along Cub Creek, through the streamside woods and tall-grass prairie, past

The Palmer-Epard cabin, built by pioneers in 1867, was moved to Homestead National Monument from a nearby farm to represent dwellings of the homestead era.

various building sites and the Freeman family cemetery. Restoration work on the prairie began in 1939, one of the first such programs in the United States. Exhibits in the visitor center recount the history of the homestead movement, beginning with the efforts of Missouri senator Thomas Hart Benton in 1825. Many documentary photographs and pioneer artifacts are on display.

The **Freeman School,** a one-room brick schoolhouse used from 1872 until 1967, also served as a church and polling place. In 1899 Daniel Freeman took the school board to court because the teacher was giving Bible instruction in the school. The case attracted national attention. Freeman lost in county court, but in 1902 the Nebraska Supreme Court, upholding the principle of separation of church and state, ruled in Freeman's favor.

LOCATION: Route 4, 4.5 miles west of Beatrice. HOURS: *Visitor Center:* 8:30–5 Daily; *Trail and Outdoor Exhibits:* Dawn–Dusk Daily. FEE: None. TELEPHONE: 402–223–3514.

In nearby **Beatrice,** the **Gage County Historical Society Museum** (2d and Court streets, 402–228–1679) is housed in the 1906 Classic Revival Burlington Depot. Its exhibits pertain to the railroad and local farming, industry, and community life. The historical society also owns the three-story limestone **Elijah Filley Stone Barn** (1874), which was built into the side of a hill.

ROCK CREEK STATION
STATE HISTORICAL PARK

Rock Creek Station, set amid prairie etched with rugged ravines, is steeped in the history of the Oregon Trail, the Pony Express, and the saga of "Wild Bill" Hickok. Rock Creek Station was established in 1857 as a road ranch for travelers on the Oregon Trail. In 1859 David McCanles abandoned his plans to go to the Colorado gold fields and bought Rock Creek Station, building a toll bridge across the creek. The buildings on the facing banks came to be known as the East and West Ranch. McCanles leased, and later sold, the East Ranch to the overland freight company of Russell, Majors & Waddell, who used the facilities as a stagecoach stop and remounting station for their Pony Express riders. Early in 1861 James Butler "Wild Bill" Hickok, then 23 years old, was hired as a stable hand. On July 12 at the East Ranch, Hickok and two other stage company employees killed McCanles and two of his hired hands, perhaps in a dispute over

The Freeman School, now part of the Homestead National Monument, opened in 1872 with an enrollment of fourteen students. OPPOSITE: *Freeman's students used the enormously popular, heavily moralistic* Eclectic Readers, *anthologies of American classics developed in the 1830s by William Holmes McGuffey.*

money that the stage company owed McCanles. Hickok and his accomplices were tried for murder in nearby Beatrice and acquitted on pleas of self-defense. The "Rock Creek Massacre" became part of the gunfighting lore that would follow Wild Bill wherever he went. Shortly after the trial Hickok headed for Missouri to fight in the Civil War on the Union side. Colonel Ward Nichols presented a thrilling but groundless account of the fray at Rock Creek Station in the February 1867 issue of *Harper's*. The article portrayed Hickok as an adroit and heroic gunman outnumbered by "blood-thirsty devils." Though Hickok repudiated the account, it was the first of many literary embellishments on the career of the dashing frontier scout and marshal. Hickok was shot dead in Deadwood, South Dakota, in 1876.

Replicas of the toll bridge and the East and West Ranch buildings have been constructed on site. The visitor center presents photographs and artifacts gathered during archaeological investigations.

LOCATION: Off Route 136, 6 miles south of Jansen. HOURS: Grounds: 8–Dusk Daily; *Visitor Center:* June through August: 9–5 Daily; Mid-April through May and September through October: Saturday 9–5, Sunday 1–5. FEE: Yes. TELEPHONE: 402–729–5777.

In nearby **Fairbury,** the 1892 **Jefferson County Courthouse** (5th and E streets) is a massive Richardsonian Romanesque limestone edifice. The **Woral C. Smith Lime Kiln and House** (four miles north of Fairbury on River Road) preserves the vestiges of the lime-burning industry, which produced quick lime used in plastering. Smith opened the kiln on the banks of the Little Blue River in 1874 and built his limestone house two years later. The house contains family memorabilia and items of local history.

REPUBLICAN RIVER VALLEY

WILLA CATHER
STATE HISTORIC SITE

Readers of Willa Cather who make a pilgrimage to Red Cloud, her childhood home on the rolling Nebraska prairie, will be struck by how much the contemporary town resembles Black Hawk, Sweet

The simple house in Red Cloud to which Willa Cather's family moved when she was nine. The Pulitzer Prize-winning novelist described the house in several of her works.

Water, Frankfort, and the other fictional settlements in her writings. The quiet, unassuming town of Red Cloud lies in the Republican River valley along the route of the old Burlington Railroad. In the 1880s eight passenger trains a day passed through en route to Kansas City, Chicago, and Denver.

The Cather home, built around 1878, has been carefully preserved, as have the **Farmers' and Merchants' Bank, Burlington Depot,** and **Pavelka Farmstead,** also associated with her writings. The Cathers, originally from Virginia, moved to Red Cloud in 1884, after an eighteen-month attempt at Nebraska farming. By today's standards the two-bedroom house with an attic seems inadequate for four (later seven) children, parents, a grandmother, servant girl, and cousin. Cather spent six years in Red Cloud, during which time her family recognized her precocious interest in reading, writing, languages, and drama. As a young woman, Cather wanted to be a surgeon, and one of her earliest extant pieces of writing is an oration on the importance of scientific investigation, which she presented at her

The parlor of the Cather House contains a stove similar to those described in Cather's fictional accounts, along with many furnishings that belonged to the Cather family.

high school graduation. Its opening sentence, "All human history is a record of an emigration, an exodus from barbarism to civilization," encapsulates the pioneer experience on the Great Plains. In 1890 she left Red Cloud to attend the university in Lincoln. The Cather House resembles the one described in *Song of the Lark:* "a low storey-and-a-half-house, with a wing built on at the right and a kitchen addition at the back, everything a little on the slant—roofs, windows, and doors." It contains both original and period furnishings. Cather eventually turned to Southwestern themes in her writing.

LOCATION: 326 North Webster Street, Red Cloud. HOURS: 8–5 Monday–Saturday, 1–5 Sunday; Call for times of scheduled tours. FEE: Yes. TELEPHONE: 402–746–2653.

The stately Chateauesque **Farmers' and Merchants' Bank** stands on the main thoroughfare in **Red Cloud.** The bank was built in 1889 by Silas Garber, founder of Red Cloud, two-term governor of Nebraska, and Red Cloud's most prominent citizen in the late 1800s. Garber was the model for Captain Forrester in Willa Cather's *A Lost Lady.*

McCOOK

This farming community in the Republican River valley was a division point on the Burlington Railroad. From 1902 until 1944, the town was the home base for the maverick politician George Norris. The Ohio-born lawyer moved to Nebraska in 1885 and threw himself into local politics. In 1902 he was elected to the U.S. House of Representatives, where he served until 1912, when he ran successfully for the Senate. He was a senator for thirty years. Ostensibly a Republican, he supported Franklin D. Roosevelt and other Democrats. Norris drafted the Tennessee Valley Authority Act (1933) and the Rural Electrification Act (1935)—legislation that had an enormous impact on the lives of rural Americans. The simple stucco **Senator George Norris House** (706 Norris Avenue, 308–345–8484) was built in 1886 and remodeled in the 1930s. It contains original furnishings and memorabilia from Norris's long tenure in Congress. A block away stands the **H. P. Sutton House** (602 Norris Avenue, private). Built in 1908, it is the only work in Nebraska of Frank Lloyd Wright. The nearby **High Plains Museum** (421 Norris Avenue, 308–345–3661) contains nineteenth-century costumes, kitchen

implements, apothecary items, farm tools, railroad memorabilia, and
military uniforms.

Just east of **Trenton** on Route 34 is the **Massacre Canyon Monument,**
which marks the site of the last clash between the Sioux and
Pawnee. The longstanding antipathy between the Sioux and Pawnee
had been aggravated by the Pawnee alliance with whites. Many
Pawnee served as scouts for the U.S. Army, and others under Sky
Chief guarded railroad construction crews. On August 5, 1873, the
Sioux attacked a hunting party of Pawnee, killing about 150, includ-
ing Sky Chief. Likenesses of the Sioux John Grass and the Pawnee
Ruling-His-Sun are carved on the granite monument.

CHAMPION MILL STATE HISTORICAL PARK

Champion Mill, a looming frame structure with handsome clerestory
windows, stands on the Frenchman River in the southwestern corner of Nebraska. The original 1888 mill was destroyed by a fire and
rebuilt in 1892. In the 1930s and 1940s, Champion Mill produced
two grades of flour—Valley Pride and Prairie Rose. Flour milling was
discontinued during World War II, but as the last functioning water-
powered mill in Nebraska, Champion Mill continued to grind and
mix feed until 1968. The machinery at Champion Mill is still run by
water power to produce flour for souvenirs. The mill pond is used
for swimming, canoeing, and fishing.

> LOCATION: 2d and Mill streets, Champion. HOURS: Memorial Day
> through Labor Day: 9–5 Daily. FEE: Yes. TELEPHONE: 308–882–5860.

PLATTE RIVER VALLEY

The Platte River runs the entire length of Nebraska. Its two forks,
the North Platte and South Platte, enter western Nebraska from
Wyoming and Colorado respectively. These two rivers join at the
town of North Platte to form the main stem of the river, which flows
eastward to join the Missouri River at Plattsmouth, twenty miles
south of Omaha. The river valley is a shallow, wide trough lipped
with low sandy hills and mesas. Between 1841 and 1866, 500,000
immigrants passed through this valley along the Oregon and
Mormon trails. In the 1860s the tracks of the Union Pacific followed

the Platte Valley to Cheyenne, Wyoming, and points west. Today Route I-80 retraces a good part of that route. In the nineteenth-century, the Platte River was a shallow, treeless, sand-laden watercourse that flooded sometimes to two or three miles wide. A series of dams on the North Platte in Wyoming and western Nebraska—most of them built during the New Deal era—radically altered the character of the river, so that today Nebraska's most historic landmark is a narrow, tree-lined stream. This tour travels east to west.

GRAND ISLAND

Grand Island is named for a cluster of wooded islands in the Platte River that early French-Canadian fur traders called *La Grande Ile.* The first settlers were German immigrants who arrived from Davenport, Iowa, in 1857. The Union Pacific Railroad laid out the present town in 1866. The **Hall County Courthouse** (1st and Locust streets) is a splendid Beaux-Arts structure built by Thomas Rogers Kimball in 1904. The **William Stolley Homestead** (Stolley Park Road) was the home of the leader of the Germans who founded Grand Island. The original log portion of the house was built in 1859; the two-story clapboard addition dates to 1893.

Stuhr Museum of the Prairie Pioneer

The Stuhr Museum is a 200-acre compound that includes a re-created railroad town and three exhibit halls. Indoor exhibits feature pioneer clothing, tools, furnishings, and documentary photographs of frontier life. The Fonner rotunda houses Great Plains Indian artifacts and memorabilia associated with the frontier cattle industry. The railroad town consists of more than fifty nineteenth-century structures that have been relocated from the area, including a bank, general store, church, farmstead, and the cottage where Henry Fonda, a Grand Islander, was born; all contain period furnishings. A steam locomotive of 1908 travels the site. In summer about 200 antique automobiles and farm machinery are displayed on the museum grounds.

LOCATION: Junction of Routes 34 and 281. HOURS: *Attractions:* May through mid-October: 9–5 Daily; *Main Building and Rotunda:* 9–5 Monday–Saturday, 1–5 Sunday. FEE: Yes. TELEPHONE: 308–385–5316.

A Danish Lutheran Church with an unusually patterned steeple, built in 1888 by two members of its congregation, has been preserved in the Stuhr Museum of the Prairie Pioneer. OVERLEAF: *The sons of Zachariah Perry enjoy watermelon and cards at their homestead in Custer County in 1886.*

In **Aurora** the **Plainsman Museum** (210 16th Street, 402–694–6531) features murals and mosaics depicting an Indian buffalo hunt, the Coronado expedition of 1541, and a stagecoach stop on the Oregon Trail. It has displays of china, clocks, agricultural implements, and firearms, as well as a log cabin of 1859, sod house, and a rural chapel.

The town of **Hastings** was founded in 1872 at the junction of the Saint Joseph & Denver City Railroad and the Burlington Railroad; by 1880 it was an important division point between Chicago and Denver. The **Burlington Station** (1st Street and Saint Joseph's Avenue) suggests the importance of the railroad to the town; the charming Spanish Colonial Revival station of 1902 was designed by Thomas Rogers Kimball. The **Hastings Museum** (1330 North Burlington Avenue, 402–461–4629) features dioramas of Great Plains natural history and Indian culture and period rooms from a sod house and Victorian residence. In addition, collections of firearms, coins, china, glassware, and clothing are also on display.

The town of **Kearney** began as the junction of the Union Pacific and Burlington lines on the north bank of the Platte River. It was platted in 1871 and named for the military outpost south of the river; the misspelling of General Stephen Watts Kearny's name has

The one-room, red brick Antioch School, near Pauline, built in 1912 to replace earlier sod and frame schools. Classes were held in this modest building until 1965.

endured. The **George W. Frank House** (308–234–8284), on the Kearney State College campus, evokes the town's boom years before the Panic of 1893. Built in 1889, the house combines elements of the Shingle and Richardsonian Romanesque styles and contains both original and period furniture.

FORT KEARNY STATE HISTORICAL PARK

Established in 1848, Fort Kearny was the first in a chain of military installations along the Oregon Trail and was originally located near present-day Nebraska City. That site, however, proved to be about a hundred miles east of the main Oregon Trail and thirty miles south of the Mormon Trail, so the army sent out scouts to choose a better location. They found the perfect place south of the Platte River at the point where the Oregon Trail converged with the Mormon Trail. The relocated Fort Kearny was just west of the heavily forested La Grande Ile, which provided the lumber to build the fort.

With the opening of the California gold fields, Fort Kearny became a busy way station. Between 1849 and 1850, 30,000 people bound for California, Oregon, and the Great Salt Lake passed by the fort. Fort Kearny was the base for the Pawnee scouts, organized in 1864 by Frank North, a white settler and trusted companion of the Indians. Frank's brother Luther served as a company officer of the Pawnee scouts. Known as the "Fighting Norths," the brothers later went into the ranching business with Buffalo Bill Cody. Probably the most harrowing time at the fort was during the summer of 1864, when Sioux and Cheyenne raids on wagon trains along the Platte and Little Blue rivers peaked. Afterward, Indian troubles shifted to the west and south. The last task of Fort Kearny personnel was to provide protection for Union Pacific crews from 1866 to 1867; the fort closed four years later.

Replicas of the blacksmith-carpenter shop, built of adobe brick with a sod roof, and of one of the three original stockades and the powder magazine can be seen on site. Two veteran cottonwoods remain from the stand that bordered the parade ground. Even as saplings, these trees were landmarks on the vast prairie: An early visitor to the fort wrote, "They are the only bushes that can be seen in any direction except a few straggling ones on the banks of the Platte a few miles distant."

LOCATION: Route 10, 8 miles southeast of Kearney. HOURS: Memorial Day through Labor Day: 9–5 Daily. FEE: Yes. TELEPHONE: 308–865–5305.

Just west of Fort Kearny stood **Dobytown,** a staging area for Russell, Majors & Waddell's freight operations and a gathering place for merchants, blacksmiths, stock tenders, and drivers. Dobytown had a thriving subculture of saloons, gambling houses, and brothels, serving travelers and soldiers alike. A soldier from Ohio wrote that the tables in the gambling houses were always full, and the "languages used were Mexican, French, English, and profanity. Occasionally some exultant winner would express his delight by firing his pistol through the roof or into the sod walls and a little loose dirt would trickle down." The town faded rapidly after the fort was closed. A historical **marker** on Route 50A about one-and-a-half miles west of the fort indicates the site of Dobytown.

Located in the small farm community of **Minden,** the **Harold Warp Pioneer Village** (Routes 6/34 and 10, 308–832–1181) is a virtual encyclopedia of Americana. More than 50,000 historical items, from antique automobiles, airplanes, bicycles, farm machinery, and a steam-powered carousel to household appliances and musical instruments, are on display. Crafts such as spinning, weaving, broom making, and glass blowing are demonstrated on the grounds. The village includes a sod house, a land office, a store, and a country school.

In **Lexington** the **Dawson County Historical Museum** (805 North Taft Street, 308–324–5340) preserves artifacts from the Union Pacific Railroad and pioneer settlements in the area. These include a depot from the 1880s, a steam locomotive built in 1903, a log cabin, a one-room schoolhouse, and a biplane designed by a local inventor. The museum features an exhibit on the importance of corn and alfalfa to the area. **Fort McPherson National Cemetery** (Route N-56A), located two miles south of **Maxwell,** was established in 1873 on the grounds of Fort McPherson, a military outpost which was active from 1863 to 1887.

BUFFALO BILL RANCH
STATE HISTORICAL PARK

Scout's Rest Ranch, on the outskirts of the town of North Platte, was once the 4,000-acre ranch of the frontier guide, buffalo hunter, and showman William F. "Buffalo Bill" Cody. Born in Iowa and raised in Kansas, Cody went to work for Russell and Majors when he was eleven years old. From 1867 to 1868 he shot buffalo to feed the Kansas Pacific construction crews; he is said to have killed 4,280 buffalo in an eight-month period.

Cody's first exposure to show business occurred in 1872 when he performed in a play about the frontier. His own famous Wild West Show evolved from a Fourth of July extravaganza that he staged in North Platte in 1882. From 1883 until 1913, his traveling show attracted large audiences both here and abroad; the dapper Cody became rich and famous. Cody lived at Scout's Rest Ranch off and on until the turn of the century. In 1902 he moved to Cody, Wyoming, a town he had founded six years before. Cody suffered a series of financial reversals and sold his ranch in 1911. He died in Denver in 1917 at the age of 70. The handsome ranch house, built in 1886, was largely conceived by his sister Julia and her husband, Al Goodman, who managed the ranch. It contains both original and period furnishings. Outbuildings include a horse barn and a log

"Buffalo Bill" Cody made his home here in the 1880s and 1890s when he was not touring with his Wild West Show.

cabin, both built in 1877, that originally stood on another Cody ranch on the Dismal River.

LOCATION: Buffalo Bill Avenue, North Platte. HOURS: August: 10–8 Daily; May and September through October: 9–5 Monday–Saturday, 1–5 Sunday; April: 9–5 Monday–Friday. FEE: Yes. TELEPHONE: 308–535–8035.

California Hill, just west of **Brule,** is another important landmark on the Oregon Trail. This was the first major grade that westward-bound travelers had to climb after leaving the Missouri River. The thousands of wagons that crested the hill have left deep ruts.

LAKE McCONAUGHY

The Reclamation Act of 1902 and New Deal legislation during the Depression established programs intended to develop the water resources of the Great Plains. The resulting water-control projects undertaken across the western United States remain marvels of engineering. The last in the chain of reservoirs on the North Platte River is Lake McConaughy, an immense body of blue water edged with white-sand beaches that lends a Mediterranean touch to a region of wheat farms and cattle ranches. The reservoir, with a storage capacity of 2 million acre-feet of water, is held in check by **Kingsley Dam,** a massive earth-fill structure 162 feet tall and 3 miles long. The hydroelectric dam was completed in 1941; the impounded water is used to irrigate crops in three counties. The **Central Nebraska Public Power and Irrigation District** (308–284–2332) conducts tours by appointment and for groups.

Just west of Lake McConaughy, **Ash Hollow State Historical Park** (Route 26, 308–778–5651) preserves an old campsite on the Oregon Trail. The visitor center has exhibits and information on the historic route, and the summit of nearby Windlass Hill affords a panorama of the old wagon trail; down below the ruts in the road are still visible.

In the town of **Sidney** on the Lodgepole Creek, **Historic Fort Sidney** (6th and Jackson streets, 308–254–2150), was originally a military post mandated to protect Union Pacific construction crews. The fort was used from 1875 until 1894. Several buildings have been restored. A museum is located in the married-officers' quarters, an unusual building with two front doors, two sets of banisters, and so on.

T H E   S A N D   H I L L S

The Sand Hills are windblown sand dunes covered with prairie grass that cover thousands of square miles in northwest Nebraska. This area north of the Platte River and west of the Loup River system was one of the last strongholds of the Sioux. With white settlement, the Sand Hills became cattle country, and ranching remains the principal industry today. The undulating dunescapes along Route 83 to Valentine and along Route 2 toward Chadron offer some of the most beautiful landscapes in America. The northwest edge of the Sand Hills borders the Pine Ridge area, a narrow band of sandstone bluffs covered with ponderosa pine that stretches for some twenty miles along Route 20. The southern edge of the Sand Hills is punctuated with oddly eroded sandstone buttes and mesas that once served as trail markers for pioneers on the Oregon and Mormon trails. The first of the landmarks to greet westward-bound travelers was the **Courthouse and Jail Rocks,** which can be seen today from Route 88, about five miles south of **Bridgeport.**

CHIMNEY ROCK NATIONAL HISTORIC SITE

The most awe-inspiring of the Oregon Trail formations is Chimney Rock, an elegant spire rising from a conical base that towers 450 feet above the North Platte River. Fur trappers heading to the Rocky Mountains in the early 1800s used the needle as a landmark. The first record of the name Chimney Rock occurs in Joshua Pilcher's 1827 report about his trip through the Platte Valley. Virtually every diarist who traveled the Oregon Trail mentioned the formation, and contemporary artists sketched and painted the rock. A reliable spring at the base of the rock made it a traditional campground for travelers. During the summer a portable museum features exhibits about the Oregon and Mormon trails and the Indians of the area. Chimney Rock is located south of the Platte River, three-and-a-half miles south of Bayard at the intersection of Routes 26 and 92.

SCOTTS BLUFF NATIONAL MONUMENT

The Plains Indians called this huge ship-shaped bluff *Me-a-pa-te,* "the hill that is hard to go around." Seven explorers employed by John

The Courthouse and Jail Rocks were reportedly named by early travelers from Saint Louis after landmarks in their home city.

Buffalo, as North American bison are commonly called, were once ubiquitous on the open prairie, providing food and other basic necessities for the Plains Indians for

Jacob Astor were the first recorded white adventurers to encounter the landmark in 1812. It was later named for Hiram Scott, a fur company clerk thought to have died in the vicinity around 1828. The national monument comprises 3,000 acres of mid-grass prairie. Hiking trails and a paved road to the top of the bluff provide splendid views of the North Platte River valley, Chimney Rock, and the Oregon Trail approach to Mitchell Pass. The **Oregon Trail Museum** has geological, paleontological, and historical exhibits, along with reproductions of watercolors and sketches by the photographer and artist William Henry Jackson. Jackson bivouacked at Scotts Bluff on his trip west in 1866; a trail leads to his campsite. There is also a display about the history of the Mormons and information on the Robidoux trading post, eight miles south of Scotts Bluff at Robidoux Pass, which was active from 1848 until 1851. Robidoux Pass in the scenic Wild Cat Hills was part of the Oregon Trail until 1851, when

centuries. Beginning in the 1830s, they were slaughtered for their hides, for sport,
and to clear the land for settlement. By 1900, there were fewer than 1,000 surviving.

the more northerly route through Mitchell Pass became standard.
Robidoux Pass is on private property but accessible.

> LOCATION: Route 92, 3 miles west of Gering. HOURS: *Museum:* 8–5
> Daily. *Summitt Road:* 8–4:30 Daily. FEE: Yes. TELEPHONE:
> 308–436–4340.

In **Gering,** the **North Platte Valley Museum** (10th and J streets,
308–436–5411) features a pioneer kitchen, general store, and cattle
ranch tack room. A display of fur-trapping artifacts includes a bull
boat of about 1812, a peculiar tublike vessel covered with a buffalo
hide that Indians and trappers used to navigate rivers. Also on the
grounds are a log cabin and a sod house with pioneer furnishings.

Thirty-four miles north of Mitchell is the **Agate Fossil Beds**
National Monument (Route 29, 308–436–4340). This remote landscape of low hills along the Niobrara River contains a rich concen-

tration of 19-million-year-old fossils. Captain James H. Cook discovered the fossil beds in the late 1870s and later acquired the site. Today trails lead to exposed beds that display fossils in situ. A visitor center displays fossils and Indian artifacts from Chief Red Cloud and the Sioux Indians.

FORT ROBINSON STATE PARK

Fort Robinson and the site of the old Red Cloud Indian Agency lie in the rugged White River valley in the Pine Ridge section of northwestern Nebraska. They are now part of this state park, a large recreational area offering frontier and dude-ranch activities.

Fort Robinson was established in 1874 to keep order at the Red Cloud Agency, where Sioux under the leadership of Red Cloud lived for part of the year and collected their government rations. During the spring and summer many Sioux left the agency to hunt buffalo in "unceded territory" to the north and west reserved for them by a treaty Red Cloud signed at Fort Laramie in 1868. Other bands refused to have anything to do with the agencies. Sitting Bull derided the Indians who took government hand-outs: "You are fools to make yourselves slaves to a piece of fat bacon, some hard-tack, and a little sugar and coffee."

The U.S. government renewed hostilities in January 1876 in order to force the Sioux to give up the Black Hills. After the defeat of Custer at the Little Bighorn in June, the army's campaign against the Sioux and Cheyenne was more successful. Sitting Bull fled to Canada and Crazy Horse decided to surrender. On May 6, 1877, Crazy Horse led a two-mile-long train of 900 Indians, including 200 warriors, into Fort Robinson, where they turned over their guns and 2,000 ponies. Rumors spread that the government planned to move the Sioux elsewhere, and that Crazy Horse himself would be sent to a prison in Florida. On September 5, 1877, the chief was arrested on the order of General George Crook, commander of the Department of the Platte. During the arrest Crazy Horse was bayoneted by a private and died from the wound that night. It was later said that he had resisted and pulled a knife, but it is likely that the killing had been planned in advance.

OPPOSITE: *A Conestoga wagon in front of Eagle Rock near Scotts Bluff. Monoliths such as these were important landmarks for pioneers traveling across the flat prairie.*

Fort Robinson's bloodiest incident, the Cheyenne Outbreak, occurred in 1879. Cheyenne chief Dull Knife led his tribe out of Oklahoma's Indian Territory to seek shelter with Red Cloud, unaware that the Red Cloud Agency had been moved. A cavalry troop was dispatched from Fort Robinson. When the Cheyenne were confronted by the troop, Dull Knife agreed to follow them to the fort. Once there, Dull Knife and his people awaited word of their fate from the War Department. The order came that they should be returned to Indian Territory immediately. When Dull Knife refused, the Cheyenne were chained inside the barracks by the army, in an effort to freeze and starve them into submission. After six days the Cheyenne, armed with weapons they had hidden among their possessions, broke out of the barracks and killed three sentries. The ensuing battle between the Cheyenne and the army lasted nearly two weeks. In the end, 64 of the 149 Cheyenne who fled Fort Robinson were killed and 78 were captured. Dull Knife and his family escaped safely but were later captured.

The **Fort Robinson Museum**, housed in the former post head-quarters, contains a collection of Indian objects and artifacts collected by an early agent at the Red Cloud Agency, along with military artifacts and implements. Fort buildings have been restored or replicated and contain period furnishings and artifacts. These include the original adobe officers' quarters (1887), the harness repair shop (1904), the blacksmith shop (1906), the veterinary hospital (1908), and replicas of the guardhouse and adjutant's office, where Crazy Horse was killed. The **Trailside Museum** (308–665–2929) features geological, natural-history, and paleontological exhibits, including a fourteen-foot mammoth excavated in the vicinity. It is housed in the 1904 fort gymnasium.

The site of the **Red Cloud Indian Agency** is about two miles east of the fort complex. It was established in 1873; its agent was to oversee the 13,000 Indians in the area. No structures remain, but a monument stands on the site, and a series of historical markers explain the history of the agency.

LOCATION: Route 20, 3 miles west of Crawford. HOURS: Phone for specific times. FEE: Yes. TELEPHONE: 308–665–2919.

OPPOSITE: *The reconstructed post adjutant's office at Fort Robinson, where the Sioux chief Crazy Horse died in September 1877, after being bayoneted when troops tried to place him under arrest.*

MUSEUM OF THE FUR TRADE

The Museum of the Fur Trade is located in the Pine Ridge area on Bordeaux Creek, on the site of an old fur-trading post and warehouse. One section of the museum displays goods traded between 1500 and 1900, including beads, kettles, knives, silverwork, tomahawks, and Indian blankets. Firearms made for the Indian trade from 1650 to 1900 and buffalo robes and pelts of beaver, wolf, mink, and badger are on display. Exhibits chronicle the history of fur trading from colonial days to the early twentieth century, covering French, British, and Spanish traders, voyageurs, mountain men, and professional buffalo hunters and the Indian tribes with whom they traded. The trading post on the museum grounds was established around 1837 by the American Fur Company. In 1849 it was taken over by James Bordeaux, who ran it as an independent trading post for the Sioux. From 1872 to 1876 it was operated by Francis Boucher, until the army discovered that ammunition was being sold illegally to Indians. The trading house has been reconstructed on the original site and furnished with typical furnishings and trade goods.

LOCATION: Route 20, 3 miles east of Chadron. HOURS: June through August: 8–5 Daily. FEE: Yes. TELEPHONE: 308–432–3843.

Just northeast of Merriman, the **Arthur Bowring Ranch State Historical Park** (Route 61, 308–684–3428), on the site of Bowring's 1890s homestead, has a reconstruction of his sod house. Located four miles east of the ranch town of Valentine, the **Fort Niobrara National Wildlife Refuge** (402–376–3789) is situated in the Sand Hills on the Niobrara River. The fort was established in 1879 to maintain peace between settlers and the Sioux on the nearby Rosebud Reservation. It was abandoned in 1906. All that remains is a barn, old foundations, and earthworks.

FORT HARTSUFF STATE HISTORICAL PARK

Fort Hartsuff stands near the North Loup River on the eastern fringe of the Sand Hills. It was established in 1874 to protect settlers and local Pawnee from the Sioux. Built amidst drought, grasshopper plagues, and depression, the fort provided a welcome source of employment for settlers. Its garrison was small and had only one major encounter with the Sioux, the Battle of the Blowout in 1876.

Three troopers won Medals of Honor for their parts in this battle, fought a few miles northwest of Burwell. The outpost, an important gathering place for Loup Valley settlers in an otherwise eerily empty landscape, was abandoned in 1881. Because of abundant supplies of gravel in the area, the fort's buildings were made of grout, which has withstood the rigors of time. Nine original structures remain, and these have been restored and furnished with period items. Firearms, military uniforms, and frontier tools are on exhibit.

> LOCATION: 10 miles north of Ord on Route 11, then 3 miles north of Elyria. HOURS: Memorial Day through Labor Day: 9–5 Daily. FEE: Yes. TELEPHONE: 308–346–4715.

Located near Halsey, the evergreen silhouette of the **Nebraska National Forest** (Route 2, 308–533–2257) stands like a mirage against the backdrop of the treeless, rolling Sand Hills. The forest was established in 1902 at the instigation of President Theodore Roosevelt to provide a nearby source of lumber to settlers.

The Bordeaux Trading Post, where James Bordeaux lived and carried on trade with the Brule Sioux Indians between 1849 and 1872, has been restored on its original foundations by the Museum of the Fur Trade.

C H A P T E R F O U R

IOWA

G rant Wood and Marvin Cone's placid farmscapes, painted in the 1930s and 1940s, still capture the essence of Iowa. Among the states Iowa typically ranks second after California in total cash farm income. Much of the population is engaged in the production, processing, or shipment of four commodities: corn, soybeans, cattle, and hogs. The state remains a province of scattered farmsteads and small towns, many scarcely more than a gathering of buildings at a crossroads. Iowa is a place where the term village means something. Iowa's history is also relatively tranquil, a circumstance that can be explained in part by an abundance of fertile soil, which promoted the influx of no-nonsense agrarians, coupled with an absence of the precious minerals that tend to bring out the cupidity and disorderliness in human beings.

At different times during the Pleistocene age, several glaciers spread out across the land that is now Iowa. As these ice sheets melted, they left behind a rich composite of clay, sand, and gravel. This soil produced an ocean of prairie grass and eventually proved ideal for farming. Iowa's prairies, now waving with grain instead of grass, have the reputation of being flat, but in many places—in the vicinity of Des Moines, for instance—the terrain rises and falls in huge swells. At the eastern and western boundaries of Iowa, these vast, undulating prairies terminate abruptly at two great rivers, the Mississippi and the Missouri. The river bluffs abound in scenery and history. The French explorers Father Jacques Marquette and Louis Jolliet were the first Europeans to record their arrival in this terrain. The event occurred during their landmark excursion to the Mississippi River in 1673. But hundreds of years before their visit, the Mississippi and Missouri and their tributaries provided abundant forage and hospitable haunts for prehistoric people. Ceremonial centers and burial grounds were perched on the scenic cliffs and river terraces. There are three important sites of this type in Iowa: Blood Run (not accessible) on the Big Sioux River, a tributary of the Missouri, and Effigy Mounds and Toolesboro on the Mississippi.

The Indians inhabiting present-day Iowa in 1682, the year that La Salle claimed the Mississippi Valley for France, were themselves fairly recent arrivals. They were not destined to stay long. The Ioway, for whom the state is named, migrated onto the prairies from the Great Lakes. While they were widely spread along tributaries of the

OPPOSITE: *In 1844 George Catlin painted this portrait of the Iowa Indian Little Wolf wearing full war paint, which was believed to protect the wearer during battle.*

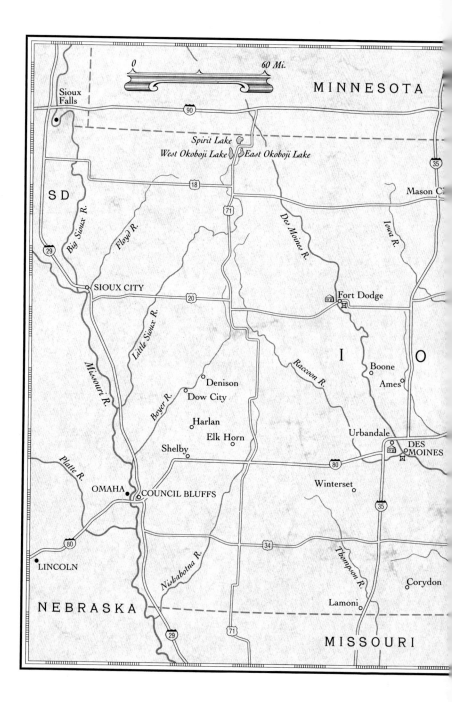

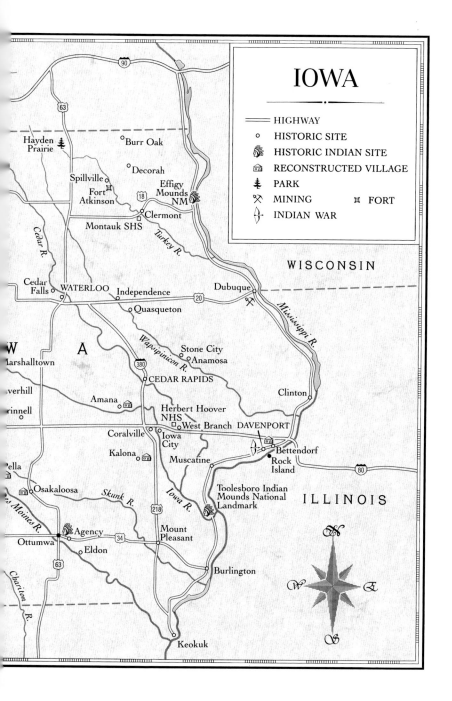

IOWA

- ═══ HIGHWAY
- ○ HISTORIC SITE
- HISTORIC INDIAN SITE
- RECONSTRUCTED VILLAGE
- ⁂ PARK
- ✕ MINING
- ⊞ FORT
- ⌿ INDIAN WAR

WISCONSIN

ILLINOIS

Hayden Prairie
Burr Oak
Decorah
Spillville
Fort Atkinson
Effigy Mounds NM
Clermont
Montauk SHS
Cedar R.
Turkey R.
Cedar Falls
WATERLOO
Independence
Dubuque
Quasqueton
Mississippi R.
Wapsipinicon R.
Stone City
Anamosa
Marshalltown
CEDAR RAPIDS
Clinton
Amana
Herbert Hoover NHS
West Branch
DAVENPORT
Coralville
Iowa City
Bettendorf
Rock Island
Kalona
Muscatine
Osakaloosa
Skunk R.
Iowa R.
Toolesboro Indian Mounds National Landmark
Mount Pleasant
Agency
Eldon
Ottumwa
Burlington
Des Moines R.
Chariton R.
Keokuk

Mississippi, the Ioway never resisted white settlement, and in 1838 they sold their Iowa lands and moved west to reservations in Nebraska, Kansas, and Oklahoma.

The Sauk (Sac) and Mesquakie (Fox) left a larger mark on Iowa history. In the 1600s these two Algonquian tribes were living in Wisconsin. The Mesquakie were traditional enemies of the Ojibwa, whose strong trade ties with the French quickened the Mesquakie dislike for the European interlopers. By the early 1700s, however, the French and Ojibwa had driven the Mesquakie south along the Mississippi into present-day Iowa and Illinois. At about the same time, the Mesquakie temporarily combined forces with the Sauk to fight their common enemy, the Illinois. A large concentration of Sauk and Mesquakie lived in the area on the Mississippi River where the Quad Cities stand today. In 1804 a group of Sauk were tricked into signing a treaty that ceded their tribal lands in Illinois. Many members of the allied tribes, especially those under the leadership of the Sauk chief Keokuk, realized the futility of fighting the treaty, and with the steady advance of white settlement in the 1820s, they favored a peaceful retreat across the Mississippi. The Sauk leader Black Hawk and his followers were less receptive to this notion. In 1832 Black Hawk and a band of men, women, and children returned to their village on the Illinois side of the river, precipitating the so-called Black Hawk War. The three-month-long confrontation was hardly a war—the woefully outnumbered Indians were ruthlessly chased down across Illinois and Wisconsin and slaughtered—but it did mark a turning point in trans-Mississippi history. The terms of the Black Hawk Treaty of 1832 opened up the eastern quarter of Iowa to settlement, and Iowa's population burgeoned to 200,000 by 1850. The Sauk and Mesquakie lived in Iowa until 1842, when they sold their lands and moved first to Kansas and then to Oklahoma. A small group of Mesquakie purchased land in Iowa in the 1850s and continue to live in the vicinity of Tama. The other tribes associated with Iowa—the Winnebago, who lived in northeastern Iowa from 1840 to 1848, the Potawatomi, who lived in western Iowa from the 1830s to 1847, and the Sioux, who roamed throughout the northern part of the state—had all been relocated by 1851.

From the late 1600s until 1838, when Iowa was named a territory, the land between the two rivers was in limbo. It was passed from France to Spain in 1762, then reclaimed by Napoleon in 1800, only to be sold to the United States in 1803 as part of the Louisiana Purchase. Reapportionment continued: At various times Iowa belonged to the territories of Indiana, Louisiana, Missouri, Michigan, and Wisconsin, and from 1821 to 1834 it was not attached to any territory at all. In 1838 the Territory of Iowa was created, a body that included present-day Iowa, much of Minnesota, and the Dakotas.

Aside from some fur trading, the only activity in this part of the continent prior to the Louisiana Purchase was Julien Dubuque's venture on the west bank of the Mississippi. In 1788 Dubuque began to mine lead in the vicinity of the city that now bears his name, and in 1796 Spain accorded him a large land grant to continue his mining operations. The French-Canadian entrepreneur ultimately lost his fortune and his land, but he is nonetheless considered Iowa's first permanent white resident.

Two important exploratory missions skirted Iowa—the Lewis and Clark expedition on the Missouri River from 1804 to 1806 and the Zebulon Pike expedition up the Mississippi in 1805. One of Pike's objectives was to locate appropriate sites along the river for forts. Although he recommended two excellent places in Iowa—on the bluffs across from Prairie du Chien and at present-day Burlington—his advice was not heeded. In 1808 the U.S. Army constructed the virtually indefensible Fort Madison on a site between a ridge and a ravine. Continual harassment by Black Hawk and his followers forced the soldiers to abandon the outpost in 1813, under cover of darkness, burning the fort as they left.

Iowa was the backdrop for another historic journey, in February 1846. After the murder of their leader, Joseph Smith, Jr., some 15,000 Mormons began the exodus from Nauvoo, Illinois. They cut a network of roads across southern Iowa, setting up transient villages, which they called Camps of Israel, and leaving behind bridges, wells, and gardens for those who followed. Routes 34 and 2 parallel portions of the Mormon Trail in Iowa. At the vanguard of the trek, the new Mormon leader, Brigham Young, reached the Missouri River in the summer of 1846. The encampment he established on the east bank of the river was one of the villages from which the future city of Council Bluffs grew. At the same time, the wife and son of Joseph Smith, Jr., and another group of Mormons did not follow Brigham Young west. Instead, they established the Reorganized Church of Jesus Christ of Latter Day Saints, headquartered from 1881 until 1906 in Lamoni, Iowa.

OVERLEAF: *A farm complex in central Iowa, where the topsoil is exceptionally fertile. Over ninety percent of the land in the state is farmland.*

Dinner for Threshers, *painted by Grant Wood, shows Iowa farmers coming in to a farm house for a hearty lunch after a long morning's work. Born on an Iowa farm,*

The first settlers who came to Iowa in the 1830s and 1840s were mainly native-born Americans. The largest number of foreign-born immigrants to Iowa came from Germany, especially during the years between 1890 and 1910. By 1920 over half of the farmers in Iowa were of German descent. The agrarian life was congruent with the principles of such religious groups as the German Inspirationists who founded the Amana Colonies and the Amish and Mennonites who continue to live in the vicinity of Kalona. Other nineteenth-century foreign immigrants whose descendants still predominate in the rural areas of Iowa include Swedes, Norwegians, Dutch, Danes, and Czechs. A number of Czechs also settled in Cedar Rapids.

Iowa entered the Union in 1846 as a free state. Tabor, Des Moines, Grinnell, West Branch, Iowa City, Clinton, and Springdale were among the towns whose citizens provided shelter for runaway slaves on the Underground Railroad. From 1857 to 1858 the fiery abolitionist John Brown sequestered himself with a Congregational minister in Tabor, in southwestern Iowa, and later with Quakers in Springdale, near Iowa City, while making plans for the raid on Harpers Ferry in Virginia.

*Wood traveled to the East Coast and Europe before discovering that his subject mat-
ter was to be found in the people and landscape of his native state (detail).*

An early combatant against racial discrimination in Iowa was
Alexander Clark, a free black who in 1842 settled in Muscatine,
where he opened a barbershop. He founded the first African
Methodist Episcopal Church west of the Mississippi in 1849 and was
the second black graduate from the University of Iowa Law School
(his son was the first). He fought for black suffrage and the right to
hold office; in 1868 he argued before the Iowa State Supreme Court
that his daughter had been unjustly denied admission to public high
school on the basis of race. The court ruled in his favor. Few blacks,
however, obtained land for agriculture in Iowa; consequently their
numbers are low in rural areas. In 1850 about 300 blacks worked in
the lead mines at Dubuque and as laborers in the river towns of
Keokuk, Burlington, Davenport, Sioux City, and Muscatine.
Beginning in the 1880s, several thousand blacks, hired frequently as
strike breakers, worked in the coal mines in rural southern Iowa
until the mines were depleted in the 1920s.

The first railroad in Iowa was the Mississippi & Missouri, which
was completed between Davenport and Iowa City in 1856. In that
same year, the Chicago & Rock Island Railroad opened the first

bridge across the Mississippi. Connecting the cities of Rock Island and Davenport, the bridge was viewed with foreboding by the steamboat industry, which took the Chicago & Rock Island Railroad to court on grounds that the bridge was an obstruction to river commerce. An Illinois lawyer, Abraham Lincoln, was one of a team of attorneys who argued the railroad company's case. Although they lost the jury trial, the railroad company's right to span the river was eventually upheld by the Iowa Supreme Court.

Recognizing that Iowa sat squarely in the path of any future transcontinental railroad route, Congress in 1856 gave the state 4 million acres of land (one-ninth of the state's total area) to entice railroad companies to build there. The Civil War slowed the pace of construction, but after the war General Grenville Dodge helped orchestrate the completion of the first transcontinental railroad from his home in Council Bluffs. By 1880 five major railroad lines cut west across the state. With the guarantee of distant markets for its farm products, Iowa's agrarian tradition became even more firmly entrenched. Before the end of the century, virtually all of the prairie had been plowed for cultivation.

The complicated and discriminatory rate schedules of the railroads provoked the ire of farmers, river port businessmen, and state politicians throughout the Midwest. This grievance was one of the rallying forces behind the National Grange of the Patrons of Husbandry, widely known as the Grange, which was founded by Oliver Kelley in 1867. In the 1870s the Grange attracted a large national following among farmers: 100,000 of its 1 million members were Iowans, the largest membership from any state. Iowa, along with its neighbors Illinois, Wisconsin, and Minnesota, became an important testing ground for the public's right to regulate the operations of a business. In the 1870s and 1880s, the Iowa legislature passed increasingly tighter restrictions on the railroads, culminating with the 1888 Railroad Commissioner Law, which was a state equivalent of the federal Interstate Commerce Act passed in 1887.

As farming is a fairly egalitarian pursuit, Iowa claims an abundance of vernacular structures and a distinct shortage of the baronial edifices that accompany great wealth. The state's most lavish nineteenth-century estate, Terrace Hill in Des Moines, was built with money made in real estate and banking, while the mansions found in the Mississippi River towns of Dubuque and Clinton manifest the fortunes of a handful of lumber barons. The structures that perhaps best embody Iowa's agrarian past are the beautiful gristmills that

early settlers built on the banks by streams and rivers in the nineteenth century. Examples may be found in remote parts of the state
such as in the small towns of Decorah and Independence and in
Wildcat Den State Park north of Muscatine. Many farms throughout
Iowa have been preserved as outdoor museums, but that effort on
the part of historians does not imply that the classic farmstead is
obsolete. Even though metal structures may take the place of frame
barns and trailer homes are supplanting traditional farmhouses,
many nineteenth-century farm structures are still actively used. Iowa
also possesses a number of early-twentieth-century buildings
designed by prominent architects of the time, including Frank Lloyd
Wright's Cedar Rock at Quasqueton, Louis Sullivan's church in
Cedar Rapids, and commercial structures in Clinton and Grinnell,
Walter Burley Griffin's residences in Mason City, and the magnificent
Prairie School–Baroque Woodbury County Courthouse in Sioux City,
by William Steele, William Gray Purcell, and George Elmslie.

The chapter begins along the bluffs of the Mississippi River, which
was the first area of Iowa to be settled. It then moves to the cities in
the eastern and central part of the state, which grew up along rivers,
usually at propitious mill sites. It next tours rural south-central Iowa,
which includes the Amana Colonies, the Amish center of Kalona,
and glimpses of Mormon history at Corydon and Lamoni. The
chapter concludes in western Iowa, at the site of the Spirit Lake
Massacre and in the cities along the Missouri River.

MISSISSIPPI   RIVER   BLUFFS

The **Great River Road,** a system of county, state, and federal high-
ways skirting the west bank of the river, affords beautiful vistas of the
bluffs and terraces along the Mississippi—terrain that is particularly
stunning in autumn. Along the route, numerous small towns, such
as the German settlement of **Guttenberg** and Luxembourger village
of **Saint Donatus,** preserve their nineteenth-century architecture.

EFFIGY MOUNDS NATIONAL MONUMENT

Situated along 300-foot-high bluffs above the Mississippi, this tranquil site preserves a number of prehistoric burial mounds and offers
a spectacular panorama of the river valley. Most of the mounds are
conical or linear in shape, but twenty-nine take the form of birds or

The Chapel on the Mount, built of local limestone by the Luxembourgian settlers of Saint Donatus, is modeled on the Chapel du Blichen in their native land.

bears. This distinctive type of effigy mound, thought to have been built between A.D. 600 and 1000, predominates in southern Wisconsin, with a few found on the fringes of Iowa, Illinois, and Minnesota. Great Bear Mound, one of the most monumental of the animal forms here, is 70 feet across the shoulders, 137 feet long, and 3.5 feet high. The visitor center offers tours of the earthworks, as well as archaeological exhibits.

LOCATION: Route 76, 3 miles north of Marquette. HOURS: 8–5 Daily; Tours: Memorial Day through Labor Day: 10:30 and 2. FEE: Yes. TELEPHONE: 319–873–3491.

DUBUQUE

The handsome town of Dubuque is one of Iowa's oldest settlements. When the city was incorporated in 1837, it was already an active community. It lays claim to the state's first church (1834), first bank (1836), and first newspaper (1836). The city is named for the French-Canadian Julien Dubuque, who in 1788 began mining lead on the west bank of the Mississippi; in 1796 he obtained a grant from Spain for several thousand acres of land in the area. Dubuque's mines flourished at first, but then he fell on hard times and was forced to deed most of his lands to the Saint Louis fur trader Auguste Chouteau. Chouteau's claim was ultimately declared invalid by the U.S. Supreme Court. Dubuque died in 1810 at the age of 48 and was buried with pomp on a bluff overlooking the Mississippi River by the local Mesquakie, who held him in considerable awe. The **Julien Dubuque Monument** (ca. 1897), which marks his grave, stands at the confluence of Catfish Creek and the Mississippi River in the **Mines of Spain State Recreation Area.** The Mesquakie controlled the mines until 1832, when the Black Hawk Treaty opened up the region to white settlement. By the 1850s the Dubuque mines, along with those around Mineral Point in southwestern Wisconsin, and Galena, Illinois, were producing most of the nation's lead. An important landmark from Dubuque's lead-mining days is the 150-foot limestone and brick **Shot Tower** (Commercial Street and River Front), built in 1856 to manufacture lead munitions. Molten lead was dropped from the ninth floor, through screens, into the river, which cooled it into finished shot.

By the late 1850s, lumber processing had begun to supplant lead mining as Dubuque's major industry. Logs were rafted down the Mississippi from northern pine forests to sawmills, where much of the timber was sawn into building materials. Dubuque was a bustling river port, manufacturing center, and railroad hub as well as lumber town, and during the latter part of the nineteenth century it was the second-largest city in Iowa. This prosperity fueled considerable public and private construction in Dubuque. In 1857 John F. Rague, architect of the Old Capitol in Iowa City, designed two structures in Dubuque. The **Dubuque City Hall** (50 West 13th Street) is an Italianate building. Nearby is the **Dubuque County Courthouse** (720 Central Avenue), a monumental structure of Richardsonian Romanesque and Beaux-Arts styling, with a 200-foot central tower topped by a 14-foot Statue of Justice. The building, completed in 1893, is constructed of Indiana limestone and brick, with terra-cotta decorations and marble columns. Adjacent to the courthouse is the **Old Jail Art Gallery** (36 East 8th Street, 319–557–1851), one of three surviving examples of Egyptian Revivalist architecture in the country. It is believed to have housed Confederate prisoners during the Civil War. Constructed in 1857–1858 of native blue limestone and cast iron, it now features exhibits from the Dubuque Museum of Art. The **Majestic Theatre**

(405 Main Street) is an exuberant eclectic vaudeville house designed in 1910 by Chicago architects C. W. and George L. Rapp.

Among the several Victorian mansions that have been restored are the **Redstone** (504 Bluff Street, 319–582–1894), a massive brick-and-stone residence of 1894 combining chateauesque and Queen Anne elements. It was built for the daughter of A. A. Cooper, whose wealth derived from his wagon and buggy works. The **F. D. Stout House** (1105 Locust Street, now private) is a Richardsonian Romanesque mansion built in 1890 by lumber baron F. D. Stout. The **Fenelon Place Elevator** (4th Street at the foot of the bluff) is a cable railway that scales the precipitous cliffs between downtown and the bluff-top neighborhood of Fenelon Place. It began operation in 1882 and still runs seasonally, providing splendid views of Dubuque and the Mississippi.

The **Mississippi River Museum** (3d Street Ice Harbor, 319–557–9545) focuses on the history of boating and commerce on the upper Mississippi River. Exhibits display artifacts related to Indians and the fur trade, logging and mining, Lewis and Clark, Mark Twain, Robert Fulton, and other famous people associated with river lore, exploration, and industry. Open for tours are the decks and pilothouse of the side-wheeler *William M. Black* (1934), which affords excellent views of the Port of Dubuque.

Mathias Ham House

Mathias Ham, one of the first settlers to cross the Mississippi River into Iowa, established the town of Eagle Point. He proceeded to amass a fortune in lead mining and lead smelting. His stately home, constructed in 1856–1857 of native limestone, is a distinctive example of the Italianate villa style. It contains period furnishings as well as exhibits explaining the history of Dubuque. Several other buildings have been moved to the site, including a miner's log cabin, built ca. 1833 (2241 Lincoln Avenue, 319–557–9545).

In the belief that if it is opened to the public, tourists will come, the ***Field of Dreams* movie site** (Lansing Road, northeast of Dyersville, off Route 20 Exit 294, 319–875–8404), consisting of a baseball diamond in the middle of a cornfield, is accessible to visitors.

OPPOSITE: *The Dubuque County Courthouse, designed by the local architects Fridolin Heer & Son and completed in 1893.*

This ca. 1833 log cabin, possibly the oldest extant building in Iowa, was occupied by William Newman, an early Iowa settler. It is now located on the grounds of the Mathias Ham House.

Located forty-five miles south of Dubuque, **Clinton** began in the 1830s as a ferry crossing on the Mississippi River. In the 1880s the town was a booming sawmill center. The **George M. Curtis House** (420 Fifth Avenue South, 319–242–8556) is one of the few extant mansions of Clinton's lumber barons. It has terra-cotta trim, stained-glass windows, and handsome interior woodwork produced in the Curtis Brothers millwork factory. Another highlight in Clinton is the **Van Allen and Company Department Store** (200 Fifth Avenue South), the last multistory steel-frame building designed by the Chicago-based architect Louis Sullivan. Completed in 1914, the four-story flat-roofed brick building is adorned with the voluptuous terra-cotta ornamentation that is a signature of Sullivan's designs. The structure is currently being restored.

DAVENPORT–BETTENDORF

Sited on the bluffs of the Mississippi River, Davenport and its smaller satellite, Bettendorf, are the Iowa components of the Quad

Cities, a large metropolitan area that includes the Illinois cities of Rock Island and Moline. This stretch of the river was the heartland of the Sauk and Mesquakie Indians. During the War of 1812, many of their ranks fought on the side of the British, in part because the Indians preferred the trading practices of the British and also because they were outraged by a "treaty" with Americans in 1804, to which only a few of them had assented. On September 5, 1814, British soldiers and about a thousand Indians under the Sauk leader Black Hawk routed the Americans in a battle fought near present-day Davenport. In 1816 Black Hawk signed a treaty ratifying the land-relinquishing terms of the earlier one. By 1829 white settlers were beginning to infringe on the Indians' major village, Saukenuk, which stood on the Rock River, just upstream from the Mississippi, in Illinois. This encroachment precipitated the Black Hawk War of 1832, a brave but futile campaign across present-day Illinois and Wisconsin led by the aging but obdurate leader. At the same time, Black Hawk's more accommodating counterparts, Chief Keokuk of the Sauk and Chief Wapello of the Mesquakie, conveyed their followers peacefully across the Mississippi into Iowa. In 1832 Keokuk and Wapello signed the so-called Black Hawk Treaty, which relinquished 6 million acres of land and pushed the Indians beyond a line fifty miles west of the Mississippi River. On one tract of this land, the town of Davenport was established in 1836. Antoine LeClaire, a fur trader of French and Indian parentage, was interpreter at the treaty signing and a founder of the town. One of Davenport's more colorful patriarchs, LeClaire was a negotiator of many Indian treaties and instigator of numerous enterprises in the area, including the first railroad bridge across the Mississippi, completed in 1856. The **Antoine LeClaire House** (630 East 7th Street) is a brick Italianate structure constructed in 1855.

The town of Davenport was named for another founder, Colonel George Davenport, who came to the area in 1816 to serve at Fort Armstrong on nearby Rock Island and later established a fur-trading outpost here. With the advent of the steamboat, Davenport became a thriving river port, and in the 1880s the quarrying of local limestone prompted the rise of the cement-manufacturing industry. The **Putnam Museum** (1717 West 12th Street, 319–324–1933) offers splendid views of the Mississippi River as well as fine exhibits of regional history, natural history, and anthropolo-

Walnut Grove Pioneer Village centers around Alfred Ehler's blacksmithing shop, with the original fittings intact. Established in the 1860s, it operated into the 1950s.

gy. Founded in 1867, the Putnam is one of the oldest museums west of the Mississippi.

Bettendorf, formerly Gilbertown, was named for the local industrialist W. P. Bettendorf, who moved his railroad-car factory here in the early 1900s. The **Family Museum of Arts and Science** (2900 Learning Campus Drive at 18th Street, 319–344–4106) is a hands-on museum emphasizing science and history. Exhibits range from home, farm, and school life around 1900 to the science of music and the human heart, and even optical illusions.

On February 26, 1846, William F. "Buffalo Bill" Cody was born in the family home near **Le Claire,** a small river town just north of Bettendorf. In 1853 the family moved to Kansas, where Cody began a career as a horseman, scout, and buffalo hunter. The **Buffalo Bill Museum** (200 North River Drive, 319–289–5580) in Le Claire contains Cody memorabilia, Indian and pioneer artifacts, and exhibits pertaining to the riverboat era. Nestled in the scenic valley of the Wapsipinicon River, the **Cody Homestead** (Route F33 off Route 61, 319–225–2981) is located about twelve miles north of Bettendorf near the town of **McCausland.** Buffalo Bill Cody lived here from 1847 to 1850, and it is the only standing structure in Iowa associated with him. The limestone-and-frame house is furnished with typical nineteenth-century items. The nearby **Walnut Grove Pioneer Village** (Route F33, 319–285–9903) preserves structures from this bygone crossroads as well as several buildings relocated from the vicinity, including a blacksmith shop (ca. 1860), equipped with forge and tools, and a rural Catholic church, the vestry of which dates from 1853. The altar and stained-glass windows have been restored.

Wildcat Den State Park (319–263–4337), situated fifteen miles southwest of the Quad Cities, preserves the **Pine Creek Gristmill.** Built in 1848, the large frame mill has been restored and displays the original milling equipment. In the river town of **Muscatine,** twenty miles southwest of the Quad Cities, the **Muscatine Art Center** (1314 Mulberry Avenue, 319–263–8282) has an important collection of paintings, drawings, prints, maps, and photographs portraying the Mississippi River. A gallery is also devoted to local history. The museum is housed in the **Musser Mansion** (1908); original furnishings belonging to a lumber-milling family remain in several rooms. Muscatine has a footnote in literary history. In 1919, as he was struggling to start his career as a novelist in New York, F. Scott Fitzgerald worked for an advertising agency and was assigned to write a slogan for a steam laundry in this city. The future author of *The Great Gatsby* came up with "We Keep You Clean in Muscatine."

TOOLESBORO INDIAN MOUNDS NATIONAL HISTORIC LANDMARK

Standing near the mouth of the Iowa River on bluffs overlooking the Mississippi, this group of six conical burial mounds is typical of the ancient (200 B.C. to A.D. 400) Hopewell culture. They are the best-preserved examples of this prehistoric civilization in Iowa. A large number of mounds in the area were discovered by settlers in the 1830s, but many were subsequently destroyed by farming. When archaeologists excavated some of the mounds in the late nineteenth century, they found skeletal remains and items characteristic of the Hopewell period, including effigy pipes, mica ornaments, and copper tools. The visitor center contains replicas of some of these artifacts as well as dioramas depicting Hopewell culture; the Marquette and Jolliet expedition of 1673, which ventured onto Iowa soil in this vicinity; and the Black Hawk War Council, which met in 1832 on the nearby banks of the Iowa River. In addition, the site offers a demonstration prairie plot, planted with the wildflowers and grasses once abundant on the Great Plains.

> LOCATION: Route 99, 7 miles east of Wapello. HOURS: Memorial Day through Labor Day: 12–4 Daily; Day after Labor Day through October 31: 12–4 Saturday–Sunday. FEE: None. TELEPHONE: 319–766–4018.

BURLINGTON

The town of Burlington clings to the hills and bluffs along the Mississippi River, rugged terrain known as the Flint Hills. Prior to the Black Hawk Treaty of 1832, which opened the west bank of the river to settlement, this area was occupied by Indians who gathered flint for tools and weapons. Burlington stands near the site of a former Mesquakie village called Shoquoquon that was presided over by Chief Tama. White settlement began in 1833, and in 1834 one of the newcomers christened the village Burlington for his hometown in Vermont. The town served as capital of both the Wisconsin and Iowa territories. Pork packing became a major industry in Burlington, and sawmills sprouted to process logs rafted down the Mississippi from Wisconsin forests. Burlington was also an important frontier gateway for immigrants. People and goods moved first by river, then by rail. The first train arrived from Chicago in 1855, Iowa service began in 1856, and a railroad bridge spanning the Mississippi was completed in 1868.

In addition to American-born settlers, many Germans, Irish, and Swedes settled in Burlington. The Germans in particular found

OPPOSITE: *The Pine Creek Gristmill, built in 1848 in what is now Wildcat Den State Park near Muscatine, is one of several such structures remaining from an important early Iowa industry.*

the craggy landscape reminiscent of their homeland and were not daunted by the engineering challenges that the topography presented. **Snake Alley** (North 6th Street between Washington and Columbia streets) is a steep and winding lane along which stand several Victorian-era residences designed by three German immigrants—an architect, engineer, and paving contractor. The **Phelps House** (521 Columbia Street, 319–753–2449) on Snake Alley commands a ridgetop view of Burlington. Built in 1851, with extensive additions in the 1870s, the house includes Second Empire and Italianate elements. It contains many furnishings and memorabilia of the original occupants. The **Apple Trees Museum** (1616 Dill Street, 319–753–2449) of the Des Moines County Historical Society is housed in the only remaining wing of the sprawling residence once owned by Charles E. Perkins, an official with the Chicago, Burlington & Quincy Railroad. Perkins called his estate The Apple Trees because it encompassed land on which a pioneer settler had built his log cabin and planted an apple orchard in 1833. The museum contains Indian crafts and artifacts, Victorian furnishings, glassware, china, pioneer tools and household implements, and memorabilia associated with nineteenth-century Burlington. The historical society also maintains the **Hawkeye Log Cabin Museum** (Crapo Park, 319–753–2449). Standing on a bluff overlooking the Mississippi River, the cabin was built in 1909 by the Hawkeye Natives Association, an early Iowa history society and social club. It contains pioneer tools and furnishings.

Keokuk, tucked into the southeasternmost corner of Iowa, is named for the influential Sauk chief. The **Keokuk River Museum** (Victory Park at Johnson Street, 319–524–4765) is housed in the *George M. Verity,* a 1927 stern-wheel steamboat of the type used in the barge industry prior to the introduction of diesel-powered towboats. The steamboat's fixtures and machinery are intact, and photographs and memorabilia throughout pertain to Mississippi River history. The **Miller House Museum** (318 North 5th Street, 319–524–5055) was built in 1857 by Samuel Freeman Miller, a Kentucky lawyer who moved to Keokuk in 1850 because of his antislavery views. At the age of 46, President Lincoln appointed him to the Supreme Court, where he served for twenty-eight years. The museum, a Federal-style house, has nine rooms filled with period furniture.

The Painter-Bernatz Mill, built in 1851 and the oldest extant building in Decorah, displays the Vesterheim Norwegian-American Museum's collection of farm machinery.

THE   EASTERN   INTERIOR

DECORAH

Set in the deep cleft of the upper Iowa River valley, Decorah retains much nineteenth-century charm. The town took its name from a Winnebago leader, Chief Waukon-Decorah. The Iowa River provided mill sites for early settlers from the Northeast, but it was Norwegian immigrants who left their fastidious and thrifty stamp on the village and outlying farmlands. After 1850 Decorah served as both a center and gateway of Norwegian settlement west of the Mississippi.

Norwegian-American Museum (Vesterheim)

Vesterheim, a Norwegian word meaning "western home," was established in 1877 and is one of the oldest and largest immigrant museums in the United States. A major portion of the collection is housed in a handsome Italianate brick structure built in 1877 as a hotel, which later served as offices for the Lutheran Publishing

House. Vesterheim's exhibits focus first on eighteenth-century folk culture in Norway and then on the immigrants' new life in America. A wealth of furnishings, household items, folk costumes, and textiles is presented in typical interior settings or in extensive display cases. Many of the hand-carved objects—including furniture, mangle boards, walking canes, cupboards, and church-related pieces—bear the characteristic Norwegian acanthus motif. A variety of trunks, buckets, tankards, and bowls are decorated with rosemaling, Scandinavian folk painting that emphasizes floral designs.

The museum has also gathered onto its grounds an impressive assortment of eighteenth- and nineteenth-century structures, including two immigrant log houses, a log parochial school, and the **Norris Miller House,** a simple frame structure of 1856, which is a rare example of stovewood construction. The centerpiece of this assembly, however, is the **Painter-Bernatz Mill,** a magnificent stone-and-frame building with a distinctive gabled clerestory. Constructed in 1851, the mill soon became an economic and social hub for local Norwegian farmers. It still stands on its original site and is the oldest extant building in Decorah. The buildings in this outdoor museum are appointed with period furnishings, while the mill contains nineteenth-century agricultural and industrial implements.

> LOCATION: 502 West Water Street. HOURS: May through October: 9–5 Daily; November through April: 10–4 Daily. FEE: Yes. TELEPHONE: 319–382–9681.

The **Porter House Museum** (401 West Broadway) is an Italianate villa of 1867, surrounded by an impressive rock wall of stones collected in the United States and abroad. Its second occupant, Adelbert Porter, was a naturalist and collector, and the home contains many of his furnishings and collections.

The Vesterheim museum maintains the **Jacobson Farmstead** (319–382–9681), a ten-acre site about seven miles east of Decorah. Settled in 1850 by an immigrant Norwegian family, the farm includes a log house, stone barn, granary, and several other outbuildings. These have been restored to the turn of the century and contain period furniture, some of which is original to the Jacobson family. Twelve miles north of Decorah, in the village of **Burr Oak,**

is the **Laura Ingalls Wilder Park and Museum** (319–735–5916), one
of the several sites scattered about the Midwest and Great Plains
that are associated with the children's author who wrote about the
nineteenth-century pioneer experience. In 1876, following a disastrous scourge of grasshoppers that ruined crops in Minnesota,
Charles Ingalls moved his family to Burr Oak to try his hand in the
hotel business. He managed the **Master's Hotel** with the help of
his wife and two daughters, Mary and Laura, who was then nine
years old. During this time Burr Oak was a stop on one of the
wagon trails across Iowa. The Ingalls family stayed about a year
before returning to Minnesota. The simple hotel has been
restored and furnished with nineteenth-century items.

Hayden Prairie, forty miles west of Decorah and about three
miles south of the small town of **Chester,** is one of the few remnants of native grassland in Iowa. The 200-acre site is particularly
impressive in late May and again in early September when the
spring and fall wildflowers are in full bloom. Hayden Prairie is
maintained by the Iowa Department of Natural Resources
(515–281–5145).

Spillville, twelve miles south of Decorah, is one of several villages in this corner of Iowa settled in the mid-nineteenth century
by Czechs. In 1893 the composer Anton Dvorak, living in New York
at the time but homesick for his native Bohemia, spent the summer in Spillville with immigrants from his country. Dvorak and his
family stayed in a modest brick building that now houses the **Bily
Clock Museum** (Main Street, 319–562–3569). Of Czech descent,
the brothers Frank and Joseph Bily grew up near Spillville around
the turn of the century. Farmers and carpenters by trade, the two
men were gifted woodcrafters who designed an array of large, elaborately carved clocks, many of which have musical features or mov-
able figures.

Five miles south of Spillville, on the outskirts of the small town
of **Fort Atkinson,** the **Fort Atkinson State Preserve** (off Route 24,
319–425–4161) stands amid what was once called the Neutral
Ground—a strip of territory 40 miles wide and 150 miles long
stretching across northern Iowa that was established in 1830 as a
buffer zone between the Sioux and their perennial enemies, the
Sauk and Mesquakie. In 1840, due in part to the pressure of white
settlement, federal agents decided to move the Winnebago out of
Wisconsin and into the Neutral Ground, where their presence

would serve as an additional deterrent to the feuding Indians. The Winnebago were rightfully hesitant to leave their homelands to enter this potentially hostile precinct. To provide them some measure of protection from marauding Sioux, Sauk, or Mesquakie, the military built Fort Atkinson in 1840. A wooden stockade surrounding stone blockhouses, the fortress perched conspicuously on a promontory above the Turkey River. Perhaps because the fort looked so imposing, no conflicts ever arose here among the Indians. The Winnebago were relocated to a reservation in Minnesota in 1848, and the fort was abandoned a year later. The stockade and portions of some buildings have been restored, and remnants of several foundations can be seen.

MONTAUK STATE HISTORIC SITE

Montauk, the estate of the prominent nineteenth-century Iowa businessman and politician William Larrabee, is set on a wooded

Montauk, the restrained Italianate house built by Iowa Governor William Larrabee in 1874, was occupied by members of the Larrabee family until 1965.

hillside overlooking the Turkey River near the town of Clermont. Born in 1832 in Connecticut, Larrabee came to Iowa in 1853. He served as state senator from 1867 to 1885 and governor from 1886 to 1890. Larrabee was a founder of the Republican party in Iowa, an advocate of stricter regulation of the railroads, a progressive in education, and a supporter of women's suffrage. He died in 1912. Both Larrabee and his wife, Anna Appelman, came from seafaring backgrounds, and they named their Iowa estate after the easternmost tip of Long Island, New York. Built in 1874, Montauk is a brick structure with Italianate ornament. Crowning the roof is a captain's walk with a broad view of the river valley. The mansion contains family memorabilia, original furnishings, paintings, and books, and many objects gathered by Larrabee on world travels.

> LOCATION: Route 18E, 1 mile northeast of Clermont. HOURS: Memorial Day through October: 12–4 Daily. FEE: Yes. TELEPHONE: 319–423–7173.

Two sites in nearby **Clermont** are associated with the Montauk State Historic Site. The **Union Sunday School** (McGregor and Larrabee streets, 319–423–7173) is a brick Greek Revival church built in 1858. For 108 years the Union Sunday School was home to a number of denominations. It contains a large, handsomely cased Kimball pipe organ, given to the church in 1896 by William Larrabee, an early proponent of allowing students to have access to historical artifacts. The **Clermont Museum,** which he founded in 1912 in a bank building he owned, focuses on this "hands-on" approach to teaching history.

CEDAR FALLS

The attraction on this stretch of the Cedar River was the cascades, which offered mill possibilities, and by 1845 a few families had settled on the west bank of the watercourse. First called Sturgis Falls, for town founder William Sturgis, Cedar Falls acquired its permanent name in 1849. During the nineteenth century, Cedar Falls became a bustling milling and manufacturing center and home to Iowa State Normal School, now the University of Northern Iowa. The **Cedar Falls Historical Society** (303 Franklin Street, 319–266–5149) maintains four buildings: Their offices are within the **George Wyth House and Viking Pump Museum** (303 Franklin

Street), a 1907 residence combining elements of the Mission and Prairie styles. It contains Art Deco fixtures and furnishings and items pertaining to the Viking Pump Company, of which George Wyth was the founder. the **Victorian House Museum** 308 West Third) is a Civil War-era Italianate structure that contains period furnishings, clothing, and memorabilia. The **Ice House Museum** (First and Clay streets) is a circular building used to store blocks of ice cut from the Cedar River. It displays ice-harvesting equipment and nineteenth-century agricultural implements. **The Little Red Schoolhouse** (First and Clay streets) was moved to Sturgis Park in 1988. More formally known as Bennington Township Schoolhouse #5, it was built in 1909 and restored in 1968. On display in the schoolhouse are a bell tower and bell, blackboards, a potbellied stove, books, and other period furnishings.

WATERLOO

Waterloo, which straddles both banks of the river, was first known as Prairie Rapids. Prospering as an industrial and distribution hub, the town became particularly well known for the manufacture of tractor engines. Because Waterloo secured not only the county seat but also division offices of the Illinois Central Railroad, it soon became larger than Cedar Falls. A relic from mid-nineteenth-century Waterloo, the **Rensselaer Russell House Museum** (520 West 3d Street, 319–233–0262) is a handsome residence in the Italianate villa style. Completed in 1861, it was one of the first brick houses in Waterloo. Several pieces of period furnishings are original to the house.

The **Grout Museum** (503 South Street, 319–234–6357) displays a broad array of items in the areas of natural history, geology, anthropology, and pioneer history. Many of the objects are from the collection of the museum's namesake, the turn-of-the-century Waterloo businessman Henry W. Grout. One section of the museum contains full-scale dioramas depicting a log cabin, tool shed, blacksmith shop, carpenter shop, and general store.

Along the Wapsipinicon River in the town of **Independence** is one of the oldest structures in northeastern Iowa, the **Wapsipinicon Mill** (100 1st Street, 319–334–3472). The massive stone-and-brick building, built in 1867, operated as a feed mill for many years; it now houses the museum of the **Buchanan County Historical Society.**

CEDAR ROCK

Cedar Rock, designed by Frank Lloyd Wright, stands on the left bank of the Wapsipinicon River in the village of Quasqueton, about thirty miles east of Waterloo. Completed 1950, the residence and the riverside pavilion were owned by Lowell and Agnes Walter. The house is constructed of reinforced concrete, brick, steel, and glass and has ample views of the landscape. It is one of Wright's "Usonian" houses—inexpensive housing for workers. Wright also designed the furniture and fixtures and selected the carpets and many of the household implements.

LOCATION: Route 282, 7 miles south of Route 20, Quasqueton.
HOURS: May through October: 11–5 Tuesday–Sunday. FEE: None.
TELEPHONE: 319–934–3572.

CEDAR RAPIDS

Cedar Rapids stands on the Cedar River amid the former lands of the Sauk and Mesquakie Indians. White settlers arrived in the late 1830s, and within a few years, they had harnessed the river to power gristmills and sawmills; Cedar Rapids was on its way to becoming an industrial and manufacturing center. Cedar Rapid's most famous product is Quaker Oats, and several of its citizens took part in the development and national promotion of this breakfast cereal. In 1853 John Stuart and his son Robert started the North Star Oatmeal Mill in Cedar Rapids, which became known as Douglas and Stuart, after local businessman George Douglas purchased an interest in the mill. In 1888 the Stuarts and Douglas joined ranks with Ferdinand Schumacher of Akron, Ohio, and other oatmeal magnates to form the American Cereal Company, which evolved in 1901 into the Quaker Oats Company.

Czechs began coming to Cedar Rapids in 1852, attracted by work in Cedar Rapids's booming meat-packing industry. By the turn of the century, they formed the city's largest immigrant population. Ultimately they clustered in the southwestern section of town, a neighborhood that is now near downtown Cedar Rapids. The **National Czech and Slovak Museum and Library** (30 16th Avenue SW, 319–362–8500), amid ethnic shops and restaurants, keeps Old World arts and crafts traditions alive.

The Iowa painter Grant Wood was born in 1891 on a farm near Anamosa, eighteen miles east of Cedar Rapids. From the age of 10, after his father's death, he lived in or near Cedar Rapids, except for periods of study in Minneapolis and Chicago and travel in Europe. In high school Wood met and became lifelong friends with another artist, Marvin Cone, an important regional painter whose landscapes are particularly evocative of the expansive, rolling farm country of the Midwest. The **Cedar Rapids Museum of Art** (410 3d Avenue SE, 319–366–7503) has a large collection of the works of Wood and Cone. The two artists were active in the formation of the Stone City Art Colony, a gathering of regional artists that met at the John Green Estate in the village of Stone City, about twenty miles east of Cedar Rapids. The colony was short-lived (the artists gathered only in the summers of 1932 and 1933); nonetheless the rural landscape around Stone City provided Wood and Cone with the setting for some of their best works.

Also in Cedar Rapids is **Saint Paul's United Methodist Church** (1340 Third Avenue SE), one of the last works of Louis Sullivan, who received the commission in 1910. His design for a brick structure with a semi-circular front and a rear tower was pronounced too expensive. His former designer, George Elmslie was hired to finish the building; he completed it as faithfully as possible to Sullivan's original plans.

Brucemore

Brucemore is a twenty-six-acre estate surrounding a mansion built in 1886 for Caroline Sinclair, widow of Thomas Sinclair, a wealthy industrialist and meat packer. After 1906 it became home to the George Bruce Douglas family, whose fortune was made in Quaker Oats and transportation. The Douglases expanded the estate, developed the gardens, and built several outbuildings. The last occupants, Howard and Margaret Douglas Hall, kept a small menagerie at Brucemore; lions are buried in the pet cemetery on the grounds. Many of the Victorian furnishings in the brick mansion are original to the Douglas and Hall eras, and photographs and memorabilia of its occupants are throughout the house.

LOCATION: 2160 Linden Drive SE. HOURS: February through December: Tours on the hour, 10–3 Tuesday–Saturday FEE: Yes. TELEPHONE: 319–362–7375.

The butternut-wood staircase at Brucemore, a Queen Anne house.

IOWA CITY

Iowa City was founded in 1839 to be the capital of Iowa Territory, and after statehood in 1846, the town continued for some years to serve as the seat of government. However, with steady growth westward in the state, pressure increased to find a more central location for the capital. In 1857, over Iowa City's protests, the state government was moved to Des Moines. To placate the city, legislators established a state university at Iowa City. Chartered in 1847, the institution opened in 1855, and since then the University of Iowa has shaped the character and economy of Iowa City.

Old Capitol

The University of Iowa lies in the heart of the city along the banks of the Iowa River, and the centerpiece of the campus is the Old Capitol. A handsome exercise in Greek Revival, the limestone building has Doric porticos on its east and west faces and is capped with a tall dome. It was designed by John Francis Rague, who had just completed work on a similar capitol in Springfield, Illinois. It was constructed from 1840 to 1842 and expanded in 1856. After its role in state government had ended, the structure served as the first permanent building of the university. The interior of the Old Capitol has been restored with furnishings and fixtures that reflect the different periods of use in the building's history. A highlight is the unusual reverse spiral staircase that dominates the central hall.

LOCATION: Clinton Street and Iowa Avenue on the University of Iowa campus. HOURS: 10–3 Monday–Saturday, 12–4 Sunday. FEE: None. TELEPHONE: 319–335–0548.

Plum Grove (1030 Carroll Street, 319–337–6846) was the retirement home of Robert Lucas, who served as first territorial governor of Iowa from 1838 to 1841. In 1844 he and his wife, Friendly, built this handsome brick house in a thicket of plum trees on the southern edge of Iowa City. The Greek Revival structure contains period furnishings, some from the Lucas family.

In the suburb of **Coralville,** the **Johnson County Heritage Museum** (310 5th Street, 319–351–5738) is housed in the Coralville Public School (1876). The second floor is furnished as a turn-of-the-century school, while the first floor contains exhibits of area history.

HERBERT HOOVER
NATIONAL HISTORIC SITE

The village of West Branch, ten miles east of Iowa City, was the birthplace and childhood home of Herbert Hoover. Born in 1874, he was the second of Jesse and Hulda Hoover's three children. The Hoovers were active members of the Quaker community. Jesse, a successful blacksmith and farm machinery merchant, died when Herbert was six; three years later Herbert's mother also passed away. Within a year the boy moved to Oregon to live with an uncle. In 1895, with a degree in engineering (he was a member of the first class of engineering students at Stanford University in 1891), Hoover embarked on a career in mining that took him from the

OPPOSITE: *Iowa's Greek Revival Old Capitol, in Iowa City, is constructed largely of Devonian limestone quarried from the banks of the Iowa River.*

This modest two-room board-and-batten cottage was the birthplace of Herbert Hoover, the thirty-first president of the United States. It is furnished (opposite) as it would have been when occupied by the Hoover family, who were devout Quakers.

California gold mines to Australia and China and made him a millionaire by the age of 40. With the outbreak of World War I, he became involved in public service projects that led to several governmental appointments, including secretary of commerce under Presidents Warren Harding and Calvin Coolidge. In 1928 Hoover ran for president on the Republican ticket and soundly defeated his Democratic opponent, Alfred E. Smith. He entered office on a wave of popularity, which crashed along with the stock market in 1929. In the 1932 presidential election, Hoover was defeated by Franklin D. Roosevelt. Returning to California, he devoted himself to the Hoover Institution on War, Revolution, and Peace at Stanford. He died in 1964 and is buried at West Branch with his wife, Lou.

The **cottage** where Hoover was born still stands on its original site in a setting reminiscent of a mid-nineteenth-century Midwestern farm community. Built in 1871 by Jesse Hoover and his father, the two-room house has been restored and contains many original furnishings. The **blacksmith shop** is typical of the one operated by Jesse Hoover in the 1870s. Other structures moved to the site include an 1853 **schoolhouse** and the **Friends Meetinghouse** (1857), where Herbert and his family attended Quaker services. Herbert and Lou Hoover's grave site overlooks West Branch and Wapsinonoc Creek. Memorabilia are on display at the **Presidential Library and Museum.**

LOCATION: Parkside Drive and Main Street, West Branch. HOURS: 9–5 Daily. FEE: Yes. TELEPHONE: 319–643–2541.

C E N T R A L   I O W A

MASON CITY

Mason City is a manufacturing, trade, and transportation center for outlying farms, so named because many of its settlers were Freemasons. The first colonists to arrive in 1853 were temporarily repulsed by Indians, but most returned within a year. Mason City stands upon huge quantities of glacially deposited clay, an ingredient in the making of cement; by the early twentieth century, this northern Iowa town was one of the nation's largest producers of portland cement. The looming mills of **Northwestern States Portland Cement** and **Lehigh Portland Cement** (2100–2500 blocks of North Federal Avenue) form one of the impressive sights in Mason City. Opening up the region to agriculture demanded a method of draining the boggy prairies. The solution was found in lining fields with tiles, and from the 1880s until the advent of plastic tiling, Mason City was a major manufacturer of clay tiles.

Mason City has a trove of Prairie School architecture. The **City National Bank** (4 South Federal Street) and adjacent **Park Inn Hotel** (15 West State Street) were a double commission designed in 1909 by Frank Lloyd Wright. Although both structures have been altered, they still possess the flat rooflines, overhanging eaves, and terra-cotta and brick exterior trimwork that the architect favored. In the early twentieth century, Mason City developers called upon Prairie School architect Walter Burley Griffin to plan the residential areas of **Rock Glen** and **Rock Crest** (Rock Glen, East State Street, and River Heights Drive, west of the Willow Creek Foot Bridge). Among the neighborhoods' many Prairie School homes is the **J. G. Melson House** (56 River Heights Drive, private), which Griffin designed in 1912. The residence is constructed of rough-cut stone and poured concrete and seems to be growing out of the cliff edge on which it is poised.

Located seven miles west of Mason City on Route 18, the **Kinney Pioneer Museum** (515–423–1258) exhibits Indian artifacts, wagons, steam engines, early automobiles, and a variety of pioneer furniture, household items, tools, musical instruments, dolls, and toys. Also on display are memorabilia of Meredith Willson, composer of the musical *The Music Man,* who was born in Mason City in 1902. A log cabin (1856) and schoolhouse (1900) are preserved on the grounds.

FORT DODGE

This town on the Des Moines River grew out of the short-lived military outpost built in 1850 to protect settlers from the Sioux. Fort Dodge was abandoned in 1853 and purchased by William Williams, sutler for the troops, who laid out the town of Fort Dodge in 1854. An early settler named Henry Lott was both a victim and an avenger in the chain of violence that led to the Spirit Lake Massacre. In revenge for the deaths of his wife and son, Lott killed the Sioux Sidominadota, whose brother Inkpaduta led the massacre of settlers at Spirit Lake several years later. During the 1862 Indian uprisings in southern Minnesota, settlers from Fort Dodge volunteered to man Fort Williams, one of five militia outposts built by the Northern Border Brigade along the Iowa–Minnesota line.

Fort Dodge Historical Museum

This outdoor compound includes an assortment of structures, some original and some replicas, typifying the early village of Fort Dodge, and a military stockade representing Fort Williams. Front Street, as it is called, is lined with a general store, blacksmith shop, log chapel, and one-room schoolhouse, all of which contain period fixtures. The fort museum contains Indian artifacts, items of military interest, and pioneer tools, furniture, and clothing.

LOCATION: Just east of junction of Routes 20 and 169. HOURS: May through mid-October: 9–6 Daily. FEE: Yes. TELEPHONE: 515–573–4231.

AMES

Ames is a college town on the prairie. In 1858 the state legislature established the State Agricultural College and Model Farm, now **Iowa State University,** and Story County was selected as the site of the new institution. The college opened in 1862, after passage of the federal Morrill Land Grant Act, which provided the school with additional lands. The arrival of the Cedar Rapids & Missouri Railroad in 1864 and drainage of the prairie's sloughs and marshes attracted settlers as well as students. The town was called College Farm until 1866, when it was named for Oakes Ames, a railroad official. In **Parks Library** on the university campus are a series of Grant Wood murals painted in 1934 and 1936 under a program sponsored by the Works Progress Administration. They depict various agrarian and industrial activities.

The Farm House

The Farm House was originally a home for the college's farm superintendents and later for deans. Built in 1860 of local brick, stone, and timber, it was the first building constructed on campus. The simple, stuccoed house with Greek Revival elements served as the social center of the college, especially during the thirty-year deanship of C. F. Curtiss, who lived in the house with his family from 1896 to 1946. Other inhabitants included James "Tama Jim" Wilson, who served as secretary of agriculture under presidents William McKinley, Theodore Roosevelt, and William Howard Taft. The Farm House has been restored and decorated with period furnishings. The kitchen contains fixtures from the early 1860s, while articles in other rooms reflect the home's appearance from 1869 to 1910.

> LOCATION: Knoll Road, Iowa State University. HOURS: February through December 12–4 Sunday–Friday. FEE: None. TELEPHONE: 515–294–3342.

In **Boone** is the **Mamie Doud Eisenhower Birthplace** (709 Carroll Street, 515–432–1896), where the former First Lady was born in 1896. The family moved to Cedar Rapids when Mamie was a baby and from Iowa to Colorado when she was 10. Mamie Doud met Lieutenant Dwight D. Eisenhower in San Antonio, Texas, in 1915, and they were married several months later. The house has been restored and furnished with items typical of the 1890s. The master bedroom furnishings are original to the home, and many other pieces are from the Doud, Carlson, and Eisenhower families. Exhibits of memorabilia pertain to Mamie Doud Eisenhower's life and the political career of her husband.

DES MOINES

The capital of and largest city in Iowa sits amid rolling hills where the Raccoon River joins the larger Des Moines River. The area was home to the Sauk and Mesquakie. The prospect of fur trade with the Indians attracted French explorers, who referred to the bigger river as La Rivière de Moingona. Historians speculate about the origins of the name: It may trace to an Indian word for "middle" (the river being the principal watercourse between the Mississippi and Missouri) or to the French word for Moingona Indians.

By the 1830s American settlers were appearing in the valley. In 1835 Colonel Stephen W. Kearny and Lieutenant Albert M. Lea explored the confluence of the two rivers as a possible garrison site. In 1841 John C. Frémont, who became known as the "Pathfinder" because of his explorations of the American West, surveyed the territory around the Des Moines River. In 1842 the Sauk and Mesquakie (represented by Chiefs Keokuk and Poweshiek) ceded the area to the federal government. To ensure peace among these Indians, the incoming settlers, and the Sioux who appeared occasionally, the army opened Fort Des Moines at the river fork in 1843. It was actually the second Fort Des Moines, Stephen Kearny having established the first one in 1834 at Keokuk Rapids in the Mississippi River near present-day Keokuk. The fort was not garrisoned for long—the Sauk and Mesquakie were removed to a Kansas reservation in 1845—but it provided the nucleus around which the civilian settlement of Fort Des Moines grew. The city's name became simply Des Moines in 1857, the same year that a decade-long political fight to move the state capital west from Iowa City was won.

Besides serving as the seat of state government, Des Moines became a hub for life insurance, publishing, and hybrid seed development. Frederick Hubbell arrived in Des Moines from Connecticut in 1855, at the age of 16, and went on to become one of Iowa's richest citizens by serving the expanding state's twin demands for investment capital and insurance. After he and his associates founded the Equitable Life Insurance Company of Iowa in 1867, many similar companies established offices in Des Moines. The city ranks third internationally, after London and Hartford, Connecticut, as an insurance center. Printing and publishing, which began in Des Moines in the 1850s, grew rapidly with the demand from local insurance companies for printed forms. The industry soon expanded into the realm of journals and magazines, mainly for farmers, including *Wallaces' Farmer, Swine World,* and *Successful Farming.* Des Moines is also the headquarters of the country's oldest black newspaper, *The Iowa Bystander,* which began publication in 1894. In 1904 Henry A. Wallace began experimenting with breeding corn, an endeavor that led to the formation of a hybrid seed company, Pioneer Hi-Bred. During the New Deal years, Wallace served as secretary of agriculture and vice president under Franklin Roosevelt and in 1948 ran unsuccessfully for president against Harry Truman on the Progressive party ticket. The **Iowa State Fairgrounds** (East 30th Street and Grand Avenue) is the site of the annual agriculture exposition, established in 1878 and at its present site since 1886.

In 1903 Fort Des Moines was established a third time as a cavalry post. In 1917 it became the nation's first officers' training camp for blacks. Their presence here, combined with the availability of work in skilled and entrepreneurial positions during World War I, drew friends and relatives to Des Moines, and during the 1920s the city became a hub of middle-class black enterprise. On May 15, 1942, Fort Des Moines became the first training center for the Women's Auxiliary Corps. The **Polk County Heritage Gallery** (2d and Walnut streets, 515–286–3215) is housed in the restored lobby of the former U.S. post office, a handsome Beaux-Arts Classical building constructed in 1908. The gallery displays changing cultural exhibits.

Iowa State Capitol

The Iowa State Capitol was conceived in the grand tradition of Greek Revival and Classic Revival public buildings. The building stands on a hilltop with a commanding view of downtown Des Moines. Especially conspicuous are its five domes—one on each of the four corners and a central one that shimmers with gold leaf.

OPPOSITE: *The gold-leaf-covered dome of the Iowa State Capitol in Des Moines is modeled on Les Invalides in Paris.*

The capitol was begun in 1871 but not completed until 1886; construction was prolonged by funding as well as structural problems. The original architects, John Cochrane (who resigned early on) and Alfred Piquenard (who died), were followed by W. F. Hackney and M. E. Bell. The interior is lavishly appointed with marble, carved woodwork, murals, mosaics, and statuary.

> LOCATION: East 9th Street and Grand Avenue. HOURS: 8–4:30 Monday–Friday, 8–4 Saturday–Sunday. FEE: None. TELEPHONE: 515–281–5591.

State Historical Building of Iowa

This museum, ensconced in a new (1987) Postmodern facility one block west of the capitol, contains the state archives, a library, and exhibits that chronicle Iowa's Indian heritage, the history of white settlement, and the state's natural history. The museum has an excellent collection of Indian beadwork and fine examples of the arts and crafts made by members of the Amana Colonies and Amish community, the state's preeminent folk cultures.

> LOCATION: 600 East Locust. HOURS: 9–4:30 Tuesday–Saturday, 12–4:30 Sunday. FEE: None. TELEPHONE: 515–281–5111.

Terrace Hill

Terrace Hill is a splendid Second Empire mansion in the midst of a fine nineteenth-century estate. In 1867 Benjamin F. Allen, one of Iowa's early millionaires, commissioned a Chicago architect, W. W. Boyington (best known for the Chicago Water Tower), to design Terrace Hill. The mansion was completed in 1869. In 1884, after Allen lost his fortune, he sold the house to insurance magnate Frederick Hubbell. Terrace Hill remained in the Hubbell family until 1976, when it became the Iowa governor's residence. The villa is Franco-Italian, built of brick with decorative quoining and a mansard roof fenestrated with arched and hooded windows. The most conspicuous Italianate feature is the tall central tower encircled with a balcony. The interior features marble mantelpieces,

OPPOSITE: *The rotunda of the Iowa State Capitol is ringed with statues by S. Cottin; these three represent Peace, Commerce, and Agriculture. The dome is decorated with the symbol of the Grand Army of the Republic and the dates of the Civil War.*

carved woodwork, and stenciled walls and ceilings. Some of the Victorian furnishings are original to the Allen and Hubbell eras.

LOCATION: 2300 Grand Avenue. HOURS: March through December: Tours 10–1:30 Tuesday–Saturday. FEE: Yes. TELEPHONE: 515–281–3604.

Hoyt Sherman Place

Hoyt Sherman was a pioneer Des Moines businessman who began as a land agent for Southern investors in Iowa farmlands. He was involved in banking and city services and was one of the founders of the Equitable Life Insurance Company of Iowa, incorporated in 1867. Born in Ohio, he was one of eleven children, including William Tecumseh, of Civil War fame, and John, author of the Sherman Anti-Trust Act. Sherman arrived in Des Moines in 1848. He and his wife, Sarah, had five children. He built this handsome

The drawing room of Terrace Hill, the Iowa Governor's mansion since 1976, contains ornate Belter furniture that belonged to a Des Moines family. OPPOSITE: *Terrace Hill was completed in 1869 for Benjamin F. Allen, the richest man in Iowa.*

home in 1877 and lived here until his death in 1904. The house contains a large number of antiques, glass, silver, decorative arts, and a collection of nineteenth-century paintings.

> LOCATION: 1501 Woodland Avenue. HOURS: 8–4 Monday–Friday; Reservations required for guided tours. FEE: Yes. TELEPHONE: 515-243-0913.

The Hoyt Sherman Place is located in the **Sherman Hill Historic District** (Woodland, Cottage Grove, 15th, and 19th streets). One of the city's oldest residential neighborhoods, it contains many examples of turn-of-the-century domestic architecture. The **Salisbury House** (4025 Tonawanda Drive, 515–279–9711) is an unusual Tudor mansion composed of architectural fragments gathered from fifteenth-century structures in England. It was constructed from 1923 to 1928 by cosmetics manufacturer Carl Weeks and his wife, Edith.

A re-created na-ha-che, or tree skin house, like those built by the Ioway tribe ca. 1700, at Living History Farm. Next to it is a ramada, a shaded work space.

The mansion contains furnishings and tapestries from the fifteenth, sixteenth, and seventeenth centuries, other decorative arts, and rare books and manuscripts. The **Des Moines Art Center** (4700 Grand Avenue, 515–277–4405) is a noted Iowa architectural landmark. The first structure was designed in 1948 by the Finnish-born, American-naturalized architect Eliel Saarinen. Two newer wings are the work of I. M. Pei (1968) and Richard Meier (1985).

Living History Farms

Living History Farms is a 600-acre outdoor historical compound where interpreters dressed in pioneer clothing grow crops and grow livestock using nineteenth-century methods. In addition, there are many related demonstrations of canning, sewing, and cooking. The complex includes a representation of an **Ioway Indian Village,** which includes replicas of *na-ha-ches,* the Indians' oval bark lodges; tools

A log cabin at the Living History Farm re-creates an Iowa farmhouse of the mid-1800s, with skeins of wool and dried apples hanging over a one-legged bed.

and implements commonly used by the Ioway; and garden plots where traditional plants are cultivated. An 1850s **Pioneer Farm** includes a log cabin, log barn, and pastures enclosed with split-rail fencing. Nearby is the dogtrot-style **Oak Grove Educational Center. Walnut Hill** is a town composed of many nineteenth-century structures original or moved to the site, creating a community dating to about 1875. Included are an Italianate villa, a general store, blacksmith shop, pottery, cabinetmaker's shop, and school. A farmhouse, barn, corn crib, and large collection of horse-drawn farm machinery make up the **1900 Farm**. The **Farm of Today and Tomorrow** focuses on current and future agricultural practices.

LOCATION: 2600 Northwest 111th Street. HOURS: May through third Sunday in October: 9–5 Daily. FEE: Yes. TELEPHONE: 515–278–2400.

Thirty miles southwest of Des Moines, in **Winterset,** is the **John Wayne Birthplace** (224 South 2d Street, 515–462–1044), where Marion Michael Morrison, the future movie star, was born in 1907. The **Madison County Museum and Historical Complex** (815 South 2d Avenue, 515–462–2134), fourteen buildings on eighteen acres, includes an 1856 Gothic-style mansion, stone barn, schoolhouse, church, and depot. The *Bridges of Madison County,* six of them, made famous by novelist Robert Waller, are nearby. **Francesca's House** (3271 130th Street, 515–981–5268), home of a character in the *Bridges* movie, dates from the late 1800s.

RURAL EAST–CENTRAL IOWA

The small towns and rural byways between the cities of Ames and Cedar Rapids still retain a sense of nineteenth-century agrarian life. In the village of **Haverhill,** about thirty miles east of Ames, the **Matthew Edel Blacksmith Shop** (515–752–6664) preserves a German immigrant's workshop and tools. Edel opened his blacksmith shop in 1883 and operated it until his death in 1940. In addition to repairing farm implements and shoeing horses, Edel made and patented several tools, including dehorning clippers and garden hoes, and also crafted iron grave markers. In the industrial and farming community of **Marshalltown** five miles north is the **Marshall**

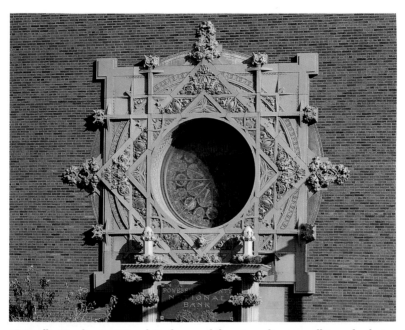

Grinnell's Merchants National Bank, one of the extraordinary small-town banks in the midwest designed by Louis Sullivan near the end of his career.

County Courthouse, a charming nineteenth-century exercise in profusion. The limestone structure, constructed from 1884 to 1886, was conceived by Chicago architect John C. Cochrane, a designer of the Iowa State Capitol. The **Marshall County Historical Museum** (202 East Church Street, 515–752–6664) contains fine examples of crinoids and Native American stone weapons and tools as well as items related to local history. Adjacent is the **Glick-Sower House** (201 East State Street), a brick structure (ca. 1865) containing the original furnishings of a pre–Civil War home. The museum also administers the **Taylor #4 Country School,** dating to the early 1900s.

    Grinnell is home to Iowa's most famous building, the **Merchants National Bank** at Fourth Avenue and Broad Street, designed by Louis Sullivan and completed in 1914. The Grinnell bank is internationally celebrated for its severe geometric form, ornamented by the terra-cotta cartouche and circular window about and above the entryway. The interior contains original chandeliers and replicas of other brass wall and ceiling light fixtures.

AMANA COLONIES

The seven villages of Amana are situated along the Iowa River amid rolling farmland about twenty miles southwest of Cedar Rapids. The colonies were founded in 1855 by a utopian religious group whose members had immigrated from Germany to America in 1843. They were known as Inspirationists, for their belief that God spoke through prophets rather than ordained ministers. Before moving to Iowa, they had lived for some ten years in a group of six villages called Ebenezer, near Buffalo, New York, where they had established a communal system of work and landownership. The colonists prospered in Iowa and became especially well known for goods produced in their woolen mill, which is still in operation. Throughout their seven villages, they constructed handsome vernacular struc-

The main hearth at the Communal Kitchen Museum in Middle Amana, covered with cooking equipment once used to prepare meals for up to forty people.

tures of brick, stone, and frame. These large, simple buildings served as communal kitchens, shops, mills, and factories.

In 1932 the people of the Amanas voted to abandon the communal system and incorporated their holdings into the profit-sharing Amana Society. Members of the community continue to farm, make wine and a variety of specialty foods, and manufacture furniture, appliances, and woolens. Among the small museums scattered about the villages are the **Communal Agricultural Exhibit** (319–622–3567), the **Barn Museum** (319–622–3058), and the **Communal Kitchen Museum** (319–622–3567) in **Middle Amana.** In the main village of **Amana,** the **Museum of Amana History** (Routes 151 and 220, 319–622–3567) is housed in three nineteenth-century structures. The **Noe House,** built in 1864, served as a communal kitchen and later as a doctor's residence. It has exhibits of Amana

The dining area of the Communal Kitchen at Middle Amana is still heated by the stove that stands in the center of the room.

history, church furnishings, and crafts made by the Inspirationists. The **schoolhouse** (1870) contains toys, dolls, Christmas ornaments, and school furnishings. The **washhouse-woodshed** has wine-making and gardening displays.

KALONA HISTORICAL VILLAGE

Many Amish and Mennonites live and farm in the rolling prairies around Kalona, eighteen miles south of Iowa City. Their forebears immigrated to America 250 years ago, having been persecuted for their religious beliefs in their homelands of Germany and Switzerland. The Amish in particular are noted for their adherence to simple styles of dress and nineteenth-century modes of farming. Although some orders of Amish permit use of certain twentieth-century amenities, the Old Order Amish shun cars, telephones, and electricity. The Kalona Historical Village is a gathering of nineteenth-century buildings, including a railroad depot (1879), a one-room schoolhouse, a log cabin, and a country store, containing period furnishings and memorabilia. Also on the grounds, the **Wahl Museum** exhibits glassware and pioneer items, while the **Iowa Mennonite Museum and Archives** contains material relating to Mennonite history.

LOCATION: Route 22, on east edge of Kalona. HOURS: April through mid-October: 10–4 Monday-Saturday; Rest of year: 11–3 Monday–Saturday. FEE: Yes. TELEPHONE: 319–656–3232.

Pella, forty miles southeast of Des Moines, was founded in 1847 by Henry Peter Scholte and a religious group from Holland. The white frame **Scholte House** (728 Washington, 515–628–3684), built about 1850, was the home of the pastor and his family. It contains church and family memorabilia, and a collection of French and Italian furniture. The **Pella Historical Village** (507 Franklin, 515–628–2409) is a compound of nineteenth-century structures from the area, which includes the boyhood home of Wyatt Earp, restored to the 1850s period, and a replica of the Scholte Church.

Located two miles northeast of **Oskaloosa,** the **Nelson Pioneer Farm Museum** (Glendale Road off Route 63, 515–672–2989) comprises several original structures of the Daniel Nelson Farm, which was homesteaded in 1844, and other nineteenth-century rural buildings that have been gathered onto the site, including the **Daniel Nelson House** (1852). Constructed of local brick and native timber, it contains period furnishings. The **Daniel Nelson Barn,** a classic frame structure of 1856, houses pioneer farm equipment. Buildings moved onto the farm include a rural school (1861), a log cabin (1867), and a country store (ca. 1910), all of which contain period fixtures and pioneer memorabilia. There is also a museum containing historical exhibits, including a collection of Indian artifacts. A machinery exhibit displays antique machinery and tools.

The town of **Mount Pleasant** lies amid rolling hills dotted with barns, silos, and farmsteads. The **Midwest Old Threshers Museum** (Threshers Road, 319–385–8937) displays an array of antique agricultural equipment and implements as well as an electric trolley operation, schoolhouses, and other nineteenth-century structures. Also on site is the **Museum of Repertoire Americana,** displaying a large collection of early-day tent, repertoire theater, opera house, and Chatauqua memorabilia tracing the American theater tradition. Twenty-five miles west of Mount Pleasant, in **Eldon,** is the **American Gothic Home** (Burton and Gothic streets, private). The board-and-batten house of 1881, with its Gothic-inspired window, was the backdrop for Grant Wood's famous painting *American Gothic* of 1930, which captures the humorless, foursquare mien of a rural father and daughter. The town of Agency was once the federal Indian agency for the Sauk and Mesquakie during the nineteenth century. **Chief Wapello Memorial Park** (southeast of Agency, off Route 34) contains the grave of the Mesquakie leader and marks the site of the treaty in 1842 that arranged for land purchases from the two tribes and helped open the gate to homesteaders in Iowa Territory.

The town of **Corydon** lies on the **Mormon Trail.** In 1871 Jesse James and several colleagues robbed a bank here. The **Wayne County Historical Society Museum** (Route 2, 515–872–2211) has Indian artifacts, pioneer items, Mormon memorabilia, and an exhibit re-creating the James robbery. In **Lamoni,** near the Iowa-Missouri border, is **Liberty Hall Historic Center** (1300 West Main Street, 515–784–6133), an eighteen-room Victorian farmhouse that was the home of Joseph Smith III and his family from 1881 to 1906. Smith was the son of Joseph Smith, Jr., founder of the Church of Jesus Christ of Latter-day Saints. After the elder Smith was murdered in 1844, near Nauvoo, Illinois, members of the church split into several groups. One assembly followed Brigham Young west to Utah. The other major contingent, calling itself the Reorganized Church of Jesus Christ of Latter Day Saints, remained in the Midwest and Joseph Smith III became its president in 1860. During the late nineteenth century, the headquarters for the Midwestern group was at Lamoni; it later moved to Independence, Missouri, where it remains. The Smith farmstead contains period furnishings and church memorabilia.

WESTERN IOWA

IOWA GREAT LAKES

This cluster of ten water-filled basins near the Iowa-Minnesota border was created by glaciers. The three largest lakes in the group are **Spirit** and **East** and **West Okoboji.** Prior to the arrival of white settlers in the mid-1850s, these beautiful lakes were a gathering place for bands of Sioux. It was here in 1857 that the Spirit Lake Massacre occurred. The previous year, a group of six families settled in the area between East and West Okoboji lakes in the vicinity of present-day Arnolds Park. The Sioux, who had been induced to leave Iowa in 1851, resented the infestation of the land around their sacred lakes by white settlers. This widespread ill feeling formed a backdrop for a massacre precipitated by Inkpaduta, who was so dangerous that he had been banished by his kin and wandered northwestern Iowa with a band of like-minded folk. Inkpaduta justified their maraudings on the grounds that his brother, Sidominadota, had been killed some years previous by a white trader from Fort Dodge.

The winter of 1856–1857 had been especially harsh, and by the first thaw in early March, both the Spirit Lake settlers and Inkpaduta's band were hard pressed for rations. Because the whites had scattered their cabins along the lakes, they were easy targets. Beginning on the morning of March 8 at the house of Rowland and Frances Gardner, the Indians roamed from cabin to cabin, killing thirty of the Spirit Lake settlers. Because of the remoteness of the settlement, it was almost two weeks before a passerby discovered the bodies and a month before a search party was launched from Fort Dodge. Inkpaduta and his followers were never apprehended. The only extant structure from the period of the massacre, the **Gardner Cabin,** stands in **Arnolds Park** on Pillsbury's Point overlooking West Okoboji Lake. Nearby, a mass grave is marked by the **Spirit Lake Massacre Monument,** a stone obelisk dedicated in 1895.

SIOUX CITY

On August 20, 1804, 23-year-old Sergeant Charles Floyd, Jr., a member of the Lewis and Clark expedition, died of what is now thought to be a ruptured appendix. He was buried on a river bluff near where Sioux City stands today, his grave marked since 1900 by the **Sergeant Floyd Monument** (Glenn Avenue and Lewis Road), a hundred-foot obelisk. Floyd was the only member of the party to die during the arduous two-and-a-half-year trek across the continent.

Sioux City stands at the confluence of the Big Sioux, Floyd, and Missouri rivers in the former territory of the Omaha, Oto, and Sioux Indians. The first white settler was William Thompson of Illinois, who platted Thompsonville in 1848. He was followed, a year later, by a French-Canadian trader, Théophile Bruguier, who was accompanied by his Sioux wives and his father-in-law, Chief War Eagle. Born into the Santee tribe in the 1780s, War Eagle was later embraced by the Yankton Sioux and served as a chief of that band for a number of years. In 1856 the settlement was voted the county seat and the freighter *Omaha* steamed up the Missouri River from Saint Louis—two events that boded well for Sioux City. The first railroad arrived in 1868 and enhanced the river town's importance as a shipping hub. Situated in a corn- and livestock-farming region, Sioux City grew to be a large meat-packing center, an industry represented by the massive brick **Midland Packing Company** (2001 Leech Avenue) in the heart of the stockyards.

Woodbury County Courthouse

The Woodbury County Courthouse is of national importance as a landmark in early-twentieth-century design. A Sioux City architect, William Steele, got the job, and called in William Gray Purcell and George Elmslie to give verve and finesse to the plans for the structure. The three men had previously worked together in the Chicago office of Louis Sullivan, and they brought to the project many of

ABOVE *and* OPPOSITE: *Sioux City's Woodbury County Courthouse, designed by William Steele with Purcell & Elmslie, is the largest public building in the United States constructed in the Prairie Style. Its rich ornamentation is in the style of Louis Sullivan, in whose firm all three architects had worked.*

the design principles that were fermenting in Chicago at the turn of the century. Completed in 1918, the courthouse possesses none of the Greco-Roman attributes that characterize most public buildings from the period. An angular brick-and-granite structure out of which rises a flat-roofed tower, it is an original work of art, akin to neither the domestic work associated with the Prairie School of architecture nor the skyscrapers of the Chicago School.

The building inside and out is appointed with leaded stained-glass windows, beautiful Sullivanesque terra-cotta ornament, and mosaics. Elmslie had been, in effect, Sullivan's design partner. Midwestern taste was turning conservative, and this was the final exuberant outburst of its most fruitful period. The terra-cotta figures were executed by an Illinois sculptor, Alfonso Ianelli. Four murals on the second level of the rotunda were painted by the

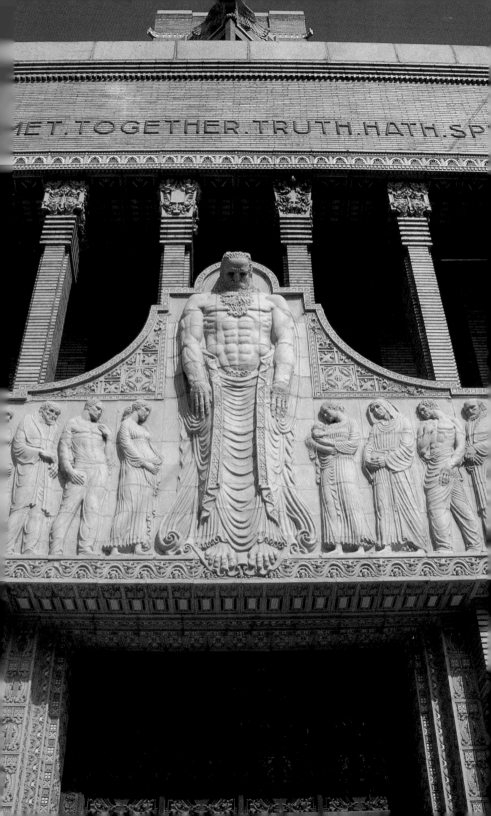

Chicago artist John W. Norton. The courthouse is still in use and open to the public during normal business hours.

LOCATION: 7th and Douglas streets.

Another impressive structure in Sioux City is the **Sioux City Central High School** (1212 Nebraska Street), a massive Richardsonian Romanesque building constructed of rough-hewn sandstone. The facility was built in 1892 with additions in 1911 and 1930. The **Sioux City Public Museum** (2901 Jackson Street, 712–279–6174), housed in the **Pierce Mansion** (ca. 1890), displays exhibits on geology and natural history, the pioneer period in Iowa, the Civil War, and the settlement of Sioux City. There is also a large collection of Indian artifacts, clothing, and crafts.

In **Denison,** the **William A. McHenry House** (1428 First Avenue North, 712–263–3806) is a handsome Queen Anne structure with Stick-style elements. Built in 1885, the mansion has fine interior woodwork and contains period furnishings and fixtures. Overlooking **Dow City** and the Boyer River valley, the **Simeon E. Dow House** (Prince Street off Route 30, 712–674–3734) was home to the founder of the town, who was also a successful farmer, stock raiser, and businessman. The red-brick Italianate structure of 1874 is decorated with period furnishings.

COUNCIL BLUFFS

Council Bluffs spreads from the stark precipices of the Missouri down onto the broad flats along the river and offers views of Omaha, its west-bank Nebraska neighbor. The city takes its name from the first formal conclave that Lewis and Clark conducted with Indians on their historic expedition from 1804 through 1806. The meeting, during which the captains discussed future trade matters with the Oto and Missouri Indians, occurred on August 3, 1804, on the west bank of the river about fifteen miles upstream from present-day Council Bluffs.

The town coalesced from a number of trading posts and settlements ensconced along this stretch of the river, including Trader's Point, established around 1824; Hart's Bluff, a trading post of the American Fur Company active in the 1840s; Father Pierre-Jean De

Smet's Indian mission, which the Jesuit priest started among the Potawatomi in 1838; and Kanesville, the Mormon community organized by Brigham Young and his followers in 1846. Council Bluffs lies at the gateway to the broad Platte River valley, a natural pathway across the plains. With the California gold rush, the settlement became a rough-and-tumble staging point for wagon trains heading west. Entrepreneurs, including Grenville Mellen Dodge, soon recognized Council Bluffs' potential as a rail hub, and much of the town's history is tied to the western expansion of the railroads.

General Dodge House

With its commanding bluff-top view, this mansion is an opulent confirmation of the long, colorful, and prosperous career of Grenville Méllen Dodge. A military and civil engineer, Dodge carried out survey work on the Mississippi & Missouri (Rock Island) Railroad that

A late nineteenth-century portrait of Mrs. Grenville Mellen Dodge hangs in the back parlor of the General Dodge House in Council Bluffs. Both the front and back parlors contain many original furnishings, including parlor chairs and pier glass.

brought him to Council Bluffs in 1853, and a year later he summoned his wife, parents, and siblings to join him on the frontier.
Dodge threw himself into many ventures, including the freight
business, banking, milling, surveying, and real estate. In this last
endeavor, he invested heavily in land along proposed railroad
routes. When Abraham Lincoln visited Council Bluffs in 1859,
Dodge had a fruitful discussion with the soon-to-be president about
railroads, which ultimately contributed to Lincoln's decision in 1864
to select the Platte Valley as the route for the nation's first transcontinental railroad.

During the Civil War, Dodge organized a network of spies for
the Union army and orchestrated the repair of war-ravaged railroads. In 1866 he resigned his army commission and returned to
building railroads. As chief engineer of the Union Pacific from 1866
to 1869, he directed the westward construction of the transcontinental railroad, shaking hands with his Central Pacific counterpart,
Samuel Montague, at Promontory Summit, Utah, where the two railroads met on May 10, 1869. Dodge was subsequently involved in rail
construction in Texas, Louisiana, Missouri, Kansas, Colorado, and
Mexico. His last venture was in Cuba in 1903.

The Dodges began construction on their home in 1869.
Completed a year later, the three-story brick mansion is in the
Second Empire style. Ornate dormers jut from its mansard roof, and
a handsome Doric-columned porch wraps around two sides of the
structure. The interior is lavishly appointed with parquet floors and
marble-manteled fireplaces. Many of the furnishings are original
family pieces. The house also contains memorabilia of Dodge's long
career, including artifacts relating to his involvement in the Civil War.

LOCATION: 605 3d Street. HOURS: February through December:
10–5 Tuesday–Saturday, 1–5 Sunday. FEE: Yes. TELEPHONE:
712-322-2406.

Near the Dodge House is the **Pottawattamie County Squirrel Cage
Jail** (226 Pearl Street, 712–323–2509), built in 1885. The brick
Victorian structure preserves an unusual detention center design
concept: A rotary cell system composed of a metal drum encircles
three floors, each tier divided into ten wedge-shaped cells. The jailer
gained access to a prisoner by turning a crank that aligned the cell
door with the opening on the outer drum.

The **Rock Island Depot** (South Main and Sixteenth Avenue, 712–323–5182), built in 1900, is now a railroad museum featuring extensive displays of passenger and freight trains as well as a restored central office and waiting rooms. On display outside are a caboose, postal, and baggage cars. The **Ruth Anne Dodge Memorial,** also known as the **Black Angel** (North 2d Street and Lafayette Avenue), is an imposing bronze sculpted by Daniel Chester French in 1919. It was commissioned by General Dodge's daughters shortly after their mother's death.

In Harlan is the **Pioneer Trails Historical Settlement,** a complex of four buildings in Potters Park (Pine Street and Morris Avenue, 712–755–2114), including two log cabins (ca. 1857) containing original mid-nineteenth century furniture; **Pioneer Hall,** which displays such pioneer artifacts as a covered wagon of 1860, blacksmith's tools, and various Indian artifacts; and the **Prairie Trails Museum,** which houses the archives of Shelby County's eleven incorporated towns, Civil War and World War I memorabilia, antique furniture, and paintings.

Located just south of Shelby, the **Carsten Memorial Farmstead** (Routes M16 and 83, 712–322–5519) preserves the house, numerous outbuildings, and eighty acres of an original section of land settled by German immigrants in the 1870s. Many household items and farm implements are on exhibit.

Elk Horn is the heart of a large concentration of Danes who settled in western Iowa in the 1870s. The **Danish Windmill** (Main and Elm streets, 712–764–7472), built in 1848 in Norre Snede, Denmark, has been reassembled in Elk Horn and put back into service as a gristmill. Many nineteenth-century structures here and in nearby **Kimballton** reflect rural Danish architectural styles as well as the immigrants' carpentry and masonry skills. In Elk Horn, the **Bedstemor's House** (Union and College streets, 712–764–6082) is a local application of a popular early-twentieth-century pattern-book design, built ca. 1908.

SOUTH
DAKOTA

OPPOSITE: *1880 Town, west of Murdo, preserves more than thirty buildings from the South Dakota prairie dating from the 1870s to 1919.*

Much of South Dakota's history has been shaped by the Missouri River, slicing through the middle of the state, and the Black Hills, looming in the southwest. In a realm of scant rainfall and unpredictable weather, the river's banks provided hospitable places where prehistoric and historic peoples alike built villages and planted crops. The big muddy river also served as a gateway: With the arrival of Europeans, the Missouri became the major highway on the midcontinent for exploration, commerce, and settlement. Then, for a time in the nineteenth century, the river became a barrier, the official boundary beyond which white settlement was forbidden.

The prehistoric peoples had disappeared from the northern Great Plains in the thirteenth century, possibly forced out by drought. Into this void migrated the Caddoan-speaking Arikara, also called the Ree, and two Siouan-speaking tribes, the Mandan and Hidatsa. Although they did not always get along, the three groups shared a number of customs. Farmers and hunters, they built earthen lodges in villages perched on the bluffs of the upper Missouri River. The Arikara, particularly able middlemen, held trade fairs in the autumn at their villages at the confluence of the Grand and Missouri rivers, where they traded to the Sioux horses obtained from the Cheyenne. Smallpox, brought by European explorers and traders, was the curse of these early Indians. The epidemic of 1780–1781 alone killed an estimated 75 percent of the Arikara population.

During the 1600s and 1700s other tribes, pushed west by adversaries, began moving onto the Great Plains. Formerly sedentary farmers, they acquired horses from the Spanish and quickly evolved into nomadic buffalo hunters. Present-day South Dakota became the haunt of the Cheyenne, an Algonquian-speaking group ousted from the Great Lakes region by the hostile Sioux and Ojibwa. The Black Hills were a particularly favored retreat of the Cheyenne. In the early 1800s, however, they were pushed south and west by the Sioux, who emerged as the dominant force on the plains of South Dakota for the next half century. The Teton—the largest of the major branches of the Sioux—held sway over large parts of South Dakota, while the more peaceable Yankton settled around the confluence of the James and Missouri rivers near present-day Yankton.

OPPOSITE: *A large rawhide medallion, decorated with dyed porcupine quills, seed beads, and eagle feathers, which was worn by the Oglala Sioux chief Red Cloud on his buffalo robe.*

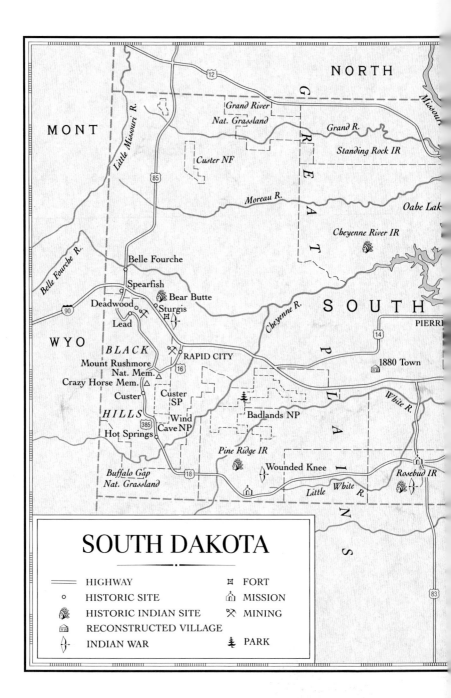

SOUTH DAKOTA

———— HIGHWAY

○ HISTORIC SITE

HISTORIC INDIAN SITE

RECONSTRUCTED VILLAGE

INDIAN WAR

FORT

MISSION

✕ MINING

🌲 PARK

In 1743 the sons of French explorer Pierre Gaultier de Varennes, sieur de La Vérendrye, left a dated plaque on a bluff overlooking the Missouri River near present-day Pierre, marking the first recorded visit by white adventurers to South Dakota. Throughout the remainder of the eighteenth century, a small number of trappers and traders ascended the Missouri from Saint Louis to do business among the Indians. The journals of Jean-Baptiste Truteau, field manager for the Missouri Company, and the river maps of James Mackay and John Thomas Evans, other explorers for the Missouri Company, were of great use to Meriwether Lewis and William Clark on their monumental expedition up the Missouri River in 1804.

One of the first entrepreneurs to exploit the discoveries of Lewis and Clark was Manuel Lisa, a Saint Louis-based trader. He established Fort Manuel around 1809 as part of a system of trading posts located among the upper Missouri Indians. Fort Manuel stood on the Missouri River near an Arikara village in what is now extremely northern South Dakota. The interpreter at this trading post was Toussaint Charbonneau, who along with his Shoshone wife,

Prospective homesteaders from Nebraska, who had traveled to the end of the rail line near Pierre in Dakota Territory in 1890, were transported in a variety of buggies, wagons, carriages, and surreys to view available land.

Sacajawea, had accompanied Lewis and Clark across the continent a few years earlier.

In 1823 General William Ashley and Major Andrew Henry, along with a party of adventurers, including mountain men Jim Bridger, Jedediah Smith, and Hugh Glass, embarked on what became one of the most famous trapping expeditions up the Missouri River. In the summer of 1823, while out scouting ahead of the party, Hugh Glass was attacked and mauled by a grizzly bear. Glass managed to crawl from the forks of the Grand River (in what is now northwestern South Dakota) to Fort Kiowa (near present-day Chamberlain), a feat marked by a monument near the forks of the Grand River just south of the town of Shadehill. The group also had several bloody but inconclusive encounters along the Missouri River with the Arikara, who resented the incursions of the white traders.

In 1831 the *Yellow Stone,* the first steamboat to ply the upper Missouri, docked at Fort Pierre (present-day Pierre) and launched the era of steamboat travel in the Dakotas, a period that lasted until the advent of railroads in the 1870s and 1880s. Forts and trading posts sprang up along the river. Many were destroyed by Indians or dismantled to provide cordwood for steamboats, and all were without purpose after the Indians were subdued and the buffalo extirpated. Several evolved into cities—the prime examples being Pierre, Chamberlain, Yankton, and Vermillion. The steamboats brought entrepreneurs and curious onlookers. The American artist George Catlin was on the *Yellow Stone's* first Missouri voyage, followed in 1833 by a Swiss artist, Karl Bodmer, in the company of Maximilian, prince of Wied, an indefatigable anthropologist and natural historian. These men made valuable records of the Great Plains Indian cultures. The first whites, mainly farmers, settled in the valley of the Big Sioux River in what is now southeastern South Dakota. They were initially discouraged by the Dakota Conflict of 1862 in nearby Minnesota Territory and by scourges of grasshoppers. But with improvements in farm machinery (especially in the sod-breaking capabilities of the plow) and the access to outside markets brought by the railroads, the agrarians began to inch, then scramble, into the fertile valleys of the James and Missouri rivers. Wheat was the favored crop.

Treaties in 1853 and 1864 established, respectively, the Yankton and Sisseton reservations, which lie in what is now eastern South Dakota. For the Teton the 1868 Treaty of Fort Laramie established the Missouri River as the boundary of white settlement, and lands west of the river became the Great Sioux Reservation. For the Cheyenne and Sioux, who arrived on the Great Plains only a few generations before white settlers, the Black Hills were a sacred refuge. Though this ground was hallowed for the Indians, rumors of gold in the hills interested the whites. When these tales were confirmed in 1874, a tide of gold seekers poured into the Black Hills. Their presence, in breach of treaties with the Indians, helped precipitate the Indian wars of the Great Plains. The various bands of the Teton Sioux were led by charismatic chiefs and warriors who became legends of the American West: Red Cloud and Crazy Horse of the Oglala, Spotted Tail of the Brule, Big Foot of the Miniconjou, and Sitting Bull of the Hunkpapa. The most famous battle of these wars, the Battle of Little Bighorn, took place in Montana. Although it was a victory for the Indians, their final defeat was inevitable. After Little Bighorn the Sioux warriors broke off into groups that were each defeated. Crazy Horse, leader of the largest band, surrendered in the spring of 1877. Sitting Bull retreated into Canada, then decided to surrender in 1881. Meanwhile, the settlement of their former lands had continued apace.

South Dakota's non-Indian population swelled from 12,000 in 1870 to 348,000 in 1889, the year it achieved statehood. Among the Czech, Norwegian, Swedish, and Finnish immigrant farmers were German-Russians, including members of the Mennonite and Hutterite sects. These peoples had fled religious persecution in Germany, emigrating to Russia and then to Canada and the United States. They arrived in Dakota Territory in 1873 and 1874. The majority of immigrants clustered in the eastern part of South Dakota, although a number of Finns went to work in the gold mines in the Black Hills. Some of the West's most colorful characters—Wild Bill Hickok, Calamity Jane, and Texas Jack, among others—were also lured to the Black Hills by gold. They were celebrated in the works of dime novelists and Western writers, who helped create the myth of the romantic West.

From 1878 to 1887, bonanza wheat farming boomed in the eastern half of the state, but farmers found that the region west of the 100th meridian had too little rainfall to support agriculture. The spacious plains west of the Missouri River became the grazing ground for vast herds of cattle. One of the largest cattle ranches in western South Dakota was founded by Henry J. Frawley, who arrived in the Black Hills in 1877 to practice law. As he prospered, he began acquiring property for his ranch from homesteaders whose attempts at farming 160-acre plots had failed in this arid region.

Many of the cattle in the Black Hills region were driven north from Texas to graze on summer grass before being shipped via railroad to eastern markets. The most romantic figure to emerge from this era of the wide-open range and the great cattle drives was the cowboy. Writers, and later moviemakers, gave this character mythic proportions, and their sentimentalized rendition of the nineteenth-century cowboy has long outlasted the fleeting period in which he thrived. By the late 1880s, the cattle boom had come to an end, a collapse brought on by an overstocked range and several years of killer blizzards on the Great Plains.

In 1889 General George Crook and a party of politicians traveled to the various Indian agencies. Over a period of months, they convinced the Sioux to yield another 9 million acres of their lands. Sitting Bull, who refused to go along with the settlement, made the famous statement to a newspaperman, "Indians? There are no Indians left but me." Today there are nine reservations in South Dakota, five of which are remnants of the Great Sioux Reservation: Standing Rock, Cheyenne River, and Lower Brule, skirting the Missouri River; and Pine Ridge and Rosebud, on the edge of the Badlands in the southwest. South Dakota remains the heartland of the Sioux, whose population of 30,000 constitutes one of the largest tribal groups in the country.

This chapter begins in the southeast, where settlers established the first towns in the Dakota Territory. It then moves to the agricultural centers that grew up along the James River, which cuts through the eastern third of the state. The next section covers the Missouri River, the dividing line between South Dakota's farming and ranching cultures. Alongside the river in the center of the state is the capital, Pierre. The chapter concludes in the southwest, where South Dakota's plains form a minimalist vista before giving way to the unequivocal scenic luster of the Badlands and the Black Hills. This corner of the state is steeped in Indian lore and gold rush history and was the scene of the final confrontation between American soldiers and Plains Indians, the 1890 massacre at Wounded Knee.

OVERLEAF: *Evidence found in prehistoric Indian settlements shows that sunflowers have been cultivated in South Dakota for more than 1,000 years.*

YANKTON

Yankton is named for the Yankton Sioux, whose traditional home-land was centered here at the confluence of the James and Missouri rivers. The frontier town flourished during the steamboat era, but by the late 1870s, with the coming of the railroads, Yankton began to wane in importance. The great flood that came during the spring thaw of 1881, following a winter of record snows, struck another blow to the riverboat industry. This deluge carried huge blocks of ice down the Missouri River, reportedly crushing the fleet of steam-boats docked at Yankton. As a gateway to the vast Missouri country, Yankton was capital of Dakota Territory from 1861 until 1883, when the seat of government was moved to Bismarck. A Yankton man, John Pearson, is credited with initiating the Black Hills gold rush with his discovery of gold deposits near Deadwood in 1875. Jack McCall, the man who killed James Butler "Wild Bill" Hickok in Deadwood in 1876, was sent to Yankton to stand trial—he was hanged in 1877 two miles north of town.

The **Excelsior Mill** (2d and Capital) remains from the era when milling locally grown wheat was one of Yankton's major industries. It was constructed in 1872 of chalk rock (soft yellow sandstone) and Sioux quartzite, two indigenous building materials, and now houses Gurney Seed and Nursery, in business since 1894. Adjacent to the mill are the studios of WNAX radio, where Lawrence Welk began his radio career in the late 1920s. The **African Methodist Episcopal Church** (508 Cedar Street), built by former slaves in 1885, is the old-est black church in the Dakota Territory. The **Cramer-Kenyon Heritage House** (509 Pine Street, 605–665–7470) dates to Yankton's riverboat heyday. Built in 1886, the Queen Anne residence contains Victorian fixtures and period antiques.

Dakota Territorial Museum

This museum contains Sioux artifacts, memorabilia from Yankton's steamboat era, period furnishings, and clothing. It also exhibits musical instruments and papers of Felix Vinatieri, an Italian-born musician who immigrated to Dakota Territory. General George Custer heard a band concert conducted by Vinatieri in Yankton in

OPPOSITE: *A portrait of Sitting Bull taken in the 1880s. He had visions that predicted the Indian victory at the Battle of Little Bighorn.*

1873 and asked him to join ranks as bandmaster. Vinatieri enlisted and served as chief musician of Custer's Seventh Cavalry Band until the death of the general at the Battle of the Little Bighorn in 1876. Custer usually liked to have his band playing when he went into battle. But Vinatieri and his musicians missed the Last Stand because this time Custer had ordered them to stay behind. Vinatieri was then discharged from the army and returned to Yankton. Several nineteenth-century structures have been moved to the museum's grounds, including the **Territorial Council Building,** a white frame structure where the Dakota Territory legislature first met in 1862.

LOCATION: 610 Summit Street, Westside Park. HOURS: June through August: 1–5 Wednesday–Monday; September through December: 1–4 Wednesday–Sunday. FEE: None. TELEPHONE: 605–665–3898.

YANKTON RESERVATION

This reservation, about forty miles west of Yankton, was established by treaty in 1853. In **Greenwood,** the **Holy Fellowship Episcopal Church** is a simple clapboard structure built in 1886 to serve the Sioux. The southern boundary of the Yankton Reservation is formed by the Missouri River, a portion of which has been impounded by **Fort Randall Dam.** Completed in 1954, it is one of the four South Dakota dams envisioned by the Pick-Sloan Missouri River Basin Development Plan. At the base of the dam stands **Fort Randall Historic Site** (605–487–7845). The fort was established in 1856 to help keep peace between white settlers and the Sioux and served as an active military outpost through the 1880s. Its roster of visitors included Philip Sheridan, William Tecumseh Sherman, and George Custer. After four years of exile in Canada and his subsequent surrender in 1881, Sitting Bull was held here as a prisoner for two years before being allowed to return to the Standing Rock Reservation. The only structure standing at the outpost is the **Fort Randall Chapel,** a chalk rock structure built in 1875.

VERMILLION

Vermillion was established on the bluffs above the confluence of the Vermillion and Missouri rivers after an earlier settlement on the flats was swept away by the flood of 1881. The town takes its name from the river's red clay banks. The earliest outpost in the vicinity was Fort Vermillion, a trading post built by the American Fur Company in 1835. Vermillion was founded in 1859 following the treaty with the Yankton Sioux. The tide of white settlement began after passage of the Homestead Act in 1862. In that same year, the legislature selected Vermillion to be the site of Dakota Territory's first university but failed to provide funding. Local citizens underwrote the institution, which opened in 1882. One of the university's promoters was frontier banker and politician Darwin Inman. The **Inman House** (415 East Main Street, private) is a handsome Georgian Revival structure, which serves as a residence for the University of South Dakota's president. Another relic of frontier prosperity is the **Austin-Whittemore House** (15 Austin Avenue), a brick Italianate structure built in 1882 by an early Dakota Territory settler, Horace J. Austin. The house, which is maintained by the Clay County Historical Society, contains Victorian furnishings.

Operated by the University of South Dakota, the **Shrine to Music Museum** (Clark and Yale streets, 605–677–5306) displays a large collection of musical instruments from around the world. Two of the six galleries in the museum are devoted to American musical history. The Graese Gallery exhibits musical instruments used by North and South American Indians, Civil War military bands, Appalachian folk musicians, and jazz performers. The Lewison Gallery focuses on nineteenth-century American keyboard instruments, including melodeons, reed organs, and a variety of pianos.

The **W. H. Over State Museum** (1110 Ratingen, 605–677–5228) is named for the prominent early-twentieth-century naturalist of the northern Great Plains, and his specimens form the core of the museum's natural-history collection. Also on display are archaeological exhibits, a large collection of Plains Indian art and artifacts, nineteenth-century photographs documenting South Dakota's territorial period, and pioneer tools, firearms, and clothing.

Spirit Mound, visible from Route 19 about seven miles north of Vermillion, provides the only relief in the notably flat prairie landscape. On a hot, windy August day in 1804, Meriwether Lewis and William Clark, along with several men from their expedition and Lewis's Newfoundland dog, Seaman, walked to the mound, which an Oto Indian had told them was inhabited by fierce midget-sized warriors. The explorers took note of a swarm of swallows feeding on insects on the lee side of the mound, and from atop the formation they were afforded a splendid view of the surrounding grasslands.

SIOUX FALLS

Sioux Falls is named for the picturesque cascades on the Big Sioux River, around which the town grew to be the largest city in South Dakota. The first settlers, rival land speculators from Minnesota and Iowa, arrived in 1857, but the nascent village was abandoned in the summer of 1862 as violence from the Dakota Conflict in the Minnesota Valley rippled westward. On August 25 Indians killed two Sioux Falls citizens—a father and son haying on the outskirts of town—and two days later the entire population fled to nearby Yankton. Indians burned the empty town to the ground. Three years later, Fort Dakota was established at the site of the falls, and settlers began to trickle back. The military outpost was active until 1870. In 1871 a plague of grasshoppers destroyed crops in the river valley, and many discouraged townspeople deserted Sioux Falls again. The town began to stabilize in the late 1870s with the advent of grist milling (using the falls as power), the arrival of the railroads, and the development of the quarry industry. Many nineteenth-century buildings were constructed of a native material, a distinctive red stone called Sioux quartzite. In the 1890s, as a result of South Dakota's then lax divorce laws, the city's lawyers, hoteliers, and merchants thrived on business brought by the colorful colony of people sitting out the required six months in Sioux Falls to attain their divorces. Religious leaders united to have the term lengthened in 1908.

The **Old Minnehaha County Courthouse Museum** (200 West 6th Street, 605–367–4210) is housed in a mammoth structure built of Sioux quartzite and dominated by a lofty clock tower. It is the finest example of Richardsonian Romanesque architecture in the state, and when it was completed in 1890 it was the largest building between Chicago and Denver north of Saint Louis. Vacated in 1962, the courthouse was subsequently restored and now contains interpretive exhibits about pioneer settlement and the Plains Indians.

Pettigrew Home and Museum

Born in Vermont, Richard Franklin Pettigrew came to the Dakota Territory in 1868. He staked a claim near Fort Dakota and com-

OPPOSITE: *Busts of Senator Richard F. Pettigrew and his brother Fred flank the fireplace in the foyer of the Pettigrew Home.*

menced to make money in milling, meat packing, and other business ventures. In the late nineteenth century, he was also elected to several territorial, state, and federal offices, where he earned a reputation as a stormy public servant. When he opposed the U.S. entry into World War I, he was indicted for sedition, but the charges were later dropped. Completed in 1889, the Pettigrew Home is a handsome Queen Anne structure built of Sioux quartzite and brick and filled with period furnishings. Pettigrew was interested in archaeology and natural history. His collection of artifacts and specimens is on display.

LOCATION: 131 North Duluth Avenue. HOURS: 9–12, 1–5 Tuesday–Friday, 9–5 Saturday, 1–5 Sunday. FEE: None. TELEPHONE: 605–367–7097.

The Pettigrew Home and Museum is within a neighborhood comprising many fine nineteenth-century residences, as well as the commanding **Saint Joseph Cathedral** (North Duluth Avenue and 5th Street), a church in the French and German Romanesque style designed in 1916 by the French architect Emmanuel L. Masqueray, who designed the great cathedral in Saint Paul.

Located on the campus of **Augustana College,** the **Center for Western Studies** (2111 South Summit Avenue, 605–336–4007) is a library and research facility that also has regular displays pertaining to the history of the Great Plains. These exhibits cover prehistoric and Sioux cultures, pioneer settlement, ethnic history, nineteenth-century medical practices, and Western art. The **Great Plains Zoo and Museum** (805 South Kiwanis Avenue, 605–367–7059) includes among its collections a North American Plains Exhibit, which displays native mammals and waterfowl in a natural setting along a tributary of the Big Sioux River.

MITCHELL

In 1879 a Chicago, Milwaukee & Saint Paul Railroad representative selected the site for Mitchell, which was named for the company's president, Alexander Mitchell. Backed by competing railroads, Mitchell and Pierre were the last contenders in the state capital contest. The battle reached a fever pitch in the summer of 1904 when, to woo voters, the vying railroad companies gave free tickets to passengers to entice them to visit their respective cities. Mitchell subsequently lost the election to Pierre. The centerpiece of Mitchell's commercial district and one of South Dakota's architectural landmarks is the **Corn Palace** (604 North Main Street, 605–996–7311). The exhibition hall and auditorium first opened in 1892 as part of the state's Corn Belt Exposition. To accommodate ever larger crowds, three different palaces have been built, the last in 1921. The exotic Moorish-style structure is famous for its facade, which is decorated each year with murals composed of thousands of bushels of corn, grains, and grasses grown by local farmers. **The Friends of the Middle Border Pioneer Museum** (1311 South Duff Street, 605–996–2122) exhibits Indian arts and crafts as well as farm equipment, clothing, and toys from the homestead era. Also on the grounds are several nineteenth-century structures including a one-room schoolhouse (1885) and the Victorian home (1886) of Louis Beckwith, founder of the Corn Palace, which contains period furnishings. In addition, the **Case Art Museum** features works of artists of the era, including James Earle Fraser, John Innes, Harvey Dunn, and Nancy Coonsman Hahn.

Mitchell Prehistoric Indian Village

A testament to the long agricultural heritage of the James River Basin, this fortified village on a tributary of the James River was occupied by a group of farmer-hunters about 900 years ago. A thousand people are estimated to have lived here in seventy timber-frame mud-plastered lodges. Visitors can walk through a replica of one of these rectangular dwellings. The villagers hunted buffalo in the spring, foraged for a variety of small game and wild plants, and grew corn, beans, squash, tobacco, and sunflowers. A garden plot contains plantings representative of remains found at the site. The museum displays artifacts excavated from the site, including animal and plant remains and implements made of stone, bone, shell, and fired clay. A geodesic dome has been built over a part of the village's archeological deposits, and the Archeodome Research Center was scheduled to be opened in 1998.

LOCATION: Indian Village Road, on the west bank of Lake Mitchell. HOURS: June through August 8–8 Daily; May and September: 9–4 Daily; October: 9–4 Monday–Friday. FEE: None. TELEPHONE: 605–996–5473.

The James River valley town of **Huron** dates to 1879, when surveyors for the Chicago & Northwestern Railroad set up camp here on the banks of the river. Beginning in the mid-1880s, Huron vied with Pierre, Watertown, Sioux Falls, Mitchell, and Chamberlain to become the state capital, a much coveted designation that Pierre finally secured in 1904. In that same year, Huron was selected to be the site of the South Dakota State Fair. The **Dakotaland Museum** (West 3d Street, on the South Dakota State Fairgrounds, 605–352–4626) contains exhibits of Indian crafts and artifacts and pioneer tools, household items, and toys.

DE SMET

The small town of De Smet, forty-five miles west of Brookings, is closely associated with Laura Ingalls Wilder, whose children's books chronicle the pioneer experience on the Great Plains. After unsuccessful attempts at homesteading in Kansas and Wisconsin, Laura's father, Charles Ingalls, moved to De Smet in 1879 to work for the

Moorish-inspired domes and minarets were added to the "World's Only Corn Palace" in Mitchell in 1937, transforming the angular 1921 building into a fantastic structure that more closely resembled the original Corn Palace.

Corn cobs, sawn in half, and other local argricultural products are nailed to panels to create the intricate designs on the Corn Palace in Mitchell.

railroad. That first winter, the Ingalls family lived in the **Surveyors' Shanty** (101 Olivet Street), built originally to house Chicago & Northwestern Railroad workers. The **Ingalls House** (210 West 3d Street, 605–854–3383) is a frame structure built in 1887. The shanty and house contain period furnishings and Ingalls memorabilia. Laura Ingalls lived in De Smet from the age of 12 until 27, when she and her husband Almanzo Wilder moved to Mansfield, Missouri.

MADISON

A small town amid numerous glacial lakes, Madison was founded in 1875 and is home to the state's first normal school, now Dakota State College, founded in 1881. On campus is the **Smith-Zimmermann State Museum** (North 8th Street, 605–256–5308). Exhibits of clothing, furnishings, household items, and agricultural implements focus on the settlement of eastern South Dakota, which began with the Homestead Act of 1862. The museum also maintains a large collection of memorabilia from the Chautauqua resort on nearby Lake

Madison, an important cultural center in this part of South Dakota from 1890 to 1932. **Prairie Village** (Route 34, 605–256–3644) is a compound of restored nineteenth-century structures and equipment relocated from the Madison vicinity. It includes a steam carousel of 1893, a frame church of 1906, and the **Chapel Car Emmanuel.** One of seven Barney and Smith railroad cars equipped with pews, organ, and pulpit, the Chapel Car Emmanuel was dedicated in 1893 by Baptist minister Boston Smith, whose idea it was to send clergymen out in the railroad cars to minister to churchless frontier settlements.

A mile south of Prairie Village is the **Herman Luce Cabin** (Lake Herman State Park, 605–256–5003) of 1871, a fine example of rustic homestead architecture. The cabin, which stands on its original site, is constructed of hewn oak logs and contains pioneer furnishings and household utensils. The house was part of a small community that withered when the railroad bypassed it for Madison. Near the cabin, the graves of Luce's wife and two in-laws make manifest the severity of frontier life.

BROOKINGS

Brookings is home to the state's land grant college, South Dakota State University, which was established in 1881. The town was platted in 1879, the day after the first train pulled into the frontier village. It was named for Judge Wilmot W. Brookings, an early and tireless promoter of South Dakota. Located on the university campus, the **State Agricultural Heritage Museum** (11th Street and Medary Avenue, 605–688–6226) has exhibits of pioneer household items and farm implements and machinery, dating from 1860 to 1940. One wing contains a homesteader's claim shanty of 1882 with many original furnishings. The museum is housed in the university's old **Stock Judging Pavilion,** a handsome Prairie-style structure built in 1918.

WATERTOWN

Platted in 1878, Watertown lies on the Big Sioux River, near the shores of Lakes Kampeska and Pelican, two glacial lakes characteristic of northeastern South Dakota. Citizens originally called their village Kampeska, but later named it after Watertown, New York. The **Codington County Courthouse** (First Avenue SE, between South Broadway and Maple Street), built in 1929, is a Classic Revival gray limestone structure with Renaissance exterior elements and an elaborate marble interior. The **Carnegie Free Public Library** (27 First

Eastern South Dakota consists of rolling farmland like that of neighboring Minnesota and Iowa. Across the Missouri River are grass lands suitable for grazing cattle.

Avenue SE, 605–886–7335) of 1905, also in the Classic Revival style, houses the collections of the **Kampeska Heritage Museum,** which include pioneer artifacts, period furnishings, and local natural-history and military-history exhibits. The **Mellette House** (421 Fifth Avenue NW, 605–886–4730) of 1883 was home to Arthur Calvin Mellette, the last appointed governor of Dakota Territory, who went on to be elected first state governor of South Dakota in 1889. The red brick Italianate house contains original family furnishings.

FORT SISSETON STATE HISTORIC PARK

This park is on the Coteau des Prairies ("highland of the prairies"), a distinctive expanse of elevated prairie in southwestern Minnesota, eastern South Dakota, and northeastern Iowa. The state park contains seventeen original and reconstructed structures of Fort Sisseton, a military outpost built in 1864 in response to the 1862 Dakota Conflict in the nearby Minnesota River valley. The well-fortified installation was intended as a show of force to discourage further insurrections. Until it closed in 1889, Fort

Fort Sisseton, a mid-nineteenth-century outpost on the Dakota frontier, included commissary, hospital, and a commodious stable.

Sisseton was an important way station on the Western frontier for wagon trains, fur trappers, and gold prospectors. The North Barracks now houses the visitor center. Other structures include the Guardhouse, Officers' Quarters, Commanding Officer's Residence, and Trading Post.

> LOCATION: 10 miles southwest of Lake City. HOURS: Memorial Day through Labor Day: 10–6 Daily. FEE: None. TELEPHONE: 605–448–5701.

About fifty miles northwest of Aberdeen is the 7,800-acre **Samuel H. Ordway, Jr., Memorial Prairie** (Route 10 West, nine miles west of Leola, 605–439–3475). Owned and maintained by the Nature Conservancy, the preserve is one of the last fragments of the tall-grass and mixed-grass prairie that once characterized the eastern, moist portion of the Great Plains.

The reconstructed northwest block house at Fort Sisseton. Its two levels face eight directions, permitting defenders to meet attacks from all sides.

ABERDEEN

Aberdeen, the third-largest city in South Dakota, sprang up in the 1880s at the junction of several railroads. It lies amid the rich agricultural lands of the James River valley. The town was named for Aberdeen, Scotland, once the home of one of the town's prominent railroad representatives. The tree-lined streets of the town attest to the early efforts of Great Plains settlers to relieve the monotonous prairie landscape with tree plantings. In a similar effort, they named an early residential neighborhood Highlands, embellishing on the fact that the area is three feet higher in elevation than Aberdeen's commercial district. By 1906 four railroad companies had converged on Aberdeen, bringing settlers and entrepreneurs and linking local farmers with Eastern markets. Handsome remnants of those bustling days are the **Minneapolis & Saint Louis Railroad Depot** (1100 South Main Street), a brick-and-stone Classic Revival structure of 1900, and the Prairie-style **Chicago, Milwaukee & Saint Paul Depot** (901 Southeast Second Avenue) of 1911. The **Dacotah Prairie Museum** (21 South Main Street, 605–626–7117) is housed in the Western Union Building (1888–1890). The museum contains a prairie grasslands diorama, Sioux and Ojibwa decorative arts, and pioneer tools, furnishings, and clothes.

CHEYENNE RIVER AND STANDING ROCK RESERVATIONS

The vast arid plain west of the Missouri River and north of the Cheyenne River comprises the Cheyenne River Reservation and the Standing Rock Reservation. In the 1880s the Cheyenne River Reservation became a center of the ghost dance religion, a spiritual movement inspired by a Paiute named Wovoka. According to Wovoka, the white man would vanish from the plains and the buffalo reappear if the Indians performed certain ritualized dances. The practitioners wore supposedly bullet-proof white shirts, which is how the ritual came to be called ghost dancing.

The Standing Rock Reservation, which extends into North Dakota, was home to Sitting Bull, the leader of the Hunkpapa Sioux. Born in 1831 near the Grand River, he came back to the Standing Rock Reservation in 1883 after his release from imprisonment at Fort Randall. With the spread of the ghost dance religion, white authorities became concerned that the movement might coalesce into a general uprising with Sitting Bull as its leader. Several thousand army reinforcements were dispatched to the South Dakota reservations, and Standing Rock Reservation police attempted to arrest Sitting Bull on December 15, 1890. A struggle ensued in which Sitting Bull and several other people were murdered. After this incident, Chief Big Foot of the Cheyenne River Reservation, who was a proponent of the ghost dance movement, crossed the Badlands with a group of followers seeking refuge in the Pine Ridge Indian Reservation. Their flight culminated in the massacre at Wounded Knee two weeks after the death of Sitting Bull.

OAHE LAKE

Six miles north of Pierre is Oahe Lake, a 230-mile-long reservoir formed by Oahe Dam, a massive earthen rampart 242 feet high and 1.9 miles long. Named for an Indian mission established nearby in the 1870s by Thomas Riggs, *oahe* is a Siouan word meaning "a safe place on which to stand." The project is the largest of four reservoirs built on the Missouri River as part of the Pick-Sloan Plan, a program initiated by the U.S. Army Corps of Engineers and the Bureau of Reclamation to harness the mighty and unpredictable Missouri River. As with most dam-building projects in the western United States, Oahe Dam sparked controversy—in this case among farmers concerned about the valuable agricultural lands the reservoir would inundate—and it irrevocably altered the character and environment of the river it restrains. Nevertheless the structure is an engineering feat and vivid reminder of the historic era of mammoth dam projects that were begun under the New Deal in the 1930s.

The **Oahe Mission School and Chapel,** which stands at the east end of Oahe Dam, was saved from the rising waters of the reservoir. The church was built in 1877 by Indian laborers and Thomas Riggs, a missionary to the Sioux who was carrying on the work of his father, Stephen Return Riggs, an Ohioan who came to Dakota Country in 1835 to minister to the Indians.

PIERRE

Pierre (pronounced PEER), the capital of South Dakota, is located in the approximate center of the state on the east bank of the Missouri River. On the opposite bank, where the Bad River joins the Missouri, stands the small town of **Fort Pierre,** the first permanent white settlement in South Dakota and the nucleus from which Pierre grew. This site has a long history of human occupation and was visited by a steady stream of explorers from the sons of French explorer Pierre Gaultier de Varennes, sieur de La Vérendrye, in 1743 to Lewis and Clark in 1804 to the anthropologist Prince Maximilian of Wied and his artist, Karl Bodmer, in 1833. The prehistoric Indians who lived along the river were followed by the Mandan, who were driven out by the Arikara, who were in turn displaced by the Sioux. The La Vérendryes laid claim to this territory for Louis XV in 1743. Almost 200 years later, in 1913, a group of schoolchildren on an outing along the west bank of the Missouri River found the metal plate inscribed in Latin with the La Vérendryes' claim. In Fort Pierre, the **Vérendrye Monument**

OVERLEAF: *Fort Pierre, the first white settlement in South Dakota, was established by the Chouteau Fur Trading Company. The United States government purchased it in 1855 for $36,500 on the basis of this drawing by Frederick Behman, an employee.*

Oahe church, built in 1877 by Sioux laborers under the direction of a missionary, Thomas Riggs, was moved to its current site in the 1950s during the construction of the Oahe Dam.

(Vérendrye Drive off Route 83) stands on the hillside where the plaque was discovered.

In September 1804 Lewis and Clark spent several anxious days at the Bad River negotiating with a group of troublesome Teton to let the Corps of Discovery pass up the Missouri River. These Indians, in an effort to dominate trade along the Missouri, had repulsed previous traders and seemed intent on barring Lewis and Clark from doing business with their enemies, the Mandan and Arikara. The expedition eventually departed with two amiable chiefs, Buffalo Medicine and Black Buffalo, on board (their presence probably helped prevent an attack from more belligerent Indians who trailed the boats on land). The French-Indian trader Joseph La Framboise established the first permanent white settlement in the region in 1817 when he opened a trading post at the confluence of the two rivers. This outpost evolved over time, and in 1832 an influential Saint Louis–based French trader rebuilt the settlement and renamed it after himself—Fort Pierre Chouteau, Jr. It served as the center for his Upper Missouri fur trade for two decades. In 1855 the U.S. Army bought the fort, but the dilapidated compound was never activated.

The east-bank town of Pierre came into being with the arrival of the Chicago & Northwestern Railroad in 1880. A frontier village sprouted quickly at the railroad's terminus and was soon busy with gold seekers bound for the Black Hills via stagecoach or wagon train. Pierre was named temporary state capital in 1889, a designation that became permanent in 1904, after prolonged competition with rival cities. Completed in 1910, the **State Capitol** (500 East Capitol Avenue, 605–773–3765) is a domed Classic Revival structure of dressed limestone and sandstone. As a cost-saving measure, the supervising architect, C. E. Bell, adapted his designs for the Montana state capitol. The ornate interior contains a grand staircase lined with Corinthian columns, Italian marble floors, and murals depicting the influence of agriculture, livestock, and mining in the state's economy. In contrast to the highly embellished capitol, the **Governor's House** (southeast corner of the Capitol Complex) is a two-story clapboard structure built in 1934 by the Works Progress Administration.

Pierre's grand State Capitol, constructed between 1907 and 1910, settled the question of which town was to be the permanent seat of South Dakota's government.

The **Cultural Heritage Center** (900 Governors Drive, 605–773–3458), built completely underground, is the headquarters of the South Dakota State Historical Society and contains their archives, library, and museum. On display is the Vérendrye Plate, placed at the site of present-day Fort Pierre in 1743 by François and Louis Joseph, sent by their father, the explorer Pierre Gaultier de Varennes, sieur de La Vérendrye, to claim the region for France.

More than thirty buildings dating from the 1870s to 1919 have been brought together to form **1880 Town** (605-344-2259), located west of Murdo on Route 90. Included are the 1910 Draper Hotel, originally in Draper, Saint Stephen's Church from Dixon, and the Two Strike Fire Company.

BADLANDS NATIONAL PARK

Located in southwestern South Dakota, the park preserves a sweep of dramatic landscape where rain has carved out rugged canyons, ridges, and spires. (Although the rainfall in the region is sparse, thunderstorms bring heavy downpours that rapidly erode the land.) This distinctive landscape is formed of volcanic ash and soft sediment left by inland oceans as long as 80 million years ago. In 1848 the French missionary Pierre-Jean De Smet wrote a vivid description of the region: "Viewed at a distance, these lands exhibit the appearance of extensive villages and ancient castles, but under forms so extraordinary, and so capricious a style of architecture, that we might consider them as appertaining to some new world, or ages far remote." In the eighteenth and nineteenth centuries, this formidable terrain presented such an obstacle that early French-Canadian trappers called the region *les mauvaises terres à traverser* (bad lands to travel across). Badlands National Park also preserves remnants of the grasslands that once covered the middle of North America from southern Canada to Mexico. The park's mixed-grass prairie is recognized as the finest that survives. Beginning in the mid-nineteenth century, cattle replaced bison, and wheat and corn supplanted the prairie grasses. Bison and

OPPOSITE: *Allegorical paintings by Edward Simons representing agriculture and the livestock industry decorate the rotunda of the Capitol. On the other side are Simons's representations of mining and family life.*

South Dakota's Badlands National Park preserves a region of eroded gullies, spires, and buttes. This spectacular landscape has been created in the course of more than three million years by water washing through soft sediments and volcanic ash.

bighorn sheep have been reintroduced into the **Sage Creek Basin** of the Badlands.

The headquarters of Badlands National Park is at the **Ben Reifel Visitor Center** (605–433–5361), some two miles northeast of the small town of Interior off Route I-90. It offers exhibits of natural and cultural history. Interpretive exhibits pertaining to the Oglala Sioux are on display at the **White River Visitor Center,** located on the Pine Ridge Reservation, twenty miles south of Scenic.

At the park's east entrance is the sod-and-log **Prairie Homestead** (Route 240, 605–433–5400), a rare extant example of pioneer prairie architecture. Edgar and Alice Story Brown homesteaded 160 acres of the Badlands in 1909 and lived here for some twenty years with their two children. The house, which is dug partially into an embankment, is constructed of cottonwood logs and buffalo grass sod. It contains pioneer furnishings, some of which are original. Also on site are a claim shanty and barn used by the Browns.

PINE RIDGE AND ROSEBUD RESERVATIONS

The Pine Ridge and Rosebud Reservations are situated in south-central South Dakota. The Rosebud Agency, which served the Brule Sioux, and Pine Ridge Agency, for the Oglala, were established in 1878, two years after several Sioux chiefs had relinquished the near-by Black Hills in return for food and supplies. Conditions were grim on the reservations following this major land cession. Congress cut beef rations, disease was rampant among the Indians, and federal surveillance increased with the spread of the ghost dance movement. The tensions culminated in the massacre on the banks of Wounded Knee Creek on the Pine Ridge Reservation. On December 29, 1890, a confused fight broke out while soldiers of the Seventh Cavalry were disarming a group of Sioux who had fled here with Chief Big Foot in the aftermath of Sitting Bull's death. The Sioux had spent the night of December 28–29 surrounded by the soldiers, who were reinforced during the night. In the morning, 500 troopers formed a box around the camp; then some of them

The Prairie Homestead, established by Mr. and Mrs. Ed Brown in the South Dakota Badlands in 1909, has been preserved as a typical early twentieth-century homestead.

Sioux Indians unenthusiastically await their handout on ration day at Pine Ridge Indian Reservation. The Indians did not prosper at farming after their traditional way of life was no longer possible, and some died of starvation when they refused to eat the unfamiliar food that was available at the reservation.

entered the camp to collect weapons. A shot was fired, perhaps inadvertently, but it touched off gunfire from both sides and desperate hand-to-hand struggles. The soldiers pulled back to allow a fearsome weapon to be used—four rapid-firing Hotchkiss guns, firing fifty rounds per minute, opened up on the Sioux. About 250 men, women, and children were killed. The Wounded Knee massacre marked the end of the Indian wars on the Great Plains. A **monument** stands at the mass grave where the dead were buried.

On the Rosebud Reservation in the small town of **Saint Francis** is the **Saint Francis Mission and Buechel Memorial Lakota Museum** (350 South Oak Street, 605–747–5509). The Catholic congregation was established among the Sioux in 1886 and administered by Franciscans and Jesuits from Germany. The museum contains the collections of Father Buechel, the indefatigable Jesuit priest who assembled Indian artifacts and photographs and wrote a number of books in the Lakota language, one of the dialects of the Sioux.

THE BLACK HILLS

The pine-clad Black Hills are noted for their dramatic pinnacles and mammoth rock outcrops. Sacred to the Indians, the Sioux called the mountains Paha Sapa. Reports of gold in the Black Hills were widespread on the Great Plains in the early nineteenth century, and even though the territory was within the domain of the Sioux, the federal government came under increasing pressure to confirm rumors of the precious metal. In the summer of 1874, George Armstrong Custer led the Seventh Cavalry on a military expedition into the Black Hills, and in late July the two experienced miners in his party, Horatio N. Ross and William McKay, found traces of gold in French Creek. By September the world at large had news of the discovery, and pressure increased for the government to renege on its treaty. A Chicago paper editorialized: "Pleasant as be the pastures in which [the Indians'] children have sported, and the slopes that hold the bones of their dead, they must leave them for the land of the stranger, and stand not upon the order of their going. There is gold in the hills and rivers of the region, and the white man desires to take possession of it." And take possession he did. The rush for gold spurred the War for the Black Hills (also known as Sitting Bull and Crazy Horse's War), of which the most famous fight was the Battle of the Little Bighorn in 1876. Within a year, however, the Indians lost a series of battles across the Great Plains (including the Battle of Slim Buttes, which occurred near the present-day town of Reva in northwestern South Dakota), and white miners had an irrevocable hold on the Black Hills.

HOT SPRINGS

On the southern edge of the Black Hills, Hot Springs grew up as a turn-of-the-century spa nestled among the scenic sandstone cliffs of the Fall River Canyon. Discovered in 1974 during excavation for a housing development, the **Mammoth Site** (19th Street and Evanston Avenue, 605–745–6017) is an ancient sinkhole where countless mammoths were entrapped as they came to drink. Consuming 500 pounds of vegetation a day, the ten-ton herbivores were the dominant creatures on the Pleistocene landscape. More than forty mammoths have been unearthed at the site, and their fossilized bones are estimated to be 26,000 years old. Exposed bones in situ are on view at the visitor center, which has been constructed over the sinkhole.

CUSTER

The town of Custer lies beside French Creek near the spot where gold was discovered on the Custer Expedition. Founded in 1875, this town claims to be the oldest settlement in the Black Hills, but it never thrived on the gold rush: The town boomed for about a year, after which many of its inhabitants hastened to the richer fields of gold in Deadwood and Lead. Custer's population began to stabilize in the late nineteenth century, especially after the railroad arrived in 1890. The **Custer County Courthouse** (411 Mount Rushmore Road), built in 1881, was the scene of many trials to settle cattle thefts, stolen mine property, and other matters of frontier strife. The red-brick Italianate structure houses the **Custer County Historical Society Museum** (605–673–2443), which contains exhibits of the Custer Expedition, Sioux arts and crafts, rocks and minerals, and pioneer clothing.

Custer State Park

Custer State Park lies in the heart of the Black Hills on terrain closely associated with the area's early gold rush frenzy. After Custer's party discovered gold nearby in 1874, an impatient group of gold seekers from Sioux City, Iowa, headed for the mountains, violating the 1868 Treaty of Fort Laramie. The Gordon Party, named for its leader John Gordon, erected a hasty fortification for protection from the Indians and the bitter weather. Custer State Park encompasses the party's wintering ground, and a replica of the **Gordon Stockade** stands on the site where they built their stronghold in early 1875. In the spring, military escorts accompanied the prospectors out of the Black Hills to Cheyenne, Wyoming. The twenty-eight-member party included a boy and his mother, Annie D. Tallent, who is often cited as the first white woman to reach the Black Hills.

Custer State Park was promoted by Peter Norbeck, an influential early conservationist and politician in South Dakota. When established in 1919, it was the largest state park in the nation. Norbeck was instrumental in developing scenic roads in the area, including the spectacular Needles Highway (Route 87), which enters the park from the northwest. The **Peter Norbeck Visitor Center,** a Civilian Conservation Corps project constructed in 1934 of native stone, contains exhibits on local history. In 1927 Norbeck built a summer retreat in the park called **Valhalla,** a rambling log structure used primarily for state government functions. The **Badger Clark Home** (ca. 1910) is a rustic structure of native stone and wood shingles built by South Dakota's first poet laureate. Scorning electricity and fetching water from a nearby spring, Clark lived and worked in this pastoral cabin for thirty years. It contains his library and original furnishings.

LOCATION: Route 16A, 5 miles east of Custer. HOURS: *Park:* Always open. *Visitor Center:* Spring and Fall: Schedule varies; June through August: 8–8 Daily. *Badger Clark Home:* Memorial Day through Labor Day: 10–5 Monday–Friday, 1–4 Saturday–Sunday. FEE: Yes. TELEPHONE: 605–255–4515.

MOUNT RUSHMORE NATIONAL MEMORIAL

The sixty-foot faces of Presidents George Washington, Thomas Jefferson, Abraham Lincoln, and Theodore Roosevelt chiseled into this granite outcrop form one of the most imposing monuments in the country. Gutzon Borglum was the sculptor who designed the grouping and orchestrated the dynamiting and jackhammer work, which brought the faces out of the rock. Funding and weather, both unpredictable, slowed the progress of the project. Borglum worked on Mount Rushmore on and off between 1927 and 1941, when he died at the age of 74. His son, Lincoln, continued for some months afterward until funds were exhausted. The federal government financed $836,000 of the $990,000 spent on the memorial. Exhibits in the visitor center explain events leading up to the construction of Mount Rushmore and display equipment used in sculpting the faces. **Borglum's Studio,** the second he had built during his work on the project, contains the sculptor's scale models and smaller tools, such as bits, chisels, and hammers.

LOCATION: Route 244, 3 miles south of Keystone. HOURS: *Visitor Center:* June through August: 8 am–10 pm Daily. Rest of year: 8–5 Daily. FEE: None. TELEPHONE: 605–574–2523.

Mount Rushmore nearing completion. The sculptor, Gutzon Borglum, trained a group of local miners and laborers to carry out his design for the massive rock face.

CRAZY HORSE MEMORIAL

Echoing the monumentalism of Mount Rushmore, the Crazy Horse Memorial is a 563-foot-high, 641-foot-long sculpture-in-progress of the Oglala Sioux warrior who defeated General George Armstrong Custer at the Battle of the Little Bighorn. The work, which is being blasted from a granite mountain, will depict the bare-breasted warrior on a charging horse. Sioux chiefs invited the sculptor Korczak Ziolkowski to work on the project in 1939. After serving in World War II, he settled in the Black Hills, where he remained to work on the project until his death in 1982. **Korczak's Studio-Home,** a log structure built in 1947, contains memorabilia and examples of his art. The **Indian Museum of North America** displays art, artifacts, tools, and clothing of Plains Indians as well as of other North American tribes.

LOCATION: 4 miles north of Custer off Route 16/385. HOURS: Dawn–Dusk Daily. FEE: Yes. TELEPHONE: 605–673–4681.

Each of the four presidential faces on Mount Rushmore is sixty feet high. The memorial can be seen to its best advantage in morning light.

RAPID CITY

Rapid City sits on the east slope of the Black Hills. The town was founded in 1876 by a group of dispirited gold miners who decided to turn their talents to business. At the time, white settlement of the Black Hills violated Indian treaties, so agents of the federal government and embittered Sioux both discouraged the early growth of Rapid City. Nonetheless, the town grew steadily and boomed with the arrival of the first railroad in 1886. Rapid City's **Commercial Historic District** (Main and Saint Joseph streets between 6th and 7th streets) retains the tenor of the late nineteenth century, when the town was a business center for miners.

The Journey (222 New York Street, 605–394–6923), a museum complex revolutionary in design and concept, opened in 1997. It incorporates holdings of four museums and a private collection that span 2.5 billion years in the Black Hills. At the **Museum of Geology,** a field tent and two excavation sites introduce visitors to techniques of discovery and data-collection used by geologists and paleontologists. The **South Dakota State Archaeological Research Center** brings together artifacts from thousands of sites. The **Sioux Indian Museum** presents the diversity of Northern Plains Sioux arts. A hologram storyteller recounts tales of Sioux life. Three bison-hide tipis and a horse and travois (an early means of transport) are among the exhibits. The **Minnilusa Pioneer Museum Collection** surveys early military and scientific expeditions, the cattle and ranching industries, homesteading and agriculture, and the colorful characters who populated the local historical stage. The **Duhamel Collection** includes hundreds of Sioux artifacts that are among the country's finest.

STURGIS

This town, founded in 1878 on the northern edge of the Black Hills, grew out of Camp Sturgis, a U.S. military outpost established in 1876 in an attempt to protect white settlers and instill order in the chaos of the gold rush. The town is named for Lieutenant Jack Sturgis, the youngest officer killed at the Battle of the Little Bighorn and the son of Colonel Samuel Sturgis, commander of nearby Fort Meade, which succeeded the military camp. Sturgis was home to two celebrated Black Hills women. The **Annie Tallent House** (1603 Main Street, private) was home in later years to the only female member of the Gordon Party, which went into the hills in the winter of 1874 to search for gold. She was a teacher and author of *The Black Hills; or the Last Hunting Ground of the Dakotahs*. The stone cottage was built in 1898. The **Poker Alice House** (North Junction Street, private) was the home, casino, dance hall, and brothel of Alice Tubbs, a colorful Englishwoman who opened her notorious establishment in Sturgis in about 1890. Before she moved to Sturgis she had won fame throughout the West as a gambler. The simple clapboard house dates from 1895.

Old Fort Meade Museum

Established in 1878, Fort Meade replaced Camp Sturgis as the headquarters of the peace-keeping force in the Black Hills. The site, which reportedly was selected by General Philip Sheridan, stood on a main Indian trail into the mountains and near the Bismarck, Fort Pierre, and Sidney trails, by which the pioneers poured into the Black Hills. The first garrison at the fort was the

U.S. Seventh Cavalry, reorganized after the 1876 Battle of the Little Bighorn and under the command of Colonel Samuel Sturgis. Major Marcus A. Reno, a colorful and controversial survivor of the Little Bighorn, was court-martialed and discharged from service at Fort Meade for disorderly conduct, which included surreptitiously peeking in Colonel Sturgis's window at his comely daughter Ella. Fort Meade was also home from 1879 to 1887 to the illustrious horse Comanche, the lone survivor of the main battle at the Little Bighorn.

The fort was a key post during the Sioux unrest in 1890, which culminated in the massacre at Wounded Knee, and also during the Ute uprising from 1906 to 1908. In 1944 Fort Meade became a Veterans Administration hospital. Several original nineteenth-century frame buildings remain at the fort as well as numerous structures from the 1900–1910 period. Exhibits at the **Old Fort Meade Museum** interpret life at the frontier outpost.

LOCATION: Route 34, 1 mile east of Sturgis. HOURS: Memorial Day through Labor Day: 8–6 Daily; May and September: 9–5 Daily. FEE: Yes. TELEPHONE: 605–347–9822.

DEADWOOD

The town of Deadwood, in the northern Black Hills, sprang up along the narrow gulch where Yankton prospector John Pearson discovered gold in 1875. By the summer of 1876, an estimated 25,000 people rushed to the area, lured by news of the find. Placer mining—washing gold from coarse streambed gravel—was the first method of extracting the precious metal. As the placer claims were worked out, miners began digging underground shafts for gold. Although a fire in 1879 and an equally ruinous flood in 1883 destroyed many of the early wooden structures in the gulch, the **Deadwood Historic District,** which encompasses the entire town, preserves numerous late-nineteenth-century buildings from Deadwood's heyday. **Adams Memorial Hall Museum** (54 Sherman Street, 605–578–1714) contains Indian items, mining equipment, mineralogical specimens, antique firearms, costumes, and gold rush memorabilia. The **House of Roses Museum** (15 Forest Avenue, 605–578–1879) was built in 1879 and contains period furnishings.

Although his tenure in Deadwood was brief, Wild Bill Hickok is perhaps the most famous person associated with the town. James

Butler Hickok, born in Illinois in 1837, was a scout and sharpshooter for the Union army during the Civil War and a marshal in the Kansas towns of Hays City and Abilene from 1869 to 1872. He toured with Buffalo Bill Cody's Wild West Show for one season, from 1872 to 1873. In the summer of 1876, along with a tide of other gold seekers, Hickok came to Deadwood. However, only a few weeks after his arrival, on the afternoon of August 2, he was shot and killed by Jack McCall while playing cards at Saloon # 10. A replica of the original structure, which was destroyed by the 1879 fire, stands at 657 Main Street. Hickok is buried, along with other Deadwood luminaries, in the **Mount Moriah Cemetery,** also known as **Boot Hill,** which lies on the eastern slope of Deadwood Gulch. One of these fabled characters was Martha Jane Cannary, known as Calamity Jane. Born in 1852, she came to the Black Hills as a young woman during the height of the gold rush. Calamity Jane was described by nineteenth-

By 1876, the gold-mining boom town of Deadwood had a lively main street and some 25,000 residents, even though gold had only been discovered in the vicinity the previous year, and the land was still Indian territory.

century adventure writers and dime novelists as a remarkable rider and shot, who was also distinguished for her stamina, colorful language, and ability to imbibe quantities of liquor. She died in 1903 and at her request was buried near Wild Bill Hickok, with whom she purportedly had a liaison many years earlier.

LEAD

While Deadwood lies in a gulch, Lead (pronounced LEED), three miles to the south, is built on precipitous mountain slopes. The town's name, which means a lode or vein, derives from the renowned Homestake Lead, which proved to be the richest gold strike in the Black Hills. The first discovery of gold ore was made by Fred and Moses Manuel on April 9, 1876. The sprawling compound of the **Homestake Mine** (605–584–3110) dominates the hillsides of Lead. Still in operation, the Homestake extracts gold both underground and in a surface open pit and is considered the most productive gold mine in the Western Hemisphere. The **Black Hills Mining Museum** (323 West Main Street, 605–584–1605) recounts the history of mining in the Black Hills and has a simulated tour of underground mining operations.

Virtually the entire town is included in the **Lead Historic District.** Clinging to the hillsides are many nineteenth-century miners' houses and a number of more elaborate Queen Anne structures. Because of the size of the Homestake's operations, the mine employed a large number of immigrant workers from Great Britain, Scandinavia, Italy, and the Balkans at the turn of the century. A reminder of Lead's rich ethnic heritage, the **Sweatman Art Memorial** (100 East Main, 605–584–3478), formerly a Finnish Lutheran church, is a simple frame structure built in 1891. During the turn of the century it served a congregation of miners, domestic workers, and merchants. It contains an eleven-foot wall mural painted by a Homestake miner in 1907.

BEAR BUTTE

Rising 1,400 feet from the flats just north of the Black Hills, Bear Butte is a distinctive conical mountain formed by volcanic action and subsequent erosion. The term for this geologic consequence is laccolith. For several centuries the butte has been a holy place

among the Indians. The mountain figures in important myths of the Cheyenne. After the Sioux displaced the Cheyenne in the Black Hills, they too made pilgrimages to the butte to pray and fast. The lone mountain now stands within Bear Butte State Park.

LOCATION: Bear Butte State Park, Route 79, 8 miles northeast of Sturgis. HOURS: *Park:* Open Daily; *Visitor Center:* May through September: 9–7 Daily. FEE: Yes. TELEPHONE: 605–347–5240

SPEARFISH

Set at the mouth of scenic Spearfish Canyon, Spearfish was founded in 1876 during the Black Hills gold rush, but its economy was sustained by the area's ranchers and farmers. A handsome Spearfish landmark is the **Episcopal Church of All Angels** (129 West Michigan), a High Victorian Gothic structure built in 1895 of locally quarried cut stone.

The **D. C. Booth Historic Fish Hatchery** (423 Hatchery Circle, 605–642–7730) began in 1899 as the Spearfish National Fish Hatchery, to stock streams in the Black Hills with trout, which were not native to the waterways. Active continuously for ninety years, the hatchery was central in the development of trout fisheries here, in Yellowstone Park, and in other parts of the West. The site was renamed for D. C. Booth, its first superintendent. The **Hatchery Building,** completed in 1899, a sprawling frame structure with Victorian elements, houses a collection of nineteenth-century aquaculture equipment. The 1905 **Superintendent's House** is a two-story white frame Victorian residence containing period furnishings.

The town of **Belle Fourche,** ten miles north of Spearfish, developed as a trade and livestock shipping center for South Dakota's cattle and sheep country. Dreams of converting the semi-arid terrain into irrigated farmland prompted construction of the **Belle Fourche Dam.** Built between 1905 and 1911, it was one of the first projects conceived under the 1902 Reclamation Act. An enormous structure for its time, the earth-fill dam is 122 feet high and just over a mile long.

OPPOSITE: *Spearfish Canyon, at the northern end of the Black Hills National Forest, with a dusting of snow.*

NORTH DAKOTA

OPPOSITE: *A blockhouse at Fort McKeen, near Fort Abraham Lincoln, where General George Custer was stationed with the Seventh Cavalry in 1873. During the Civil War Custer had achieved the brevet (temporary) rank of Major General; after the war, he first reverted to his earlier rank of captain, then was appointed lieutenant colonel, although many referred to him as "General."*

During the bitterly cold winter of 1804–1805, Lewis and Clark and the Corps of Discovery camped along the Missouri River across from its confluence with the Knife River in what is now North Dakota. On a day in late January, Captain Clark made this entry into his journal: "Attempt to Cut our Boat and Canoos out of the Ice, a deficuelt Task I fear as we find water between the Ice, I bleed the man with the Plurisy to day & Swet him, Capt. Lewis took off the Toes of one foot of the Boy who got frost bit Some time ago." North Dakota, then and now, is defined by a climate of extremes and by immense vistas that consist mainly of sky and plain, where the wind may blow for days on end. This elemental, often harsh environment nonetheless nurtured a vast array of wildlife on the nutritious tall and short grass prairie lands, and in their journals Lewis and Clark noted with awe the multitudes of waterfowl and herds of browsing bison. By 1895 hunters had all but eliminated the buffalo.

About 12,000 years ago, Paleo-Indians arrived on the vast plains of the Dakotas. These big-game hunters found abundant prey—mammoths, mastodons, and giant bison—in what was then a humid landscape of lakes and marshes. The Paleo-Indians became nomadic Archaic hunters about 6000 B.C., hunting herds of modern bison and collecting plants from the rich prairies. By about 600 B.C., the North Dakota plains were occupied by mound-building semi-sedentary farmers who raised corn, beans, sunflowers, squash, and tobacco. In present-day North Dakota, they inhabited the fertile river valleys and the area around Devils Lake. The burial mounds they built ranged from individual round mounds to complexes of round and linear mounds covering as much as half a square mile in area. The Mandan and Hidatsa, like their mound-building ancestors, lived in villages along the bluffs of the Missouri River. They were farmers who periodically hunted buffalo out on the prairie, a task that became decidedly easier in the mid-eighteenth century, when they acquired horses through the vast prehistoric trade network in which they were a major hub.

The Mandan built snug earthlodges, which housed extended families, an assortment of dogs, and occasionally even horses. The lodges consisted of wooden frames covered with willow branches, grass, and a layer of sod. For defense, they sometimes enclosed their villages in sturdy log palisades. They used tub-like vessels called bull boats to ferry across the Missouri River. Made of wooden frames cov-

Tub-shaped boats, made by covering willow frames with a buffalo hide, landing near a Mandan village located on a promontory overlooking the Missouri River, painted by the young Swiss artist Karl Bodmer in the winter of 1833-1834.

ered with a buffalo hide, these small circular boats were unstable and difficult to pilot in a straight line. A major Mandan center on the Missouri was at the confluence of the Heart River, where the city of Mandan stands today. In this area in 1738 the French-Canadian adventurer Pierre Gaultier de Varennes, sieur de La Vérendrye, and his three sons and a nephew encountered the Mandan; this was the first recorded contact between the Mandan and Europeans.

In the 1400s another Indian tribe—the Arikara—began moving into Mandan territory along the Missouri River from the south. They too were village-dwelling farmers. The settled habits of these Indians made them particularly susceptible to smallpox, a virus brought to North America by Europeans. In 1782 a smallpox epidemic ravaged the northern Plains. The Mandan and Hidatsa suffered additional trauma when their enemies, the Sioux, attacked two of their villages. They moved northward to the area around the confluence of the Knife and Missouri rivers, where they were living when Lewis and Clark arrived in the winter of 1804. In 1837–1838 the Indians again were devastated by smallpox. In 1871 the federal

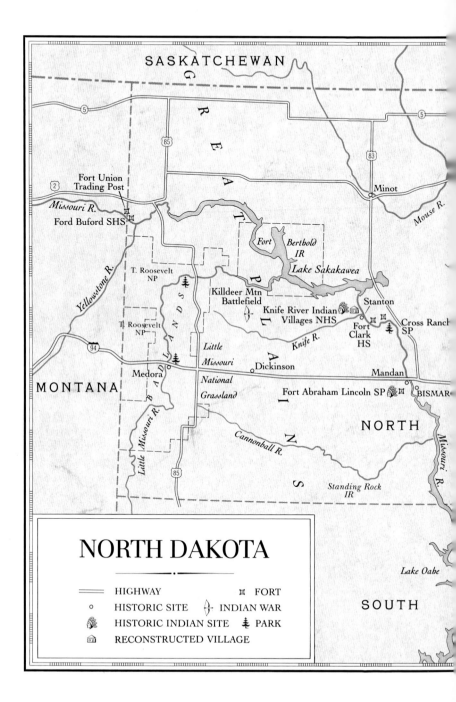

SASKATCHEWAN

5

85

83

Minot

2
Fort Union
Trading Post

Missouri R.

Ford Buford SHS

Mouse R.

Fort Berthold
IR

Lake Sakakawea

Yellowstone R.

T. Roosevelt
NP

Killdeer Mtn
Battlefield

Knife River Indian
Villages NHS

Stanton

Fort
Clark
HS

Cross Ranch
SP

T. Roosevelt
NP

Little
Missouri

94

Medora

National

Grassland

Knife R.

Dickinson

Mandan

Fort Abraham Lincoln SP

BISMAR

NORTH

MONTANA

Little Missouri R.

85

Cannonball R.

Standing Rock
IR

Missouri R.

Lake Oahe

SOUTH

NORTH DAKOTA

———— HIGHWAY   ⊟ FORT

   ○   HISTORIC SITE   ⊹ INDIAN WAR

   HISTORIC INDIAN SITE   ♠ PARK

   RECONSTRUCTED VILLAGE

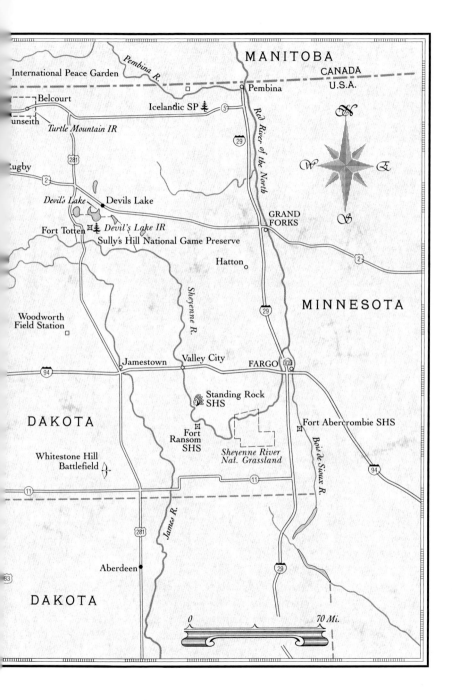

MANITOBA

International Peace Garden

Pembina R.

CANADA
U.S.A.

Pembina

Belcourt

Icelandic SP

⑤

unseith

Turtle Mountain IR

Red River of the North

②⑨

N

Rugby

②⑧①

W

E

S

Devil's Lake — Devils Lake

GRAND
FORKS

Fort Totten — Devil's Lake IR
Sully's Hill National Game Preserve

②

Hatton

Woodworth
Field Station

Sheyenne R.

MINNESOTA

②⑨

Jamestown — Valley City

FARGO

DAKOTA

Standing Rock
SHS

Fort Abercrombie SHS

Whitestone Hill
Battlefield

Fort
Ransom
SHS

Sheyenne River
Nat. Grassland

Bois de Sioux R.

⑨④

①①

⑧③

James R.

②⑧①

Aberdeen

②⑨

DAKOTA

0   70 Mi.

government established Fort Berthold Reservation for the Mandan, Hidatsa, and Arikara, who are now known as the Three Affiliated Tribes. The reservation surrounds the western half of Lake Sakakawea, a reservoir on the Missouri River. Chippewa and Sioux reservations are also located in the state, and Native Americans number 30,000 in North Dakota today.

The first manager at Fort Union, Kenneth McKenzie, and an American Fur Company trader, Pierre Chouteau, devised the plan of employing small steamboats on the upper Missouri. They arranged for the construction of the *Yellow Stone,* which reached Fort Pierre in 1831 and Fort Union in 1832, landmark events in the history of the Dakotas. With the assistance of the American Fur Company, a succession of scientists, naturalists, and artists visited Fort Union, including George Catlin (who arrived in 1832 on the *Yellow Stone*), Karl Bodmer and Prince Maximilian of Wied, and John James Audubon. The drawings, paintings, and writings of these explorers form an invaluable, and often poignant, historical record of the upper Missouri country.

Another, much later but important nineteenth-century outpost on the North Dakota stretch of the Missouri River was Fort Abraham Lincoln. Established in 1872 near the mouth of the Heart River, adjacent to a former village of the Mandan, the fort's purpose was to protect settlers and railroad workers, and in so doing it helped stimulate the growth of Mandan and Bismarck. The latter town became the territorial capital in 1883 and the state capital in 1889. Fort Abraham Lincoln's first commanding officer was General George Armstrong Custer, who rode out with the Seventh Cavalry from this outpost on May 17, 1876, to chastise the Sioux and Cheyenne and met with disaster at the Battle of the Little Bighorn in Montana.

The first non-Indian settlement in North Dakota began not along the Missouri River but in the Red River valley, which now forms the state's boundary with Minnesota. The fertile valley has had European residents since 1797, when a North West Company employee built a fur-trading post at the confluence of the Pembina River and the Red River of the North. This remote corner of the state was the heartland of the Métis, people of mixed European and Indian parentage who were noted for their skill as fur traders.

The area's history and development are closely linked to Saint Paul and Winnipeg. The Métis transported their buffalo hides overland via ox cart to trade them in Saint Paul. The advent of steamboat travel on the Red River of the North established trade lines between Saint Paul and Winnipeg and opened the valley to further settlement, developments enhanced by the completion of railroads that connected Saint Paul to Winnipeg and the Red River valley.

Minnesota, which experienced rapid growth after the Civil War, seeded the Red River valley with settlers, and as the fur trade began to ebb in the mid-nineteenth century, farming followed in its stead; it remains the economic mainstay in the fertile valley. The fits and starts of the Northern Pacific Railway significantly affected the placement and growth of towns in southern North Dakota, as well as the boom-and-bust economy of the area. Construction of the railroad, which was to span the wilderness between Duluth and Puget Sound, commenced in the 1870s. The Philadelphia financier Jay Cooke was in charge of selling bonds for the project, which at that time was the largest business venture in the United States. The railroad reached Bismarck by 1873, but Cooke was forced into bankruptcy, an event that helped push the nation into the Panic of 1873. Not until 1879 did the Northern Pacific resume laying track west of Bismarck. The railroad's eastern and western sections were finally linked in Montana in 1883. Route I-94 roughly parallels the Northern Pacific tracks across southern North Dakota.

The depression of the 1870s was followed by the Great Dakota Boom of the 1880s, a period of prosperity and optimism partially the result of railroad expansion. From 1878 to 1890, the population in this northern part of Dakota Territory grew by more than 1,000 percent, a surge that helped to justify statehood, which was conferred in 1889. The orchestrator of much of this growth was the Saint Paul tycoon James J. Hill, the financial wizard behind the St. Paul, Minneapolis & Manitoba (usually called the Manitoba) Railroad. Although he never lived in North Dakota—Hill lived in a Richardsonian Romanesque mansion perched on a bluff overlooking Saint Paul—he had more than an absentee landlord's interest in the state. In 1889 Hill and his associates turned the Manitoba Railroad into the Great Northern, which by 1893 linked the Midwest with the Pacific. (The Great Northern cut across northern North Dakota through Grand Forks and Minot, a path paralleled today by Route 2.) When the Panic of 1893 forced the Northern Pacific into its second bankruptcy, Hill bought securities in the reorganized railroad, thereby giving him a hand in controlling what had been Great Northern's major competitor.

A steam plow easily cuts through prairie land in Hettinger County, as shown in a photograph used by a land company to promote North Dakota farmland early in the twentieth century. The advertising emphasized that the prairie was free of stones.

A breakthrough in the processing of hard spring wheat further contributed to the Great Dakota Boom. Developed in the 1870s by millers in southern Minnesota, the technique was picked up by the flour mills in Minneapolis, which was then the largest milling center in the country. With a guaranteed market, farmers turned to producing the amber waves of grain—red fife, bluestem, and the various kinds of durum wheats—for which North Dakota is famous.

Although the average North Dakota farm in 1890 was under 300 acres, the 3,000-acre (and larger) bonanza farms were an element of the Great Dakota Boom. The farms were formed by men who were left holding bonds in the bankrupt Northern Pacific Railway They exchanged the bonds for railroad lands and began planting wheat. Often 15,000 or 20,000 acres in size, the farms required transient labor. The call for seasonal work attracted loggers from Minnesota and Wisconsin, as well as Norwegian and German immigrants just beginning their own homesteads.

The drier, more rugged western half of North Dakota, known as the Missouri Plateau, was not settled at the same time as the eastern portion. Even the arrival of the Northern Pacific (1880) and Great Northern (1886) did not spur much immigration. For much of the nineteenth century, most European inhabitants in this territory clustered around the four army outposts on the Missouri River (Rice, Abraham Lincoln, Stevenson, and Buford) and on widely scattered ranches. Army suppliers, railroad workers, and big-game hunters were the first to recognize the potential of the western Dakota grasslands to support cattle. The craggy Badlands, spreading along the Little Missouri River in western North Dakota, became the center of ranching in the state. The backbone of the early Dakota cattle business was formed by large Texas-based land and cattle companies, which drove their herds north to fatten on summer grass. The cattle boom was short-lived. Among other problems, cattlemen overstocked the range and failed to anticipate the severity of Great Plains winters. Several blizzards in the late 1880s virtually wiped out the industry.

Farming came slowly to western North Dakota in the late nineteenth century. The confluence of the Knife and Missouri rivers,

Members of several generations of the Pendroy family working on a quilt in the Double Irish Chain pattern in their home in 1888. The house also served as the post office for the small community of Pendroy. OVERLEAF: *Farms near Valley City.*

near the town of Stanton, was one of the first areas to be settled, and many of the original immigrants were German-Russians. Frugal homesteaders and expert farmers, they extended the range of wheat westward and left their cultural mark on the central-southern part of the state. The literature associated with the Dakotas forms one genre of nineteenth-century descriptive writing. The journals of Lewis and Clark have appeared in various editions and condensations since the explorers' diaries were edited and rewritten by Nicholas Biddle and published in 1814. George Catlin published his observations and renderings of Native Americans. Prince Maximilian of Wied, Karl Bodmer, and Theodore Roosevelt, among others, shared their travels of the region.

This chapter covers the state of North Dakota by roughly following the routes of the two railroads that opened up the state, the Great Northern (paralleled by Route 2) and the Northern Pacific (paralleled by Route I-94).

PEMBINA

In the northeastern corner of North Dakota on the Canadian border where the Pembina River joins the Red River of the North lies the town of Pembina. Its name derives from a Cree word for the highbush cranberry, a colorful plant found along the rivers. Pembina maintains the distinction of being the cradle of European settlement in the state. At the confluence of the two rivers, fur traders from the North West Company, XY Company, and Hudson's Bay Company built rival trading posts in the late eighteenth and early nineteenth centuries. In 1801 an outpost was established by Alexander Henry, Jr., an industrious North West Company partner who, with an entourage of Indians and voyageurs, stimulated trade and settlement in the Red River valley. Henry's men devised the Red River carts, rather crude but serviceable ox-drawn vehicles made entirely of wood. Known for the creaking sounds they made as they rolled across the prairie, these carts helped American fur traders open overland routes to markets at Saint Paul and points east. In 1812 a group of dispossessed Scots and Irish peasants, under the proprietorship of Thomas Douglas, the fifth earl of Selkirk, were granted permission by the Hudson's Bay Company to settle in the area. It was hoped that the colonists would grow food for Hudson's

Bay employees. The "Selkirkers" called their colony Fort Daer. However, many of them were unprepared for frontier life, and their presence was resented by the rival North West Company fur traders. The strife among the trappers and farmers culminated in the Massacre of Seven Oaks in 1816, when twenty of the immigrants were killed. By 1818 they had formed an agrarian settlement in the Red River valley. By the mid-1850s European settlement of the area was under way. Fort Pembina, a U.S. military post on the west bank of the Red River, was active from 1870 to 1895. Exhibits at the **Pembina State Museum** (Route 59, 701–825–6840) survey the area's history, from Native Americans to miners to soldiers to settlers.

This area of North Dakota was an enclave of the Métis, a group of mixed-blood peoples who, in the nineteenth century, achieved a proud identity through the melding of their Indian and European cultures, dress, religion, and language. Many Métis were of French-Ojibwa ancestry or, to a lesser extent, Scot-Ojibwa. An important Métis landmark, as well as a rare extant structure from North Dakota's fur-trade era, is the **Gingras Trading Post State Historic Site** (off Route 32, two miles northeast of Walhalla), one of a chain of outposts owned and built in the 1840s by the successful Métis fur trader Antoine B. Gingras. The house, in particular, exhibits a high degree of workmanship and attention to detail, reflecting Gingras's wealth. The compound remains on its original site, between the Pembina River and an old Red River ox-cart trail.

In the 1880s farmers from Iceland began settling this far corner of Dakota Territory. A relic from that period, the **Gunlogson Home,** stands in **Icelandic State Park** (off Route 5, five miles west of Cavalier, 701–265–4561), in the heart of the Icelandic settlement. The simple white frame house was constructed between 1882 and 1890. Located within the park is the **Pioneer Heritage Center,** which has exhibits documenting the numerous ethnic groups that settled North Dakota in the nineteenth century.

GRAND FORKS

Grand Forks was named for its position at the confluence of the Red River of the North and Red Lake River. The town's nineteenth-century prosperity is linked to James J. Hill, the Minnesota financier who scouted Dakota Territory in 1860 and later dispatched Alexander

The original log section of the Campbell Homestead, the birthplace of Thomas Campbell, furnished as it would have been at the turn of the century, with wood stove, washing machine, and ice box.

Griggs to explore the Red River valley. Griggs settled at the outpost with his family in 1871, developed a thriving flatboat freight business, and filed a plat on the town in 1875. In 1879 the Manitoba Railroad arrived, followed two years later by the Northern Pacific. The first gristmill in the Red River valley opened in Grand Forks in 1877, and the city remains the agricultural center for the wheat farmers in the valley. A dominant silhouette on the city's skyline is the **North Dakota Mill and Elevator** (1823 State Mill Road, 701–795–7000), which opened in 1922 and is the nation's only state-owned mill. The mill is a legacy of North Dakota's Nonpartisan League, an aggressive but short-lived (1915–1920) populist political group that tried to achieve fair trading practices for the state's grain farmers.

Myra Museum and Campbell House

The Myra Museum contains exhibits of nineteenth-century farm tools and household items and furnishings, which emphasize the area's Norwegian and Swedish heritage, and displays of World War I memorabilia. The Campbell House was the birthplace and home of Thomas Campbell, whose successful early-twentieth-century achievements in farming vast acreages in North Dakota and Montana earned him the nickname "Wheat King." The original log cabin section of the house was built in 1879, with additions in 1900. Also on the grounds are the original 1870s Grand Forks post office, a 1917 rural one-room schoolhouse, and a replica of a nineteenth-century carriage house.

LOCATION: 2405 Belmont Road. HOURS: Mid-May through mid-September: *Museum and Campbell House:* 1–5 Daily. FEE: Yes. TELEPHONE: 701–775–2216.

FORT TOTTEN STATE HISTORIC SITE

General Alfred Terry established Fort Totten on the south shore of Devils Lake in July 1867 to protect an overland route from Minnesota to western Montana and to oversee the Sioux on the adjacent Fort Totten Reservation. Although the outpost never witnessed any fighting, members of the Seventh Cavalry from Fort Totten were among the soldiers killed at the Battle of the Little Bighorn in Montana in 1876. In 1890 the fort was decommissioned and the buildings turned over to the Bureau of Indian Affairs. The compound served thereafter as a boarding school (1891–1935), tuberculosis sanitarium (1935–1939), and reservation school (1940–1959) for the Indian community in the northern United States. Fort Totten is the best preserved of the frontier military outposts on the northern Great Plains. Its parade ground is surrounded by handsome buildings, which include enlisted men's barracks, officers' quarters, a hospital, surgeon's and chaplain's quarters, and a quartermaster's storehouse. Erected between 1868 and 1871, the structures were built of bricks made from local clay. Several buildings contain period furnishings and historical exhibits. Within the former commissary is an interpretive center displaying artifacts and memorabilia from the different phases in the fort's tenure.

Musical productions are presented in July.

LOCATION: Off Route 57, 14 miles south of Devils Lake. HOURS: Grounds: 8–5 Daily. Buildings: Mid-May through mid–September: 8–5 Daily. FEE: Yes. TELEPHONE: 701–766–4441.

One mile northeast of Fort Totten is **Sullys Hill National Game Preserve** (701–766–4272), a refuge for bison, elk, prairie dogs, and other wildlife characteristic of the Great Plains before the era of European settlement. The four-mile bison auto trail traverses a prairie dog town, grasslands, and bison wallows where the animals roll in the dirt to get relief from insects. A tower at the top of Sullys Hill provides a view of historic Fort Totten.

The tribal headquarters of the **Turtle Mountain Reservation** is in **Belcourt.** The **Turtle Mountain Chippewa (Ojibwa) Heritage Center** (West on Route 5, 701–477–6451) contains exhibits of Ojibwa arts and crafts and items from the fur trade era, when the Ojibwa of the area engaged in commerce with the French, Cree, and Métis.

A joint venture between Canada and the United States, the 2,339-acre **International Peace Garden** (Route 281, 701–263–4390) sits astride the boundary just north of the North Dakota town of **Dunseith.** Founded in 1932, the garden is a botanical commemora-

A row of barracks at Fort Totten, established in 1867 and decommissioned in 1890. Between 1890 and 1959, the buildings housed an Indian school and a tuberculosis sanitarium. It became a State Historic Site in 1960.

tion of the peaceful association between the two countries. To the south, the town of **Rugby** celebrates its central position on the North American continent with the **Geographical Center Historical Museum** (Route 2, 701–776–6414) which has exhibits of farm machinery, firearms, and antique cars. On site is a pioneer village composed of twenty-six structures, including a livery barn, schoolhouse, and general store, each containing period furnishings.

Minot is a farm community amid the wheat-growing region of northwestern North Dakota. The **Ward County Historical Society** (North Dakota Fairgrounds, 701–839–0785) maintains a pioneer village with a church, schoolhouse, and other historic structures. In **Kenmare,** the 1902 **Danish Mill** (City Park) is a rare extant example of a Danish-style wind-powered grist mill. It was in operation until World War I. The **Lake County Historical Society Pioneer Village and Museum** (701–385–4368) contains exhibits of pioneer artifacts and sixteen turn-of-the-century buildings, including a bank, post office, dentist office, church, and schoolhouse, each restored and furnished with period items.

YELLOWSTONE–MISSOURI CONFLUENCE

The bountiful territory around the upper Missouri and Yellowstone rivers was inhabited by the Assiniboine, Crow, and Blackfoot. British fur traders of the Hudson's Bay Company had established ties with these tribes in the eighteenth century, but after the Lewis and Clark expedition, the confluence of these rivers became an important base of operations for American traders as well.

FORT UNION TRADING POST

In 1829 the Scottish-born fur trader Kenneth McKenzie established the Fort Union Trading Post for the American Fur Company on the Missouri River near the mouth of the Yellowstone. The indomitable McKenzie had learned the fur trade working from the North West Company in Canada before joining the Upper Missouri outfit of John Jacob Astor's American Fur Company. One of his first accomplishments during his tenure as manager at Fort Union was convincing the Blackfoot to make use of their trading post. The pro-British Blackfoot had hostile feelings toward Americans in part because of British incitation and in part because, in 1806, two of them were killed in a confrontation with Meriwether Lewis and several members of the Corps of Discovery. Fort Union soon grew to be the most important of the Missouri River trading posts. During the fort's early years, traders watched the demand for beaver plews decline (the fashion was shifting to silk hats) while the call for buffalo hides increased. Fort Union did a brisk business in buffalo furs for about a decade until 1837, when the first smallpox epidemic, carried by passengers on the steamboat *Saint Peter,* killed nearly a thousand Assiniboine beyond Fort Union. Twenty years later an epidemic took a similar toll among the Indians of the Yellowstone. The diminished tribes were harassed by the Sioux, who were moving into the Yellowstone and upper Missouri country. After the 1857 epidemic, fewer and fewer Indians came to Fort Union. It was sold to the North West Fur Company, which was unable to revive trade at the fort, and the once flourishing post was abandoned in 1867.

Fort Union stood on a broad terrace with a commanding view of the Missouri River and a receding horizon of rugged buttes. The

Fort Union, established in 1829 for the American Fur Company near the confluence of the Missouri and the Yellowstone rivers, was the major trading center on the northern Plains. This 1833 painting by Karl Bodmer shows Assiniboine Indians breaking camp after a trading visit.

The main house at Fort Union has been reconstructed by the National Park Service after archaeological excavation of the site uncovered the foundations, along with arti-facts such as eating utensils, buttons, beer bottles, china, and glass.

outpost was enclosed by a palisade of squared timbers. The structures within included the manager's house, a bell tower, kitchen, and trade house; two impressive stone bastions stood at the southwest and northeast corners of the fort. All have been reconstructed on their original sites. During trading season, Indians pitched their tepees on the grassy plain around the fortification. The bourgeois house contains a National Park Service visitor center and museum, with extensive displays of Fort Union and American Fur Company artifacts.

LOCATION: Buford Route, 24 miles southwest of Williston via Routes 2 and 1804. HOURS: June through August: 8–8 Daily; September through May: 9–5:30 Daily. FEE: None. TELEPHONE: 701–572–9083.

FORT BUFORD STATE HISTORIC SITE

In response to increasing unrest among the Sioux, an infantry company began building a military post at the confluence of the Yellowstone and Missouri rivers in 1866. For an expansion in 1867,

the soldiers dismantled the virtually defunct Fort Union, which stood nearby, for materials. Fort Buford, as it was called, was occupied by soldiers until the conclusion of the Indian wars and eventually housed six companies of infantry and cavalry. It was discontinued in 1895. Many influential Indians surrendered or were briefly interned here, including Chief Joseph of the Nez Percé and Gall and Sitting Bull, leaders of the Sioux. This fort was the place where Sitting Bull at last laid down his arms and submitted to U.S. authority. He was brought here in July 1881 after he had crossed the Canadian border to surrender. He returned to the United States reluctantly, probably because his few remaining followers were starving, saying, "The country there is poisoned with blood." At the formal surrender ceremony, he refused to hand over his rifle to the officer in charge, passing it instead to his 8-year-old son, Crowfoot.

Gall was one of the greatest of the Sioux warriors. Soldiers had killed two of his wives and three of his children, but Gall had his revenge at the Battle of the Little Bighorn, when, wielding a hatchet, "I killed a great many." In his later years, Gall fell out of favor with the Sioux because he became friendly with whites. A photographer remembered that while at Fort Buford Gall enjoyed listening to Mendelssohn's "Wedding March" played on the captain's piano. Extant structures at Fort Buford include a stone powder magazine (ca. 1874) and the frame officers' quarters (1872), which now houses exhibits on the history of the site. The post cemetery may also be visited.

LOCATION: Route 1804, 22 miles southwest of Williston. HOURS: Mid-May through mid-September: 6–5 Daily; Mid-September through mid-May: By appointment. FEE: Yes. TELEPHONE: 701–572–9034.

THEODORE ROOSEVELT NATIONAL PARK

Theodore Roosevelt National Park preserves a swath of the majestic landscape where the enthusiastic outdoorsman and future president hunted big game, dabbled in ranching, pursued his interest in natural history, and began to formulate his concerns about the environment. His first ranching venture was a partnership that began in 1883 with two other men in the Maltese Cross Ranch, which was

OPPOSITE: *Theodore Roosevelt National Park preserves more than 70,000 acres of Badlands first visited by the future president in 1883, when he was on a buffalo hunt.*

Theodore Roosevelt mounted on his favorite horse, Manitou, during his ranching days in western North Dakota in the 1880s.

located about seven miles south of present-day Medora. The next year he started his own open-range ranch, which he called the Elkhorn. Theodore Roosevelt National Park is divided into three large tracts, the North Unit, south of Watford City, the South Unit, accessible from Medora, and the Elkhorn Ranch. Each offers a wealth of dramatic geology and native plants and wildlife, including bison and elk that have been reintroduced to the grasslands.

The Medora visitor center, at the South Unit, contains personal effects of Roosevelt, ranching implements, and natural-history exhibits. The restored **Maltese Cross cabin,** a log structure originally located on Roosevelt's first Badlands ranch, stands behind the visitor center. It contains period furnishings and items, some dating to Roosevelt's involvement with the Maltese Cross enterprise.

LOCATION: *North Unit:* West of Route 85, 15 miles south of Watford City. *South Unit:* Off Route I-94, north of Medora. *Elkhorn Ranch:* 35 miles north of Medora, between South and North units. HOURS: *Park:* Always open, however some roads are closed in winter. *Visitor Center:* Hours vary, phone for information. FEE: Yes. TELEPHONE: 701–623–4466.

MEDORA

Medora lies near the Little Missouri River in the heart of the beautiful and rugged North Dakota Badlands. It grew out of a military outpost established here in 1879 to protect railroad workers. By the late nineteenth century, Medora was a rough-and-tumble cattle town surrounded by large ranching operations, where tens of thousands of

Theodore Roosevelt's Maltese Cross Cabin, where he lived from 1883 to 1885. In 1904, the North Dakota Commission sent it to the Saint Louis World's Fair.

Reconstructed earth lodges at On-A-Slant Indian Village, a Mandan settlement that once contained sixty-eight such structures.

heads of cattle grazed on the open range. The most famous person associated with Medora was Theodore Roosevelt, who came to the Badlands in 1883 to hunt bison and other big game.

The frontier village was named for Medora von Hoffman, the American wife of the marquis de Mores, a Frenchman who arrived in the Badlands town in 1883 to develop a meat-packing plant where range-fed beef would be dressed, then shipped to eastern markets via the Northern Pacific Railway in refrigerated cars. Several things conspired against the novel plan, including the unpredictable supply of beef, fierce competition from Chicago meat packers, a growing preference among consumers for corn-fed beef, and de Mores's own faulty business practices. In 1886 the plant closed and the marquis and his wife left Medora for other exploits. De Mores joined a Franco-Islamic alliance to force the British out of Africa and was killed in the Sahara in 1896. A brick smokestack and some of the foundation are all that remain of the **Marquis de Mores Packing Plant,** which burned down in 1907. On the east bank of the Little

Missouri River, the lone chimney, a conspicuous landmark in Medora, is a state historic site.

Chateau de Mores State Historic Site

In 1883 the Marquis de Mores built this rambling twenty-six-room frame house overlooking the Little Missouri River and the frontier town that he platted and named. The plain clapboard exterior belies its lavish interior, which the marquis and his wife appointed with fine furniture, carpets, and china. The couple entertained frequently, and among their guests was Theodore Roosevelt. Chateau de Mores contains many of its original furnishings. Inside the visitor center are a scale model of the packing plant, the marquis's stagecoach, hunting coach, and buckboard, and other exhibits pertaining to de Mores history.

> LOCATION: Off Route I-94. HOURS: Mid-May through mid-September: 8:30–5:30 Daily; other times by appointment. FEE: Yes. TELEPHONE: 701–623–4355.

In **Dickinson,** the **Joachim Regional Museum** (200 Museum Drive, 701–225–3466) is housed in one of several buildings of a prairie outpost park; other structures include a country church, a one-room schoolhouse, a railroad depot, and replicas of sod and stone houses. Within the museum is a permanent collection of fossilized dinosaur bones, prairie artifacts, and photographs of the pioneer settlement. About ten miles west of the small town of Killdeer, the **Killdeer Mountain Battlefield Historic Site** marks the scene of fierce combat between some 2,200 American cavalry and infantrymen and several thousand Sioux warriors on July 28, 1864. The American troops were under the command of General Alfred Sully, while the Indians were ensconced in a rugged stronghold, which Sully described as "a small chain of very high hills filled with ravines and thickly timbered." The Indians, however, proved no match to the army artillery, and after six hours of fighting they began to take down their tipis and scatter.

FORT ABRAHAM LINCOLN STATE PARK

Four miles south of Mandan, this state park encompasses two important North Dakota historic sites: **Fort Abraham Lincoln** and **On-A-Slant Indian Village,** a Mandan village site occupied from around

A view of George Custer's residence at Fort Abraham Lincoln, from which he set out with the Seventh Cavalry on the campaign that ended in defeat at Little Bighorn.

1650 to 1780. The Lewis and Clark expedition camped near this abandoned village in October 1804, and a **marker** in the park makes note of their famous exploratory passage up the Missouri River.

In an effort to protect settlers and railroad workers on the Dakota frontier, Fort Abraham Lincoln was started in 1872 near the mouth of the Heart River on the west bank of the Missouri. The fort grew out of an adjacent infantry post, called Fort McKeen, that had been established a year earlier at the site. By 1874 Fort Abraham Lincoln accommodated three companies of infantry and six of cavalry, totaling about 650 men, and ranked as one of the larger forts on the northern Great Plains. For the first three years, the commanding officer at Fort Abraham Lincoln was General George Armstrong Custer. Custer arrived in nearby Bismarck in the fall of 1873 via the Northern Pacific Railway with his wife, Elizabeth. The Custers' house burned down in 1874. It was replaced with a handsome frame structure, commodious for its time and place, which boasted a bay window, dormers, and a large verandah. This house was dismantled in 1891, but a replica of the **Custer House,** filled with furnishings reminiscent of the period, now stands on its original site facing the fort's parade ground. In the late 1990s, other buildings that originally stood nearby were being reconstructed or were scheduled for reconstruction.

Custer and the Seventh Cavalry embarked on two now-famous expeditions from Fort Abraham Lincoln: the 1874 exploration of the Black Hills, which confirmed the presence of gold in those mountains, and the 1876 campaign that culminated in the annihilation of Custer's command at the Battle of the Little Bighorn. Before departing from the fort, one of Custer's soldiers wrote a letter summing up the overconfidence that led to disaster: "Old Sitting Bull has sent word that if we come up there, he will have all our scalps, but I think the old boy is mistaken; he has got a bad crowd to fool with and had better keep quiet."

In 1882 the headquarters of the Seventh Cavalry was moved to Fort Meade, at the edge of the Black Hills, and Fort Abraham

An 1875 photograph of an informal musicale in Custer's house at Fort Abraham Lincoln shows the general turning the pages of sheet music for his sister, Margaret, seated at a square piano, with his wife, Elizabeth, and brother in the audience.

The reconstructed Custer House at Fort Abraham Lincoln has been furnished using photographs taken in the house during Custer's time.

Lincoln was finally closed in 1891. Three reconstructed blockhouses from the original infantry outpost of 1872 occupy commanding lookouts on the bluffs overlooking the Missouri River. There are also replicas of several Mandan earthlodges at On-A-Slant Village, a name derived from how the Indians built their houses on a hillside. The visitor center contains exhibits of Mandan artifacts, items from the railroad and homestead era, and military memorabilia.

LOCATION: Route 1806, south of Mandan. HOURS: June through August: 9–9 Daily; Rest of year: Shorter hours. FEE: Yes. TELEPHONE: *Park:* 701–663–9571. House: 701–663–1464.

BISMARCK

Bismarck, the capital of North Dakota, stands on the east bank of the Missouri River at a ford long used by Indians and buffalo. In 1883 the territorial capital was moved from Yankton, in present-day South Dakota, to Bismarck, and when North Dakota achieved statehood in 1889 Bismarck remained the seat of state government. The town was named for the nineteenth-century chancellor of the German Empire, Prince Otto Eduard Leopold von Bismarck-Schönhausen, in the hopes of attracting German capital for railroad investment. Settlers began arriving at the river crossing in 1871 in anticipation of the coming of the Northern Pacific in 1873, and Bismarck owes its origins and early prosperity to that railway. Until 1879 Bismarck was the terminus of the Northern Pacific, a situation that spurred river traffic, and at least in the summer months when the Missouri River was high and not frozen, the town was a bustling port. With the discovery of gold in the Black Hills in 1874, Bismarck became an important stop for stagecoaches and wagon trains headed for the gold-rich hills.

North Dakota State Capitol

In 1930 North Dakota's capitol burned down. The disaster precipitated debate about moving the state government to another city, but popular vote kept the capitol at Bismarck. Work commenced on a new capitol in 1933 amid much public debate over its dramatic but unorthodox style, and it was occupied in 1935. Seeking a capitol that was both efficient and modern, monumental and impressive,

A grand staircase leads up to Memorial Hall, which connects a nineteen-story tower with the lower quarters of the state legislature at the North Dakota State Capitol.

the Chicago firm of Holabird and Root (John Holabird and John W. Root, Jr.) designed the building in collaboration with North Dakota architects Joseph Bell DeRemer and William F. Kurke. The Depression-era building that emerged was partially inspired by the statehouses of Louisiana and Nebraska, though with far more functional use of space. The building was also designed to fully exploit a magnificent site of rolling prairie and is visible for many miles. Portending institutional styles that would prevail in the 1950s, the exterior of the North Dakota statehouse exhibits none of the flamboyance of turn-of-the-century government buildings. It is an unadorned nineteen-story structure faced with white Indiana limestone and appointed on the interior with sleek marbles and hardwoods in the Art Deco manner. An exercise in fiscal restraint, it was constructed for a cost of $2 million. By comparison, Nebraska's more elaborate capitol, built at about the same time, cost $11 million.

LOCATION: 600 East Boulevard. HOURS: Call for information on tours, offered hourly during week, weekends in summer. FEE: None. TELEPHONE: 701–224–2480.

North Dakota Heritage Center

The North Dakota Heritage Center contains the state's major museum as well as the archives and collections of the state historical society. Extensive permanent and special exhibits interpret the natural and human history of the northern Great Plains, featuring five areas of Dakota history: the natural setting; North Dakota prehistory; the Frontier, 1738–1870; the settlement period, 1870–1915; Bright Dreams and Hard Times: North Dakota, 1915–1941; and the Modern Era: North Dakota since 1941.

LOCATION: Capitol Grounds. HOURS: 8–5 Monday–Friday, 9–5 Saturday, 11–5 Sunday. FEE: None. TELEPHONE: 701–224–2666.

Built in 1884, the **Former Governor's Mansion** (4th Street and Avenue B, 701–224–2666) dates from one of Bismarck's boom eras, which commenced after the town was named territorial capital. The state bought the house in 1893, and it was used as the governor's residence for the next sixty-seven years. A frame structure with Stick-

style elements, it contains some original furnishings and gubernatori-
al memorabilia, as well as exhibits about the restoration process. The
military installation of **Camp Hancock** (First and West Main streets,
701–224–2666), was established in 1872 to provide protection for
work crews on the Northern Pacific Railway. After it was decommissioned in 1894, the site was used as the Bismarck weather station and
then by the U.S. Soil Conservation Service. An original log building
serves as a museum; a ca. 1885 church and a 1909 Northern Pacific
Steam locomotive also stand on the site. The Renaissance Revival
U.S. Post Office and Courthouse (304 East Broadway), completed in
1913, was one of the last designs by James Knox Taylor in his capacity
as supervising architect of the U.S. Treasury.

The towns of Mandan and Bismarck sit astride an eighty-mile stretch
of the Missouri River little changed from steamboat days. Broad
swatches of bottomland are dotted with the remains of some two
dozen earthlodge village sites, a few of which are marked with interpretive markers. The town of **Fort Yates,** some fifty miles south of
Bismarck and Mandan, is the tribal headquarters of the **Standing
Rock Indian Reservation.** After Sitting Bull and several of his followers were killed in the skirmish at his home on the reservation on
December 15, 1890, their bodies were brought to Fort Yates for burial. Although some historians submit that his remains were later
removed from the cemetery, the **Sitting Bull State Historic Site**
(701–854–7291) marks the original burial spot and is a monument
to the famous Hunkapapa Sioux.

K N I F E   R I V E R   R E G I O N

The area surrounding the confluence of the Knife and Missouri
rivers, between the present-day towns of Washburn and Hazen,
abounds in history. The bluffs along the Knife and the meandering,
muddy Missouri were the heartland of the Arikara, Hidatsa, and
Mandan nations, who maintained gardens on the floodplain terraces
and hunted buffalo on the prairies. Construction of huge reservoirs
on the Missouri River during the twentieth century has altered much
of the river's character, but **Cross Ranch State Park** (701–794–3731)
and the adjacent **Cross Ranch Nature Preserve** (701–794–8741)

encompass seven of the last free-flowing miles of the Missouri. They provide a glimpse of the unfettered river cutting through native prairies, a scene not unlike the landscape that sustained horticultural Indians in the eighteenth and early nineteenth centuries. The preserve and park are located about five miles south of **Hensler.**

KNIFE RIVER INDIAN VILLAGES NATIONAL HISTORIC SITE

By the eighteenth century, the Mandan, Hidatsa, and Arikara had established flourishing villages and gardens along the Missouri River as well as complex trade dealings with such far-flung tribes as the Crow, Cheyenne, and Blackfoot. By the beginning of the nineteenth century, the Missouri River in present-day North Dakota supported a population of over 20,000 people. The Knife River Indian Villages National Historic Site encompasses two Indian villages visited by Lewis and Clark in 1804 and depicted by George Catlin and Karl

A birds-eye view of a Mandan village, painted by George Catlin between 1837 and 1839, shows "The Big Canoe," a cylindrical enclosure in the center of the village, which contained the tribe's sacred medicines.

Mandan tribesmen dressed as buffalo perform a Bull Society Dance to attract buffalo herds to the vicinity of the village, as painted by Karl Bodmer in the 1830s.

Bodmer in the 1830s. These villages—now called the **Hidatsa (Big Hidatsa) Village** and the **Awatixa (Sacajawea Village**—were inhabited variously by the Mandan and Hidatsa (it is difficult to distinguish the two in the archaeological record). Large circular depressions approximately three feet deep and thirty to sixty feet in diameter mark the locations of the Indians' earthlodges. The Awatixa (Sacajawea) Village is where historians believe the young Shoshone woman and her husband Charbonneau lived at the time of Lewis and Clark's visit. The Awatixa (Sakakawea) Village is of particular interest because, as the Knife River has eroded the riverbank, different cultural layers of the village have been revealed. Interpretive tours are given of village sites. A visitor center at the **Awatixa Xi'e (Lower Hidatsa) Village** has exhibits explaining the culture of the Mandan and Hidatsa and their Arikara neighbors, including a full-scale model of an earthlodge. Research at Knife River and nearby sites has documented 11,000 years of human habitation.

LOCATION: 1 mile north of Stanton. HOURS: June through August: 8–6 Daily; Rest of year: 8–4:30 Daily. FEE: None. TELEPHONE: 701–745–3309.

One side of the street at Jamestown's Frontier Village contains a re-created late nineteenth-century dentist's office and post office.

A smallpox epidemic in 1837–1838 extirpated nearly 60 percent of the three tribes. In 1845 a group of surviving Mandan and Hidatsa, harassed by the Sioux, left their Knife River villages and went some forty miles northwest to where they formed Like-a-Fishhook Village. The American Fur Company subsequently established a trading post there called Fort Berthold. In 1862 they were joined by the last Arikara, and in 1871 the federal government established the **Fort Berthold Reservation.** The original Fort Berthold and Like-a-Fishhook Village were inundated by Lake Sakakawea, created by the Garrison Dam. Located on Route 23 three miles west of New Town, the **Three Affiliated Tribes Museum** (701–627–4477) displays arts, crafts, and historical items.

In November 1804 Lewis and Clark's Corps of Discovery settled in for the winter on the east bank of the Missouri about six river miles below the mouth of the Knife River. They felled cottonwoods to build a log compound, which was christened Fort Mandan. During their stay Lewis and Clark tried to carry out one of the directives of the expedition—to establish rapport with the Indians in hopes of developing trade with them. Enduring a bitterly cold winter, the party remained at the fort until early April. It was here that the resident trader Toussaint Charbonneau signed on with the Corps of Discovery as an interpreter, a task that his Shoshone wife, Sacajawea, also shared as the party proceeded westward. At the time, Sacajawea was about 18 years old and pregnant. Her baby boy was born that winter at Fort Mandan. The **Fort Mandan Overlook State Historic Site,** twelve miles west of Washburn, overlooks the area where Lewis and Clark established their winter headquarters.

The church in Frontier Village was originally the Eldridge, North Dakota, school, converted in 1920. The furnishings are from several local churches.

The **Lewis and Clark Interpretive Center** (Routes 83 and 200 in Washburn, 701–462–8535) provides an overview of the expedition, emphasizing the winter at the fort. The Native American display includes artifacts from nearly all the tribes encountered by the expedition. Visitors can try on a buffalo robe and a cradleboard like the one in which Sacajawea carried her baby. Not far away is the full-scale reconstruction of **Fort Mandan,** in a wooded area on the banks of the Missouri River.

The 2,650-acre **Chase Lake Prairie Project** (701–752–4218) is located about forty miles northwest of Jamestown amid the undulating prairies of the Missouri Coteau, a range of hills pushed up by the glacier that receded 10,000 years ago. The field station preserves a suggestion of the vast unbroken prairie prior to the era of intensive agriculture, when the Missouri Coteau supported multitudes of nesting waterfowl, herds of bison and elk, bears, wolves, and mountain lions. The station is operated by the Northern Prairie Wildlife Research Center, a branch of the U.S. Fish and Wildlife Service.

JAMESTOWN

Northern Pacific Railway workers formed the nucleus of the town in 1871, and farmers were drawn to the fertile James River Valley. Fort Seward, built on a bluff above the village in 1872, protected rail workers and settlers. The **Fort Seward Interpretive Center** (north on Route 281, 701–252–8421) displays military equipment and memorabilia from the fort. Exhibits of pioneer life can be found at the **Stutsman County Memorial Museum** (321 Third Avenue SE, 701–252–6741) and at **Frontier Village** (17th Street SE, 701–252–6307), a complex that has a schoolhouse, church, depot, and jail. Adjacent are the world's biggest bison—60 tons of steel and cement, 26 feet tall—and the **National Buffalo Museum** (701–252–8648), which tells the story of the dark beast that Americans find so fascinating; Native American hunting artifacts and works of art depicting the bison are among the exhibits.

OPPOSITE: *The High Line Bridge carried the Northern Pacific Railway across the Sheyenne River at Valley City in eastern North Dakota.*

WHITESTONE HILL BATTLEFIELD

In the fall of 1863 Generals Alfred Sully and Henry Sibley embarked on a two-pronged mission in the upper Missouri country to punish the Sioux for their 1862 uprising in Minnesota. On September 3 Sully and his troops came upon a large hunting camp of about 3,500 Sioux, 1,000 of whom were warriors. Although it is not certain that the Indians at Whitestone Hill were involved with the events in Minnesota, Sully's cavalry attacked the camp, killing about 200 men, women, and children, capturing another 156 Indians, and burning some 400,000 pounds of dried buffalo meat. The massacre at Whitestone Hill helped hasten the settlement of increasingly destitute Sioux on reservations. This conflict, added to the many others to exacerbate Sioux-white relations, resulted in almost thirty years of warfare, which ended in 1890 in South Dakota at the Wounded Knee massacre. The site, which commemorates both Indian and white participants, is marked with several monuments, and a small museum interprets the events of the battle.

LOCATION: Southeast of Kulm via Routes 56, 3, and 2. HOURS: Mid-May through mid-September: 9–5 Thursday–Monday. FEE: None. TELEPHONE: 701–396–7731.

One of the most impressive feats of engineering in the state is the **High Line Bridge,** which spans the Sheyenne River in Valley City. Opened in 1908 and still in operation, the Northern Pacific Railway trestle is 3,838 feet long and stands 126 feet above the river. About twenty miles south is the **Standing Rock State Historic Site,** a four-foot-tall conical rock long held sacred by the Sioux, who call the geological formation *Inyan Bosendata.* The rock stands atop a complex of prehistoric burial mounds that date from the Woodland Period (A.D. 1 to 1400). Ten miles further south, just west of the town of Fort Ransom, the **Fort Ransom State Historic Site** marks where General Alfred Terry established a 200-man military outpost in 1867 to aid overland travelers. The fort was abandoned in 1872; outlines of the buildings and dry moat are still discernible.

FARGO

The Red River valley town of Fargo, like its sister city, Moorhead, Minnesota, grew up at a fording place on the river and became a

The Richardsonian Romanesque Northern Pacific Railway Depot in Fargo, designed by the noted architect Cass Gilbert.

thriving railroad, riverboat, and agricultural center. The town is named for William G. Fargo, a Northern Pacific Railway director and cofounder of American Express and Wells-Fargo Express. The arrival of the Northern Pacific Railway in Fargo in 1872 guaranteed markets for grain and prompted the boom in wheat farming in the surrounding valley. Many of the immigrants and goods that came in on the railroad were transported north to such places as Fort Garry (present-day Winnipeg) on steamboats and barges. The riverboat heyday, which lasted about a decade, drew to a close with the arrival of the Great Northern Railway in 1880, which quickly supplanted boat traffic in the Red River valley. A handsome reminder of the nineteenth-century ascendancy of the railroads is the **Northern Pacific Railway Depot** (701 Main Avenue, 701–241–1350), a brick building (1898) combining elements of the Richardsonian Romanesque and Shingle styles. The depot was designed by Cass Gilbert, a deft practitioner of prevailing turn-of-the-century styles.

Bonanzaville, U.S.A.

Bonanzaville takes its name from the nineteenth-century bonanza farms, which proved the feasibility of growing wheat on a large

The U-R Next Barber Shop, built in Buffalo, North Dakota, in 1900, is preserved with all its fittings in Bonanzaville, U.S.A.

scale in the Red River valley. The forty buildings in the village compound are either originals or replicas of late-nineteenth- and early-twentieth-century structures significant to the history of the Fargo area, including a town hall, a rural church, and a replica of a sod house. The buildings contain period furnishings and fixtures, and several house collections of specific historic items, such as telephones, antique cars, and airplanes. The farmstead barn shelters the animals that were typically employed on nineteenth-century farms. The centerpiece of the village is the **Houston House,** a handsome white frame structure of 1881 that was the home of David H. Houston, a Scottish immigrant who prospered as a Red River valley wheat farmer. An inventor as well, Houston designed various photographic items, including roll film, which were among the first products manufactured by Eastman Kodak. The **Red River and Northern Plains Regional Museum,** the principal interpretive

center at Bonanzaville, contains exhibits of pioneer tools and
household items and a large collection of Indian artifacts.

LOCATION: Exit 343 off Route I-94, West Fargo. HOURS: June through
August: 9–5 Daily. September through October: 9–5
Monday–Friday, 1-5 Saturday–Sunday; May: 9–5 Monday–Friday;
Museum open in winter. FEE: Yes. TELEPHONE: 701–282–2822.

In the small town of Hatton, the **Hatton–Eielson Museum and
Historical Association** (405 8th Street, 701–543–3726) is within the
Victorian home of Carl Ben Eielson, the World War I cold-weather
pilot and arctic explorer who established air mail routes to the
Pacific northwest. Eilson died in 1929 on a rescue mission in Siberia.
On display are many original furnishings as well as exploration gear,
maps, and photographs.

FORT ABERCROMBIE STATE HISTORIC SITE

As nearby Minnesota was rapidly filling with settlers and pioneers
pressed into the Red River valley, the United States established Fort
Abercrombie on the west bank of the Red River of the North in 1857.
Construction of the fort was completed in the fall of 1858. The first
permanent U.S. military post to be built in what is now North
Dakota, Fort Abercrombie was a link in the chains of outposts that
protected traffic heading downriver into Canada and travelers moving west on the overland route into Montana's gold fields. The only
unrest that stirred Fort Abercrombie's otherwise peaceful existence
occurred during the 1862 Dakota Conflict. The rising of the Siouan
nations centered in the Minnesota River valley to the south and east,
but word of it spread, and white settlers and traders along the Red
River sought refuge at the fort. Indians attacked Abercrombie for a
few days in late September, but they were repulsed by howitzers. One
original building remains on the site, and the palisade wall and several blockhouses have been reconstructed. A museum contains artifacts from the fort and area settlements.

LOCATION: East edge of Abercrombie. HOURS: Mid-May through mid-
September: 8–5 Daily. FEE: Yes. TELEPHONE: 701–553–8513.

NOTES ON ARCHITECTURE

FRENCH COLONIAL

BOLDUC HOUSE, MO

Built largely in the Mississippi Valley, French Colonial structures followed models developed in the French West Indies. The main floor was one full story above the ground and was ringed by a full-length porch, or gallery, which allowed the main rooms to be insulated from both the damp earth and the sun. Vertical log walls were either *poteaux en terre*, set in the ground, or *poteaux sur sole*, set on a stone sill. A prominent hipped roof, extending over the gallery, provided shade.

GREEK REVIVAL

OLD CAPITOL, IA

The Greek Revival manifested itself in severe, stripped, rectilinear proportions, occasionally a set of columns or pilasters, and even in a few instances Greek-temple form. It combined Greek and Roman forms—low pitched pediments, simple moldings, rounded arches, and shallow domes, and was used in public buildings and many private houses.

GOTHIC REVIVAL

The Gothic Revival brought darker colors, asymmetry, broken skylines, verticality, and the pointed arch to American buildings. New machinery produced carved and pierced trim along the eaves. Roofs became steep and gabled; "porches" or "piazzas" became more spacious. Oriel and bay windows became common and there was a greater use of stained glass.

ITALIANATE

KENNARD HOUSE, NB

The Italianate style began to appear in the 1840s, both in a formal, balanced "palazzo" style and in a picturesque "villa" style. Both versions of the style had round-headed windows and arcaded porches. Commercial structures were frequently made of cast iron, with a ground floor of large arcaded windows and smaller windows on each successive rising story.

SECOND EMPIRE

GOVERNOR'S MANSION, MO

After 1860, Parisian fashion inspired American builders to use mansard roofs, dark colors, and varied textures, including shingles, tiles, and increasing use of ironwork, especially on balconies and skylines. With their ornamental quoins, balustrades, pavilions, pediments, columns, and pilasters, Second Empire buildings recalled many historical styles.

QUEEN ANNE

TRUMAN HOUSE, MO

The Queen Anne style emphasized contrasts of form, texture, and color. Large encircling verandahs, tall chimneys, turrets, towers, and a multitude of textures are typical of the style. The ground floor might be of stone or brick, the upper floors of stucco, shingle, or clapboard. Specially shaped bricks and plaques were used for decoration. Panels of stained glass outlined or filled the windows. The steep roofs were gabled or hipped, and other elements, such as pediments, Venetian windows, and front and corner bay windows, were frequently employed.

RICHARDSONIAN ROMANESQUE

DOUGLAS COUNTY
COURTHOUSE, KS

Richardsonian Romanesque made use of the massive forms and ornamental details of the Romanesque: rounded arches, towers, stone and brick facing. The solidity and gravity of masses were accentuated by deep recesses for windows and entrances, by rough stone masonry, stubby columns, strong horizontals, rounded towers with conical caps, and repetitive ornament based on botanical models.

RENAISSANCE REVIVAL OR BEAUX ARTS

KANSAS CITY MUSEUM, MO

In the 1880s and 1890s, American architects who had studied at the Ecole des Beaux Arts in Paris brought a new Renaissance Revival to the United States. Sometimes used in urban mansions, but generally reserved for public and academic buildings, it borrowed from three centuries of Renaissance detail—much of it French—and put together picturesque combinations from widely differing periods. The Beaux Arts style gave rise to the "City Beautiful" movement, whose most complete expression was found in the late nineteenth– and early–twentieth century world's fairs in Chicago and San Francisco.

PRAIRIE STYLE

WOODBRIDGE COUNTY
COURTHOUSE, IA

From about 1900 to 1920, Frank Lloyd Wright and several other Midwestern architects developed a style of building that attempted to reflect the rolling prairie. Wright claimed "The prairie has a beauty of its own and we should recognise and accentuate this natural beauty, its quiet level. Hence, gently sloping roofs, low proportions, quiet sky lines, suppressed heavy-set chimneys and sheltering overhangs, low terraces and outreaching walls sequestering private gardens." Prairie style buildings, primarily houses, were built until the end of World War I, when the fashion returned to buildings based on architectural styles of the past.

I N D E X

460

The editors gratefully acknowlege the assistance of Claire Blackwell, Ann J. Campbell, Rita Campon, Fonda Duvanel, Virgil Dean, Julia Ehrhardt, Ann ffolliott, Virginia Heidenreich, Loren N. Horton, Brigid A. Mast, James E. Potter, Paul M. Putz, Robin P. Robinson, Tonice Sgrignoli, Catherine Shea Tangney, Linda Venator, Wendy Wilson, and Patricia Woodruff.

Composed in ITC New Caledonia and ITC New Baskerville by Graphic Arts Composition, Inc., Philadelphia, Pennsylvania. Printed and bound by Toppan Printing Company, Ltd., Tokyo, Japan.